The Comparative Law Yearbook of International Business

The Comparative Law Yearbook of International Business

Volume 25, 2003

PUBLISHED UNDER THE AUSPICES
OF THE CENTER FOR INTERNATIONAL LEGAL STUDIES

General Editor

Dennis Campbell
Director, Center for International Legal Studies
Salzburg, Austria

Volume Editor

Susan Woodley

A C.I.P. Catalogue record for this book is available from the Library of Congress.

ISBN 90 411 2222 2 (HB)
ISBN 90 247 3002 3 (Series)
ISSN 0962-0435

Published by Kluwer Law International,
P.O. Box 85889, 2508 CN The Hague, The Netherlands.
sales@kluwerlaw.com
http://www.kluwerlaw.com

Sold and distributed in North, Central and South America
by Aspen Publishers, Inc.
7201 McKinney Circle, Frederick, MD 21704, USA

Sold and distributed in all other countries
by Extenza-Turpin Distribution Services,
Blackhorse Road, Letchworth, Hertfordshire,
SG6 1HN, United Kingdom

Printed on acid-free paper

Printed in the Netherlands.

The Center for International Legal Studies

The Center for International Legal Studies is a non-profit research and publications institute established and operating under Austrian law and with its international headquarters in Salzburg, Austria.

The Center has operated since 1976 in Salzburg, and it has had a close cooperation with the Faculty of Law of the University of Salzburg, the Austro-American Institute in Vienna, and numerous other universities and educational institutions in Europe and the United States.

The Comparative Law Yearbook of International Business prints matter it deems worthy of publication. Views expressed in material appearing herein are those of the authors and do not necessarily reflect the policies or opinions of the Comparative Law Yearbook of International Business, its editors, or the Center for International Legal Studies.

Manuscripts proposed for publication may be sent to:

The Editor
Comparative Law Yearbook of International Business
Postfach 19
A-5033 Salzburg, Austria

Table of Contents

Investment and Taxation

General Commercial Issues

Editor's Note

The 2003 volume of the *Comparative Law Yearbook of International Business* deals with a variety of topics in the field of commercial law. These range from mergers in Nigeria and joint ventures in Thailand and Hungary to the fight against curruption on an international level, as well as corporate fraud in the United States, with attention being focused upon the new Sarbanes-Oxley Act of 2002.

Some authors have dealt with subjects that involve finance, such as foreign investment in e-commerce in China, employees' stock purchases and option plans in the United States, pension funds in Nigeria and preferential tax regimes in Madeira. There is also a review of the Agreement on Trade-Related Investment Measures.

Other popular areas of commercial law that are covered in this volume include consumer protection in Bulgaria and alternative dispute resolution. Arbitration in Paraguay is discussed, along with the conducting of mediation by legal professionals. In addition, European Union law arises in relation to the likelihood of association, with another chapter detailing the economic association between Mexico and the European Union.

The commentators in this book are leading professionals in their respective fields and the interesting mix of topics should be of value to those involved in business in the international arena and their legal advisers.

Susan Woodley, Editor
Center for International Legal Studies
Salzburg, Austria

Joint Ventures

Joint Ventures in Thailand

Apichart Phankeasorn
Johnson Stokes & Master
Bangkok, Thailand

Introduction

The explosive growth of foreign investment in Thailand during the past decade has resulted in the development of new forms of business, new regulations and increased incentives for foreign investment in Thailand. Thailand is an ideal location for doing business in South East Asia, as the availability of natural resources, productivity of the labor force and the policies on foreign investment combine to offer significant development incentives.

The Thai Government has encouraged foreign investment in many ways, such as establishing the Board of Investment (the BOI) to provide incentives to stimulate investment and to conduct extensive investment promotion. The BOI aims to promote businesses that strengthen Thailand's industrial and technological capabilities, make use of domestic resources, create employment and develop infrastructure, together with conserving natural resources. Besides the BOI, the Government has also enacted many regulations that meet the needs of foreign entities doing business in Thailand, for example, the Investment Promotion Act,[1] the Foreign Business Act,[2] and the Condominium Act.[3] These regulations will help foreign investors to work and reside in Thailand.

A joint venture has no defined legal status, rights or duties under the Thai Civil and Commercial Code (the CCC). However, the Thai Revenue Code has defined a joint venture in Articles 39 as a business or profit-seeking enterprise carried out jointly by:

(1) A company and a company;
(2) A company and a juristic partnership; or
(3) A company and/or a juristic partnership, on the one hand, and

1 Investment Promotion Act BE 2520 (1977).
2 Foreign Business Act BE 2542 (1999).
3 Condominium Act BE 2522 (1979).

D.Campbell and S.Woodley (eds.), The Comparative Law Yearbook of International Business 2003, 3-34

an individual, a non-juristic body of persons, an ordinary partnership or another juristic person, on the other hand.

The Thai Revenue Code has defined a joint venture as a tax entity having the duty to pay taxes and duties corresponding to an ordinary partnership. From its definition, a joint venture must be an activity operated jointly for a commercial or profit-seeking purpose, and at least one party among the joint investors must be a juristic person.

Presently, joint ventures are considered to be the most popular vehicle for investment in Thailand and have been used extensively in various forms of business, including construction projects and the manufacture of food, beverages, textiles, jewelry, leather products, furniture and fixtures, paper, chemical products, petroleum, coal, rubber products, plastic products, basic metal products, fabricated metal products, machinery, electrical and electronic products, transportation equipment and scientific and measuring equipment.

Thai investors have a positive attitude towards joint ventures with foreign participation. Possible reasons for this could be that foreign investors can provide new sources of capital and technology and permission to use brand names, fund business expansion and provide access to foreign markets. At the same time, the foreign investor also acquires benefits from joint operations with Thai investors. For example, if a foreign investor joins with a Thai investor, they are allowed to conduct their business in ways that are not permitted under the Foreign Business Act, and they are allowed to acquire the ownership of land and to obtain an Investment Promotion Certificate. Foreign investors will also be assisted with respect to the providing of information on marketing, raw materials and labor from the Thai investor.

In choosing a business vehicle, the foreign investor should consider the commercial and legal factors of conducting business in Thailand. A foreign investor is able to operate his business in any form though a branch office, limited company or joint venture. It is not always easy to decide which is the appropriate form of vehicle to be used for doing business, as there are no ready-made patterns or well-defined criteria for foreigners to adopt. The choice of vehicle will, therefore, differ depending on the size, complexity and nature of the operation, as well as the business policies of the investors. However, the choice of vehicle must comply with Thai law. The most important factor which influences the decision on which business vehicle to use seems to be the size and nature of the business.

Legal Forms in Structuring a Joint Venture

A joint venture in Thailand may take the form of either an incorporated or unincorporated business. Generally, a joint venture takes the form of a limited company, although a joint venture may be established through other forms of business organization.

Incorporated Joint Ventures

Joint ventures generally take the form of a business organization recognized under the CCC and conduct their business either in the form of a partnership or a company. In a general joint venture, partners adopt private limited companies.

Registered Ordinary Partnership

An ordinary partnership may register with the Registrar of Partnerships and Companies in the Ministry of Commerce. Consequently, the partnership becomes a juristic person as a registered ordinary partnership, which has a legal entity separate from its partners.

A partner in a registered ordinary partnership has liability similar to that of a partner in an ordinary partnership in terms of having joint and unlimited liable for all partnership obligations. However, there are some differences. An ordinary partnership's creditors are entitled, as soon as the partnership is in default, to seek performance of the obligation from any of the partners. In addition, the liability of a partner in a registered partnership is limited to a period of two years after he ceases to be a member.

Limited Partnership

Under the CCC, the meaning of limited partnership is defined as a kind of partnership which has two groups of partners:

(1) One or more partners whose liability for the partnership's obligations is limited to the capital contributed; and
(2) One or more partners who have joint and unlimited liability for all the partnership's obligations.

A limited partnership is required to register with the Ministry of Commerce. Upon registration, it becomes a juristic person distinct from its partners. The unlimited partner may contribute in the form of monies, property or services, whereas the limited partner must contribute in the form of cash and property only. The management of the partnership is the responsibility of the unlimited partner who has unlimited liability for the obligations of the partnership. If the limited partners participate in such management, they will be liable for all liabilities in the same way as the unlimited partners.

Private Limited Company

Under Thai law, there are two types of limited company: a private limited company and a public limited company. A private limited company is the most common form of business that has been used for conducting joint ventures between Thai and foreign investors in Thailand.

A private limited company is a juristic person which must be registered with the Ministry of Commerce. The company must consist of at least seven promoters in order to register. Shareholders can be either natural or juristic persons. The company's capital is divided into equal shares. The shareholder is liable in a private limited company to any unpaid amount on the shares held by him. Therefore, if a shareholder has fully paid for his shares, he is not subject to further liability. In addition, at least twenty-five per cent of the registered capital must be paid by each shareholder on the date of the company's formation.

In a case where a foreign investor establishes a private limited company, this company may obtain an incentive under the Investment Promotion Act because a business that is eligible to obtain an investment promotion certificate must be in the form of a company. This is one of the reasons why most of the businesses in Thailand use a company form rather than a partnership.

Public Limited Company

A public limited company is a company established for the purpose of offering shares for sale to the public, and the liability of the shareholders is limited to the amount paid for these shares. The public limited company should have at least fifteen promoters and be established in accordance with the Public Company Act.[4] All shares in a public limited company must be fully paid. The objective of the company is contained in the memorandum of association.

Unincorporated Joint Ventures

An unincorporated joint venture can be carried out in the form of a contractual joint venture or ordinary partnership.

Contractual Joint Venture

The contractual joint venture is a purely contractual relationship between parties who jointly undertake a project without establishing a separate entity. A joint venture is commonly used for contracted projects which a single company cannot undertake alone. The parties maintain a separate identity and are independent from each other. They will, however, be bound by the terms and condition of an agreement. Thai law considers a contractual joint venture to be an unregistered partnership or a form of ordinary partnership pursuant to which the joint venturers shall have joint, several and unlimited liability towards third parties. A joint venture contract usually states that the parties should establish a company to operate their business. There is, however, no precedent regarding the legal status of an incorporated joint venture. Therefore, the parties to a joint venture may agree on their respective liabilities in a joint venture agreement. The parties can agree whatever terms and conditions they wish in the joint venture agreement as long as they do not violate public policy or good morals.

Ordinary Partnership

An ordinary partnership is one out of the three partnership forms provided by the CCC that is not a juristic person. Therefore, it is not regarded as a separate legal entity. Each party shall maintain a separate identity in the venture. An ordinary partnership can conduct business under its name, but it may not sue, be sued or acquire rights and obligations in its name. Each partner in an ordinary partnership shall have joint and unlimited liability for all obligations of the

4 Public Company Act BE 2521 (1978).

partnership towards a third party. A partner may contribute in the form of monies, property or services.

An ordinary partnership may be simply established because it does not require any filings or other public formalities of formation. The ordinary partnership is deemed to be a voluntary association which may arise through the agreement of the partners. However, in forming an ordinary partnership, the parties should specify in a well-drafted agreement before commencing their business the terms and conditions concerning, *inter alia*, management responsibility, liability, the share of each partner in the profits and losses, procedures for the settlement of disputes between the parties and termination of the partnership.

The relationship between the co-investors will depend on an agreement signed by both parties. However, their liabilities towards third parties are joint and unlimited for all obligations of the partnership. Therefore, a creditor may seek performance of obligations from any of the partners in an ordinary partnership. In addition, a former partner can still incur liability for the obligations of the partnership while he was a partner.

Thai business people do not commonly use an ordinary partnership to conduct their business. However, it seems to be the preferred option by Thai-foreign joint ventures, the objective of which is limited to a single undertaking covering a short period of time. Moreover, it is generally used between partners who do not differ much in size and financial stability.

Aspects Influencing Choice of Legal Form

In choosing the form of business operation, the choice will depend on a number of factors, including capital, liability and tax obligations. In general, there are several factors which influence the investors' decision as to which form is most suitable for their business.

Capital Investment

Some projects or businesses, such as a power plant or an expressway, require a large amount of capital investment. An investor, therefore, needs to seek co-investors in order to raise the funds necessary to implement such a project.

Risk Sharing

Some projects that invest a large amount of capital may be too risky for an investor to undertake alone. Therefore, if he can find co-investors, they can share the risk and he avoids having to bear the entire liability and burden of the projects.

Expertise

Human resources often being a major problem in implementing a project, the investors need to seek expert co-investors with technical knowledge and specialist skills in certain areas. Foreign partners might be able to assist in passing on technical knowledge to Thai workers so that, eventually, they will be capable of performing the work themselves without foreign experts.

Liability

In an unincorporated joint venture, a joint venture partner has joint, several and unlimited liability towards third parties. In the case of disputes, a third party may claim against any joint venture partner because a partner's liability is not limited to his capital contribution to the joint venture. This is in contrast to an incorporated joint venture, where a partner's liability as regards third parties is limited to any unpaid amount on the shares held by him.

Tax Consequences

Tax planning is one of the most important factors influencing the decision to establish a joint venture because establishing a joint venture can reduce the tax burden of the investors. Any profit that the investors might obtain from the joint venture business shall be distributed between the participants in proportion to their interests, but income tax may be exempted by virtue of the Royal Decree which was issued following the Revenue Code.[5] This benefit applies to companies or juristic partnerships regardless of whether they were established under Thai or foreign law provided, however, that their business operates in Thailand. In cases where the joint investor is a

5 Revenue Code, Volume 10, BE 2500, as amended by Volume 108, BE 2524, Section 5*bis*.

foreign company with no business activities in Thailand, the joint investor will pay corporate income tax on its share of the profits in the same manner as a dividend.

Governing Law and Language

There are no restrictions with regard to the governing law of the agreement. According to the principles of conflict of laws in Thailand, the parties to the agreement may select the governing law for such agreement provided that the parties are of different nationalities. The Thai courts will only recognize and apply foreign law when such law is not contrary to good morals or public order and is proven to the satisfaction and discretion of the Thai courts. However, in respect of property situated in Thailand, Thai law shall govern the provisions and clauses required for the validity of a contract, document or other juristic act relating to such property.

Judgments obtained in foreign jurisdictions are not enforceable in Thailand and may only form part of the evidence presented in a Thai court case. Enforcement against a debtor's property requires a judgment from the Thai courts. In addition, the law governing movable and immovable property situated in Thailand must be Thai law.

An agreement between the parties may be in any language, depending on the consent of the parties, although English is commonly used in joint venture agreements.

Scope of Joint Venture and its Business Activity

In order to consider the scope of business to be undertaken by the joint venture, there are many issues of concern, such as the availability of natural resources, the infrastructure, the law and government policies, the educational level and productivity of the labor force and the list of promoted activities and products.

Thailand has a flourishing agricultural sector and a rapidly growing industrial sector. Thailand, rich in agricultural resources, is a leading producer and exporter of agricultural products, such as rice, sugarcane, sugar, maize, cassava, tapioca, rubber, palm oil, meat, milk and fruits. In addition, Thailand's fishing industry exports a significant amount of frozen seafood and canned seafood products.

Thailand is also a leading producer and exporter of high quality natural rubber which, in turn, boosts the manufacturing of rubber-based products.

Most industries in Thailand involve agricultural products, which include food processing, beverages, tobacco and textiles. The textile industry is also considered one of the major industries of the country. However, in the past decade, the country's industries have expanded to the areas of electrical parts and components, petrochemicals, plastics, pharmaceuticals, cement, ceramics and paper products, which have now become major sources of foreign exchange.

Thailand has a population of approximately 625-million and a workforce of around 33-million, with the majority of the workforce being under thirty years of age. The minimum wage in Thailand is currently Baht 169 per day in Bangkok and between Baht 133 and Baht 168 in the provinces. The cost of labor in Thailand is not the lowest in the region, but the efficiency of the workers is more competitive than in other countries. Thai workers have a reputation for being hard-working and skillful. The education level of workers varies from uneducated to university graduates.

The Thai language is predominant in all parts of the country. Education is conducted in Thai, but English is taught as a second language at all academic levels and is widely used in business sectors. French and German are also taught as optional subjects from high school level.

Thailand has high standards of infrastructure, including electricity, water supply, telephone, sea ports, airports, highways and railways, which are available throughout the country. Thailand's transportation system consists of well-developed road networks, rail networks serving all major regions of the country and mass transit systems in Bangkok. The sea ports are of a high standard, and there are eight international deep-sea ports in operation situated in Bangkok, Laem Cha Bang, Map Ta Put, Phuket, Sattahip and Songkha. The development of the sea ports, especially those on the East Coast, is creating a base for new industries.

Thailand has six international airports and more than twenty-nine domestic airports around the country. International airports are situated in Bangkok, Chiang Mai, Chiang Rai, Hat Yai, Phuket and U-Taphao. Thailand also has major air transport infrastructure projects that will be completed in the near future: the New Bangkok International Airport (NBIA) at Nong Ngu Hao, the Global Transpark

(GTP) at U-Taphao and the Heavy Aircraft Maintenance Center (HAMC) at U-Taphao. Thailand has a plan to achieve its goal of becoming an air transportation center of South East Asia.

Investors may obtain BOI promotion if their business is on the list of activities eligible for investment promotion, which is set out in Appendix 1. Activities that have been designated as priority activities are those that involve agriculture, technology, infrastructure and environmental protection.

Financing the Joint Venture

Thailand has a number of local commercial banks, international commercial banks and finance companies which have schemes to support businesses. The list of financial institutions in Thailand appears in Appendix 2. The commercial banks provide normal banking services by way of loans, international loan refinancing and expert assistance.

Finance companies in Thailand must be either limited companies or public companies and obtain a license from the Ministry of Finance. They provide loans and a variety of lending services, including working capital loans, project loans, term loans, loan arrangements and guarantees. Finance companies may conduct leasing business, housing, revolving mortgage lines, project finance and selling of government bonds. The financial sector underwent significant restructuring during the financial crisis in 1997, and fifty-six finance companies were closed down. Thus, finance companies that survived the economic crisis are considered to have good performance records and the ability to conduct their business well.

The Industrial Finance Corporation of Thailand (the IFCT) is a government organization established according to the Industrial Finance Corporation Act.[6] The IFCT is an industrial bank which was established to promote domestic industries and to ensure that the country's industrial development is comparable with foreign countries.

The IFCT offers various services, such as financial services, credit guarantee, investment in IFCT's promissory notes, bills of exchange and debentures, investment banking, foreign exchange transactions, trade financing and even a search for a joint venture

6 Industrial Finance Corporation Act BE 2502 (1959).

partner. Businesses wishing to obtain loan assistance from the IFCT should carry out a feasibility study. The project must demonstrate capability in marketing, financing and engineering in order to qualify for financing services.

The small and medium-enterprises (SME) industry has been widely recognized in the past few years as an important tool for driving the economy. The business generated by SMEs is considered crucial for improving the economic situation. The Small Industry Finance Corporation of Thailand (the SIFCT) was established by the Small Industry Finance Corporation Act[7] for the purpose of supporting and financing the SME industry. An SME is defined as an operation which has permanent assets in a total amount not exceeding Baht 100-million. The SIFCT supports areas including industrial, retail, wholesale and services, as well as businesses operating on industrial estates.

The Export-Import Bank of Thailand (EXIM Bank) is a financial institution wholly owned by the Thai Government under the Ministry of Finance's supervision. EXIM Bank offers short-term and long-term credit in both the domestic and overseas markets. EXIM Bank can borrow from local or overseas financial institutions, as well as issue short-term or long-term financial institutions for sale to financial institutions and the general public. Moreover, EXIM bank can engage in any financial activities that are customary for commercial banks, apart from accepting deposits from the general public. In 1999, EXIM Bank expanded its objective and scope of operation to provide support to Thai investors overseas, as well as local investors in businesses relating to export or involving foreign exchange.

Antitrust and Competition Law

The Thai Government passed important new legislation, the Trade Competition Act[8] (the TCA), which came into force on 30 April 1999. The TCA replaces the Price Fixing and Anti-Monopoly Act.[9] The purpose of enacting the TCA is to encourage fair competition and to prevent the actual existence or potential establishment of a monopoly

7 Small Industry Finance Corporation Act BE 2534 (1991).

8 Trade Competition Act BE 2542 (1999).

9 Price Fixing and Anti-Monopoly Act BE 2522 (1979).

or unfair competition in the market. This is especially important to prevent a dominant business operator from abusing its power by maintaining unfair pricing levels, limiting customer choice, causing the supply of goods or services to be restricted and interfering with other businesses.

Pursuant to this Act, there are five main prohibitive trade practices:

(1) Abuse of dominant position;
(2) Merger arrangement possibly creating anti-competition;
(3) Anti-competitive co-arrangement;
(4) Deprivation of the local end user's opportunity to purchase goods or services directly from abroad; and
(5) Unfair competitive actions causing damage to other businesses.

Dominant position, as defined in the TCA, refers to the number of shares and the total turnover of any particular product or services in a market attributable to one business operator. Pursuant to the TCA, any business operator enjoying over seventy-five per cent market share is deemed to have power over the market or to be in a dominant position.

Any businesses involved in the prohibited area set out in the TCA shall require permission to operate. For example, if a company is considering a merger or joint venture and there is legitimate concern that the establishment of the new entity or the existence of the merged entity may create a monopolistic position or limit fair competition in the market, then the company may submit an application for preliminary approval, which is a pre-condition to such acquisition. Breach of the TCA or an order of the Trade Competition Board (the Board) may result in a fine of up to Baht 6-million or three years' imprisonment.

The Board will consider an application to jointly establish and maintain a restrictive trade practice, having considered the business efficacy and likely duration of the business activity. Permission will be granted if the activity is considered commercially necessary or beneficial to the country and upon the condition that it is not detrimental to consumer interests.

While only certain trade practices were controlled in the past, the TCA covers all businesses in Thailand, including joint ventures, but there are some exceptions for government sectors; state enterprises; groups of farmers, co-operatives or co-operative communities recognized by law; and other businesses as prescribed by Ministerial Regulations. Thus, the burden of determining the impact of the application of the law is shifted from the Government to individual business operators.

Formation Agreement

A joint venture formation agreement should follow standard legal provisions, such as the nature of the joint venture, the date of commencement of the business, the composition of the board of directors, the capital contribution to be made by the parties, the management control of the company, the voting rights of the parties and restrictions on the transfer of shares.

Furthermore, other issues that must be considered are the provision of technology transfer and methods of transfer as well as the governing law, restrictions on assignment of the rights of the parties and termination of the agreement. Conventionally, the joint venture agreement has an international element, either a foreign natural person or foreign juristic person, so in the joint venture agreement it is also necessary to mention the choice of law and dispute settlement in order to avoid any future dispute.

There are no specific regulations governing joint ventures in Thailand. The laws that apply to joint ventures are those relating to contracts, land, partnership, companies, agencies, taxation, exchange control and investment.

Thai authorities have not published a standard agreement for a joint venture. The parties may negotiate the rules and procedures that are to govern all the liabilities, duties and responsibilities of the parties under the terms and conditions in the agreement as long as it does not contravene public policy or good morals.

Where joint venture parties have agreed to form a limited company in Thailand, there are no rules that relate to the relationship between the joint venture agreement and the articles of association. However, if the joint venture takes the form of a limited company, the articles of association shall bind the shareholders and the parties and govern all matters of the company.

Procedure in Establishing a Corporate Vehicle

To establish a company for the purposes of a joint venture, a Thai private limited company is required to have at least seven promoters, of which at least fifty-one per cent must be Thai shareholders with a maximum foreign shareholding of forty-nine per cent. It is not necessary for all joint venture agreements to be approved by or registered with government authorities. There are no specific rules which govern joint ventures relating to the establishment of a company. Therefore, the parties need not present any specific document to set up a company. However, where the parties would like to establish a company in Thailand, the parties are required to follow the following procedure with the Ministry of Commerce.

The first step in forming a private limited company is to reserve the name at the Ministry of Commerce. The company can easily reserve the name at the website www.thairegistration.com. The name to be reserved must not be the same or similar to other companies. Upon approval, such name will be valid for thirty days, whereby no other person can apply for the same name.

The next step involves the memorandum of association (the MOA) and objectives of the company being filed with the Department of Business Development. The names, addresses, ages and occupations of the seven promoters will be required at this stage. Upon receipt of all the details, the application will be filed with the Company Registration Office and normally takes one to two days for approval. The fee for registration of the MOA is Baht 50 per Baht 100,000 of registered capital. The minimum fee is Baht 500 and the maximum fee Baht 25,000.

Once the MOA is duly registered, a statutory meeting should be called, and at least twenty-five per cent of the value of each share must be paid up. After the statutory meeting, the promoters pass the business of the company to the directors and, within three months of the statutory meeting, the directors must apply to register the company. An application for registration of the company can be filed along with the articles of association with the Company Registration Department. The number of shareholders should not be less than seven, and it is essential that the names of the seven promoters be on the list of shareholders at the time of registration of the company. When the application is approved, a registration fee of Baht 500 per Baht 100,000 of registered capital is payable, subject to a minimum fee of Baht 5,000 and a maximum fee of Baht 250,000.

After registration of the company, the company must file an application for a taxpayer identification card with the Revenue Department within sixty days of completion of the registration company. It normally takes one to two days for a taxpayer identification card to be issued. A value added tax (VAT) certificate will be required when the company has generated income greater than Baht 1,200,000 or when the company wishes to enter into the VAT system following the commencement of company business.

In a case where the investor wants to obtain special privileges, tax exemptions and other incentives provided by the BOI, the investor must submit an application to the Office of the BOI. The approximate minimum period for obtaining promotion from the BOI is ninety working days from the date of submission of the application. To receive an investment promotion certificate, the applicant must submit all of the following documents to the BOI:

(1) The memorandum of association;
(2) The certificate of business registration;
(3) A certificate stating the registered capital,
(4) A list of directors indicating those empowered to bind the company and the address of the head office;
(5) A list of shareholders;
(6) A document showing the transfer of funds from overseas;
(7) A joint venture contract (if any);
(8) Licensing agreement;
(9) Technical assistance contract; and
(10) A completed investment promotion certificate application form.

The BOI will issue the investment promotion certificate after receipt of all the documents specified and approval of the application.

Ancillary Agreements

A joint venture company may have to prepare agreements ancillary to the joint venture agreement which are binding between the parties, such as distribution or supply agreements, licensing agreements, technical assistance agreements, employment agreements and other supporting agreements which are considered relevant by the parties.

A distributorship agreement is a common agreement that is used extensively when a manufacturer or supplier from abroad seeks a local natural person or company to distribute its products in the local market. The legal nature of this agreement is similar to a sales agreement under which the manufacturer or supplier acts as a seller and the distributor as a buyer.

With regard to a licensing agreement, the trademark owner should first complete the registration process for the mark with the

Trademark Registrar and then enter into an agreement for licensing the use of such registered trademark in Thailand. Furthermore, the licensing agreement must be in writing and registered with the Registrar of the Intellectual Property Department of the Ministry of Commerce in order for the same to be valid and enforceable under Thai law. The clause in the licensing agreement shall comply with the rules and procedures prescribed in the Ministerial Regulations and shall show at least the following:

(1) Conditions or terms between the trademark owner and licensee to ensure effective control by the registered owner of the trademark over the quality of the goods of the licensee; and
(2) The goods for which the trademark is to be used.

Where the licensee is a manufacturer, the licensee is required to apply for a factory license or notification for approval or consent from the Ministry of Industry prior to commencing operations. The application must be sent together with drawings and particulars of the proposed factory, its machinery and effluent treatment system. The operation of the factory shall be carried out in accordance with the criteria prescribed under the Factory Act, Ministerial Regulations and other regulations relating to the control of factory operations.

Factory licenses are valid until the end of the fifth calendar year from the year in which the business started operations, except when the factory is transferred, leased or is subject to hire purchase or has ceased operations. The company must apply for the renewal of licenses prior to the date of expiration.

Employment agreements should have minimum terms and conditions which are specified in the Labor Law. Expatriates wishing to work in Thailand must obtain a work permit from the Foreign Occupational Control Division or One Stop Services Department, a Department of the Ministry of Labor and Social Welfare. The number of expatriates allowed is dependent on many factors, including the employer's financial status, the ratio of foreign to Thai staff and the gross income of the applicant. At present, in order to obtain a work permit, the minimum registered capital of the employer must be Baht 2-million per one expatriate employee. Additionally, the ratio of foreign to Thai workers must be maintained at 1:4.

Incentives Available to Foreign Joint Venturers

The BOI, through the Investment Promotion Act, offers various investment incentives and privileges to foreign investors, such as special guarantees and tax exemptions. A foreign investor who has received an investment promotion certificate will be entitled to government investment incentives.

Guarantees

Guarantees may be obtained:
- (1) Against nationalization;
- (2) Against competition from new State enterprises;
- (3) Against State monopolization of the sale of products similar to those produced by the promoted project;
- (4) Against price control;
- (5) Against tax-exempt imports by government agencies or state enterprises; and
- (6) To grant permission to export.

Protection Measures

Protection measures utilized include:
- (1) The imposition of a surcharge on imports at a rate not exceeding fifty per cent of the cost insurance freight (CIF) value for a period of not more than one year at a time;
- (2) Import ban on competitive products; and
- (3) Authority of the Chairman of the BOI to order any assistance or tax relief measures for the income generated from promoted projects.

Permission

Permission may be granted:
- (1) To bring in foreign nationals to undertake investment feasibility studies;
- (2) To bring in foreign technicians and experts to work on promoted projects;
- (3) To own land in order to carry out promoted activities; and
- (4) To take or remit foreign currency abroad.

Tax Incentives

The promoted company may receive privileges and a number of tax incentives, which include personal income tax, corporate income taxes and withholding income tax, as well as:

(1) Exemption from or reduction in import duties on imported machinery;

(2) Exemption from or reduction in import duties on imported raw materials and components;

(3) Exemption from corporate income tax for three to eight years, with permission to carry forward losses and deduct them as expenses for up to five years; and

(4) Exclusion of dividends derived from promoted enterprises from taxable income during the corporate tax holiday.

Special Investment Promotion Zones

There are the following additional incentives for enterprises in Special Investment Promotion Zones:

(1) Reduction of corporate income tax by fifty per cent for five years after the termination of a normal income tax holiday or from the date upon which income is earned;

(2) Double deduction from taxable income of water, electricity, and transportation costs for ten years from the date of first sales; and

(3) Allowance to deduct up to twenty-five per cent of the investment costs of installing infrastructure facilities from taxable corporate income for ten years from the date upon which income is earned.

Additional Incentives for Export Enterprises

With respect to export enterprises, the following additional incentives apply:

(1) Exemption from import duties on imported raw materials and components;

(2) Exemption from import duties on re-exported items;

(3) Exemptions from export duties; and

(4) Allowance to deduct from taxable corporate income an amount equivalent to five per cent of an increase in income derived from exports over the previous year (excluding the cost of insurance and transportation).

Besides the BOI, the Industrial Estates Authority of Thailand (IEAT) plays an important role in industrial development of the country. The IEAT also provides various incentives for an industrial operator on an industrial estate. An industrial operator may be authorized to own land required for its operations and permitted to bring in a specific number of experts, technicians and their spouses or dependants for a certain period as fixed by the Board of the IEAT, even though it may exceed the length of stay permitted under the Immigration Law. Moreover, foreign industrial operators are permitted to take out or remit money abroad, including money that was imported into Thailand for investment, dividends, repayment of loans, interest on a loan and franchise or service fees.

Industrial operators and export traders in the Export Processing Zone (the EPZ), that is, industries that export at least forty per cent of what they manufacture, are entitled to additional privileges on tax incentives as follows:

(1) Exemption from payments of special fees, import duties, VAT and excise tax on machinery, equipment and tools;
(2) Exemption from import and export duties; and
(3) Exemption or refund of taxes on goods used for manufacture in the EPZ.

Restrictions on Activities of Foreign Joint Venturers

Foreign investors are free to conduct their business in Thailand. However, there are some restrictions which apply to foreign investors, such as the Exchange Control Act, Foreign Business Act, Land Code, Work Permit Act, Immigration Act and Investment Law. Furthermore, there is also a restriction on the percentage of foreign ownership in some businesses, including commercial banks, finance companies, commercial fishing, aircraft, commercial transportation, telecommunications, commodity export and mining.

Exchange Control Act

The Exchange Control Act[10] and the Ministerial Regulation[11] issued under the Exchange Control Act govern all matters involving foreign

10 Exchange Control Act BE 2485 (1942).
11 Ministerial Regulation Number 13 BE 2497 (1954).

exchange. All regulations that involve foreign currency are enacted by, and require permission from, the Bank of Thailand (the BOT). All foreign exchange transactions are to be conducted through authorized banks. There are no special requirements concerning the currency to be used for financial settlements with foreign countries, but payments are generally made in United States dollars.

In the past decade, the BOT has considerably relaxed the regulations regarding exchange control in relation to foreign investors so that, currently, a transaction in Thai Baht or foreign currency can be performed without restriction. However, in certain cases, approval from the BOT is still required.

People living in Thailand are required to surrender foreign currency received from an authorized bank or authorized person or deposit the same in a foreign currency account within seven days from the date of receipt. Travelers passing through Thailand, foreign embassies and international organizations are exempted from this rule.

Forward coverage, swaps and options are generally permitted between genuine traders and authorized banks. Thai residents are allowed to maintain foreign currency accounts under certain conditions. Non-residents may also open such accounts with any of the authorized banks in Thailand. Account transactions are, however, subject to the control of the BOT.

Exports are free from any exchange restriction, but export income must be remitted into Thailand immediately after payment is received, which may not be later than 120 days from the export date, and sold to an authorized bank or deposited in a foreign currency account with an authorized bank in Thailand within seven days from the date of receipt. Importers may freely purchase or draw foreign exchange from their own foreign currency accounts for import payments upon submission of supporting evidence. Letters of credit may also be opened without authorization. All receipts of service fees must be surrendered to authorized banks or deposited in a foreign currency account within seven days from the date of receipt. Payments for service fees related to foreign trade, educational expenses or family allowances abroad can be made freely.

Foreign investors are allowed to invest through the establishment of a business or equity participation and invest on the Stock Exchange of Thailand. Foreign investments in Thailand, which receive promotional privileges from the BOI, are accorded various incentives and special benefits.

There are no restrictions on capital investment and foreign borrowing. The remittance of investment funds and foreign loans into Thailand is unlimited and freely permitted, but foreign exchange inflows in the form of capital and loans must be surrendered to authorized banks or deposited in a foreign currency account within seven days from the date of receipt. Securities, promissory notes and bills of exchange may be sent abroad without restriction. Repatriation of investment funds, dividends and profits, as well as loan repayments and interest payments thereon, net of all taxes, may be made freely through a commercial bank in Thailand.

Foreign Business Act

The Foreign Business Act[12] came into force on 4 March 2000, replacing the old Foreign Business Law (National Executive Announcement Number 281), which was enacted in 1972. The previous Act, which had been in effect for a long time, and some of the regulations were not appropriate for the current economic and investment situation.

The Foreign Business Act is the most important law governing majority foreign-owned businesses in Thailand. The Act contains three categories of businesses which are prohibited or require permission before commencing operations. However, there remain a number of businesses, including most manufacturing businesses, which do not fall within any of the three categories and are open to investment by foreigners. Under the new Act, "foreigner" means a natural or juristic person who is not of Thai nationality, including a company with half or more of its shares held by foreigners.

The new Act refers to forty-three restricted businesses in three lists. List 1 contains nine businesses prohibited for special reasons relating to national media, agriculture, natural resources, religion, heritage and land. List 2 contains thirteen businesses related to national safety or security or affecting arts, culture, traditional customs, folk handicrafts, natural resources and the environment. A foreigner who wishes to operate a business which is in this list must obtain a license from the Ministry of Commerce. List 3 contains twenty-one businesses in which Thai people are not yet ready to compete with foreigners. The Director-General of the Department of

12 Foreign Business Act BE 2542 (1999).

Business Development, with the consent of the Alien Business Operation Committee, may issue a license to foreigners who wish to operate a business in this list.

If the business activity is governed by the Foreign Business Act, such business must apply to the Ministry of Commerce for a foreign business license, which is valid for a fixed period and subject to certain conditions, such as the ratio of capital to loan to be used in the business.

Where a foreigner wishes to operate a restricted business, the minimum capital shall not be less than Baht 3-million. Moreover, for non-restricted businesses, the minimum capital used at the commencement of the business operations shall not be less than that prescribed by ministerial regulations and shall not, in any case, be less than Baht 2-million.

Foreigners may operate a business under List 2 only if Thai national or Thai juristic persons hold at least forty per cent of the shares (this may be reduced to twenty-five per cent upon Cabinet approval). Moreover, at least two-fifths of the directors must be Thai. Businesses in Lists 2 or 3 may have conditions attached to their foreign business licenses, such as minimum debt/equity ratio, number of foreign directors resident in Thailand, amount and period of investment, technology and assets.

Exceptions to the Foreign Business Act include foreigners who engage in business with the permission of the Royal Thai Government (RTG), those who are engaged in contracts directly with the RTG or those who are covered by a treaty between the RTG and another foreign nation. The only treaty currently in existence is the Treaty of Amity and Economic Relations between Thailand and the United States. This Treaty provides that United States individuals and companies may freely engage in any of the restricted activities listed in the Foreign Business Act. The Treaty, however, lists certain activities in which United States entities are restricted, such as the provision of communications, transportation and banking.

Land Code

Under the Land Code,[13] foreigners are not allowed to own land in Thailand. However, it is possible for a company with foreign

13 Land Code BE 2497 (1954).

shareholders to own land in Thailand provided that the percentage of foreign shareholding in such company does not exceed forty-nine per cent. A company is deemed to be foreign if more than forty-nine per cent of its shares are owned by foreigners.

The new amendment to the Land Code allows foreigners who invest over Baht 40-million to own up to one Rai or 1,600 square meters of land for residential purposes, and the land must be situated in Bangkok, Pattaya or other specified areas. They must obtain approval from the Ministry of the Interior. Under the amended Condominium Act,[14] foreigners may own up to forty-nine per cent of the total area of a condominium and the foreign ownership of any condominium can exceed forty-nine per cent if such project is located in Bangkok or Pattaya and the total development area of the condominium, is less than 5 Rai (8,000 square meters). This allowance for foreign ownership of forty-nine per cent or more has been in effect for five years, since 28 April 1999. After five years, the foreign ownership quota for new developments will decrease to forty per cent.

In addition, companies granted investment promotion either by the BOI or the IEAT are authorized to own land for industrial purposes. Moreover, pursuant to the Act Governing Leasing of Immovable Property for Commercial and Industrial Purposes,[15] a foreign company may lease immovable property for between thirty and fifty years, and the lease can be renewed for another fifty years.

Investment Promotion Act

An applicant that intends to apply for an investment promotion certificate from the BOI shall be a company, a foundation or a co-operative established in accordance with the respective law. The BOI also states that the limitation on foreign shareholders is on a case-by-case basis for most projects awarded promotion. Conditions may be imposed on promoted projects, including minimum capital investment, minimum Thai shareholders, requirements to use local raw materials, nationality and number of employees, training of labor and distribution, designation and quality of products.

---

14 Condominium Act BE 2522 (1979).

15 Act Governing Leasing of Immovable Property for Commercial and Industrial Purposes BE 2542 (1999).

Dispute Resolution

The parties are able to resolve disputes either through the Thai courts or by arbitration proceedings. The courts of Thailand consist of the Court of First Instance, the Court of Appeal and the Supreme Court. There are special courts dealing with specific matters, for example, the Central Bankruptcy Court, the Central Labor Court, the Central Tax Court, the Juvenile and Family Courts and the Central Intellectual Property and International Trade Court. Cases from the special courts may be appealed directly to the Supreme Court rather than going via the Court of Appeal.

Generally, in commercial cases, the parties prefer to resolve their disputes by arbitral proceedings rather than using the courts because arbitration proceedings are faster and more effective. Therefore, the dispute settlement clause always stipulates arbitration as the method for solving disputes between the parties.

Under Thai law, arbitration can be categorized into two types, namely, arbitration in court and arbitration out of court. Arbitration in court can take place where there is a lawsuit pending in a Thai court and the parties have decided to arbitrate rather than litigate the issues. Arbitration out of court is a more common form of arbitration that is widely used to resolve commercial disputes. An arbitration agreement shall be enforceable only if made in the form of written evidence and signed by both parties or appearing in correspondence or other documents between both parties agreeing on an arbitration clause.

The joint venture agreement may also provide for arbitration under the Arbitration Act,[16] which took effect on 30 April 2002. The new Arbitration Act uses the UNCITRAL Model Law on International Commercial Arbitration as a model. This Act deals with the procedure for conducting arbitration and the enforcement of foreign arbitral awards in Thailand. Pursuant to the new Act, the parties must appoint an odd number of arbitrators, and one arbitrator will have the casting vote. Where the parties cannot determine the number of arbitrators, the number of arbitrators shall be one.

To enforce an award granted by arbitration in Thailand, it is necessary for the party seeking enforcement to file a petition with a Thai court for enforcement of the award. The court will consider enforcing the award against the other party if the issuance of the award complies with the conditions under the Arbitration Act and the contents thereof

16 Arbitration Act BE 2545 (2002).

are not contrary to public policy or good morals. Moreover, according to the new Act, an arbitration award must be enforced by a Thai court within three years from the date of the award.

Thailand is also a party to the New York Convention on the Recognition and Enforcement of Arbitral Awards of 1958. Thailand joined the New York Convention on 21 December 1959. Where one party is unable to enforce against the other's assets in Thailand or where the assets in Thailand are not sufficient to satisfy the award, the New York Convention provides for enforcement in any member country where the other party has sufficient assets.

Impact of Changes in the Law Subsequent to Formation

Generally, the promoted person acquires privileges or incentives as prescribed in the investment promotion certificate issued by the BOI. Any incentives given to the promoted person are not affected by subsequent changes in the law. It means that any promoted person receiving an investment promotion certificate will receive such incentives during the period of time stipulated in the terms and conditions of such certificate. To this end, joint ventures do not receive any favorable or special treatment.

Double Taxation Agreements and Joint Ventures

In order to promote trade between foreign countries and Thailand, the Thai Government has signed a bilateral agreement concerning double taxation with approximately forty-three other countries, which to a greater or lesser degree relieve the tax burden for persons wishing to remit income abroad. The double taxation agreement is an agreement to eliminate overlapping tax payments. Generally, these treaties place a taxpayer in a more favorable position for Thai income tax payments by providing that profits shall only be taxable if the taxpayer has a permanent establishment in Thailand, instead of on the basis that it is carrying on business in Thailand. It means that if a foreign company registers in Thailand, it will become a Thai company and, as such, double taxation agreements will not apply. It should be noted that the double taxation agreement provides relief only for income tax, not other taxes, such as specific business tax and VAT.

The countries that have a double taxation treaty with Thailand include Australia, Austria, Bangladesh, Belgium, Bulgaria, Canada, Cyprus, Czech Republic, Denmark, Finland, France, Germany, Hungary, India, Indonesia, Islamic Republic of Pakistan, Israel, Italy, Japan, Laos, Luxembourg, Malaysia, Mauritius, Nepal, The Netherlands, New Zealand, Northern Ireland, Norway, People's Republic of China, The Philippines, Poland, Republic of Korea, Romania, Singapore, South Africa, Spain, Sri Lanka, Sweden, Switzerland, United Arab Emirates, United Kingdom, The United States of America, Uzbekistan and Vietnam.

Protection of Foreign Investors

Thailand has concluded over thirty bilateral agreements concerning the encouragement and protection of investments. Agreements on the promotion and protection of investments aim to provide protection against expropriation and nationalization, as well as to create fair and equitable conditions for investment. Thailand has entered into such agreements with several countries, such as Argentina, Bangladesh, Cambodia, Canada, Croatia, Egypt, Finland, Germany, Hungary, India, Indonesia, Israel, Laos, Luxembourg, People's Republic of China, Peru, Poland, Republic of Korea, Romania, Slovenia, Sri Lanka, Sweden, Switzerland, Taiwan, The Netherlands, The Philippines, United Kingdom, Vietnam and Zimbabwe.

The agreements deal with all issues related to investments carried out by nationals of one contracting state in another contracting state. They guarantee protection for such investment against nationalization and expropriation, payment of adequate compensation when nationalization or expropriation takes place, freedom to repatriate profits and capital and settlement of disputes under the Convention on the Settlement of Investment Disputes. Thailand has based its Promotion and Protection of Investment Treaties on the standards of the most-favored nation treatment. Under the standard of the most-favored nations, investors of the contracting state shall be treated in the same manner as national investors or investors from any third state. Thus, the treatment offered to investors from other contracting states investing in Thailand is the same treatment which would be offered to investors from any other country.

Appendix 1

Industrial Activities

I. Agriculture and Agricultural Products

(1) Plant propagation or seed grading;
(2) Hydroponic cultivation;
(3) Manufacture of biological or organic fertilizers;
(4) Animal breeding;
(5) Animal husbandry;
(6) Manufacture of animal feed or mixes for animal feed;
(7) Crop drying and silo facilities;
(8) Deep sea fishery;
(9) Slaughtering;
(10) Leather tanning or finishing, or fur dressing;
(11) Manufacture or preservation of food or food ingredients using modern technology (except drinking water, confectionery and ice cream);
(12) Manufacture of oil or fat from plants or animals;
(13) Grading, packaging and storage of plants, vegetables, fruits or flowers using modern technology;
(14) Manufacture of natural rubber products;
(15) Manufacture of dextrin or modified starch;
(16) Manufacture of products from agricultural by-products or waste;
(17) Cold storage;
(18) Trading centers for agricultural goods;
(19) Agro-industry processing zones;
(20) Manufacture of products from herbs (except soap, shampoo, toothpaste and cosmetics);
(21) Inspection, analysis and certifying of quality standard of agricultural products;
(22) Inspection and analysis of diseases of plants, livestock or aquatic animals;
(23) Inspection and analysis of soil or water for agriculture;
(24) Reforestation;
(25) Processing of wood; and
(26) Manufacture of alcohol or fuel from agricultural products.

II. Mining, Ceramics and Basic Metals

(1) Mineral ore prospecting;
(2) Mining or ore dressing (except tin);
(3) Marble or granite mining;
(4) Manufacture of ceramic products;
(5) Manufacture of glass or glass products;
(6) Smelting;
(7) Manufacture of metal powder;
(8) Manufacture of ferro-alloy;
(9) Manufacture of flat-rolled steel products;
(10) Manufacture of long steel products;
(11) Manufacture of steel pipes or stainless steel pipes;
(12) Manufacture of iron or steel casting;
(13) Manufacture of forged steel parts;
(14) Rolling, drawing, casting or forging of non-ferrous metals;
(15) Manufacture of fire-resistant material or heat insulation;
(16) Manufacture of ceramic roof tiles;
(17) Manufacture of gypsum board or gypsum products; and
(18) Coil center.

III. Light Industry

(1) Manufacture of textile products or parts thereof;
(2) Manufacture of gemstones and jewelry;
(3) Manufacture of products from leather or artificial leather;
(4) Manufacture of shoes or parts thereof;
(5) Manufacture of sports equipment or parts thereof;
(6) Manufacture of toys;
(7) Manufacture of artificial flowers, trees and other artificial goods;
(8) Manufacture of lenses or spectacles or parts thereof;
(9) Manufacture of medical supplies or medical equipment;
(10) Manufacture of stationery or parts thereof;
(11) Manufacture of furniture or parts thereof;
(12) Manufacture of luggage or parts thereof;
(13) Manufacture of sanitary napkins and absorbent pads;
(14) Manufacture of scientific equipment;
(15) Manufacture of trawling nets; and
(16) Manufacture of abrasive paper.

IV. Metal Products, Machinery and Transport Equipment

(1) Manufacture of hand tools and measuring tools;
(2) Manufacture of machinery and equipment;
(3) Manufacture of metal products, including metal parts;
(4) Building or repair of steel ships of not less than 500 tons gross;
(5) Building of ships of less than 500 tons gross (except wooden or steel ships);
(6) Manufacture of trains or electric trains (only with rail system);
(7) Manufacture or repair of aircraft, including parts thereof or onboard equipment;
(8) Manufacture of vehicle parts;
(9) Manufacture of four-stroke motorcycles;
(10) Manufacture of assembling cars;
(11) Metal surface treatment or anodize surface treatment;
(12) Heat treatment;
(13) Manufacture of electric-powered vehicles or parts thereof;
(14) Manufacture of four-stroke motorcycle engines;
(15) Manufacture of automobile engines;
(16) Manufacture of multi-purpose engines;
(17) Repair of industrial machinery;
(18) Manufacture of metal containers;
(19) Fabrication of metal structural products or metal industrial equipment;
(20) Manufacture of air or gas compressors;
(21) Manufacture, repair, maintenance and refurbishment of containers; and
(22) Repair of vehicle parts, electrical or electronic equipment.

V. Electronic Industry and Electrical Appliances

(1) Manufacture of electrical equipment for industrial use;
(2) Manufacture of electrical products;
(3) Manufacture of parts or equipment used for electrical products;
(4) Manufacture of electronic products;
(5) Manufacture of parts or supplies used for electronic apparatus;
(6) Manufacture of material for micro-electronics;
(7) Electronic design;
(8) Software; and
(9) E-commerce business.

VI. Chemical, Paper and Plastic

(1) Manufacture of basic chemicals;
(2) Manufacture of other chemicals;
(3) Manufacture of fertilizers;
(4) Manufacture of pesticides or herbicides;
(5) Manufacture of petrochemicals;
(6) Oil refineries;
(7) Manufacture of dyes and pigments (except paints);
(8) Manufacture of active ingredients in pharmaceutical products;
(9) Manufacture of plastic or plastic-coated products;
(10) Manufacture of pulp;
(11) Manufacture of paper;
(12) Manufacture of paper containers or boxes;
(13) Manufacture of articles made of fiber, pulp paper or paperboard;
(14) Printing; and
(15) Manufacture of body-care products.

VII. Services and Public Utilities

(1) Public utilities and basic services;
(2) Mass transit systems and transportation of bulk goods;
(3) Tourism promotion services;
(4) Activities to support tourism;
(5) Real estate development for industrial use;
(6) Distribution centers;
(7) International distribution centers;
(8) International Procurement Office (IPO);
(9) Regional headquarters;
(10) Trade and investment support offices;
(11) Hospitals;
(12) Research and development;
(13) Scientific laboratories;
(14) Calibration services;
(15) Human resource development;
(16) Waste water treatment, services for the disposal of refuse, industrial waste or toxic chemicals;
(17) Thai motion picture production, motion picture supporting services or multimedia services;
(18) Product sterilization services;
(19) Medium or low-income housing; and
(20) Coating or thickening of pipes for petroleum.

Appendix 2

Commercial Banks

(1) Locally incorporated banks:

1. Bangkok Bank Public Limited Company;
2. Krung Thai Bank Public Limited Company;
3. Bank of Ayudhya Public Limited Company;
4. Thai Farmers Bank Public Limited Company;
5. DBS Thai Danu Public Limited Company;
6. The Thai Military Bank Public Limited Company;
7. Bankthai Public Limited Company;
8. The Siam Commercial Bank Public Limited Company;
9. Siam City Bank Public Limited Company;
10. UOB Radhanasin Bank Public Limited Company;
11. Bangkok Metropolitan Bank Public Limited Company;
12. Standard Chartered Nakornthon Bank Public Limited Company;
13. Bank of Asia Public Limited Company; and
14. Thanachart Bank Public Limited Company.

(2) Foreign Incorporated Banks

1. ABN-AMRO Bank NV;
2. Standard Chartered Bank;
3. JP MORGAN Chase Bank;
4. Overseas Chinese Banking Corporation Limited;
5. The Bank of Tokyo-Mitsubishi Limited;
6. Citibank, NA;
7. The Sakura Bank Limited;
8. RHB Bank Berhad;
9. The International Commercial Bank of China;
10. Bank of America, National Association;
11. Credit Agricole Indosuez Bank Limited;
12. Bharat Overseas Bank Limited;
13. The Hongkong and Shanghai Banking Corporation Limited;
14. Deutsche Bank AG;
15. Mizuho Corporate Bank Limited;
16. Dresdner Bank AG;

17. BNP Paribas;
18. The Sumitomo Mitsui Banking Corporation (SMBC);
19. The Industrial Bank of Japan Limited;
20. The Bank of China; and
21. The Bank of Nova Scotia.

(3) Finance Companies, Finance and Securities Companies:

1. Ayudhya Investment and Trust Public Limited Company;
2. Krungthai Thanakit Finance Public Limited Company;
3. Kiatnakin Finance Public Limited Company;
4. Tisco Finance Public Limited Company;
5. Bualuang Finance Company Limited;
6. National Finance Public Limited Company;
7. Radhanatun Finance Public Limited Company;
8. Primus Finance Company Limited;
9. The Siam Industrial Credit Public Limited Company;
10. GE Asia Finance Company Limited;
11. The Book Club Finance Public Limited Company;
12. Asia Credit Public Limited Company;
13. Bangkok First Investment and Trust Public Limited Company;
14. Global Thai Finance (Thailand) Limited;
15. Citicorp Finance (Thailand) Limited;
16. Thai Permsap Finance Company Limited;
17. BTM Finance and Securities (Thailand) Limited;
18. American Express Finance (Thailand); and
19. AIG Finance (Thailand) Public Limited Company.

Joint Ventures in Hungary

Ágnes Szent-Ivány
Sándor, Szegedi, Szent-Ivány
Budapest, Hungary

Introduction

"Joint venture" is not a legal term in Hungary. In practice, by joint venture is meant a business corporation where at least one of the parties involved is a foreign entity. The broader sense of a joint venture is when a cooperation between two or more business entities is regulated without the use of a long-term contract.

Joint ventures with foreign participation already have a long history in Hungary. The first joint ventures were formed with special government approval in 1986 to 1987, well before the "collapse of the iron curtain" in 1989 and before the first free elections held in the spring of 1990 in Hungary. In the second half of the 1980s, the Hungarian Government started to encourage foreign investments in Hungary because not only did it bring capital into the country, but also management, marketing policy and other kinds of know-how that form part of a market economy.

In 1988, Parliament passed Act VI of 1988 on Business Associations and Act XXIV of 1988 on Foreign Investment in Hungary (Foreign Investment Act). This legislation was a breakthrough because it provided that any foreign legal entity or private individual could freely invest in Hungary and establish joint ventures or subsidiaries, at first with a license from the Ministry of Finance and then, from 1 January 1991, without any kind of government approval. The Foreign Investment Act stated in its Preamble that Hungary grants foreign investors national treatment exempt from discrimination. This legislation and the more favorable business climate in comparison with other Eastern and Central European countries has led to thousands of joint ventures and subsidiaries of foreign investors being formed in Hungary, and most of them very successfully.

Hungary follows the continental legal system. Corporate forms, their structures and organs and the powers and functions of the organs

D.Campbell and S.Woodley (eds.), The Comparative Law Yearbook of International Business 2003, 35-85

are regulated by law, and business associations may only be set up in the forms regulated by the Companies Act.[1] The most important laws in respect of joint ventures in Hungary are as follows:

(1) Act IV of 1959 on the Civil Code of the Republic of Hungary, as amended (Civil Code);
(2) Act CXLIV of 1997 on Business Associations, as amended (Companies Act);
(3) Act XXIV of 1988 on Investments of Foreigners in Hungary, as amended (Foreign Investment Act);
(4) Act CXLV of 1997 on the Registration of Companies, Public Company Information and Court Registration Proceedings, as amended (Company Registration Act);
(5) Act CXX of 2001 on the Capital Market, as amended (Capital Market Act);
(6) Act XVI of 1992 on Concessions, as amended (Concessions Act); and
(7) Act LVII of 1996 on the Prohibition of Unfair and Restrictive Market Practices, as amended (Competition Act).

Alternative Legal Forms in Structuring a Joint Venture

Some basic rules on the different forms of companies are provided in the Civil Code, but the Companies Act contains specific and detailed regulation of the different types of companies. There are six legal forms regulated by the Companies Act:

(1) Unlimited partnership (*közkereseti társaság* — Kkt);
(2) Limited partnership (*betéti társaság* — Bt);
(3) Joint enterprise (*közös vállalat* — Kv);
(4) Professional association (*egyesülés*);
(5) Limited liability company (*korlátolt felelosségu társaság* —Kft); and
(6) Company limited by shares (*részvénytársaság* — Rt).

These are commonly referred to as business associations or companies (*gazdasági társaságok* or *társaságok*). Out of the above six forms, joint enterprises and professional associations are not used for joint ventures, and even Hungarian partners very rarely choose these forms. This chapter, therefore, deals in detail only with the widely used

---

1 Companies Act, Section 2.

company forms, that is, unlimited partnerships, limited partnerships and, in particular, limited liability companies and companies limited by shares.

Unlimited Partnership

The unlimited partnership is a business association without legal personality. Under Section 81(1) of the Companies Act, the members of an unlimited partnership undertake to pursue joint business-like economic activities with unlimited joint and several liability, and to make available to the partnership the assets necessary for such activities. The liability of the partners is in two stages. First, the company itself is liable with its assets. Where the assets of the unlimited partnership are not sufficient to cover the liabilities of the company, however, the partners will be liable to the extent of their personal property, their liability being unlimited joint and several.

As a general rule, pursuant to Section 4 of the Companies Act, a natural person may be a member with unlimited liability in only one business association and a minor may not be a member with unlimited liability in any business association. Also, an unlimited partnership or limited partnership may not be a member with unlimited liability in a business association.

Members of partnerships may assist personally in the activity of the partnership and be entitled to remuneration therefor. In addition to the items prescribed by the Companies Act as the mandatory contents of the articles of association, if so required by the partners, the method and content of the personal assistance undertaken by the members and the rules of operation of members' meetings must be set out in the articles of association.

Under Section 86 of the Companies Act, unless otherwise provided by the articles of association, all members are entitled to be involved in the management of the partnership. However, the members may, in the articles of association, entrust one or several members with the management, in which case the other members are not entitled to manage. A member of the partnership with legal personality must provide for management by a natural person entitled to represent such legal person.

The supreme body of an unlimited partnership is the members' meeting in which all members take part in person. This company form is traditionally used by small-scale businesses, rather than by private persons, because there is no statutory minimum capital requirement.

Limited Partnership

Like the unlimited partnership, the limited partnership is also a business association without legal personality. Under Section 101(1) of the Companies Act, the members of the partnership undertake to pursue joint business-like economic activities in a way in which the liability of at least one member (general partner) for the obligations not covered by the assets of the partnership is unlimited. Liability between the general partners is joint and several, while at least one other member (limited partner) is only obliged to provide the contribution undertaken in the articles of association and, subject to the exceptions contained in the Companies Act, is not liable for the obligations of the partnership.

Unless otherwise provided by the Companies Act, the regulations applicable to unlimited partnerships shall apply to limited partnerships. The basic difference is the limited liability of the limited partner, but limited partners bear the same liability as general partners if their names appear in the company name of the partnership. Only limited partners are entitled to undertake management of the partnership. However, limited partners may also take part in the activities of the members' meeting. This company form, like the unlimited partnership, is also generally used for small-scale businesses, but sometimes joint ventures are also established in the form of a limited partnership.

Joint Enterprise

Under Section 106 of the Companies Act, joint enterprises are business associations founded by members who are liable for their obligations with their assets. If the assets of the enterprise do not cover its debts, the members shall, in proportion to their contribution, bear joint responsibility for the debts of the enterprise as guarantors.

Professional Association

Under Section 272 of the Companies Act, a professional association is a cooperative business association with legal personality founded by the members to facilitate the success of their business activities and to coordinate such business activities, as well as to represent their professional interests. A professional association does not aim at making a profit. Its members bear unlimited joint and several liability for debts in excess of the association's assets. A professional association may also pursue other service and joint economic activities in support of its coordination duties.

Limited Liability Company

Pursuant to Section 121 of the Companies Act, limited liability companies are business associations founded with an initial capital consisting of capital contributions of a pre-determined amount (quotas). The obligation of the members (quotaholders) to the company extends only to the provision of their capital contributions, and to other possible contributions as provided for in the articles of association. Subject to certain exceptions contained in the Companies Act, members are not liable for the obligations of the company. The limited liability company is a separate legal person.

The limited liability company is the most favored company form for joint ventures as the minimum capital requirement is only HUF 3-million (approximately US $13,300). As a general rule, the liability of the members is limited to the value of their quotas, and the structure of a limited liability company is much more flexible than that of the company limited by shares. This company form is similar to the German GmbH or the French Sàrl.

A member of a limited liability company may be a foreign or Hungarian natural person or legal entity. A limited liability company may also be established by only one member (one-man company). According to the Companies Act, a one-man company cannot be established by a company which also has only one member and shareholder.[2]

The equity capital of the company consists of the amount of the members' capital contributions, which can be in cash and/or in kind. Half of the cash contributions, but at least HUF 1-million, must be provided before the submission of the request for registration of the company to the Court of Registration, the other half being paid into the bank account of the company within one year from registration of the company. In the case of a one-man company, the whole cash contribution to the capital is to be paid prior to the submission of the request for registration. Contributions in kind must be provided in full before submission of the registration request. The amount of cash

2 Companies Act, Section 4(4).

contributions may not be less than thirty per cent of the equity capital of the company and HUF 1-million. Contributions in kind constituting a part of the equity capital may be any marketable object or intellectual work having a pecuniary value or any right representing pecuniary value. Only such objects, intellectual works or rights which may be subject to execution and may be subsequently transferred by the company without the consent (permission) of a third party may be taken into account as a contribution in kind. Permission granted already on the provision of the contribution in kind qualifies as such.[3]

The capital contributions of the members may differ, but each must be at least HUF 100,000 and the amount must be divisible by 10,000. Following the registration of the company, the rights of the members and the shares due to them from the assets of the company are embodied in business quotas. The membership rights attached to equivalent business shares are identical, but the articles of association may invest certain business quotas with different membership rights (for example, voting rights or profit share).

Each member has only one business quota. If a member acquires another independent business quota, the original business quota is increased by the acquired business quota. One business quota may have several owners, and such owners qualify as one member of the company. The owners' rights, including the conclusion of the articles of association, may be exercised only by their joint representative, and they shall bear joint and several liability for the duties owed by such member. The articles of association may provide that employees of the company may acquire employees' business quotas free of charge or at a reduced price.

Business quotas are transferable, but it is an advantage of the limited liability company form that the members, in the articles of association, may limit the transfer of quotas, thereby preventing a hostile take-over. Business quotas may be freely transferred to other members of the company, and members may grant each other pre-emption rights in the articles of association. Business quotas may be transferred to non-members, but the other members, the company or a person appointed by the members' meeting, in that order, have statutory pre-emption rights over business quotas to be transferred by means of a contract of sale. It can be stipulated in the articles of association that

3 Companies Act, Sections 124–126.

quota transfers to non-members are subject to the consent of the company. In this case, the conditions for granting or refusing such consent are to be provided for in the articles of association. The transfer of business shares based on legal grounds other than a contract of sale (for example, gift, inheritance, exchange or in-kind contribution to another company) may be excluded or restricted in the articles of association.

Based on a resolution of the members' meeting passed by at least a three-quarter majority of votes, a company may acquire a maximum of a third of the business quotas from its assets in excess of its initial capital. Within a period of one year following the purchase thereof, the company is obliged to sell such business quotas or transfer them to members in proportion to their capital contributions without compensation. Alternatively, the company can withdraw them, decreasing the initial capital of the company, following the expiration of the one-year deadline.

The main organs of a limited liability company are the members' meeting (or quotaholders' meeting), the managing director(s) and the supervisory board. The members' meeting is the governing body of the limited liability company, which decides on the most important questions. A members' meeting must be convened at least once every year. In the case of a one-man company, the founder and sole member exercises the rights of the members' meeting. The following fall within the exclusive competence of the members' meeting:[4]

(1) Approval of the report prepared pursuant to the Accounting Act, including the decision on the appropriation of after-tax profits;
(2) Order and repayment of additional payments;
(3) Decision to pay interim dividends;
(4) Consent for the division of business quotas and order on the withdrawal of business quotas;
(5) Resolution on initiating the exclusion of a member;
(6) Decision on confiscated business quotas and the purchase of such by members;
(7) Appointment and removal of the managing director, the setting of his remuneration and the exercise of employers' rights if the managing director is also employed by the company;
(8) Appointment and removal of supervisory board members and the setting of their remuneration;

4 Companies Act, Section 150(2).

(9) Appointment and removal of the auditor;
(10) Approval to conclude contracts which take place between the company and one of its members, its managing director or one of their close relatives;[5]
(11) Enforcement of indemnification claims against members responsible for setting up the company, managing directors or supervisory board members;
(12) Decision upon the termination of the company without a legal successor or the alteration of the company;
(13) Amendment of the articles of association; and
(14) All issues which are assigned to the competence of the members' meeting by the law or the articles of association.

The members' meeting has a quorum if at least half of the initial capital or the majority of the eligible votes are represented. However, the articles of association may stipulate a higher rate of participation.

Members shall be invited to the members' meeting, and the agenda of the meeting shall be announced at the same time. There must be a period of at least fifteen days between the dispatch of the invitations and the date of the members' meeting. If the members' meeting has not been convened properly, it may pass resolutions only if all members are present and none of the members protests against the holding of such meeting. With the exception of resolutions on the approval of the yearly financial report and on the appropriation of after-tax profits, members may pass resolutions in writing without holding a formal members' meeting.

Unless otherwise provided by law or the articles of association, the members' meeting passes resolutions by a simple majority of votes. Under the provisions of the Companies Act, at least a three-quarter majority of votes is required in the following matters:

(1) Exclusion of a member;
(2) Removal of the managing director;
(3) Acquisition of own business quota;
(4) Amendment of the articles of association;
(5) Increase and decrease in the capital of the company; and
(6) Decision on termination of the company without a legal successor or alteration of the company.

5 Civil Code, Section 685(b).

The day-to-day operation, management and representation of the company are carried out by one or more managing directors. The managing director can be either a local or foreign citizen. If the managing director is a foreign citizen, he does not need a working permit, but other foreign employees employed by the company must obtain a working permit.

The appointment of a supervisory board is only mandatory if the equity capital of the company exceeds HUF 50-million or if the annual average of the number of full-time employees employed by the company exceeds 200, in which case at least a third of the members of the supervisory board must be comprised of employee representatives. In the case of a one-man company, a supervisory board is mandatory only in the latter case. The supervisory board consists of at least three members and acts as an independent body. It elects a chairman (and, if necessary, a deputy chairman or deputy chairmen) from among its members. It has a quorum if two-thirds of its members, but at least three members, are present and pass resolutions by simple majority. The members of the supervisory board must act in person; representation is not allowed. Apart from the mandatory rules of the Companies Act, the supervisory board must establish its rules of procedure itself, which must be approved by the company's supreme body which, in the case of a limited liability company, is the members' meeting and, in the case of a company limited by shares, is the general meeting.

The task of the supervisory board is the supervision of the management of the company on behalf of the company's supreme body. The supervisory board may request information from the executive officers or the managerial employees of the company, and may inspect the books and documents of the company. It must examine all substantial business policy reports on the agenda of the meeting of the company's supreme body, as well as any proposals relating to issues falling within the exclusive competence of the company's supreme body. The company's supreme body may pass a resolution on the yearly financial report and on the appropriation of after-tax profits only if in possession of a written report from the supervisory board. If, in the judgment of the supervisory board, the activities of the management are contrary to the law, the articles of association or deed of formation (company statutes) or the resolutions of the company's supreme body, or otherwise infringe upon the interests of the company or its members/shareholders, the supervisory board must call an extraordinary meeting of the company's supreme body and include such matter in its agenda.

Under Section 33 of the Companies Act, the deed of formation (company statutes) of a company limited by shares, or the articles of association of a limited liability company, may transfer to the competence of the supervisory board the appointment and removal of the members of the board of directors (or managing director), the setting of their remuneration and the approval of the legal transactions set out in the deed of formation (company statutes) or articles of association. The supervisory board must report at the next meeting of the company's supreme body on the measures it has taken within the competence transferred to it. If, within its competence, the supervisory board has refused to approve a legal transaction, the managing director or board of directors is entitled to convene the company's supreme body. In such cases, the members' meeting or general meeting, as the case may be, may approve the legal transaction by a majority of at least three-quarters of the votes.

The appointment of an auditor is mandatory with one-man limited liability companies, while a limited liability company having more than one member should have a registered auditor if its subscribed capital is more than HUF 50-million or another legal rule prescribes it. For example, under the Accounting Act,[6] if the annual income of the company exceeds HUF 50-million, the election of an auditor is mandatory. In such cases, at least one auditor is to be elected from among individuals or companies qualified and licensed as auditors in Hungary. A founder or member/shareholder of the company may not be an auditor. Executive officers, supervisory board members and their close relatives and employees of the company may not be appointed as auditors for a period of three years after termination of their respective positions. If the auditor is a company, in addition to the person pursuing the activities on behalf of the auditor company, the regulations relating to personal conflict of interests must also be applied to all members/shareholders, executive officers and managerial employees of the auditor company.

The authenticity and legal compliance of the report prepared pursuant to the Accounting Act are to be examined by the auditor and, without a statement of opinion by the auditor, the company's supreme body may not decide upon such report. Furthermore, the auditor shall

6 Act C of 2000 on Accountancy.

examine all substantial business reports proposed to the company's supreme body from the point of view of whether they contain true data and comply with all of the relevant legal regulations. The auditor may inspect the books of the company; request information from the executive officers, supervisory board members and employees; and examine the bank account, petty cash, stocks of securities and goods and the contracts of the company. The auditor is obliged to safeguard the information obtained regarding the affairs of the company as business secrets.

If the auditor ascertains or otherwise learns that a considerable decrease in the assets of the company is probable, or perceives any other issue which entails the liability of the executive officers or the supervisory board members, the auditor is obliged to request that the company's supreme body be convened. If the supreme body is not convened, or the supreme body fails to take the decisions required by the appropriate legal regulations, the auditor must inform the Court of Registration exercising legal supervision.

Company Limited by Shares

The most sophisticated company form is the company limited by shares. This company form is similar to the German AG or the French SA. Joint ventures are relatively rarely established in this form because it is less flexible than the limited liability company, there are strict decision-making rules and the minimum capital requirement is higher. Establishing a company limited by shares is advisable if the shareholders wish to go public and collect capital in this way or do not want to have statutory restrictions on share transfer. Certain kinds of activities may be pursued only by companies limited by shares, such as banking and insurance.

The company limited by shares is a separate legal person. Pursuant to Section 175 of the Companies Act, companies limited by shares are business associations founded with a share capital (subscribed capital) consisting of shares of a pre-determined number and face value, and the obligation of the shareholders to the company extends to the face value or issue value of the shares. With the exceptions defined in the Companies Act, shareholders do not bear liability for the obligations of the company.

A company limited by shares may be private or public (close company). A company limited by shares qualifies as public when its shares are issued, in part or in full, publicly. Shares are negotiable securities embodying membership rights. There are two types of shares: bearer shares and registered shares. The shares of a close company, as well as uncertificated shares prepared according to the statutory provisions on securities, may only be registered shares. In respect of companies limited by shares founded for certain activities set out in separate acts, the law may prescribe that such companies may have only registered shares.

Bearer shares are freely negotiable without an indication of their holder. Unless otherwise provided by law, registered shares are freely negotiable, but the deed of formation of a close company may restrict the negotiation of shares or may make such transfer subject to the consent of the company. Such restrictions can include stipulations of pre-emption rights or redemption rights attached to printed registered share certificates, as well as the right of an option to purchase, but such restrictive rights are valid in respect of a company limited by shares or third parties only if such rights have been stamped on the share certificates.

Another restriction could be when the deed of formation of a close company restricts the categories or classes of shares to be acquired by certain persons by way of transfer. The deed of formation of a close company may stipulate that the transfer of registered shares be subject to the consent of the company. Such consent may be refused on certain grounds, in particular, if the shares in question are to be acquired by a competitor of the company or, considering the purpose of the company and its shareholders, such refusal is justified by some other reason set out in the deed of formation.

Printed registered share certificates are negotiated by means of a full or empty endorsement drawn up on the back of the share certificate or the sheet attached to the certificate. With respect to the negotiation of uncertificated shares, the provisions of the Capital Market Act[7] are authoritative. According to the Act, only registered and uncertificated shares may be offered to the public. Shares placed into public circulation in printed form prior to the entry into force of the Capital Market Act must be converted into uncertificated shares by 31 December 2004.

Within the individual types of shares, several categories of shares may be issued: ordinary shares, preference shares, employees' shares

---

7 Act Number CXX of 2001.

and interest-bearing shares. Shares not belonging to any other category of shares are ordinary shares. Within preference shares, shares may belong to different classes and, within a class of shares, shares having different contents or shares representing different membership rights may be issued. Within a category or class of shares, several series of shares may be issued. Shares of the same type, content and representing the same membership rights qualify as one series of shares. Shares of the same series may not differ in their face value or method of production.

Preference shares are registered shares which grant certain preferences to their holders over other categories of shares. Within preference shares, the deed of formation (company statutes) may define:

(1) Preferred dividends;
(2) Preferred liquidation quotas upon the termination of a company limited by shares without a legal successor;
(3) Preference related to voting rights; or
(4) Classes of shares granting pre-emption rights in relation to the shares of a close company.

It is also possible that a class of preference shares jointly represents an entitlement to preferred dividends and preferred liquidation quotas. The voting rights related to preference shares (with the exception of the class of preference shares enjoying voting preference) may be restricted or prohibited in the deed of formation (company statutes). Otherwise, the voting rights of preference shares follow the face value of the shares. The sum of the face value of preference shares issued by a company limited by shares may not exceed half of the share capital of the company.

Employees' shares are registered shares issued free of charge or at a reduced price to the full-time or part-time employees of the company limited by shares. Employees' shares may entitle their holders to dividends from after-tax profits, to be distributed among the shareholders before the holders of shares belonging to other categories or classes of shares, but following shares granting preferred dividends. Employees' shares may be issued with a simultaneous share capital increase of the company limited by shares, up to a maximum of fifteen per cent of the increased share capital.

Interest-bearing shares are registered shares entitling their holders to a predetermined rate of interest, and may be issued to an extent of up to ten per cent of the share capital. From after-tax profits, owners of interest-bearing shares are entitled to the interest calculated according to the method shown on the shares on the face value thereof. No interest may be paid to shareholders if, as a result of this, the equity of the company does not reach the share capital of a company limited by shares as stated in the legal regulations on accounting. In addition to interest, owners of interest-bearing shares shall be entitled to all other rights attached to the shares, including the right to dividends.

A company limited by shares may acquire its own shares from its assets in excess of its share capital. The sum of the joint face value of own shares held by a close company may not exceed ten per cent of the share capital and, in the case of public companies limited by shares, five per cent of the share capital. A company limited by shares may not exercise voting rights on the basis of the own shares acquired, and must sell such shares within a period of one year. If a company limited by shares fails to satisfy its obligation to sell, it is required to withdraw the shares with a simultaneous reduction in its share capital.

A company limited by shares may be formed by a sole shareholder alone according to the rules of private (close) formation. A one-man company limited by shares may also be created in such a manner that the ownership rights of all the shares in an existing company limited by shares are acquired by a single shareholder. With respect to one-man companies limited by shares, the sole shareholder resolves the issues falling within the competence of the general meeting in writing, of which the executive officers must be informed. The same person may not be an executive officer or a member of the supervisory board of a one-man company limited by shares and, if such shareholder is a business organization, it cannot be the company's shareholder at the same time. In order for a contract concluded between a one-man company limited by shares and its shareholder to be valid, written form is required.

The share capital of a company limited by shares may not be less than HUF 20-million. Upon formation, the amount of contributions in cash may not be less than thirty per cent of the share capital or HUF 10-million and the rest of the capital may consist of contributions in kind. In the event that a contribution is provided in kind, an auditor's report must be attached to the deed of formation, which contains a description and valuation of such contribution and a statement by the auditor as to whether the value of such contribution complies with the number and face value of the shares to be received in exchange, as well as a description of the valuation methods applied by the auditor. A company limited by shares may be registered only if, prior to the submission of the application for registration, the founders who have undertaken to provide contributions in cash have paid at least thirty per cent of the face value or issue value of the shares undertaken to be received in the deed of formation, but an amount of at least HUF 10-million in total and contributions in kind must have been made fully available to the company.

The share capital of a company limited by shares may be increased in four ways: the issue of new shares; the debiting of assets in excess of the share capital; the issue of employees' shares; and the issue of convertible bonds, as a conditional increase of the share capital. The different types and methods of increasing the share capital may be decided upon and implemented at the same time. New shares or bonds may be issued publicly or privately. For the public formation of a company limited by shares or for a public issue of shares, not only the rules of the Companies Act, but also the strict provisions of the Capital Market Act, apply.

The main organs of a company limited by shares are the general meeting, the board of directors and the supervisory board. The appointment of an auditor is mandatory for companies limited by shares. The supreme body of a company limited by shares is the general meeting, which consists of all the shareholders. The following matters fall within the exclusive competence of the general meeting:

(1) Establishment and amendment of the deed of formation (company statutes);
(2) Decision on the change of the form of the company limited by shares;
(3) Decision on alteration or termination of the company without a legal successor;
(4) The appointment and removal of the members of the board of directors, members of the supervisory board and the auditor, and the setting of their remuneration;
(5) Approval of the report prepared pursuant to the Accounting Act, including the decision on the appropriation of after-tax profits;
(6) Decision to pay interim dividends;
(7) Decision on the alteration of types of shares;
(8) Decision to change printed share certificates into uncertificated shares;

(9) Variation of the rights attached to individual series of shares, and the alteration of categories or classes of shares;
(10) Decision on the issue of convertible bonds or bonds with subscription rights;
(11) Decision on the acquisition of own shares, unless otherwise provided by the Companies Act, and, in the case of a public company, upon the acceptance of a public offer for purchase received in respect of own shares; and
(12) Decision on all issues which are assigned to the competence of the general meeting by law or the deed of formation (company statutes).

The general meeting must pass resolutions on the issues listed above under points (1), (3) and (9) by a majority of at least three-quarters of the votes. The deed of formation (company statutes) may also stipulate that resolutions be passed by a majority of three-quarters or more of the votes in other issues.

Resolutions of the general meeting which discriminate against the rights attached to a certain series of shares may be passed only if, according to the procedure laid down in the deed of formation (company statutes), a majority of at least three-quarters of the shareholders of the series of shares in question consent thereto in advance. In the course thereof, any provisions on the possible restriction or exclusion of voting rights attached to such shares may not be applied. For the protection of the rights of minority shareholders, the Companies Act provides that a resolution of the general meeting aimed at changing the form of a public company may be passed only if, according to the procedure laid down in the deed of formation (company statutes), a majority of at least three-quarters of the shareholders representing up to one per cent each of the votes consent thereto in advance.[8]

The Companies Act does not allow, even in the case of a close company, shareholders to reach decisions in writing; it is always necessary to hold a general meeting. The general meeting must be convened as frequently as laid down by the deed of formation (company statutes), but at least once every year. If required, extraordinary general meetings may be held at any time. The general meeting shall be convened according to the method set out in the deed of formation (company statutes). In the case of a close company, this will be by means of invitations sent to the shareholders at least fifteen days

8 Companies Act, Section 238.

before the first day of the general meeting. In the case of a public company, there will be an announcement published according to the provisions of the deed of formation at least thirty days before the first day of the general meeting.

The general meeting has a quorum if shareholders representing more than half of the votes embodied by shares with voting rights are present, though the deed of formation (company statutes) may stipulate a higher rate of participation. A certified copy of the minutes of the general meeting (including the resolutions) or an abstract thereof, the attendance sheet and one copy of the publication containing the announcement on calling the general meeting shall be submitted to the Court of Registration by the board of directors within thirty days of the end of the general meeting. Any shareholder may request an abstract or copy of the minutes.

The management body of a company limited by shares is the board of directors. The board of directors consists of between three and eleven members, who must be natural persons. The board of directors elects its chairman from among its members. The office of the chairman or that of the members of the board of directors may not be carried out within the framework of an employment relationship. The directors must be appointed for a definite period of time, but not more than five years. They may be re-appointed and may be removed by the general meeting. The board of directors exercises its rights and performs its duties as an independent body. The rules of procedure approved by the board of directors provide for the division of tasks and competence among the members of the board of directors. The members of the board take part in the general meeting of the company with a right of consultation. The deed of formation of a close company may provide that no board of directors be appointed, in which case the rights of the board of directors are exercised by a general director.

The appointment of a supervisory board and an auditor is mandatory with companies limited by shares, the rules of which are the same as described above for limited liability companies.

Choice of Legal Form

In choosing the legal form for a joint venture, the parties should consider different aspects. Before making their decision, they should examine limitation of liability, capital requirements, flexibility of the company form, tax consequences and accounting rules. Regarding liability, there are two options: limited or unlimited liability companies.

From among the company forms used for joint ventures in the case of an unlimited partnership, the liability of the partners is completely unlimited joint and several. All the other company forms provide the partners with at least a certain degree of limitation of liability. The limited partnership form combines unlimited and limited liabilities. At least one of the partners bears unlimited liability, while the other partners are obliged only to provide their contribution and are liable only to that extent.

Foreign investors generally prefer their liability to be limited, so most joint ventures or subsidiaries involving foreign investors are established in the form of limited liability companies or companies limited by shares. With these two company forms, the liability of the members/shareholders, as a general rule, is limited to their capital contributions, that is, payment of the nominal or face value of their shares.

The rules of the Companies Act basically classify the types of business associations, on the basis of the liability of the members/shareholders for the debts of the company, as limited or unlimited liability company forms. However, the new Companies Act,[9] in force as of 16 June 1998, introduced the concept of piercing the corporate veil, that is, the limited liability provisions in company law.

The rule of unlimited liability pursuant to Section 56(1) of the Companies Act is that, if the liability of a member for the obligations of the business association was unlimited joint and several during the existence of the business association, the obligation of the member to accept liability shall also be unlimited joint and several for the obligations of the terminated business association. A debt incurred with regard to the obligation to accept liability among members shall be divided proportionately in relation to their share in the assets of the business association.

The basic rule of limited liability pursuant to Section 56(2) of the Companies Act is that, if the liability of a member for the obligations of the business association was limited during the existence of the business association, the liability of the member for its obligations

9 Act CXLIV of 1997, replacing the previous Companies Act, Act VI of 1988.

once terminated shall be limited to that share of the assets distributed upon termination which is due to such member.

However, pursuant to Sections 56(3) and 56(4), a member who has abused his limited liability may not invoke such limited liability. Therefore, a member of a limited liability company or a shareholder of a company limited by shares who has abused the separate legal personality and limited liability of the business association to the detriment of creditors shall bear unlimited joint and several liability for the unsatisfied obligations of such business association. Such liability of the members shall exist, in particular, if such members disposed of the assets of the business association as if they had been their own or reduced the assets for the benefit of others or for themselves in a way in which they knew, or should have known, that the business association would not be able to satisfy its obligations towards third parties as a result thereof.

Pursuant to Section 296 of the Companies Act, if, as a result of a dominant member's influencing interest amounting to at least majority control (more than fifty per cent), a controlled company pursues a permanently detrimental business policy and, as a consequence, the assets of the controlled company do not cover the satisfaction of creditors upon the liquidation of the company, the court may, upon the claim of a creditor lodged in the course of liquidation proceedings, order the unlimited and full liability of the dominant member for the debts of the controlled company.

With respect to a controlling interest (more than seventy-five per cent), if the dominant member pursues a permanently detrimental business policy as a result of its controlling interest, and this seriously endangers the discharge of the company's obligations, the court may, upon a claim by any member or creditor of the controlled company, order the unlimited and full liability of the dominant member for the debts of the controlled company already incurred during the normal course of business, not only in the course of liquidation proceedings. Such unlimited liability may only be enforced against such member after the controlled company has been terminated as a result of liquidation.

Under Section 297 of the Companies Act, the provisions of Section 296 shall be applied *mutatis mutandis*, even if a shareholder or member of a company limited by shares or limited liability company holds at least a half or three-quarters of the votes upon the formation of a business association.

Pursuant to Sections 173(3) and 271(3), the rules of liability related to a controlling interest described above are to be applied correspondingly to the liability of the member of a one-man limited liability company or a one-man company limited by shares. The provision on the prohibition against enforcement of a permanently detrimental business policy may not be applied against the sole member/shareholder of a one-man company if he has undertaken unlimited full liability for the debts of the company in the deed of formation or in an alteration thereto.

As the rules on piercing through limited liability have only been in force since 16 June 1998, there is still no published court practice on when the court would order unlimited liability of members whose liability is otherwise limited.

Joint venture partners should also consider the capital requirement of the different company forms. In the case of unlimited and limited partnerships, there is no minimum capital requirement, and the partners may freely decide on their contribution to the capital. For the establishment of a limited liability company, at least HUF 3-million initial capital is required, while, for the share capital of a company limited by shares, the requirement is at least HUF 20-million. The capital contribution for both forms can consist of cash contributions and contributions in kind. However, the proportion of contributions in cash and in kind at the establishment of the company is prescribed by the Companies Act.

Another important aspect is the flexibility of the company form and maintaining the company organization. From this point of view, the limited liability company can be recommended. With this company form, the day-to-day management is carried out by the managing director, and the supreme body is the members' meeting, which — depending on the requirements of the members — may decide only on those important matters which belong to the exclusive competence of the members' meeting under the provisions of the Companies Act. In the articles of association, however, the parties may also refer other matters to the exclusive competence of the members' meeting.

An important rule of the new Companies Act is that the supreme body of a company may deprive an executive officer or the board of directors of competence falling within the scope of management only in cases and to the extent rendered possible by the articles of association, deed of formation or company statutes. However, this strict provision may not be applied in the case of one-man companies and companies in which a member/shareholder holds a majority of three-quarters or more of the votes. In such cases, the member/shareholder may deprive an executive officer of his competence and may give him instructions in writing. The executive officer is then exempted from liability by the decision of the member/shareholder.

The appointment of a supervisory board or an auditor is required only for limited liability companies with high capital (that is, capital above HUF 50-million) or one-man companies, and no public announcement is required by law. A company limited by shares is the most sophisticated company form, where the capital requirement is higher and it is mandatory to appoint a supervisory board and an auditor. The shareholders may only decide upon company matters at general meetings, and public announcements are required by the law.

The tax rules are the same for all company forms in Hungary, but there are differences in bookkeeping rules. Unlimited and limited partnerships may keep books by single-entry and must only switch to double-entry bookkeeping when their annual net revenue from entrepreneurial activity exceeds HUF 50-million for two consecutive years. Limited liability companies and companies limited by shares, however, must always follow the rules of double-entry bookkeeping.

The domestic tax provisions for foreign investors may also influence the choice of company form because, in certain countries, investment in a limited partnership can be more advantageous, or investment in a limited liability company may provide a better tax position, for the foreign investor than an investment in a company limited by shares.

Governing Law and Language

In Hungary, companies can be established only in accordance with the Companies Act. Section 2(1) of the Companies Act prescribes that business associations may only be set up in the forms stipulated in the Act. The Companies Act contains detailed rules on the formation, organization and operation of a business association with a registered office in Hungary, as well as the rights, obligations and responsibilities of the founders and members/shareholders of the business association and the alteration, merger, de-merger or termination of a business association without a legal successor. Furthermore, the Companies Act regulates the acquisition of a dominant interest in a business association. The provisions of the Civil Code are applied to the property and relationships of business associations and their members/shareholders not regulated by the Companies Act.

There are no statutory restrictions on the language of contracts, and the parties are free to choose the language of the founding document. However, Hungarian is the official language of the courts and administrative bodies. The Civil Procedure Act[10] requires that all foreign language documents be translated into the form of a certified translation and submitted to the courts and authorities in such form. This means that, even if the parties sign the founding document in another language, for the registration of the company, an official translation of the founding document must be submitted to the Court of Registration.

If the parties, in addition to the founding document of the company, conclude another contract regulating the legal relationships between the joint venture partners (such as a syndicate agreement, joint venture agreement or shareholders' agreement), such contract can be concluded in any foreign language without translation and need not be submitted to the Court of Registration. The governing law of such agreements can be any law selected by the parties but, of course, the mandatory provisions of the Hungarian Companies Act must also be taken into consideration.

Scope of Business Activity

Under Section 11 of the Companies Act, the articles of associations, deed of formation or company statutes of a company shall contain the scope of activity of the company. Under Section 12(2)(f) of the Company Registration Act, the founding parties shall define the scope of activity of the company according to the Bulletin issued by the Central Statistical Office (CSO), which contains the Standard Sectoral Scheme of Economic Activities (TEÁOR). The CSO has developed the TEÁOR based on the classification scheme adopted by the European Union.

The TEÁOR lists all business activities in a specific order. Each activity has a four-digit number. Usually, more than one activity is covered by a "TEÁOR business activity" number, so it is possible to

10 Act II of 1952, as amended.

indicate in the founding document if a company carries out only a part of the activities within the business activity covered by one TEÁOR number.

Certain business activities can exclusively be carried out by the State or local government, for example, the operation of local public utilities, passenger transport and transportation of goods by railway and activities with the objective of organizing and operating gambling. The State or local government, through undertakings owned by the State or local government, pursue these activities, or contracts of concession are concluded according to Act XVI of 1991 on Concessions and other concession regulations. In the latter case, a concession company is established for a definite period of time according to the Companies Act and the specific regulations of the concession law and contract of concession.

There are certain business activities that require a license or the approval of the authorities, for example, insurance and banking. Pre-registration companies may pursue business activities only after submitting their application for registration. They may pursue business activities subject to official license after registration, provided that they are in possession of a license granted by the relevant authority.

Some activities can only be pursued by companies having specific forms, for example, insurance activities can only be pursued by a company limited by shares, a cooperative or an association or branch office of a foreign-registered insurance company. Banks and specialized credit institutions may only operate in the form of companies limited by shares or branch offices, cooperative credit institutions as cooperatives and financial enterprises in the form of companies limited by shares, cooperatives or branch offices. Certain activities require the shareholders or employees to hold specific qualifications, for example, the operation of pharmacies. There are also some activities that require notification by the company of the competent authority or registration with the authority.

Financing the Joint Venture

There are no special provisions for the financing of joint ventures, the same rules being applicable to a company with foreign participation or to a company where all the members/shareholders are Hungarian.

Since the beginning of the 1990s, the foreign exchange control system has gradually become completely free and, as of 16 June 2001, all foreign exchange control restrictions have been repealed and the Hungarian Forint has become fully convertible. From a practical point of view, it means that any Hungarian company may take loans from abroad, whether from a foreign bank, a foreign member/shareholder or from any other foreign company.

Hungary has a developed banking system with a number of commercial banks, most of which are privatized banks with foreign participation or wholly owned by foreign shareholders. Thus, not only foreign banks, but also Hungarian banks, are available for corporate or project finance.

Antitrust and Competition Law

Antitrust Rules

Chapter XIV of the Companies Act provides the basic and general rules for the takeover of limited liability companies and companies limited by shares. The rules have three aims:

(1) To protect the rights of minority shareholders;

(2) To ensure publicity by creating the obligation to announce the acquisition of influencing interests (twenty-five per cent + one vote: significant interest, fifty per cent + one vote: majority interest and seventy-five per cent + one vote: controlling interest); and

(3) To protect creditors' interests by establishing the direct liability of the dominant member in specific cases.

Chapter VII of the Capital Market Act deals with the acquisition of influence in public limited companies. The new regulation regarding the acquisition of influence in public companies limited by shares, effective as of 18 August 2001, was already introduced by the amendment of Act 111 of 1996 on Securities, Investment Services and the Stock Exchange, this Law later being replaced by the Capital Market Act, effective as of 1 January 2002, with these rules being completely taken over from the previous Act. The rules of acquisition of interests in public limited companies are very detailed and rather sophisticated. The term "acquisition of influence" is defined as a wide category of acquiring influence. Whenever influence is acquired in a public company limited by shares reaching five per cent, and all subsequent share acquisitions in five per cent stages (that is, ten, fifteen, twenty and so on), these should be notified by the acquiring party within two calendar days to the Supervisory Commission and to the board of directors of the company. Any acquisition of influence in a public limited company in excess of thirty-three per cent is subject to a public purchase offer approved in advance by the Hungarian Financial Supervisory Authority. If there is no shareholder in the public company limited by shares, other than the bidder, holding more than ten per cent of the voting rights, whether directly or indirectly, the public purchase offer must be made if the influence to be acquired exceeds twenty-five per cent.

Insider Trading and Unfair Price Manipulation

Part Six of the Capital Market Act regulates the prohibition of insider trading and unfair price manipulation. Sections 199 to 205 declare that it is forbidden to use insider information to conclude a transaction or order the conclusion of a transaction for securities and exchange products affected by insider information. Insider trading is also regulated by Section 299/A of the Criminal Code,[11] which provides punishments therefor.

Anti-Dumping Regulations

With regard to the rights and obligations of Hungary by virtue of joining the World Trade Organization (WTO), Hungary has regulated the rules of anti-dumping and countervailing duties in Government Decree 69/1994 (V.4). Investigations concerning the levying of anti-dumping and countervailing duties shall be conducted by the Ministry of Economy.

Consumer Protection

In Hungary, consumer protection is regulated by Act CLV of 1997 on Consumer Protection (Consumer Protection Act), which was harmonized with Council Directive 92/59/EEC on Overall Product Safety and Council Directive 87/102/EEC, amended by Council Directive 90/88/EEC, on Consumer Loans. The Consumer Protection Act

11 Act 4 of 1978.

protects the lives, health and property of consumers and, in connection with this, prescribes regulations for manufacturers and distributors. It imposes sanctions on manufacturers and distributors for the violation of legal regulations on the production, receiving, weighing, packaging, labeling, indication of price, storage, shipping and placement of goods on the market, or on the provision of services, and defrauding consumers by false weighing, calculation or adulteration of the quality of goods. For a consumer loan contract to be valid, the contract must be prepared in writing and one copy thereof must be given to the consumer.

The Consumer Protection Act also deals with manufacturers' obligations relating to labeling, users' manuals, certification of quality and packing, and the obligation of the distributor to indicate the price. If the manufacturer did not perform its obligations, the distributor should fulfill them.

An arbitration board is established for the purpose of attempting to reach an agreement between a business organization and a consumer to settle a dispute (consumer litigation) or, should this process fail to produce results, to decide on the matter in order to quickly, efficiently and simply enforce consumer rights. The resolution of the arbitration board is passed without prejudice to the consumer's right to have his claim enforced in court proceedings. The Bureau of Consumer Affairs, social organizations providing representation for consumer interests or the public prosecutor may file charges against a party causing substantial harm to a wide range of consumers by illegal activities, which is aimed at enforcing the interests of consumers even if the identity of the consumers actually injured cannot be established (*actio popularis*).

The Bureau of Consumer Affairs supervises and controls the observance of consumer protection regulations prescribed in the Consumer Protection Act and in other legal regulations. It may impose a fine, which does not have a maximum limit. The marketing of products of bad quality,[12] false attestation of quality,[13] false marking of goods,[14] deception of consumers[15] and profiteering[16] are crimes punished by the Criminal Code.

---

12 Consumer Protection Act, Sections 292–294.

13 Consumer Protection Act, Section 295.

14 Consumer Protection Act, Section 296.

15 Consumer Protection Act, Section 296/A.

16 Consumer Protection Act, Section 301.

Competition Law

Act LVII of 1996 on the Prohibition of Unfair and Restrictive Market Practices (Competition Act), as amended, is applicable to the market conduct of natural persons and legal entities, as well as unincorporated business associations within the territory of Hungary. The market conduct displayed by companies abroad, other than the forms of conduct regulated in Chapters II and III, also fall within the scope of this Act if the effect of such conduct might manifest itself within the Republic of Hungary.

In Chapter II, the Competition Act declares the general prohibition against unfair competition:

> "It is prohibited to violate or jeopardize the good reputation or creditworthiness of a competitor by stating or spreading untrue facts, and by misrepresenting true facts, as well as by any other practices."[17]

In this Chapter, the Act also prohibits:

(1) The violation of good reputation;
(2) Gaining access to or using business secrets;
(3) Making an unfair appeal to another party which is aimed at dissolving an economic relationship maintained with a third party or preventing the establishment of such a relationship;
(4) Producing or placing on the market goods or services with the typical outside appearance, packaging or marking of a competitor by which its goods are normally recognized without the express prior consent of the competitor; and
(5) Interfering with the integrity and fairness of bidding, auctions and transactions effected by way of exchange.

Chapter III prohibits the unfair influencing of consumer decisions. It is prohibited to mislead consumers in business competition or employ business methods restricting the consumer's freedom of choice unjustifiably.

Chapter IV prohibits both vertical and horizontal agreements which restrict competition. Agreements of minor importance are not subject to prohibition. Certain groups of agreements may be (and are) exempted by the Government in a decree form (block exemption).

---

17 Companies Act, Section 2.

The Office of Economic Competition exempts an agreement or planned agreement from the prohibition in a decision taken on the basis of an individual application (individual exemption).

Chapter V deals with the abuse of dominant position, which is prohibited by the Act. Dominant position means when an undertaking is in a position to conduct its economic activities in a given market in a manner largely independent of others, without having to consider the market behavior of its competitors, suppliers, buyers or other business partners insofar as to eliminate effective competition.

Chapter VI contains the regulation of mergers. Undertakings become concentrated if:

(1) Two or more previously independent (unrelated) companies merge, one merges into another or a part of an undertaking becomes a part of another undertaking which is independent of the first undertaking;

(2) One or more undertakings acquire direct or indirect control of the whole or part of one or more other previously independent undertakings; or

(3) Several independent (unrelated) undertakings jointly set up an undertaking, to be controlled by them, in which they unite their identical or complementary activities pursued earlier, provided that this does not qualify as an agreement restricting competition.

Authorization from the Office of Economic Competition is required for the merger of undertakings if the combined net sales revenue of the undertakings involved in the previous financial year exceeded HUF 10-billion and the previous year's net sales revenue of the business unit, the merging or acquired undertaking or — in respect of fusion — at least two of the undertakings directly involved, together with the indirect participants that are affiliated with the undertaking, is in excess of HUF 500-million.

The conduct of proceedings in relation to violation of the provisions contained in Chapter II falls within the competence of the court. Proceedings for the violation of other provisions of the Competition Act fall within the competence of the Office of Economic Competition. Decisions of the Office of Economic Competition cannot be appealed, but the interested party has the right to file a petition to the court within thirty days for a review of the decision.

Formation Agreement

The founding document of a company is a civil law document, which must be concluded in writing. The formation of a company is subject to the conclusion of articles of association. For one-member business associations and close companies limited by shares, approval of the deed of formation is required and, for public companies limited by shares, the company statutes must be approved. The articles of association and the deed of formation must be signed by all members (founders). The articles of association or deed of formation may be signed on behalf of a member by its legal representative (generally by the directors of the founding member if it is a legal entity) or a representative of such member having authorization in a notarial document or private document representing conclusive evidence of the authority to sign the formation document. The statutes of a company limited by shares must be adopted by the statutory general meeting.

The founding document is to be drawn up as a notarial document prepared by a notary public, or must be countersigned by an attorney-at-law or the in-house counsel of a Hungarian founder. In practice, attorneys-at-law generally countersign the founding document in Hungary, and the notarized form is only very rarely used. In the event that any document concerning the formation of a company is signed abroad, it must be notarized and, depending on the country of signature, legalized by the Hungarian consulate or supplied with an apostille in those countries which have joined the Hague Convention of 5 October 1961 on Abolishing the Requirement of Legalization for Foreign Public Documents.

The Companies Act prescribes the mandatory content of the founding documents, partly in its general part, which contains the common requirements, and also, where it regulates the different company forms, it provides for the specific requirements of the founding document for each particular form.

The mandatory content of founding documents for all company forms consists of:

(1) The company name and registered office of the company;
(2) The members of the company, indicating their names (company names) and domicile (registered office), with the exception of shareholders in the statutes;
(3) The scope of activity of the company;

(4) The subscribed capital of the company, as well as how and when the subscribed capital (contribution of the members) is to be made available;
(5) The method of signing for the company;
(6) The name and domicile of executive officers;
(7) The duration of the company, if founded for a limited period of time (if the founding document of a company does not provide for the duration of the business association, such business association shall be considered to have been established for an unlimited period time); and
(8) Any other information required by the Companies Act for the individual forms of company.

In the articles of association of an unlimited or limited partnership, in addition to the above listed items, the method and content of the personal assistance undertaken by the members and the rules of operation of the members' meeting shall also be regulated.

The specific content of the articles of association of a limited liability company in addition to the general content consists of:
(1) The amount of the initial capital and the capital contributions of the individual members;
(2) The method and due date for the payment of contributions in cash not paid up in full;
(3) The extent of voting rights;
(4) The first managing director and, in the case of several managing directors, the method of representation;
(5) The method of signing for the company;
(6) If establishment of a supervisory board is obligatory, the members of the first supervisory board;
(7) If appointment of an auditor is obligatory, the person appointed as the first auditor; and
(8) The order of calling repeated members' meetings.

If so required, the articles of association of a limited liability company must also provide for the following:
(1) Any contributions in kind and the value thereof;
(2) Other services having a pecuniary value (ancillary services) provided by the members to the company, the conditions thereof and the amount of penalty payable in the event of non-performance or insufficient performance of such ancillary services;

(3) The authorization of the members' meeting to order additional payments and to define the conditions thereof;
(4) The business quotas securing distinct membership rights;
(5) The exclusion or restriction of the transferability of business quotas or making the transfer of such quotas subject to the consent of the company;
(6) In the case of legal succession, a prohibition on the devolution or division of business quotas;
(7) The permission to withdraw business quotas;
(8) Employees' shares and the preferential rights attached thereto;
(9) The rules on quorum and the method of passing resolutions;
(10) The rules for calling a members' meeting at a place other than the registered office and the deadline for passing resolutions outside a meeting;
(11) The indication of a value limit above which transactions shall fall within the exclusive competence of the members' meeting;
(12) The distribution of after-tax profits and the proportion of assets due to members on the termination of the company, if the method of calculating such is different from the proportion of capital contributions;
(13) The entitlement of all members to management and representation;
(14) The restriction of the representation rights of managing directors;
(15) If a supervisory board is established voluntarily, the appointment of the members of the first supervisory board;
(16) If an auditor is elected voluntarily, the appointment of the first auditor; and
(17) In the case of an initial capital increase, the method of exercising preferential rights.

In addition to the general items, the following must be defined in the deed of formation of a private company limited by shares:

(1) The amount of share capital, the amount of cash contributions to be paid upon formation and the conditions for paying the face value or issue value of shares;
(2) The declaration of the founders on their obligation to receive all shares and on the division of the shares among themselves;
(3) The number and face value or issue value of the shares to be issued upon formation, the type of shares and the method of production, as well as the rules for transforming the shares into other types of shares;

(4) The number of members of the board of directors and the names and domiciles of the members of the first board of directors;
(5) The number of members of the supervisory board and the names and domiciles of the members of the first supervisory board;
(6) The period of mandate of the auditor and the name and domicile of the first auditor of a company limited by shares;
(7) The method of signing for the company;
(8) The method of calling general meetings and the conditions and method for exercising voting rights;
(9) The method of publishing announcements of the company; and
(10) The expected costs of formation.

If so required, the deed of formation shall contain the following:
(1) The object and value of in-kind contributions, the number and face value of shares to be received in exchange for such, the name (company) and domicile (registered office) of parties providing the contributions and the name (company) and domicile (registered office) of the auditor responsible for preliminary valuation;
(2) The rights attached to the individual categories and classes of shares, the possible restriction of certain rights attached to shares, the rules on transforming shares into other categories or classes of shares and the number and face value or issue value of shares belonging to certain categories or classes of shares, as per each series of shares;
(3) The series, number and face value of convertible bonds and bonds with subscription rights to be issued upon formation or thereafter, and the rules related to bonds;
(4) The authorization of the board of directors to increase the share capital, specifying the maximum amount of share capital increase to be implemented by the board;
(5) The authorization of the board of directors to issue and divide consolidated shares;
(6) Any restriction on the transfer of registered shares, or making transfers subject to the consent of the company; and
(7) Any other points for which the shareholders wish to provide in the deed of formation.

The founding document must always be submitted to the Court of Registration, where it will be available for public inspection. The Court of Registration exercises legal supervision over companies and, when registering a company, it controls the contents of the founding documents, ensuring that they meet the legal requirements and do not infringe mandatory legal rules.

As the founding document of a company is available for public inspection at the Court of Registration, it is preferable to keep the document as short as possible and to disclose internal relations only as far as required by law, avoiding the disclosure of confidential information. The internal relations and business strategy of joint venture partners, if the parties require so, are generally included in a separate joint venture agreement.

The joint venture agreement is a civil law agreement and is not governed by the Companies Act. Its governing law can be Hungarian law or any selected foreign law. When drafting the joint venture agreement, one must avoid provisions that contradict the mandatory rules of the Companies Act and the contents of the articles of association accepted by the parties. The contents of the joint venture agreement should preferably complement the provisions of the founding document. In the case of a breach of the provisions of the joint venture agreement, the court — depending on the nature of the breach and the governing law — may order specific performance in a given case or the payment of damages.

Procedure for Establishing a Corporate Vehicle

In Hungary, all companies, including partnerships, must be registered in the Register of Companies, which is maintained by the Court of Registration. The Court of Registration has offices at the county courts and, in Budapest, is situated at the Metropolitan Court. Companies are established upon their entry in the Register of Companies as of the date of such entry.[18] Between the date of the countersignature of the articles of association, deed of formation or company statutes and the date of registration of the company, the company operates as a pre-registration company, which should be indicated by affixing to its name the words "registration in progress". A pre-registration company may pursue business activities only after submitting its application for registration, but may not pursue activities subject to official license until after the registration process is

18 Companies Act, Section 16(2).

complete. The same rules are applicable for pre-registration companies as for registered companies, with the following differences:

(1) No changes may take place in the person of the members of the pre-registration company;
(2) The articles of association, deed of formation or company statutes may not be altered;
(3) Legal proceedings for the exclusion of a member of a pre-registration company may not be initiated; and
(4) No resolution may be made on termination without a legal successor or alteration into another business association or non-profit company.

If the application for registration of the business association is refused, it may not acquire further rights or assume new obligations and shall be obliged to terminate its operations. The members/shareholders shall accept liability for any debts arising from the undertakings of the executive officers according to the rules applicable to the termination of business associations. This provision is also applied to settlement between the members/shareholders.

If, as a consequence of the form of the business association to be established, the liability of the members for the obligations of the business association is limited, and outstanding claims remain despite the members/shareholders accepting liability, the executive officers shall bear unlimited joint and several liability towards third parties.

The rights, facts and data constituting part of the company registration records which relate to business associations, and the members, executive officers and supervisory board members thereof, are public information. Upon request, the Court of Registration grants Certificates of Registration to companies (similar to the German or Austrian *Firmenauszug*), which contain and provide proof to third parties of all the registered and public data of the company. Rules governing the registration of business associations are laid down in the Act on Company Registration, Public Company Information and Court Registration Proceedings (Company Registration Act).[19]

The following documents are required for company registration, regardless of the form of the company:

(1) Founding document;
(2) Specimen signature(s) of the person(s) entitled to sign on behalf of the company;

19 Act CXLV of 1997.

(3) If the registration application contains data in respect of the following:
   (a) a statement of acceptance by the executive officers, members of the supervisory board and the auditor;
   (b) the document authorizing an executive officer to transfer his right of representation in respect of certain matters or groups of matters;
   (c) the document of authorization and acceptance regarding the authorization of a foreign person's delivery agent in Hungary;
   (d) in the case of the participation of a foreign company, the extract from the Register of Companies of the foreign company and its attested translation into Hungarian;
   (e) in the case of real property being contributed as a contribution in kind, the title to such real estate issued within the last three months showing the legal title of disposition over the property;
(4) Power of attorney for the legal representative or other verification of his right of representation; and
(5) A declaration in connection with value added tax in order for a tax number to be issued.[20]

The following are additional documents required for the registration of companies or registration of amendments in relation to certain company forms:
(1) For limited liability companies:
   (a) members' list;
   (b) verification from a financial institution of the payment of monetary deposits;
   (c) statement by the managing director on the availability of in-kind contributions; and
   (d) if the company employs an auditor, the auditor's assessment of the value of in-kind contributions;
(2) For public formation of a company limited by shares:
   (a) draft of formation;
   (b) memorandum approved by the Hungarian Financial Supervisory Authority;
   (c) form for the subscription of shares;
   (d) proof of publication of the invitation to the inaugural general meeting;

---

20 Act XCI of 1990 on the Rules of Taxation, Section 14(1).

- (e) minutes and attendance sheet of the inaugural general meeting;
- (f) verification from a financial institution of payment of the portion of subscribed capital payable upon formation;
- (g) statement by the founders on the availability of in-kind contributions; and
- (h) auditor's assessment of the value of in-kind contributions.

(3) For private formation of a company limited by shares:
- (a) verification from a financial institution of payment of the portion of subscribed capital payable upon formation;
- (b) statement by the founders on the availability of in-kind contributions;
- (c) auditor's assessment of the value of in-kind contributions; and
- (d) founders' statement on having fulfilled the reporting obligations prescribed by the Capital Market Act.

The duty payable for the registration procedure with the Court of Registration is two per cent of the primary capital (registered capital) of the company. In the case of legal entities, the duty is at least HUF 60,000 (approximately US $266) and, at most, HUF 600,000 (approximately US $2,660). In the case of partnerships, the duty is at least HUF 20,000 (approximately US $88) and, at most, HUF 200,000 (approximately US $880). There is an additional cost, the publication fee of HUF 20,000 (approximately US $88), which applies in the case of legal entities. In the case of partnerships, the publication fee is HUF 10,000 (approximately US $44). This fee covers the publication costs of registration of the company in the *Company Gazette*, the official journal of the Ministry of Justice. The proof of payment of the publication fee shall also be enclosed in the application for registration.

Once the abovementioned documents have been prepared, signed and countersigned, an application for registration, together with these documents, should be submitted to the Court of Registration within thirty days from the signing of the founding document.

Upon receipt of the registration application by the Court of Registration, the Court of Registration issues a certificate containing the company's name and address, the company registration number and the company's tax number, statistical number and social security number. Following this, the company must fill out the necessary forms and submit them to the tax authorities, the social security authority and any other authorities that are necessary in the specific case of the company. From the date of submitting the application for registration and the company documents to the Court of Registration, the company may use the money paid as initial capital in its bank account and its executives and employees may dispose of the bank account.

Following the submission of the application for registration, the Court of Registration examines the application to establish whether all of the documents listed above are attached and the procedural fee specified by law has been paid. If the documents are not enclosed with the registration application or are insufficient, or if the procedural fee has not been paid or only a portion of it has been paid, the Court of Registration will reject the registration application within eight days of submission.

Further, in the case of partnerships, the Court of Registration only examines whether the data included in the registration application and the founding document complies with the legal regulations prescribed in the Company Registration Act for the given company form. In the case of companies having legal personality, such as the limited liability company and the company limited by shares, the Court of Registration examines whether the data, as prescribed in the Company Registration Act for the given company form, and the founding document comply with legal regulations. If the application fails to comply with the provisions, although the registration application is not rejected, the Court of Registration will issue a resolution on correction, ordering the missing data to be submitted in order to prevent rejection of the application.

In the case of partnerships, the Court of Registration makes its decision on the registration or rejection of applications within thirty days of receiving such applications. In the case of companies having legal personality, the Court of Registration has sixty days to decide upon the registration of the company. In practice, the Court of Registration usually registers limited liability companies within thirty or forty days.

Beyond registration by the Court of Registration, the approval of governmental or other authorities is not required for the establishment of companies in Hungary. However, there are certain exceptions in specific cases when approval of an authority is required, for example, the approval of the Hungarian Financial Supervisory Authority is required for the establishment of credit institutions or insurance companies.

Preparation of Ancillary Documents

Beyond the founding document of the company and the documents prescribed by the Company Registration Act, no other document is necessary for establishing a company in Hungary. Companies do, however, conclude agreements and contracts in connection with their operations. They may conclude joint venture agreements, employment or commission contracts with their staff and the executives of the company and commercial and market-related contracts, such as contracts of sale, supply contracts, license agreements, loan and other financial agreements and lease contracts. Companies may resolve different company policies and rules depending on their activities and needs.

Joint venture agreements are usually signed parallel with the founding document of the company. In these agreements, the parties usually define the following detailed rules for the internal operation of the company:

(1) Exercising of voting rights at the members' meeting, especially with respect to the appointment of the managing director and supervisory board members and profit distribution policy;
(2) The basics of the financial and investment policy;
(3) The basic rules of the employment policy and evaluation system;
(4) Major commercial issues, such as pricing policy;
(5) Management principles; and
(6) Other issues, such as patents, trademarks and know-how.

Incentives Available to Foreign Joint Venture Partners

In Hungary, the corporate tax rate is advantageous because it is rather low, only eighteen per cent. The general rate of withholding tax is twenty per cent for business entity shareholders and twenty per cent and thirty-five per cent for individuals,[21] although most Hungarian

21 Dividend tax is twenty per cent on the amount not exceeding thirty per cent of the portion which falls to the shareholder/owner from the equity capital of the company in proportion to the shareholder/owner's equity. Dividends in excess of this amount are subject to thirty-five per cent dividend tax and, as of 2004, an eleven per cent health contribution is no longer payable on dividends subject to thirty-five per cent dividend tax paid to domestic individuals.

tax treaties reduce this to five, ten or fifteen per cent. Dividends paid to domestic business entities are exempt from withholding tax.

After Hungary's joining the European Union, dividends payable to foreign shareholders/owners — in line with Council Directive 90/435/EEC on the common system of taxation applicable to parent companies and their subsidiaries in different Member States — will be exempt from dividend tax if the foreign dividend receiving party qualifies as a parent company of the Hungarian corporation for at least two years before the date of realizing the dividend. A parent company is a company which has at least a twenty-five per cent stake in the registered capital of another company.

Hungary offers many tax and non-tax incentives for investors. These incentives are regulated by Act LXXXI of 1996 on Corporate Tax and Dividend Tax (Corporate Tax Act), as amended, and are available to all Hungarian companies, irrespective of the nationality of the shareholders. Tax incentives may depend on the activities of the company and the size and location of the project.

Tax incentives related to investments have mainly been supporting manufacturing entities and hotel projects. The amount of the deduction from corporate tax (fifty or 100 per cent) depends on the volume of investment (HUF 1-billion, HUF 3-billion or HUF 10-billion). For certain categories, no minimum investment is required, but other conditions must be fulfilled. Investments in business zones or high priority regions, that is, economically underdeveloped regions where the rate of unemployment exceeds fifteen per cent in June of the year preceding the year when the investment was started, enjoy higher incentives. The different categories of incentives are available for five or ten consecutive years after the putting into operation of the investment, but, for certain categories of incentives, they are only available for those years when further conditions prescribed by law have been met, for example, a prescribed minimum annual increase in sales, an increase of total gross revenue or the average number of staff employed by the taxpayer exceeding by at least 100 or 500 persons the average number of staff employed in the tax year preceding commencement of the investment project.

Most of these incentives have been available for investments started after 31 December 1995 and can be claimed in respect of the tax on the tax base for the year 2002 for the last time. The incentives granted for investments in depressed areas are available for investments started after 31 December 1996 and can be claimed in respect of the tax on the tax base for the year 2011 for the last time. However, taxpayers are not entitled to the latter tax allowances for projects commencing after the Act promulgating the treaty on the accession of the Republic of Hungary to the European Union enters into force.

In June 2001, Parliament adopted an amendment to the Corporate Tax Act and introduced a new development tax incentive. The aim of this incentive is to promote long-term investment projects which significantly contribute to the development of the Hungarian economy. This tax incentive can be licensed by the Government upon the request of the taxpayer on the basis of a submitted development program, in accordance with the conditions detailed in a government decree.[22] The development program may qualify for this tax incentive if it meets the requirements prescribed in the Corporate Tax Act. This tax incentive will be available for development projects commencing after the Act promulgating the treaty on the accession of the Republic of Hungary to the European Union enters into force.

As of 2002, the Corporate Tax Act makes it possible for taxpayers to establish a tax deductible reserve of up to twenty-five per cent of their accounting profit (this amount was twenty per cent in 2002), but it may not exceed HUF 500-million in each tax year. The reserve established in 2003 and subsequent years must be applied for investment within four years. If the taxpayer ceases the reserve, wholly or in part, without investment or fails to apply it for investment until the end of the fourth year, the corporate tax must be paid together with late payment interest.

Other types of tax incentives are regional and other tax incentives. In the year of commencing operation, tax relief equivalent to six per cent of the value of the project may be claimed by taxpayers with registered offices or business premises registered with the Court of Registration and/or the local government in a high priority region and/or in a business zone, calculated after deduction of the value of investment in machinery, buildings (only in a business zone) or infrastructure development. These incentives can be claimed in respect of the tax on the tax base for the year 2002 for the last time.

Within the limits prescribed by Act C of 1990 on Local Taxes, each local government is entitled to levy local tax. Local business tax is levied on sales revenue less the material costs of goods sold and fees paid to subcontractors. The tax rate is defined by the local authority, but

22 Government Decree 162/2001 (IX.14) on the Development Tax Incentive.

may not exceed two per cent. Business and other local taxes are deductible expenses for the purposes of corporate tax. Local governments also often grant tax incentives for investments made in their area.

Non-tax incentives, such as interest-free loans or grants, are given on a case-by-case basis following a specific and detailed application. Several state-controlled funds, such as the Economic Development Fund, the Employment Fund, the Area Development Fund and the Environmental Protection Fund, grant support to investors, for example, financing 100 per cent of the employer's social security contribution for the first twelve months of employment of a person who was previously unemployed for at least six months. In addition to support at national level, local (county, town or district) support is also often given to investors, particularly for new projects and green field investments. Financial grants are rare at this level, but other valuable types of assistance, such as the recruitment and training of employees and finding of suppliers or customers, is often provided. Most cities encourage investment with different programs, and many of them have established "industrial parks" as business zones where the local authorities provide appropriate premises for new businesses with full infrastructure.

Restrictions on Activities of Foreign Joint Venture Partners

Since 1989, the Government and local authorities have been encouraging foreign investment and have almost entirely abolished the restrictions thereon. Almost the same reporting and registration requirements are applicable to foreign investors as to national investors. There are no restrictions on the percentage of foreign ownership of companies, except for specific types of companies, for example, companies limited by shares with national broadcasting rights. After an almost complete liberalization of foreign exchange that took place on 16 July 2001, only a very few restrictions are left on foreign exchange transactions and, as of 1 January 2002, the whole of Act XCV of 1995 on Foreign Exchange was repealed. By the amendment of 16 July 2001, the national currency, the Forint, became fully convertible.

Foreign natural persons and legal entities may not acquire ownership of arable land. A license from the head of the competent county or Budapest public administration office is required for such acquisition (other than by way of inheritance) of other types of real property (which are not classified as arable land or protected natural areas) by foreign legal or natural persons. Such other real property consists of:

(1) Land which does not qualify as arable land or as a protected nature conservation area;
(2) Such land and the building(s) and structure(s) thereon jointly;
(3) Buildings and structures which are owned separately from the land they are on;
(4) Residential and non-residential premises registered as independent properties; and
(5) Farmsteads up to a maximum of 6,000m^2.

Dispute Resolution

The Companies Act regulates the dispute resolution methods for disputes related to company matters. According to Section 47 of the Companies Act, any member/shareholder of a company may request a court review of resolutions passed by the organs of the company if he feels that such resolutions conflict with the Companies Act, other legal rules or the articles of association, deed of formation or company statutes. For the same reasons, any executive officer or supervisory board member may also initiate a court review of a resolution passed by the company's supreme body.

The claim for a court review of a company resolution violating the law must be lodged against the company within thirty days after learning of such resolution. Following the expiration of a ninety-day non-appealable deadline from the date of passing the resolution, the resolution may not be contested even if it has not been communicated to the person entitled to lodge a claim or he has not learned thereof. The right to lodge claims may not be validly excluded, but persons who contributed with their votes to the adoption of the resolution — except in cases of mistake, misrepresentation or duress — are not entitled to turn to the court. Lodging a claim has no delaying influence on the implementation of the resolution, but it may be suspended by the court. Company resolutions violating the law will be repealed by the court. A court judgment passed in the course of the review of such resolution also extends to the members/shareholders who were not involved in the proceedings.

Under Section 49 of the Companies Act, a member of a company may be excluded from the company by the court based on a claim initiated by the company against such member if the continued membership of the person in question would seriously endanger the achievement of the company's purpose. Such a claim may also be lodged for the exclusion of shareholders of companies limited by shares. A member may not be excluded from a company if the company has only two members. A member holding three-quarters or more of the votes may also not be excluded.

Both at first and second instance, the court acts in extraordinary proceedings for the exclusion of a member. If no other arrangements are required, the hearing shall be set for no later than the fifteenth day after receipt of the statement of claim by the court or, for arbitration proceedings, after appointment of the tribunal.

Corporate legal disputes may be resolved by the ordinary courts or by arbitration. Under Section 52 of the Companies Act, in accordance with the provisions of Act LXXI of 1994 on Arbitration (Arbitration Act), permanent or *ad hoc* arbitration may be stipulated in the articles of association, deed of formation or company statutes with regard to corporate legal disputes. According to the Act, a corporate legal dispute is a legal dispute arising in relation to the articles of association or the operation of the business association as part of the legal relationship between the business association and its members/shareholders, including former members excluded from or otherwise withdrawing from the business association, or between the members/shareholders themselves.

If the parties have stipulated arbitration in the articles of association, a review of company resolutions violating the law or the exclusion of a member from the company will be resolved by arbitration.

The Arbitration Act sets out the detailed rules for arbitration which, to a large extent, follow the Model Law on Arbitration approved by the United Nations Commission on International Trade Law (UNCITRAL) in 1985. The Arbitration Act regulates domestic arbitration and international arbitral proceedings. Pursuant to the Arbitration Act, no appeal may be lodged against the award of an arbitral tribunal; only an application to set aside the award for reasons of formality and procedure listed in the Act may be brought before the court within sixty days of the receipt of the award from the arbitral tribunal. The effect of an arbitral award is the same as that of a non-appealable court judgment, and the execution thereof is governed by the legal rules on enforcement through the courts.

There may be other legal disputes arising out of or in connection with a joint venture, not only corporate legal disputes, for example, arising out of a breach of the joint venture agreement. Such legal disputes, depending on the stipulation of the parties, may be submitted to the ordinary courts, Hungarian or foreign, having jurisdiction and competence in the matter or be submitted to arbitration.

In the case of corporate legal disputes, the stipulation of arbitration must always be included in the articles of association (or in a modification thereof), otherwise an arbitration agreement may be concluded as part of another contract or in the form of a separate agreement, but, in all cases, it must be made in writing. It is also regarded as an arbitration agreement concluded in writing if one of the parties states in the statement of claim, and the other party does not deny in the defense, that an arbitration agreement was in fact concluded between them.

Law Decree 13 of 1979 on International Private Law (International Private Law Act), as amended, regulates procedural issues of an international character. The International Private Law Act was amended by Act CX of 2000, which replaced completely Chapter 9 on Jurisdiction and Chapter 11 on Recognition and Enforcement of Foreign Resolutions (the Amendment). The Amendment entered into force on 1 May 2001. The provisions relating to the recognition and execution of foreign decisions, which were introduced by the Amendment, are applicable to those decisions which came into force after the entry into force of the Act pursuant to the law of the country where they were made. Due to the Amendment, the decisions of foreign courts shall be recognized and enforced if:

(1) The jurisdiction of the court in question is found to be legitimate under the rules of jurisdiction of Hungarian law;
(2) The decision is construed as definitive by the law of the State in which it was made;
(3) There is reciprocity between Hungary and the State of the court in question;[23] and
(4) Neither of the grounds for denial defined in the International Private Law Act exist.[24]

In respect of legal disputes pertaining to property rights and containing a foreign component, the parties may stipulate the jurisdiction of

23 Reciprocity currently exists only with Germany.

24 International Private Law Act, Section 72.

the courts of any State or of a specific court thereof. Parties may make such clause or stipulation:

(1) In writing;
(2) Verbally, if confirmed in writing;
(3) In a form that satisfies the established course of dealing between the parties; or
(4) In international commerce, in a form that conforms to trade usage with which the parties are or should have been familiar, and that is generally known and regularly applied by the parties for these particular types of contracts in the business sector in question.[25]

The Amendment introduced a substantial change in the case of a decision pertaining to property rights. If the jurisdiction of the foreign court making the decision has been stipulated by the parties to be in compliance with the provisions laid down in the Act, reciprocity is no longer a required condition for recognition and enforcement.[26] This Amendment thus makes it possible for a decision of a foreign ordinary court stipulated by the parties to be enforceable in Hungary.

Hungary is not yet a party to the European Community and European Free Trade Area Convention on Jurisdiction and the Enforcement of Judgments in Civil and Commercial Matters signed in Lugano on 16 September 1988. Commercial disputes between domestic and foreign parties are mostly resolved through arbitration, as Hungary is a party to the New York Convention on the Recognition and Enforcement of Foreign Arbitral Awards of 10 June 1958. Arbitral awards of participating countries can be enforced in Hungary subject to the limitations set out in the New York Convention and Hungarian law.

Impact of Changes in Law Subsequent to Formation

It is laid down in Hungarian law that no obligation can be imposed with retroactive effect and no conduct can be declared as illegal with retroactive effect. This means that only rights or benefits can be granted with retroactive effect.

25 International Private Law Act, Section 62/F.
26 International Private Law Act, Section 73(2)(b).

Regulations are certainly changing, and joint ventures with foreign participation, like all other Hungarian natural and legal entities, must comply with the effective rules. The rights and benefits, for example, tax incentives in the Corporate Tax Act, that have been granted to investors have always been provided for a definite period of time, usually until 2002 or 2011. Any changes in the terms of incentives are indicated by the legislator in advance. A recent example of such change occurred in connection with Hungary's European Union membership negotiations. A recent amendment to the Corporate Tax Act, effective as of 3 July 2001, declared that taxpayers are not entitled to the tax allowances defined in Sections 21(7), 21(10) and 21(11) of the Corporate Tax Act for projects commencing after the Act promulgating the treaty on the accession of the Republic of Hungary to the European Union enters into force.

It is a principle of Hungarian administration law that resolutions cannot be withdrawn or modified if this would violate rights received and exercised *bona fide*. However, this rule is applicable only to final non-appealable resolutions granting rights to a client and, according to the majority of interpretations, it cannot be applied to the withdrawal or modification of resolutions that impose obligations, for example, when the tax authority imposes a lower tax than it should under the law due to a mistake or other reason. However, there is also case law supporting the opposite view of this principle.

Double Taxation Agreements and Joint Ventures

Hungary has double tax treaties with the countries listed below, each treaty containing specific rates.

	Withholding tax rates		
Country	**Dividends**	**Interest**	**Royalties**
	%	%	%
Albania	5/10	0	5
Australia	15	10	10
Austria	10	0	0

	Withholding tax rates		
Country	**Dividends**	**Interest**	**Royalties**
	%	%	%
Belgium	10	15	0
Brazil	15	10/15	15/25
Bulgaria	10	10	10
Canada	5/10	10	0/10
China	10	10	10
Croatia	5/10	0	0
Cyprus	5/15	10	0
Czech Republic	5/15	0	10
Denmark	5/15	0	0
Egypt	15/20	15	15
Finland	5/15	0	0/5
France	5/15	0	0
Germany	5/15/25	0	0
Greece	10/45	10	0/10
India	15	15	20/40
Indonesia	15	15	15
Ireland	5/15	0	0
Israel	5/15	0	0
Italy	10	0	0
Japan	10	10	0/10
Kazakhstan	5/15	10	10
Korea	5/15	0	0
Kuwait	0	0	10
Luxembourg	5/15	0	0
Malaysia	0/10	15	15
Malta	5/15	10	10
Moldavia	5/15	10	0
Mongolia	5/15	10	5

	Withholding tax rates		
Country	**Dividends**	**Interest**	**Royalties**
	%	%	%
Morocco[27]	12	10	10
Netherlands	5/15	0	0
Norway	10	0	0
Pakistan	15/20	15	15
Philippines	15/20	15	15
Poland	10	10	10
Portugal	10/15	10	10
Romania	5/15	15	10
Russia	10	0	0
Serbia-Montenegro	10/15	10	10
Singapore	5/15	5	5
Slovak Republic	5/15	0	10
South Africa	5/15	0	0
Spain	5/15	0	0
Sweden	5/15	0	0
Switzerland	10	10	0
Thailand	15/20	10/25	15
Tunisia	10/12	12	12
Turkey	10/15	10	10
Ukraine	5/15	10	5
United Kingdom	5/15	0	0
United States	5/15	0	0
Uruguay	15	15	10/15
Vietnam	10	10	10

Hungary is currently negotiating tax treaties with Bosnia-Herzegovina, Estonia, Latvia, Lithuania, Mexico, Paraguay and Slovenia.

27 This Treaty has been concluded, but its provisions currently cannot be applied.

Protection of Foreign Investors

The Foreign Investment Act in Hungary established full protection for the investments of foreigners in Hungary. Beyond this protection, the Act and the rest of the legal system (including the Act on Corporate and Dividend Tax and international treaties) aim to promote investment by foreigners. Foreigners can establish or acquire companies without any restriction on the percentage of ownership. The Foreign Investment Act offers guarantees against nationalization and expropriation and provides that the withholding of capital cannot be limited and must be performed in the currency of the investment. Undertakings operating with foreign participation may take part in the formation of other companies, may themselves found other companies and may acquire holdings in existing companies. Companies with foreign participation may carry out foreign trade, wholesale and retail activities in accordance with the laws governing other domestic business organizations. The company's executive officers, managing directors and members of the board of supervisors may be foreigners.

Hungary has concluded numerous treaties on the promotion and mutual protection of investments with other countries. The Foreign Investment Act declares[28] that, in the event of the provisions of an international treaty deviating from the provisions of the Foreign Investment Act, the international treaty shall be applied. All of these bilateral treaties on the promotion and mutual protection of investments provide guarantees against nationalization and for repatriation of profit and capital. Hungary has effective treaties on the promotion and mutual protection of investments with the following countries:

Country	Date of Signature	Promulgation	Date of Effect
Albania	24 January 1996	Act 15 of 2000	1 April 1998
Argentina	5 February 1993	Act 16 of 2000	1 October 1997
Australia	15 August 1991	Act 37 of 1993	10 May 1992
Austria	26 May 1988	Government Decree 12/1990 (VII.24)	1 September 1989

28 Foreign Investment Act, Section 6.

Country	Date of Signature	Promulgation	Date of Effect
Belgium and Luxembourg	14 May 1986	Government Decree 7/1989 (I.15)	23 September 1988
Bulgaria	8 June 1994	Act 104 of 1996	7 September 1995
Canada	3 October 1991	Act 23 of 1995	21 November 1993
China	29 May 1991	Act 94 of 1994	1 April 1993
Croatia	15 May 1996	Act 26 of 2002	1 March 2002
Cyprus	24 May 1989	Government Decree 33/1990 (VIII.30)	25 May 1990
Czech Republic	14 January 1993	Act 105 of 1996	15 May 1995
Denmark	2 May 1988	Government Decree 6/1989 (I.15)	1 October 1988
Egypt	23 May 1995	Act 8 of 1999	21 August 1997
Finland	6 June 1988	Government Decree 91/1989 (VIII.17)	12 May 1989
France	6 November 1986	Government Decree 59/1987 (XI.29)	30 September 1987
Germany	30 April 1988	Law Decree 5 of 1988	7 November 1987
Great Britain	9 March 1987	Government Decree 5/1988 (II.12)	27 August 1987
Greece	26 May 1989	Act 38 of 1993	1 February 1992
Indonesia	23 May 1995	Act 8 of 1999	21 August 1997
Israel	14 May 1991	Act 64 of 1993	14 September 1992
Italy	17 February 1987	30/1990 (VIII.21) Government Decree	6 September 1989
Kazakhstan	7 December 1994	Act 13 of 1999	3 March 1996
Korea	28 December 1988	46/1989 (V.31)	1 February 1989
Kuwait	8 November 1989	Act 95 of 1994	1 March 1994
Latvia	10 June 1999	Act 3 of 2001	25 August 2000
Lebanon	22 June 2001	Act 52 of 2002	23 July 2002
Macedonia	13 April 2001	Act 29 of 2002	14 March 2002
Malaysia	19 February 1993	Act 97 of 1996	8 June 1995

Country	Date of Signature	Promulgation	Date of Effect
Moldavia	19 April 1995	Act 17 of 1999	16 August 1996
Morocco	12 December 1991	Act 102 of 2000	3 February 2000
Netherlands	2 September 1987	Government Decree 63/1988 (VIII.1)	1 June 1988
Norway	8 April 1991	Act 61 of 1993	4 December 1992
Paraguay	11 August 1993	Act 98 of 1996	1 April 1995
Poland	23 September 1992	Act 96 of 1996	16 June 1995
Portugal	28 February 1992	Act 22 of 1999	8 October 1997
Romania	16 September 1993	Act 23 of 1999	6 May 1996
Russia	6 March 1995	Act 20 of 1999	29 May 1996
Singapore	17 April 1997	Act 20 of 2000	1 January 1999
Slovakia	15 January 1993	Act 24 of 1999	19 July 1996
Slovenia	15 October 1996	Act 4 of 2001	9 June 2000
Spain	9 November 1989	Act 65 of 1993	1 August 1992
Sweden	21 April 1987	Government Decree 25/1987 (VII.28)	21 April 1987
Switzerland	5 October 1988	Government Decree 89/1989 (VIII.5)	16 May 1989
Thailand	18 October 1991	Government Decree 135/1992 (X.1)	18 October 1991
Turkey	14 January 1992	Act 27 of 1999	1 November 1994
Ukraine	11 October 1994	Act 29 of 1999	3 December 1996
United States	9 October 1989	Government Decree 74/1990 (IV.25)	27 December 1989
Uruguay	25 August 1989	Act 39 of 1993	1 July 1992
Vietnam	26 August 1994	Act 103 of 1996	16 June 1995

Hungary concluded a treaty on the promotion and mutual protection of investments with Lithuania on 25 May 1999 and Mongolia on 13 September 1994, but these treaties are still not in effect. The Hungarian Government has also agreed to conclude treaties on the promotion and mutual protection of investments with India, the Republic of Yemen, Yugoslavia, Cuba and Chile, and has authorized a minister or a person appointed by the authorized minister to sign such treaties.

Dispute Resolution

Effective Mediation by Professionals in the Field of Law

Carlos Darío Ruffinelli Céspedes
Moreno Ruffinelli & Asociados
Asunción, Paraguay

Introduction

This chapter will deal with a few of the general concepts regarding mediation, at the national as well as the international level, focusing on the need for mediation by professionals in the field of law, along with outlining some basic elements comprising mediation. Paraguayan law will be discussed, comparing some of its aspects with Argentinean law.

The author favors mediation by lawyers rather than mediation carried out by other professionals, though many of them have proven themselves to be excellent mediators, as lawyers know the law in general and can, therefore, immediately differentiate the matter or matters subject to mediation, helping the parties to reach an agreement, if possible. Lawyers who mediate should, however, if necessary, rely on subject matter experts to provide specifics in terms of the law and other sciences or professions. A settlement at all costs should not be sought. A mediating lawyer should feel satisfied that every effort has been made for the parties to achieve a settlement. He is only a facilitator, a third party seeking to draw the parties closer in their negotiations, with the final say being that of the parties.

Legal Framework

Paraguay's Law 1879/02, based on the United Nations Commission on International Trade Law (UNCITRAL) Model Law on International Commercial Arbitration, defines the legal framework for

D.Campbell and S.Woodley (eds.), The Comparative Law Yearbook of International Business 2003, 89-98

mediation in Title II, Articles 53 to 67. Article 53 of this Law characterizes mediation as:

> ". . . a voluntary mechanism aimed at dispute resolution, through which two or more people themselves work out a friendly solution to their differences with the assistance of a third neutral and qualified party called a mediator".

Paraguayan law very clearly defines mediation as a "voluntary mechanism", that is, it is not mandatory like the legislation of some jurisdictions, such as that of Argentina. Article 1 of Argentina's Law 24573 on Mediation and Conciliation stipulates:

> "Mediation is hereby instituted as mandatory prior to any trial and will be governed by the measures established in this Law. This procedure will promote direct communication among the parties towards an extrajudicial solution to the dispute."

This Article establishes an exception in its second paragraph:

> ". . . the parties will be exempt from complying with this step if evidence can be provided showing that mediation took place with Ministry of Justice registered mediators".

Nonetheless, it is clear that mediation is mandatory under Argentinean law.

Article 54 of Paraguay's Law 1879/02 defines matters subject to mediation. The only matters that may be submitted to mediation are those deriving from a contractual or other legal relationship, as long as such matters are subject to conciliation or arbitration. Article 2 of the Law on the object of arbitration provides that:

> ". . . every matter upon which settlement can be reached, which has a patrimonial content, may be submitted to arbitration, as long as the matter has not yet been the subject of a definitive and executable judgment".

It expressly establishes that "matters which require the intervention of the Office of the Public Prosecutor[1] may not be the subject of arbitration". The second paragraph of Article 2 stipulates that differences arising between the State, decentralized and autarkic entities, public enterprises and municipalities and private individuals, national or foreign, may be submitted to arbitration, as long as legal transactions or contracts governed by private law exist. This is true progress since, within the limits of the law, it means that such disputes may be the object of arbitration and, consequently, mediation.

The first legal issue the mediator must unravel and interpret is what is subject to mediation and what is not. This is where there is a need for the mediator to have knowledge of the law. Argentina's Law 24573 on Mediation and Conciliation is clearer in this respect. In its Article 2, it specifically states that the following matters may not be the object of mediation:

(1) Criminal cases;
(2) Actions involving separation, divorce and the nullification of marriage, except issues of patrimony deriving from these matters, where the judge will divide the actions, referring the patrimonial aspect to a mediator;
(3) Actions declaring incompetence and dealing with rehabilitation;
(4) Cases involving the State or its decentralized entities;
(5) Civil rights matters, *habeas corpus* and interdicts;
(6) Injunctions, until the time that a final decision is made exhausting all normal avenues of recourse except mediation;
(7) Preliminary proceedings and the production of pre-trial evidence;
(8) Succession;
(9) Preventive insolvency proceedings and bankruptcy; and
(10) Cases brought before the National Labor Court.

Although mediation is mandatory, a judge must make many decisions. This can be seen in cases involving a patrimonial aspect, where the judge will divide the case, referring the patrimonial issue to a mediator. In other words, matters that can be settled and which contain an element of patrimony are subject to mediation, such as rights which can be relinquished. This is subject, however, to Article 10 of

1 In Paraguay, the Office of the Public Prosecutor has jurisdiction over civil as well as criminal cases.

the Civil Code, which stipulates that rights conferred by law may be relinquished ". . . as long as it is in the interest of the individual and relinquishment is not prohibited".[2]

Matters subject to mediation are, therefore, only those that are susceptible to transactions, for example, contracts, within the limitations imposed by the law as stated above, and those with a content of patrimony, as long as no intervention by the Office of the Public Prosecutor is required. Also, differences arising between entities subject to public law and individuals, as long as they arise out of legal acts or contracts governed by private law, and, finally, anything that is open to conciliation can be the subject of mediation.

Each case requires, therefore, a serious legal analysis to determine whether the matter is subject to mediation or not. Even so, there are still the questions as to which matters require the intervention of the Public Prosecutors Office and which are susceptible to conciliation. With regard to the Public Prosecutor's Office, the mediator needs to refer to the different laws and norms to see if intervention from the Office of the Public Prosecutor is required, especially in the different areas of law: administrative, civil and commercial (including family law), labor, minors and crime.

With regard to conciliation, what is susceptible to conciliation and how is this different from mediation? What are the differences between conciliation and mediation? In Paraguay, conciliation arises from procedural law by which the judge in every civil, labor or defamation case attempts to reconcile the parties to avoid a trial. Conciliation is, therefore, a matter of procedural law that remains in the hands of the judge, while mediation is voluntary and, in general, is carried prior to any trial.

Nonetheless, prior to conciliation as established under procedural law, the parties may opt to refer their dispute to mediation, the latter having more leeway, since it may be performed at any time, before bringing suit or at any stage of the suit before judgment. It has the authority of a matter that has been judged according to the stipulations in Articles 55 and 56 of Law 1879/02. It should be noted that, particularly in matters of labor procedural law, the judge may, at any time, attempt conciliation with the litigating parties, as provided for in the current labor procedural law, which is in keeping with Articles 55 and 56.

---

2 "A future inheritance cannot be the object of acceptance or relinquishment, nor can an inheritance that has already been accepted be relinquished once the legally established period has expired": Civil Code, Article 2452.

Consequently, in order to determine what is open to conciliation, the mediator will have to refer to current procedural law and jurisdiction for each matter for effective mediation bound by law. Once again, it can be seen that knowledge of the law is essential for the mediator and that mediation becomes ever more reserved to professionals of the law. This does not take away from the merits of the enormous task carried out by psychologists, sociologists, members of religious orders and other professionals trained as mediators. These carry out successful mediations many times more successful than those carried out by untrained lawyers or by those unable to carry out effective mediation, whether because of manifest bias or by taking a position similar to that of a judge who decides who wins and who loses in a trial. In addition, the spirit of litigation imbued in lawyers consequently negates mediation as a way of resolving conflicts.

Law 1879/02 on Arbitration and Mediation

Knowledge of the Law

As already pointed out, knowledge of Law 1879/02 on Arbitration and Mediation, as well as other relevant norms of substance and procedure is essential. Additionally, the general provisions on mediation must be borne in mind. Various articles in the Law clearly describe the main elements of mediation, but this does not mean that great effort should not be taken in interpreting them, and training in the matter is still necessary. A mediator must be an upright person guided by the principles of impartiality, fairness and justice as stipulated in Article 66 of Law 1879/02.

Confidentiality: Article 57

Mediation is confidential in nature, and those who participate in the proceedings must maintain this confidentiality. The formulas proposed for agreement will not have a bearing on any lawsuit that might take place, and the mediator may not be called as a witness, or in any other capacity, in any subsequent trial between the same parties or concerning the same matter.

Request: Article 58

The parties may refer a matter to mediation jointly or separately by presenting a written request to the mediator of their choice or to the Center for Mediation upon which they agree.

Procedure: Article 59

In the absence of an agreement to the contrary between the parties, the Center will appoint a mediator or mediators and establish the date and time for the parties to carry out the mediation session within five working days after a request for mediation has been presented.

Agreements: Article 60

During the course of the hearings, the mediator will collaborate with the parties to clearly determine the alleged facts, as well as the positions and interests upon which these are based, in order to produce reconciliation formulas that may or may not be approved by the interested parties. The parties will collaborate with the mediator in good faith and, in particular, will make every effort to comply with the requests he may make and attend hearings when convened.

Effect: Article 61

An agreement arising out of the mediation binds the parties from the moment they and the mediator sign the mediation memorandum documenting it, and will have the effect of a matter settled by judgment from the time it is ratified by a competent judge. If the mediation agreement takes place while a lawsuit is pending, the judge in the case will be the competent party to ratify it, such ratification serving to bring the lawsuit to an end. If the mediation agreement is partial, this will be documented in the mediation memorandum, and the parties may discuss the non-mediated differences at the trial.

Termination: Article 62

The mediation procedure concludes by:

(1) The signing of a mediation memorandum containing the agreement reached by the parties in accordance with the stipulations in Article 61;

(2) The signing of a memorandum by which the mediator and the parties confirm that agreement through mediation is not possible; or

(3) A certificate issued by the center to which the request for mediation was presented to the effect that no hearing could be held due to the absence of one or more of the parties summoned to the hearing.

Elements of Effective Mediation

Goals

There are goals in the process of mediation[3] that must be clearly identified by the parties. Therefore, each party must set certain objectives for themselves with regard to the mediation. Even though agreement can be the result sought, such agreement may not materialize.

One goal of the mediation may, therefore, be that the parties will reach an agreement, but only through the facilitation of the mediator, who shall abstain from expressing opinions on the strengths and weaknesses of the case. The parties must come to an agreement on this approach. Likewise, the parties must have the opportunity to express themselves to the mediator and to the other party. Along the same lines, the mediation must allow the parties to share their own theories with regard to the case at hand. At this time, they may present their claims and defenses, which may lead to the other party reconsidering its position.

It is also important that the parties allow the mediator to give opinions on the case, not about the strengths and weaknesses of it, but rather with a view towards an independent evaluation that can be analyzed along with the other available data. It will also be equally important to establish time limits for the mediation process in order to create an agenda of days and times so that the parties can concentrate on what is of real importance.

Indications need to be made as to the process of mediation, that is, the parties should be aware beforehand that joint or separate sessions

3 The following sections of this chapter are based on Davidson, Richard C. and Enwall, Michael R. (members of the Legal Resolution Center of Colorado), "Effective Advocacy in Alternative Dispute Resolution" (University of Phoenix, Colorado, 7 February 2003) Chapter Four.

might be held. There are cases in which the mediator may opt to begin by separating the parties in order to listen to each individually from the beginning. This, however, may have negative effects on the mediation, as it is sometimes more effective to begin mediation in a joint session. Even more important is the designing of and decision-making on the format of the case by the mediator in coordination with the parties.

At times, one of the parties may have unreasonable expectations, and it is important that he receives objective feedback from the mediator in this regard. Carrying out mediation without bearing this fact in mind may render it inappropriate.

Selecting the Mediator

As noted by the Law on Arbitration and Mediation, the mediator must be a person acknowledged as upright, trained, impartial, fair and just. Once these general elements have been taken into account, special attention must be given to the mediator's capability to evaluate whether he is the right person for the matter in hand and whether the selection can be made to the satisfaction of both parties.

Confidentiality Agreement

Before the first session, a confidentiality agreement is needed to ensure the effectiveness of the mediation, and should include the materials to which the mediator must have access. Once the materials, documents or evidence have been evaluated, it might be important for the mediator to candidly and directly lay out the best and worst case scenarios. The parties must have the opportunity to present their case with the necessary evidence before the session, in order to be fully apprised of the case in advance.

During Mediation

The parties must be treated with respect and take for granted that the mediator is prepared and not improvising. If not, the idea that it is a waste of time may overcome either one of the parties and have a very negative effect on the process. After all discussions, an agreement between the parties should have begun to take definitive shape. The agreement can and should be re-evaluated by the parties, so it is important that, while the agreement is being discussed, it is put into written form, which can be reviewed by the parties.

After Mediation

Mediation is not always concluded by the simple fact that an agreement has been reached. Other matters or pending issues of any nature whatsoever may exist that have not been discussed. In this case, the mediator must be capable of re-evaluating the case, as the most appropriate action might be to continue with additional sessions. At this point, there could even be discussion as to a change of mediator in order to obtain a second independent opinion. The mediator must show willingness to re-evaluate the case, to submit it to further mediation sessions and even propose, if the case so warrants, the selection of a new mediator.

Ethics in Mediation

The highest standards of ethics must be upheld before, during and after the process of mediation. Lawyers should feel obligated, out of a sense of ethics, to advise clients on the different ways to resolve the case. Lawyers must always seek to avoid lawsuits and find a way for the parties to come to a friendly agreement. The conclusion may be that mediation is not the most appropriate manner in which to resolve the case, so that, for reasons of procedure and ethics, and not the spirit of litigation, the decision is to go to trial.

Confidentiality in mediation is one of the most important elements since it is intrinsically tied to possible future conflicts of interests. Therefore, Article 66 of the Law on Arbitration and Mediation stipulates what the mediator may not do. The mediator may not intervene, on behalf of either one of the parties, in any court case or arbitration regarding a conflict that is the subject of mediation, whether as arbitrator, witness, expert, representative of a party through a power of attorney or in any other capacity. The Centers for Mediation themselves may not intervene in cases in which their board members or staff have a direct interest.

Conclusion

The conduct of the mediator, the issue of capability and a sense of ethics are of such importance that some experts in the matter propose that, when a lawyer acts as a mediator, his colleagues from the same law firm may not represent a party that participated in the mediation in subsequent litigation, whether or not the latter is related to the matter which was the subject of the mediation.[4]

The capability of the mediator must necessarily include knowledge of the law as well as training in mediation at national or international centers or universities qualified for this purpose. Observing the highest standards of ethics speaks to the honorability and impartiality of the mediator, guided by the principles of justice and fairness.

4 Menkel-Meadow, Carry, "Ethics in ADR" (*Fordham University Legal Review*, April 2001).

Arbitration in Paraguay

Antonio Tellechea
Peroni, Sosa, Tellechea, Burt & Narvaja
Asunción, Paraguay

Introduction

In the Republic of Paraguay, in the matter of recognition and execution of foreign arbitral awards, Law Number 948 of 12 September 1996 was enacted whereby the Convention on the Recognition and Execution of Foreign Arbitral Awards, adopted in New York on 10 June 1958, was approved. Article I of the Convention states:

> "1) The present Convention shall be applied to the recognition and execution of arbitration awards handed down in the territory of a State not being that in which the recognition and execution of the aforesaid awards which have their origin in differences between natural or legal persons, are being sought. The same shall also apply to those arbitration awards which are not considered national arbitration awards in the States in which recognition and execution are being sought.
>
> "2) The expression "Arbitration Awards" shall not only comprise awards handed down by arbitrators appointed for specific cases, but also for awards handed down by permanent arbitration organs to which the parties shall have been subjected.
>
> "3) At the time of executing or ratifying the present Convention, upon adherence thereto or of making notification of their extension as provided in article X, every State may, on the basis of reciprocity, represent that the present Convention shall apply to the recognition and execution of the arbitration awards handed down solely in the territory of another contracting State. Likewise, it may represent that the Convention shall only apply to litigation arising from juridical relations, be they contractual or otherwise, which are deemed to be commercial pursuant to internal law."

D.Campbell and S.Woodley (eds.), The Comparative Law Yearbook of International Business 2003, 99-114

By the approval of the New York Convention of 1958, Paraguay has included in its domestic law the international regime that refers to the recognition and execution of foreign arbitral awards. It is also important to transcribe the provision of Article III of the New York Convention, which states:

> "Each of the contracting States shall recognize the authority of the arbitration award and shall grant its execution pursuant to the rules of procedure in force in the territory in which the award is being cited, according to the conditions set forth in the following articles. For recognition or execution, no conditions shall be enforced that are appreciably more severe, nor lawyers' fees or court costs that are higher, than those applicable to the recognition or the execution of national arbitration awards."

Updated Provisions of the Civil Procedural Code

In order to bring Paraguayan legislation on matters of civil and commercial arbitration in line with international commercial arbitration provisions and the procedures used in relation thereto, as well as the use of arbitration agreements, a Special Commission of Jurists was constituted by the Asuncion Stock Exchange (*Camara y Bolsa de Comercio de Asuncion*). This Commission, jointly with another commission, engaged in the preparation of mediation rules. The report that was submitted to the National Senate resulted in the enactment of Law Number 1879 on 27 April 2002, the Arbitration and Mediation Law.

Pursuant to that Law, which contains seventy articles, Articles 774 to 835 of Book V of the Civil Procedural Code, referring to the arbitration process, and Article 536 of the Civil Procedural Code, referring to the execution of arbitration awards handed down by foreign courts, were repealed. The objective of the report prepared by the Commission of Jurists was to provide a simpler and more flexible system of arbitration to be more widely applied, particularly in view of the still existing reticence among parties in conflict to resort to arbitration.

The intention to establish a regulated regime within the Civil Procedural Code itself with regard to mediation is being publicized, and the promotion is receiving interest. The report comprises two books: the first dedicated to arbitration and the second to mediation. As to arbitration, the new Law seeks to relate the arbitration process in Paraguay to the new international trends:

> ". . . acknowledging the contractual nature of the agreement, allowing the appointment of the competent judge, as well as the choice of procedure to apply in the development of the arbitration process. The new law, which constitutes part of the Civil Procedural Code, adopts the principles and solutions contained in the Model Law of the United Nations Commission for International Trade Law (UNCITRAL)".

Furthermore, guidelines for the definition of international arbitration are determined in a precise manner. A very positive contribution that the new Law affords to arbitration in Paraguay is the characteristics of an international system:

> ". . . that constitute solutions considered acceptable by the State parties and a different juridical ordinance that may finally allow Paraguay to become an arbitration center at the international and regional level".

Law Number 1879/02 provides that the arbitration court constituted in each relevant case shall decide on its own competence. Also of great importance are the provisions that allow the parties, by mutual consent, to agree upon the arbitration procedure, which shall remain within the framework of certain provisions necessary to protect the flexibility of negotiations, equity and the equality of the parties during the arbitration process. Therefore, matters such as arbitration venue, inception of actions, language, complaint and response, hearings and actions in writing, the case of default of one of the parties and the appointment of experts, among others, may be agreed by the parties. Likewise, the new Law introduces novelties pertaining to available recourse against the arbitration award.

As to the matter of execution of an award, the Law follows the criteria set forth in Article II of the New York Convention in relation to the recognition and execution of foreign arbitral awards. The most important new provision introduced by Law Number 1879/02 is the incorporation of the Mediation Institute into the Civil Procedural Code: "One of the most utilized means for the resolution of conflicts during the past years in the Latin American nations."

Thus, mediation appears for the first time in Paraguayan civil legislation, bringing it in line with MERCOSUR in the search for the peaceful solution of conflicts through a procedure that permits parties in dispute to be fundamental actors in the resolution of their conflicts, preserving confidentiality and endeavoring to remove the irritating factors causing such conflicts.

It is worth noting that Paraguay, as from a decade ago, initiated discussions on the principles, character and benefits of mediation. The Paraguayan Mediation Institute (IPAME) was the organizer, in the early years, of the initial seminars and panels on the subject, with Argentinean, Brazilian and Uruguayan speakers. Later, the Asuncion Stock Exchange showed an interest and the wish to help in this important task. Today, mediation is a part of the objectives pursued by the Center for Mediation and Conciliation, Consumer Education and Defense of the School of Juridical Sciences of the Catholic University *Nuestra Señora de la Asunción* and the Center for Arbitration and Mediation of the Paraguayan Stock Exchange.

> "The conclusions of the mediation achieved through the relevant agreement are enforceable as from the time that the parties and the mediator execute the final act documenting such circumstances and have the effect of *res judicata* as from the moment that the competent judge records such agreement, that may be the object of forcible execution."

Fundamental Provisions of Law Number 1879/02

Sphere of Application

Title I, Chapter I, Article 1 deals with the sphere of application as follows:

> "The present law shall be applied to national and international private arbitration without prejudice to the provisions of treaties executed and ratified by the Republic of Paraguay. The provisions of the present laws shall apply only if the venue of arbitration is located within the national territory. The provisions of Articles 11, 20 and 44 to 48 shall apply despite the venue of arbitration being outside national territory."

Object of Arbitration

Article 2 deals with the object of arbitration as follows:

"All matters subject to compromise and having a patrimonial content may be submitted to arbitration unless they are the subject of a final judgment which is not appealable. Those matters that require the intervention of the Office of the Public Attorney may not be the object of arbitration.

"The Government, decentralized or autarkic entities and government owned enterprises, as well as the municipalities, may submit their disputes with private enterprises, be they national or foreign, as long as they arise from juridical acts or contracts governed by private law."

Definitions in Arbitration

Article 3 defines the terms relating to arbitration as follows:

"The effects of the present law shall apply to:

"Arbitration Agreement: The agreement whereby the parties decide to submit to arbitration all or certain controversies that have arisen or may arise between them with regard to a definite juridical relationship, whether contractual or not. The arbitration agreement may adopt the form of a settlement clause included in a contract or be an independent agreement.

"Any arbitration proceedings shall be deemed arbitration regardless of being carried out by a permanent arbitration institution or not.

"International Arbitration: That wherein:

"1. The parties to an arbitration agreement, at the time of execution of that agreement, have their principal places of business in different States; or

"2. The venue of compliance with any substantial part of the obligations arising from the business relationship or the place where the object of contention has a closer relationship is located outside the State where the parties have their principal places of business."

"For the purposes of the present article:

"a) If any of the parties has more than one establishment, the establishment to be taken into account shall be that which is more closely related to the arbitration agreement;

"b) If any of the parties has no establishment at all, the venue to be taken into account shall be the principal place of business.

"Arbitration Court: That constituted by one arbitrator or several arbitrators appointed by the parties to arrive at a decision on a dispute.

"Costs: These comprise the Arbitration Court fees, travel expenses and other sundry expenses incurred by the arbitrators; costs of expert counselors or any other assistance required by the Arbitration Court; travel and other expenses incurred by witnesses, as approved by the Arbitration Court; representation and legal aid costs of the winning party if the parties have agreed to the claim of such costs during the arbitration process and only in the amount that the Arbitration Court considers reasonable; and the remuneration and expenses of the institution that has appointed the arbitrators."

Calculation of Time Period

Article 6 states:

"For the purposes of computing the time period established by the present law, the said period shall commence as from the day following the day upon which a notification, notice, communication or proposal is received. In the event that the last day of the term is an official holiday or not a working day at the place of residence or place of business of the addressee, the said period shall be extended until the first following working day. Any other official holidays or non-work days that occur during the course of the term shall be included in the computation of the term."

Non-Intervention by the Judiciary

Article 8 states in this regard:

> "Except as otherwise provided, judicial intervention shall not apply in matters governed by the present law."

Cases of Judicial Intervention

Article 9 states:

> "Whenever judicial intervention is required, the judge of first instance in civil and commercial matters at the relevant venue where the arbitration is to take place shall be the competent judge. In the event that the venue of the arbitration is outside national territory, competence in relation to the recognition and execution of the award shall lie with the judge of first instance in civil and commercial matters of the domicile of the defendant, or otherwise at the location of the goods."

Arbitration Agreement

Chapter II of Law 1879/02 deals with the arbitration agreement. Article 10 lays down the requirements with regard to the form of the arbitration agreement:

> "The arbitration agreement shall be in writing. The agreement is understood to be in writing when recorded in a document executed by the parties or by the exchange of letters or registered telegrams containing the agreement; or by the exchange of a statement of claim and reply in which the agreement and the terms thereof are affirmed by one party without being denied by the other party. Reference to a contract in a document that contains a commitment clause shall constitute an arbitration agreement as long as the contract is recorded in writing and the reference implies that the said clause constitutes a part of the contract."

Composition of the Arbitral Award

Chapter III, Article 12 discusses the number of arbitrators as follows:

> "The parties may freely determine the number of arbitrators, which shall be an odd number. In the case of lack of agreement, there shall be three arbitrators."

Competence of the Arbitration Court

Chapter IV, Article 19 sets out the power of the arbitration court to decide upon its competence.

> "The Arbitration Court shall have the power to decide upon its own competence, including matters relating to the existence or validity of the arbitration agreement. For this purpose, a commitment clause that constitutes a part of a contract shall be considered an agreement independent of the other stipulations of the contract. The decision of the Arbitration Court declaring that a contract is null and void shall not imply, *ipso jure*, the nullity of the commitment clause. Any claim of incompetence of the Arbitration Court must be made, at the latest, upon service of the reply to a complaint. The parties shall not be prevented from submitting such a claim by the fact that they have appointed an arbitrator or participated in the appointment. A claim based on the proposition that the Arbitration Court has exceeded its mandate shall be submitted as soon as the matter that purportedly exceeds its mandate arises in the course of the arbitration proceedings. The Arbitration Court may, however, consider a claim submitted late if it considers the delay justified. The Arbitration Court may decide upon the claims to which the present article refers as a preliminary matter or in an award. If, as a preliminary matter, the court declares itself competent, any of the parties, within thirty days following receipt of notice of the decision, may request that a judge resolve the matter, within a period of seven days, such resolution not being subject to appeal."

Provisional Cautionary Measures

Article 20 deals with the power of the arbitration court to order provisional cautionary measures as follows:

> "Except as otherwise agreed by the parties, the Arbitration Court may, at the request of any party, order the adoption of such provisional cautionary measures as it may deem necessary in respect of the matter subject to litigation. The Arbitration Court shall require from the petitioner such counter precautionary measures that it shall deem appropriate. The precautionary measures ordered by the Arbitration Court shall be enforced by a judicial order adopted without hearing within three days from the request of the Arbitration Court. Prior to the constitution of the Arbitration Court, precautionary measures must be applied for from the judge of first instance in civil and commercial matters. Provisional precautionary measures granted judicially shall lapse after seven days from the constitution of the Arbitration Court, which shall have the power to confirm, cancel or modify them as from the time of its constitution."

Arbitral Proceedings

Chapter V, Article 21 states that "the parties are to be treated with equality and each of them shall be afforded the full opportunity to enforce their rights". Article 22 deals with the determination of the process as follows:

> "Subject to the provisions of the present law, the parties shall be free to agree on the process to which the Arbitration Court shall conform in its actions.
>
> "Lacking agreement, the Arbitration Court may, subject to the provisions of the present law and by notice to the parties, govern the arbitration in the manner it considers appropriate. This power granted to the Arbitration Court includes that of determining the admissibility, relevance and value of evidence."

Article 23 covers the venue of the arbitration:

> "The parties may determine freely the venue for the arbitration. In the event of lack of agreement, the Arbitration Court shall determine the venue for the arbitration, taking into account the circumstances of the case, including the convenience of the parties. Without prejudice to the provisions of the previous paragraph, the Arbitration Court may, except as otherwise agreed by the parties, meet in any location that it considers appropriate to carry out deliberations between its members, to hear witnesses, experts or the parties or to examine merchandise or other goods or documents."

Article 25 deals with the language of the arbitration proceedings:

> "The parties may freely agree upon the language or languages to be used in the arbitration proceedings. Lacking such agreement, the Arbitration Court shall determine the language or languages to be used. This determination shall be applicable unless, otherwise specified, to all pleadings by the parties, all hearings and any award, decision or communication of any other kind that the Arbitration Court may issue. The Arbitration Court may order that any documentary evidence be accompanied by a translation into the language or languages agreed by the parties or determined by the Arbitration Court."

Article 32 contains rules applicable to the basis of the complaint:

> "The Arbitration Court shall resolve the complaint according to the rules of law selected by the parties as applicable to the basis of the complaint. All indications of law or judicial regulation of a determined State refer, unless otherwise stated, to the substantive law of that State and not to its conflict of laws rules. If the parties fail to indicate the applicable law, the Arbitration Court shall decide upon the applicable law, determined by the conflict of laws rules that it shall deem applicable. The Arbitration Court shall decide upon matters of equity only if the parties have expressly authorized it. In equitable arbitration or amicable arbitration, the arbitrators shall not be obliged to resolve issues on the basis of rules of law, but may use "conscience" or "the best of their knowledge". In all cases, the Arbitration Court

shall judge according to the stipulations of the contract and shall take into account the business usage applicable to the case."

Article 34 deals with compromise and conciliatory agreement as follows:

"If, during the arbitration proceedings, the parties arrive at a compromise or a conciliatory agreement that resolves the complaint, the Arbitration Court shall hand down an award or arbitral decision in which the above shall be recorded. The award under the agreed terms shall be handed down in accordance with the provisions of Article 36, stating therein that the same is an award. Such award shall have the same nature and effect of any other award handed down on the base of the complaint. Compromises and conciliatory agreements recorded by an Arbitration Court shall have the authority of *res judicata*."

Challenging an Award or Arbitral Decision

Article 40 grants the right to appeal for annulment:

"Sole recourse against an arbitration award shall be an appeal for annulment to the Court of Appeals in Civil and Commercial Matters having jurisdiction over the venue where the award was handed down."

Article 41 states:

"The appeal for annulment shall be made within a period of fifteen days from the date of notice of the award or arbitral decision."

Recognition and Execution of Arbitral Awards

Article 44 deals with the rules applicable to the recognition and execution of foreign arbitral awards:

"Foreign arbitral awards shall be recognized and executed in the country pursuant to the treaties ratified by the Republic of Paraguay on the recognition and execution of arbitral awards. In the event that more than one international treaty is applicable, unless otherwise agreed by the parties, that which is more favorable to the party requesting the recognition and execution of an agreement or arbitration award shall apply. In the event of non-applicability of any international treaty or convention, a foreign award shall be recognized and executed in the Republic of Paraguay under the terms of the present law and the specific provisions of this chapter."

Article 45 states:

"An arbitral award, regardless of the State that has handed it down, will be recognized as binding and, upon the presentation of a petition in writing to the competent judicial organ, shall be executed according to the provisions of the present chapter. At the option of the party requesting recognition and execution of the award, the judge of first instance in civil and commercial matters at the domicile of the party against whom execution of the award is intended shall have jurisdiction, otherwise the judge of first instance of the location of the goods. The party invoking the award or requesting execution thereof shall file the duly authenticated original of the award or a certified copy thereof plus the original of the arbitration agreement as stated in Article 10 or a duly certified copy thereof. In the event that the award or agreement shall not be written in Spanish, the party invoking the same shall be required to submit an official translation into that language by a certified translator."

Costs

Article 49 relates to the agreement regarding costs:

"The parties shall have the power to adopt, either directly or by reference to arbitration rules, rules relating to the costs of arbitration. In the absence of an agreement between the parties, the general provisions of the present chapter shall apply."

Mediation

Title II, Article 53 gives the definition of mediation as follows:

> "Mediation is a voluntary mechanism directed at the resolution of conflicts through which two or more parties themselves work out an amicable solution to their differences with the assistance of a neutral and qualified third party known as a mediator."

Article 54 deals with the matters subject to mediation:

> "Those matters arising from a contractual relationship or any other kind of juridical relationship, or are bound thereto, may be subject to mediation in the event that such matters are susceptible to compromise, conciliation or arbitration."

Article 57 contains provisions relating to confidentiality:

> "Mediation shall be confidential. The participants shall maintain due reserve and the forms of agreement proposed shall not affect any later trial, should one take place. The mediator may not be summoned as a witness or in any other capacity in any later dispute between the same parties or concerning the same subject matter."

Article 61 deals with the effects of mediation:

> "The mediation agreement shall obligate the parties from the time they and the mediator execute the mediation memorandum documenting the mediation, and shall have the effect of *res judicata* as from the moment the competent judge files it. In the event that the mediation agreement is arrived at while there is a pending complaint, the presiding judge shall have jurisdiction over the filing thereof, which shall have the effect of terminating the judicial process. If the mediation is only partial, a record of this shall be entered in the mediation memorandum and the parties shall be free to discuss at trial such differences as have not been mediated."

Article 63 provides details on mediation centers:

> "Mediation centers shall be institutions provided with the necessary administrative and technical elements that serve as support of the mediation action and the training of mediators."

Article 65 — MEDIATOR REQUIREMENTS

> "The mediator must be a person of recognized honorability, training and impartiality and his/her work shall be to direct freely the mediation process, guided by the principles of impartiality, equity and justice. As a previous requirement for the execution of his/her duties, the mediator shall participate in a special training course offered by a mediation center."

CONCLUSION

The objective of this work has been, essentially, to offer a general view of the Paraguayan law, in matters of application of foreign laws and of the efficacy and execution in this country of judgments and arbitration awards handed down by foreign courts, the latter being a subject that has lately sustained changes by reason of the enactment of Law Number 1879/02. To be precise, the indicated modification is designed to adjust the framework of commercial arbitration contemplated in Paraguayan law to the possibility of a more agile and better conditioned application of international commercial arbitration.

It is also worth noting the creation, within Paraguayan civil procedural legislation, of the Mediation Institute, one of the alternative modes of resolution of disputes that is now added to arbitration and conciliation, which already exist under Paraguayan Law.

Appendix

Legislative References Related to Paraguayan Arbitration

Constitution of the Republic, 20 June 1992.

Civil Code, Law Number 1183, 23 December 1985, in force as from 1 January 1987.

Law Code, Law Number 879, 2 December 1981, in force as from 1 March 1982.

Civil Procedural Code, Law Number 1337, 20 December 1988, in force as from 3 November 1989.

Organic Law of the Central Bank of Paraguay (Number 489/95).

Law Number 1879, 27 April 2002, on Arbitration and Mediation, immediately in force.

International Treaties Ratified by Paraguay

Paris Convention on the Protection of Industrial Property 1833.

Trademark and Brands Treaty, Montevideo, 1889.

Patents of Invention Treaty, Montevideo, 1889.

International Procedural Law Treaty, Montevideo, 1889.

General Inter-American Convention on Trademarks and Brands, Washington, 1929.

International Law Treaty, Montevideo, 1940.

Inter-American Convention on International Commercial Arbitration, Panama, 1975.

Inter-American Convention on Extraterritorial Efficacy of Foreign Judgments and Arbitration Awards, Montevideo, 1979.

Law Approving the Buenos Aires Protocol (MERCOSUR) on International Jurisdiction in Contractual Matters (Number 597/95).

Law Establishing the Compliance Regimen of Precautionary Measures within Mercosur.

Convention on the Recognition and Execution of Foreign Arbitral Awards, New York, 1958.

Corruption and Mismanagement

The Sarbanes — Oxley Act of 2002

Quinton F. Seamons and Stephen M. Craig
Beus Gilbert PLLC
Phoenix, Arizona, United States

Introduction

The Sarbanes-Oxley Act of 2002 (SOA) is the legislative response to the corporate and accounting scandals that are occurring in the aftermath of the dot com bubble and the investment markets frenzy during the 1990s.[1] There have been suggestions that the SOA is the most

1 Pub. L. Number 107–204, 116 Stat. 745. In late July 2002, the ever-broadening corporate and accounting scandals at Enron Corporation, WorldCom Inc., Global Crossing LLC, Adelphia Communications Corp. and, most recently, AOL Time Warner Inc. caused Congress to move swiftly to adopt legislation that had been negotiated in a Conference Committee in response to the perceived deteriorating market conditions. During the morning of 25 July 2002, the House approved the Conference legislation 423 to three and, later that afternoon, the Senate approved the same legislation ninety-nine to zero. President Bush signed the legislation into law on 30 July 2002, which has been named after its respective sponsors in the Senate and House of Representatives — Senator Paul Sarbanes (D-Md.) and Representative Michael Oxley (R-Ohio). The version originally sponsored in the House of Representatives and supported by the accounting and securities industries was not as comprehensive as the Senate version, but the widening incidences of corporate fraud "kicked-in" a compelling need for reform, and the House conferees acceded to the more comprehensive Senate legislation: "Fortified Sarbanes Accounting Bill Subject to Debate Limit, on Fast Track", 34 BNA *Securities Regulation and Law Report*, 1164 (15 July 2002); Weisman, Jonathan, "Watchdogs' Vigilance Key To Bill's Success", *The Washington Post* (25 July 2002); Vandehei, Jim, "Hill Leaders Agree on Corporate Curbs", *The Washington Post* (25 July 2002); Crenshaw, Albert B., "Congress Sends Corporate Reform Bill to Bush", *The Washington Post* (26 July 2002). The legislation was adopted fairly quickly without any substantive report from the Conference Committee, although there are reports from the House and Senate on the respective legislation before it entered the Conference Committee: H.R. Report Number 107–414 (22 April 2002) regarding H.R. 3763, the Corporate and Auditing Accountability, Responsibility and Transparency Act of 2002, and Senate Report 107–205 (3 July 2002) regarding S. 2673, the Public Accounting Reform and Investor Protection Act of 2002. There was another bill that was passed by the House on 6 July 2002 that was before the Conference Committee, H.R. 5118, the Corporate Fraud Accountability Act of 2002. H.R. 5118 was sponsored by Representative James Sensenbrenner (R-Wis.) to ensure that legislation will "punish the corporate wrongdoers and punish them harshly", and that "corporate criminals will do real time, real long time": Congressional Record at H4684–85 (16 July 2002); Bostelman, John T., "Enactment of Broad Accounting, Corporate Governance Reform Act Brings New Prohibitions, Requirements for Executives and Auditors", 34 BNA *Securities Regulation and Law Report*, 1281 (5 August 2002).

D.Campbell and S.Woodley (eds.), The Comparative Law Yearbook of International Business 2003, 117-161

comprehensive legislation in the securities markets since the "New Deal" separated commercial and investment banking in the Glass-Steagall Act of 1933 and imposed Securities and Exchange Commission (SEC) regulation on the markets in the Securities Act of 1933 and the Securities Exchange Act of 1934. This is somewhat of an overstatement because the practical impact of the SOA must be assessed in the context of the rules and regulations that the SOA requires the SEC to promulgate in most areas addressed in the legislation. Generally, the SOA enacted broad legislation, but left the actual implementation to the rulemaking powers of the SEC, which has created a huge regulatory agenda for the SEC over the next twelve or more months.

The SOA imposes federal regulation in new corporate and accounting areas and affects the fundamental structures and relationships in the securities markets. There is no doubt that the SOA continues the trend of federalizing corporate governance principles, which traditionally were determined by state law. The subjects addressed by the SOA are a patchwork of various legislative proposals that reflect the debates in hearings before various Congressional Committees regarding Enron Corporation and other "busted" companies. The patchwork addresses discrete areas such as SEC regulatory oversight of auditing standards and accounting firms, auditor independence, heightened corporate governance, increased disclosure and certification of periodically filed reports, new crimes and harsher penalties, enhanced SEC enforcement powers and analyst conflicts. The SOA also requires the SEC or the Comptroller General to undertake various studies and to prepare reports to be delivered to the President, the Senate Committee on Banking, Housing and Urban Affairs or the House Committee on Financial Services.

The SOA and the related SEC rulemaking will create new standards that will evolve and translate into benchmarks of corporate governance and auditing standards against which duty, negligence, scienter and other elements can be measured and alleged particularly in financial fraud litigation.[2]

This chapter highlights some of the more important provisions of the SOA. Most of the provisions of the SOA amend the Securities Acts of 1933 and the Securities Exchange Act of 1934, and other provisions amend the Federal Criminal Code and the Employee Retirement Income Security Act of 1974. A few of the provisions became effective when President Bush signed the SOA on 30 July 2002, but other provisions will become effective at later dates as rules and regulations are implemented. The rulemaking work is substantial, which is why the ramifications of the SOA in many areas turn on the substance of the SEC's rulemaking.

Public Company Accounting Oversight Board

Title I provides for the creation of a new Public Company Accounting Oversight Board (the Board), which will function as a non-governmental and non-profit corporation subject to direct SEC oversight and regulatory authority.[3] The involvement of direct SEC oversight is a fundamental change in the accounting professional environment. The Board will be comprised of five members chosen by the SEC in consultation with the Secretary of the Treasury and the Chairman of the Federal Reserve Board. Three members must be non-accountants and

2 The Sarbanes-Oxley Act extended to two years the statute of limitations and to five years the repose period for claims under Section 10(b) of the Securities Exchange Act of 1934 and Rule 10b-5 thereunder: Sarbanes-Oxley Act, Section 804. This changed the prior one-year statute of limitations and the prior three-year repose period that had been provided in *Lampf, Pleva, Lipkind, Prupis & Petigrow* v. *Gilbertson*, 501 U.S. 350 (1991). The Sarbanes-Oxley Act did not address the subject of aiding and abetting Rule 10b-5 claims, and the law remains that there is no such civil liability, as held in *Central Bank of Denver, N.A.* v. *First Interstate Bank of Denver, N.A.*, 511 U.S. 164 (1994), although the Securities and Exchange Commission can bring enforcement actions for aiding and abetting misconduct. However, *see* the study of aiding and abetting conduct of securities professionals to be undertaken by the Securities and Exchange Commission pursuant to Section 703. The Sarbanes-Oxley Act did not address the bar against pleading securities fraud as a RICO predicate act as provided in the Private Securities Litigation Reform Act of 1995.

3 Section 101 provides that: "The Board shall not be an agency or establishment of the United States Government, and, except as otherwise provided in this Act, shall be subject to, and have all the powers conferred on a non-profit corporation by, the District of Columbia Non-Profit Corporation Act".

two members must be accountants. If an accountant becomes the Chairman of the Board, the accountant must not have practiced as an accountant during the previous five years.[4]

Title I changes the fundamental regulatory structure for accountants from a "peer review" system to a self-regulatory mechanism that parallels the SEC oversight of registered broker-dealers through the NASD organization, that is, Board rules cannot become effective without a comment period and SEC approval. In addition, the disciplinary sanctions of the Board can be appealed to, and reviewed by, the SEC. Through its oversight regulation of the Board, the SEC is the ultimate standard setter for audits of the financial statements of public issuers — generally accepted auditing standards (GAASs). The SEC will also be involved in the Board's investigations because the Board can request the SEC to exercise its subpoena power to require the testimony of and document production by clients of the registered public accounting firms. The registered public accounting firms will be subject to direct SEC regulation and direct SEC enforcement of professional standards. In addition, the audit standard setting functions are now subject to direct SEC authority.[5] The primary responsibilities of the Board are described below.

---

4 The persons appointed by the Securities and Exchange Commission are appointed for five-year terms that will be staggered to ensure continuity. The appointments will be on a full-time basis, and no unrelated professional or business activities will be allowed. The Sarbanes-Oxley Act provides that the members shall be "prominent individuals of integrity and reputation who have a demonstrated commitment to the interests of investors and the public, and an understanding of the responsibilities for and nature of the financial disclosures required of issuers under the securities laws and the obligations of accountants with respect to the preparation and issuance of audit reports with respect to such disclosures": Sarbanes-Oxley Act, Section 101(e)(1); Cassell, Bryan-Low, "SEC Struggles To Fill Positions on Audit Board", *The Wall Street Journal* (22 August 2002); Hilzenrath, David, "SEC Considers Oversight Candidate", *The Washington Post* (22 August 2002).

5 The Sarbanes-Oxley Act provides that nothing in the Act or the Board's rules limits the authority of the Securities and Exchange Commission to regulate the accounting profession, accounting firms or associated persons for the purposes of enforcing the securities laws: Sarbanes-Oxley Act, Section 108(c). In addition, the Securities and Exchange Commission has authority to investigate in order to determine whether the Board's rules have been violated, may bring injunctive actions to prevent violations of the Board's rules and can bring cease and desist proceedings against persons violating Board rules. These Sarbanes-Oxley Act provisions under Title I rendered moot the Securities and Exchange Commission's proposal to establish a "Public Accountability Board" and related reform measures that it had proposed during June 2002: Exchange Act Release Number 46120 [Current Binder] Fed.Sec.L.Rep. (CCH) Paragraph 86,706 (26 June 2002).

Registration

The Board must provide for the registration of public accounting firms that audit the financial statements of public issuers.[6] The SOA provides that the Board can impose initial and annual fees to cover the cost of registration, including the review of applications and annual reports. The registration must occur 180 days (six months) after the Board becomes functional, and the Board was to become functional by approximately 30 April 2003, which is within 270 days (nine months) after the enactment of the SOA on 30 July 2002. Overall, the registration process must be completed no later than fifteen months after the enactment of the SOA, that is, by October 2003.

Audit and Other Standards

The Board must establish audit standards, quality control standards, ethical standards, independence standards and related standards to be used by registered public accounting firms in performing audits and preparing audit reports.[7] The audit standards must, *inter alia*, provide for the retention of audit work papers and other records for seven years "in sufficient detail to support the conclusions reached"; require a concurring or second partner review of the audits performed; and require documentation of the scope of the auditor's testing of internal controls. All of the standards adopted by the Board will be subject to the review and approval of the SEC. Furthermore, the SEC has authority to initiate rulemaking to establish standards where the Board has not taken, or will not take, appropriate action.

Inspection Program

The Board must establish an annual inspection program for registered public accounting firms and must conduct the inspections.[8] These inspections will consist of annual inspections for registered public accounting firms that prepare audit reports for more than 100 issuers and triennial inspections for firms that prepare audits for 100 or fewer issuers. The "peer review" system will not exist among registered public accounting firms and the Public Oversight Board is history.

---

6 Sarbanes-Oxley Act, Section 102.
7 Sarbanes-Oxley Act, Section 103.
8 Sarbanes-Oxley Act, Section 104.

Professional Standards

The Board must take steps to promote high professional standards among registered public accounting firms to enhance, *inter alia*: the monitoring of professional conduct; the development of intra-firm consulting and guidance on accounting and auditing issues; the day-to-day supervision of audit work; professional development; and related matters.[9]

Enforcement

The Board will have investigative and disciplinary authority, including the authority to conduct investigations and request documents and depositions.[10] However, it will not have subpoena power, although it can request the SEC to exercise its subpoena power on behalf of the Board. If a registered public accounting firm or associated person refuses to cooperate in an investigation, the Board may suspend or revoke the registration of the firm and suspend or bar a person from being associated with the accounting firm. The Board is authorized to conduct disciplinary hearings and impose sanctions, such as a suspension, bar or limitation on activities, as well as monetary penalties, and can impose a censure or other appropriate measures, including the revocation or bar of an accounting firm's registration. For intentional and knowing conduct, the Board can impose fines against an associated person up to US $750,000 and against an accounting firm up to US $15-million. The enforcement activities of the Board will be subject to SEC oversight, including a review of all disciplinary proceedings.[11]

---

9 Sarbanes-Oxley Act, Section 103.

10 Sarbanes-Oxley Act, Section 105.

11 The Sarbanes-Oxley Act adds, in Section 105(c)(6), a "failure to supervise" violation against a registered public accounting firm. This "failure to supervise" violation parallels Section 15(b)(4) of the Securities Exchange Act of 1934 that provides for a "failure to supervise" violation against registered broker-dealers.

Budget and Operations

The Board must establish a budget and an operational structure for conducting business.[12] The Board will have a working staff as Senator Sarbanes explained in the Congressional Record at S6330–31 (8 July 2002):

> "Of course, the board will have a staff. We expect staff salaries to be fully competitive with comparable private sector positions in order to ensure a high quality staff."

Funding of Standard Setting Bodies

To remove the Board from industry pressures and enhance its independence, the Board, as well as the accounting standard setting body, the Financial Accounting Standards Board (FASB),[13] will be funded by annual accounting support fees established by the Board and paid by public issuers pursuant to a formula based on the market capitalization of issuers. In this manner, the auditing and accounting standard setting bodies will no longer rely on funding from members of the accounting profession. This is a huge change in the regulatory environment, which is designed to remove the self-serving influence of the business sector and the accounting profession. The funding

---

12 Sarbanes-Oxley Act, Section 101.

13 The Sarbanes-Oxley Act provides, in Section 108, that the Securities and Exchange Commission may recognize as generally accepted accounting principles (GAAPs) any principles that are promulgated by a standard setting entity that meets the following criteria (and it is recognized that the Financial Accounting Standards Board is an entity that will meet these criteria): (1) The entity is private and has a board of trustees that serves the public interest and protects investors; (2) The entity's majority of trustees are not associated with a registered accounting firm or were last associated two years before becoming trustees; (3) The entity is funded by issuers, as the Sarbanes-Oxley Act provides in Section 109; (4) The entity has procedures to ensure prompt consideration by a majority vote on changes to accounting principles; and (5) The entity takes into consideration the development of international accounting standards. This provision continues the traditional deference that the SEC has extended to the accounting profession with respect to the development of accounting principles: Securities and Exchange Commission Accounting Series, Release Number 150 (1973) [37–82 Binder ASR] Fed.Sec.L.Rep. (CCH) Paragraph 72,172 (1973); *Arthur Andersen & Co.* v. *Securities and Exchange Commission* [78 Binder] Fed.Sec.L.Rep. (CCH) Paragraph 86,974 (N.D.Ill. 1978) (deference to accounting profession is not unlawful delegation to private body).

should similarly strengthen the independence of standard setting bodies, such as the Financial Accounting Foundation and its FASB. To enforce the payment of fees, an issuer that fails to pay the fees will automatically violate Section 13(a) or Section 15(d) of the Securities Exchange Act of 1934 (the periodic reporting requirements).

Auditor Independence

Title II addresses various standards for auditor independence through amendments to the Securities Exchange Act of 1934. These standards may well be enhanced and adjusted through rulemaking actions by the Board or the SEC. The basic independence principles set out in the SOA and auditor independence are a primary objective of the SOA because confidence in the integrity of financial statements is predicated on independence in fact and in appearance of the auditor from the audit client. The requirement under the federal securities laws that financial statements of reporting issuers must be prepared by an independent public certified accountant is, in effect, a franchise for accountants that creates a public duty and an obligation to the issuers' creditors and stockholders and the investing public.[14] Congress recognized that this independence has been eroded over the years because the auditor, in large part, has been providing substantial consulting and other services that far exceed the revenues received from audit services. Congress simply prohibited registered public accounting firms

14 *United States* v. *Arthur Young & Co.*, 465 U.S. 805, 817-18 (1984) ("An independent certified public accountant performs a different role [than a private attorney]. By certifying the public reports that collectively depict a corporation's financial status, the independent auditor assumes a public responsibility transcending any employment relationship with the client. The independent public accountant performing this special function owes ultimate allegiance to the corporation's creditors and stockholders, as well as to the investing public. This "public watchdog" function demands that the accountant maintain total independence from the client at all times and requires complete fidelity to the public trust.") (Chief Justice Burger).

from providing major non-audit services whenever audit services are being provided to restore the independent relationship.[15]

Prohibition on Non-Audit Services

The SOA provides that a registered public accounting firm rendering audit services to an issuer is prohibited from concurrently providing eight non-auditing services to the issuer:[16]

(1) Bookkeeping or other financial accounting record keeping;
(2) Design and implementation of internal financial information systems;
(3) Appraisal or valuation services, including fairness opinions;
(4) Actuarial services;
(5) Internal audit services;
(6) Management or human resource services;
(7) Financial services, such as broker-dealer, investment advisor or investment banking services;
(8) Legal and expert services; or

15 On 1 August 2002, the New York Stock Exchange approved significant changes to its listing standards that require, *inter alia*, that independent directors must comprise a majority of the Board, and that the audit committee must be comprised of independent directors only. The only compensation that an audit committee member may receive from the issuer is a director's fee. The new standards also require the compensation and nominating committees to be comprised of independent directors only. These and other corporate governance steps were taken to strengthen the accountability, integrity and transparency of listed issuers. These changes must be submitted to, and approved by, the Securities and Exchange Commission under Section 19 of the Securities Exchange Act of 1934: "NYSE Board Approves Changes to Corporate Governance Listing Standards", 34 BNA *Securities Regulation and Law Report* 1269 (5 August 2001), http://www.nyse.com/pdfs/corp_gov_pro_a.pdf.

16 Sarbanes-Oxley Act, Sections 201 and Section 208.

(9) Any other services determined by the Board or the SEC to be prohibited because it creates an independence conflict.[17] This list of prohibited non-audit services can be expanded through rulemaking by the Board or the SEC.

On a case-by-case basis, the Board may exempt a registered public accounting firm from one or more of the eight prohibited non-audit services.[18] In addition, there is a *de minimus* exception in Section 202 for non-audit services that consists of no more than five per cent of the total amount of revenue paid by the issuer to the auditor during the fiscal year in which the non-audit services are provided if such services were not perceived as non-audit services at the time of the engagement, and such services are promptly brought to the audit committee's attention and are approved.

Section 208 provides that it will be unlawful for a registered public accounting firm to prepare or issue "any audit report" if it engages in any activity prohibited under Title II.

Audit Committee Pre-Approval for Non-Audit Services

A registered public accounting firm can perform other non-audit services, such as tax work, if such services are approved by the issuer's audit committee.[19] In fact, all auditing and non-auditing services must be pre-approved by the audit committee and disclosed in the

---

17 These categories of prohibited non-audit services are generally consistent with the auditor independence rules that the Securities and Exchange Commission adopted in December 2000 in amending Rule 2-01 of the Securities and Exchange Commission's Regulation S-X, 17 C.F.R. 210.2-01: Securities Act Release Number 7919 (15 November 2000), http://www.sec.gov/rules/final/33-7919.htm. One exception, however, is the inclusion of expert services. The Securities and Exchange Commission had proposed to prohibit expert services in its independence rules, but it was not included in the final rules: Securities Act Release Number 7870 (30 June 2000). Expert services now appear in the prohibited non-audit services of the Sarbanes-Oxley Act, but the legislative history does not provide any explanation for this provision: Kursh, Samuel J., "The Quiet Conflict", *The National Law Journal* (1 April 2002).

18 The exemptions are intended to be narrow. Senator Sarbanes stated in the Congressional Record on 25 July 2002: "[t]he exemptive authority provided the Board is intentionally narrow to apply to individual cases where the application of the statutory requirement would impose some extraordinary hardship or circumstance that would merit an exemption consistent with the protection of the public interest and the protection of investors."

19 Sarbanes-Oxley Act, Section 202.

issuer's periodic reports. The SOA does not provide any standard for the pre-approval process and does not indicate how frequently the approval must be sought. Audit committees are expected to set their own standards in this area consistent with their fiduciary duties and other relevant considerations.[20] The audit committee's approvals must be disclosed in the issuer's periodic reports.

Audit Partner Rotation

The SOA provides that, every five fiscal years, a registered public accounting firm must rotate the lead audit partner who has primary responsibility for the audits and the audit partner who reviews the audit of the issuer,[21] the current practice being to rotate the lead audit partner every seven years. The "lead partner" refers to the partner who is in charge of the audit engagement, and the "review partner" refers to the outside partner brought in to review the audit work performed by the lead partner and the audit team. The SOA does not require rotation of audit firms — only rotation of the lead audit partner and the reviewing audit partner. The mandatory rotation of audit firms is the subject of a study under Section 207.

Auditor to Report to Audit Committee

A registered public accounting firm performing an audit must report to the audit committee on a timely basis: all critical accounting policies and practices;[22] all alternative treatments of financial information within the application of GAAPs; and all written communications between the auditor and the issuer's management.[23]

---

20 The audit committee can delegate pre-approval authority to one or more of its members, but approvals made by delegated authority must be reported and ratified at the next meeting of the audit committee. The Senate Report states at 19–20 that pre-approval can be at any time and can be on a delegated basis.

21 Sarbanes-Oxley Act, Section 203.

22 "Commission Statement About Management's Discussion and Analysis of Financial Condition and Results of Operations", Exchange Act Release Number 45321 [01–02 Binder] Fed.Sec.L.Rep. (CCH) Paragraph 86,617 (22 January 2002); "Cautionary Advice Regarding Disclosure About Critical Accounting Policies", Exchange Act Release Number 45149 [01–02 Binder] Fed.Sec.L.Rep. (CCH) Paragraph 86,609 (12 December 2001).

23 Sarbanes-Oxley Act, Section 204.

Congress believes that there should be a continuing dialogue between the auditor and the audit committee. The audit committee should be aware of key assumptions underlying an issuer's financial statements and of disagreements that the auditor has with management. The audit committee should be informed in a timely manner of such disagreements, so that it can independently review them and intervene if it chooses to assure the integrity of the audit.

Conflicts of Interest and "Cooling-Off" Period

The SOA provides that a registered public accounting firm cannot perform any audit services for an issuer if the issuer's chief executive officer (CEO), chief financial officer (CFO), CAO, controller or similar person of the issuer has participated in any capacity in the audit of the issuer within the one-year period preceding the initiation of the audit to be performed.[24] This provision is intended to protect against conflicts that arise in circumstances when the audit firm's personnel are employed by the audit client. The one-year period avoids the situation where top audit personnel may believe that they have the prospect of an immediate executive position with the audit client. In effect, the issuer would have to change auditors if such employment occurred.

Corporate Governance, Responsibility and Disclosure

Titles III and IV provide for numerous corporate governance measures to be implemented and require additional disclosures that are intended to make corporate governance and the financial condition of the issuer more transparent.[25] The various measures are not necessarily linked together and are a patchwork of requirements designed to be responsive to various problems identified during the hearings before Congressional Committees regarding the recent corporate scandals.

---

24 Sarbanes-Oxley Act, Section 206.

25 The Sarbanes-Oxley Act generally applies to foreign issuers that are reporting issuers under Section 13 or Section 15(d) of the Securities Exchange Act of 1934. The Securities and Exchange Commission has provided guidance to foreign issuers that may be subject to a different form of periodic reporting than domestic issuers: http://wwwsecgov/rules/final/33–8124.htm.

Certification of Periodic Reports

The SOA contains two separate certification requirements that apply to a CEO and a CFO with respect to the filing of periodic reports with the SEC by reporting issuers.[26] The certification under Section 302 must be filed under the signature block in the periodic report, and it is unacceptable to file the certifications as separate correspondence to the SEC on Edgar or included in a Form 8-K filing.[27] These two certification requirements are not identical and will require guidance and experience to understand their context fully.

The first certification requirement is in the criminal arena — the "Section 906 certification" under Title IX that addresses penalties for white-collar crime.[28] This provision requires the CEO and CFO to certify that any filed periodic report "fully complies" with all of the requirements for filing periodic reports under the Securities Exchange Act of 1934 and the regulations thereunder and fairly presents in all material respects the financial condition and results of operations.[29] If an officer certifies when "knowing" that the report does not comply with the SEC requirements, such officer can be fined up to US $1-million or imprisoned for up to ten years, or both. If the violation is "willful", such officer can be fined up to US $5-million or

---

26 Sarbanes-Oxley Act, Sections 302 and 906. "By demanding accountability at the top, the Administration hopes to prevent execs from passing the buck, as at Enron, where head honcho, Kenneth L. Lay, insisted he had no knowledge of financial engineering at his company": Walczak, Lee, "Let the Reforms Begin", *Business Week* 26, 30 (22 July 2002).

27 http://www.sec.gov/rules/final/33-8124.htm.

28 This provision of the Sarbanes-Oxley Act amends 18 U.S.C. Section 1350, which is entitled "Failure of Corporate Officers to Certify Financial Reports".

29 Unlike the Section 302 certification explained below, there is no materiality requirement with respect to compliance with the reporting requirements and no reference to the phrase "based on my knowledge" in Section 906 certifications, as with Section 302 certifications. The issue has been raised as to what is a "periodic report" for Section 906 certification purposes. Form 10-K and Form 10-Q are periodic reports, but Form 8-K is not because it does not have any regular filing date and is triggered by the happening of an event — not a pre-determined due date. Thus, a Section 906 certification may not be required for a Form 8-K report, and reporting foreign issuers are subject to Section 906 certification and must sort out which of their reports are periodic reports for the purposes of certification, for example, Form 20-F and Form 6-K. The Securities and Exchange Commission has recently provided guidance that certifications must be provided in Forms 20-F and 40-F, but not in Form 6-K: http://www.sec.gov/rules/final/33-8124.htm.

imprisoned for up to twenty years, or both. Both the "knowing" and "willful" violations are felonies and are fairly high standards. Other conduct, such as recklessness or "should have known", does not result in a violation of the Section 906 certification requirement. This certification requirement became effective on 30 July 2002, when the SOA was enacted into law.

Senator Joseph Biden (D-Del.), the Chairman of the Foreign Relations Committee, added the Section 906 certification as an amendment on the floor of the Senate, so there was not a lot of focus on this requirement in the criminal context. Senator Biden's explanation was that the "truth be told, the certification requirement only imposes criminal sanctions for top corporate officials who lie about their financial records". However, the SEC has said very little about Section 906 certification. The current practice appears to be that issuers are filing two certifications. There have been questions whether the "fairly presents" aspect of Section 906 certification can be qualified with a reference to GAAPs or whether a knowledge qualifier can be inserted into the certification, but there has been no guidance on these questions to date. The Section 906 certification appears to be broader than the Section 302 certification described below because it requires the officers to certify that the relevant periodic report "fully complies" with the requirements of Section 13(a) or Section 15(d) of the Securities Exchange Act of 1934 and the related reporting regulations.

The second certification (the Section 302 certification) is required under the Securities Exchange Act of 1934. The SOA required the SEC to adopt rules by 29 August 2002 that require the CEO and the CFO to certify that:

(1) The executing person has reviewed the periodic report;[30]
(2) Based on such person's knowledge, the report does not contain an untrue statement or omission of a material fact;

30 Section 302 certification expressly applies to each annual (Form 10-K) or quarterly report (Form 10-Q) which is "filed or submitted" to the Securities and Exchange Commission, so there is no ambiguity that Section 302 certification does not apply to Form 8-K. On 29 August 2002, the Securities and Exchange Commission clarified that the certification requirements apply to Forms 10-K, 10-Q, 20-F and 40-F, but do not extend to Forms 6-K, 8-K or 11-K: http://www.sec.gov/rules/final/33–8124.htm.

(3) Based on such person's knowledge, the financial statements and financial information fairly present in all material respects the financial condition and results of operation;[31]
(4) The internal controls have been designed to disclose material information to such officers and have been evaluated within the last ninety days;[32]
(5) Any significant deficiencies in the design or operations of the internal controls have been disclosed to the auditor and audit committee; and
(6) All significant changes in internal controls since their evaluation have been disclosed.[33]

The SEC had already initiated regulatory steps on 14 June 2002 to require certification on annual and quarterly reports by 14 August 2002, which certification is similar to the Section 302 certification. Corporate officers have been making these certified filings as reported.[34] The SEC issued a release on 2 August 2002 reiterating that comments on its certifications remained due on 19 August 2002, and explained that the SEC would make adjustments in its

31 The Securities and Exchange Commission has stated that the term "fairly presents" encompasses far more than generally accepted accounting principles presentation and emphasized that generally accepted accounting principles may be insufficient to disclose all material information: http://www.sec.gov/rules/final/33–8124.htm.

32 Section 906 certification does not refer to internal controls.

33 Exchange Act Release Number 46079 [Current Binder] Fed.Sec.L.Rep. (CCH) Paragraph 86,702 (14 June 2002). With regard to the differences between the two certifications, Senator Michael Enzi (R-Wyo.) stated in the Congressional Record on 25 July 2002 that: "inconsistencies appear in Sections 302 and 906. The SEC is required to complete rulemaking within thirty days of enactment with regard to chief financial officer certification under Section 302. However, Section 906 suggests that certification would be required upon enactment, thus the penalties would go into effect before the certification requirement is completed through the rulemaking process. I believe it was the intent of the Conferences that the penalties under Section 906 should not become effective until the rulemaking process is finalized".

34 Grimsley, Kristin, "Signing the Bottom Line", *The Washington Post* (1 August 2002); Williams, Krissah, "A Two-Way Race to Certify Financial Statements", *The Washington Post* (13 August 2002). Day, Kathleen, "CEO Deadline Brings Some Restatements", *The Washington Post* (15 August 2002); McKinnon, John D., "Firms Rush to Meet Deadline by SEC to Certify Statements", *The Wall Street Journal* (16 August 2002); McKinnon, John D., "SEC Boosts Tally of Firms Failing to Certify Results", *The Wall Street Journal* (19 August 2002).

existing requirements by 29 August 2002, so that its then certification would ultimately conform to the Section 302 certification requirements.[35] The SEC did not make any statement regarding the Section 906 certification, although the staff indicated on 28 August 2002 that it is working with the Justice Department on compliance with Section 906.[36]

The SEC adopted its proposed rules in final on 29 August 2002, which implemented the Section 302 certification.[37] The new rules provide for extensive disclosures regarding internal controls in terms of disclosure and financial disclosure. In addition to the Section 302 certification, the new rules require CEOs and CFOs to certify that they are responsible for the control of disclosures and have made certain disclosures to the audit committee, as well as to the auditors, regarding the issuer's financial reporting controls. Issuers must also maintain controls and procedures relating to the disclosure process, which is a new requirement that results in two sets of controls for certification purposes:

(1) Controls and procedures for effecting disclosures; and
(2) Internal controls for financial reporting purposes.

The new disclosure controls will require issuers to adopt and enforce procedures for collecting and processing information to be disclosed within the proper reporting periods. The regulations do not mandate or identify specific controls, and each issuer will have to customize disclosure procedures to best fit its environment and reporting requirements. As with internal controls, the CEOs and CFOs must evaluate the effectiveness of the disclosure controls and procedures

---

35 Exchange Act Release Number 46300 (2 August 2002), http://www.sec.gov/rules/proposed/34–46300.htm; Exchange Act Release Number 46079 [Current Binder] Fed.Sec.L.Rep. (CCH) Paragraph 86,702 (14 June 2002); "SEC Supplements Certification Proposal in Light of Sarbanes-Oxley", 34 BNA *Securities Regulation and Law Report*, 1336 (12 August 2002).

36 Schroeder, Michael, "SEC Gives Broad Interpretations of Rules for Accounting Statute", *The Wall Street Journal* (28 August 2002). Section 1001 of Title X of the Sarbanes-Oxley Act provides that: "It is the sense of the Senate that the Federal income tax return of a corporation should be signed by the chief executive officer of such corporation". While this does not have the effect of law, this sense of the Senate reflects the concern of Congress that the chief executive officer and chief financial officer have personal responsibility for the integrity of the filings made by reporting issuers which explains, in large part, the reasons for the certification requirement.

37 http://www.sec.gov/rules/final/33–8124.htm.

during the ninety-day period immediately preceding the filing date of the periodic report. The SEC recommended that issuers establish a "disclosure committee" consisting of management personnel to consider the materiality of information and to consider the timeliness of material disclosures. The disclosure committee should report to senior management.

Enhanced Audit Committees of Public Companies

The SOA[38] provides that the SEC must adopt regulations to require national securities exchanges and NASDAQ to prohibit the listing of securities the issuers of which do not have an audit committee that complies with the following corporate governance principles:[39]

(1) The audit committee is responsible for the appointment, compensation and oversight of the auditor, and the auditor must report directly to the audit committee;
(2) The audit committee members are all independent;
(3) The audit committee has independence standards that prohibit any member from having any consulting, advisory or other fee relationships with the issuer and from being an affiliate of the issuer or any subsidiary;
(4) The audit committee has procedures for the receipt, retention and treatment of complaints regarding accounting or auditing matters involving the issuer;
(5) The audit committee has procedures for confidential and anonymous submissions by employees concerning questionable accounting or auditing matters;
(6) The audit committee has authority to hire independent counsel and other advisers; and
(7) The issuer has provided for appropriate funding to pay compensation to any auditor and any advisers employed by the audit committee.

---

38 Sarbanes-Oxley Act, Section 301.

39 The Sarbanes-Oxley Act provides in Sections 2(3)(A) and (B) that an "audit committee" means "the entire Board of Directors of the issuer" if no committee of the Board is established to oversee the accounting, financial reporting and auditing process. While virtually all reporting issuers have audit committees, in any event, an issuer cannot avoid audit committee requirements by not creating an audit committee. In the absence of a committee, the Sarbanes-Oxley Act provides that the entire Board of Directors becomes, in effect, the audit committee.

These criteria, as well as the requirement to pre-approve non-audit services, move the audit committee into a substantive monitoring mode of crucial financial developments, and quite possibly into a "target rich environment" in the litigation world.[40] The responsibility to appoint the registered public accounting firm and to have that firm report directly to the audit committee will certainly enhance the power of the audit committee within corporate governance. Indeed, the SEC Division of Enforcement has stated that the agency "will scrutinize the behavior of corporate audit committees in every investigation it begins into companies' financial reporting".[41]

Prohibition on Personal Loans to Directors and Executive Officers

The SOA amended Section 13 of the Securities Exchange Act of 1934 to provide that it is unlawful for any issuer:

> "To extend or maintain credit, to arrange for the extension of credit or to renew an extension of credit in the form of a personal loan to or for any director or executive officer (or equivalent thereof) of that issuer".[42]

This provision was proposed by Senator Charles Schumer (D-NY). A number of traditional compensation arrangements will have to be evaluated in light of this provision, such as housing and relocation expenses, cashless exercises of stock options, split-dollar insurance policies and the advancing of expenses in litigation. There are a number of exemptions for loans made by FDIC-insured banks and thrifts that are subject to the existing bank regulatory insider lending restrictions. There is also an exemption for extensions of credit and credit card debt provided in the ordinary business of consumer credit and

40 Reddy, Anitha, "Audit Committees Using New Power", *The Washington Post* (17 August 2002). The ability of the audit committee to employ outside and separate advisers places pressure on audit committees to take action when problems are identified. This is a factor that may lead to more active audit committees and also encourages the outside advisers to become involved with the audit committee because the compensation arrangement should be in place at the time of engagement.

41 "SEC Says Corporate Audit Panels Under Scrutiny in Agency Probes", *Bloomberg News* (23 February 2002), http://quote.bloomberg.com/newsarchive/?sidenav=front (Director of Enforcement, Stephen Cutler).

42 Sarbanes-Oxley Act, Section 402.

made on market terms. The arrangements made in a business context, such as the reimbursement of travel expenses, should not be a problem because such expenses are not a personal loan. Also, the SOA provides a "grandfather" clause that permits companies to continue to maintain loans that are already in place. This provision became effective upon the enactment of the SOA on 30 July 2002.

Forfeiture of Certain Bonuses and Profits

The SOA amends the Securities Exchange Act of 1934 to provide that, if an issuer is required to restate its financial statements due to a material non-compliance which is the result of misconduct regarding any financial reporting requirement under the securities laws, the CEO and CFO of the issuer must reimburse the issuer for any bonus or other incentive-based or equity-based compensation that such officers received during the twelve-month period following the filing of the financial document that had to be restated.[43] In addition, any profits realized from the officers' sales of securities during that twelve-month period must be tendered to the issuers. The SEC has authority to exempt any person from the forfeiture of bonuses and profits as it deems necessary and appropriate.

This provision became effective upon the enactment of the SOA and does not require any rulemaking by the SEC. In effect, this provision creates a new derivative claim on behalf of an issuer parallel to that which exists for insider trading profits under Section 16(b) of the Securities Exchange Act of 1934.

Insider Trading and Pension Fund Blackout Periods

The SOA amends the Securities Exchange Act of 1934 to provide that directors and executive officers (but not ten per cent shareholders) cannot purchase, sell or otherwise acquire or transfer any equity security of the issuer during any "blackout period" if the officer or director acquires such equity security in connection with his service or

43 Section 304 of the Sarbanes-Oxley Act does not indicate whether the misconduct must be attributable to the chief executive officer or the chief financial officer. In other words, if another person's misconduct caused the restatement, the chief executive officer and the chief financial officer may nevertheless have to forfeit their previously paid compensation and profits. Also, Section 304 does not provide a definition of a "restatement", and further guidance may be necessary in this area.

employment with the issuer.[44] For the purposes of this prohibition, "blackout period" means any period of more than three consecutive business days during which the ability of not fewer than fifty per cent of the participants or beneficiaries under individual account plans are suspended from making any transactions in the issuer's securities.

Similar to the remedies under Section 16(b) of the Securities Exchange Act of 1934, the SOA creates a derivative action whereby any profit realized by such director or executive officer is recoverable by the issuer irrespective of the motives of the director or officer effecting the transaction. The issuer may bring the action against the director or executive officer, or an owner of the security may bring a derivative action, as is the practice under Section 16(b) of the Securities Exchange Act of 1934. There is a statute of limitations for such actions of two years from the date upon which the profit is realized. There is also a demand requirement that must be made to the issuer sixty days before the action is filed, although plaintiffs may assert that such a demand would be futile. A security owner can also proceed with a lawsuit if the issuer fails diligently to prosecute the action within the sixty-day period. The SOA requires the ERISA plan administrator to send notices of blackout periods to plan participants thirty days in advance of the blackout period, although there are certain exceptions to such notice.

Code of Ethics for Senior Financial Officers

The SOA requires the SEC to adopt rules requiring issuers to disclose whether they have a code of ethics that applies at least to the principal financial officer and controller or principal accounting officer.[45] The code of ethics is defined broadly to govern honest and ethical conduct and must contain provisions that require financial officers to provide full, fair, accurate, timely and understandable disclosure in periodic reports and to disclose how actual or apparent conflicts will be handled between personal and professional relationships. The rules must provide that a filing on Form 8-K (or on some comparable form for

44 Sarbanes-Oxley Act, Section 306.

45 Sarbanes-Oxley Act, Section 406.

foreign issuers) will be made whenever there is a change or a waiver of the code of ethics for the senior financial officers.[46]

G. Rules of Professional Responsibility for Attorneys

The SOA requires the SEC to promulgate rules that set forth minimum standards of professional conduct for attorneys who appear and practice before the SEC in any capacity in representing issuers. Section 307 mandates the SEC to adopt a rule:

> ". . . requiring an attorney to report evidence of a material violation of securities law or breach of fiduciary duty or similar violation by the company or any agent thereof, to the chief legal counsel or chief executive officer of the company (or the equivalent thereof); and if the counsel or officer does not appropriately respond to the evidence (adopting, as necessary, appropriate remedial measures or sanctions with respect to the violation), requiring the attorney to report the evidence to the audit committee of the Board of Directors of the issuer or to another committee of the Board of Directors comprised solely of directors not employed directly or indirectly by the issuer, or to the Board of Directors".[47]

This "blow the whistle" provision (at least within the corporate entity) is controversial, particularly with respect to the reporting of a breach of fiduciary duty or "similar violation", whatever that means. The requirement that an attorney report "evidence of a material violation" upstream in the issuer's hierarchy is not as extensive as Section 10A of the Securities Exchange Act of 1934, which requires

46 The recently adopted New York Stock Exchange Listing Standards require listed companies to adopt a formal code of business conduct, including provisions to address conflicts of interest. These codes must be disclosed on the issuers' websites, and any waivers from the codes must be promptly disclosed. Some of these provisions may have to be adjusted depending on the rules and regulations that the Sarbanes-Oxley Act requires the Securities and Exchange Commission to adopt in this area. *See also In re Caremark International Inc. Derivative Litigation*, 698 A.2d 959, 968–69 (Del. Ch. 1996).

47 Sarbanes-Oxley Act, Section 307.

the independent accountant to ultimately report an "illegal act" outside the issuer to the SEC.[48]

The SOA provides, for the first time, that the SEC will be involved substantively in the attorney-client relationship between counsel and the issuer, which is the true client — not management personnel or other agents of the issuer.[49] A Task Force of the American Bar Association on Corporate Responsibility has urged that changes to professional responsibility should occur through traditional channels of state court regulation and not through a federal agency such as the SEC.[50] Issuers are concerned that, while they are entitled to effective representation, their counsel will be subject to regulation by the SEC at the same time that the SEC may be antagonistic to the issuers in an investigation or disclosure dispute. Issuers believe that this regulatory relationship over counsel will inhibit their SEC counsel from zealously representing issuers before the SEC.

Senator John Edwards (D-NC) was the sponsor of the Section 307 provision along with Senator Michael Enzi (R-Wyo.) and Senator Jon Corzine (D-NJ). Senator Edwards stated in the Congressional Record at 6552 (10 July 2002):

> "Three important details about this amendment address some of the concerns that I have heard voiced. First, the way

---

48 Remarks of Senator Enzi (R-Wyo.) on the Senate floor, Congressional Record (10 July 2002); Riesenberg, Thomas L., "Trying To Hear the Whistle Blowing: The Widely Misunderstood 'Illegal Act' Reporting Requirements of Exchange Act, Section 10A", 56 *Business Lawyer* 1417 (August 2001).

49 The Sarbanes-Oxley Act requirement "to report evidence" is perceived as more rigid than Model Rule 1.13(b) of the American Bar Association: "SEC Must Issue Attorney Conduct Rules Under New Federal Accounting Reform Law", 34 BNA *Securities Law and Report*, 457 (31 July 2002); Crimmins, Stephen J., "New Legislation Will Require Attorneys to Report Evidence of Their Corporate Clients' Violations", 34 BNA *Securities Law and Report*, 1340 (12 August 2002).

50 The Section 307 provision quoted above is "nearly identical" to a proposal of the Task Force which the American Bar Association House of Delegates rejected in February 2002: Grimaldi, James V., "Congress Steps Up to Force Lawyers to Look Closer at Corporate Clients", *The Washington Post* (29 July 2002) ("While the [ABA] talked to death proposed ethics rules for lawyers who stumble on corporate fraud, the wave of Wall Street scandals effectively took the issue off the ABA's hands. Congress last week mandated the changes."). The American Bar Association had lobbied the Conferees against Section 307 asserting that the Securities and Exchange Commission rules would "pre-empt state law and override the existing state court ethical rules". The American Bar Association intends to continue consideration of the proposals of its Task Force on Corporate Responsibility.

we have drafted the bill, the duty to report applies only to evidence of material violation of the law. That means no reporting is required for piddling violations or violations that do not amount to anything. The obligation to report is triggered only by violations that are material — violations that a reasonable investor would want to know about so we have been very careful there.

"Second, when the evidence is reported within the company, we have not specified how a CEO or general counsel should act to rectify the violation. That is because the truth is that the appropriate response to cure the problem will very dramatically depending on the circumstance. If the CEO can do a short investigation, for example, and figure out that no violation occurred, then the obligation stops there. However, if there is a serious violation of law, the appropriate response is clear: the CEO must act promptly to remedy the violation. If he does not, the lawyer must go to the Board. It is that simple.

"One final point. Nothing in this bill gives anybody a right to file a private lawsuit against anybody. The only people who can enforce this amendment are the people at the SEC."

The impact of this regulation will be determined largely by the language of the SEC rules that implement Section 307. There are definitional issues that must be resolved regarding the language of Section 307 quoted above, including:

(1) What constitutes "evidence" and does it extends to any minimal amount of evidence or only substantial or clear and convincing evidence?
(2) What does "similar violations" mean?
(3) To what extent do discussions or disputes regarding disclosure constitute evidence that must be disclosed?
(4) What conduct or violations trigger reporting?
(5) How does materiality apply in these circumstances? and
(6) What is an appropriate response by management?

There will also be issues regarding the relationship between the SEC's standards of professional conduct and the codes of legal ethics adopted among the various states.[51] There is also a concern that this "whistle-blowing" requirement violates the attorney-client privilege, even though the provision only requires ultimate disclosure to the Board of Directors, which is the client for all purposes, rather than requiring disclosure to outside governmental authorities or third parties.

In addressing the Committee on Federal Regulation of Securities at the American Bar Association (ABA) Annual Meeting on 12 August 2002, SEC Chairman Pitt indicated that the SEC would proceed cautiously in formulating regulations affecting the attorney-client relationship and solicited comments regarding what should be the breadth and substance of the rules to be adopted, including comments from the ABA Task Force on Corporate Responsibility. Chairman Pitt noted that the rules should focus on egregious conduct and made reference that the poet Dante had placed "Evil Counselors" below thieves in the eighth realm of the Inferno which was provided for counselors who work by hidden ways and sin by glibness of tongue.[52] The Chairman added that attorneys "cannot escape their role in giving assistance to corporate wrongdoers by hiding behind their ability to craft a clever phrase to circumvent what they know to be the right answer". He also added that "although some lawyers believe the role of outside auditors and corporate lawyers are vastly different, lawyers representing public companies have responsibilities quite similar to those of outside auditors".

It should be noted that violations of the rules promulgated by the SEC would be grounds for the SEC to take action against attorneys

---

51 For example, *Checkosky* v. *Securities and Exchange Commission*, 139 F.3d 221, 225–26 (DC. Cir. 1998); Seamons, Quinton F., "Inside the Labyrinth of the Elusive Standard Under the SEC's Rule 2(e)", 23 *Securities Regulation Law Journal* 57 (Spring 1995) ("professionals are trapped in the Rule 2(e) labyrinth with no clear standard to guide them and no means of escape").

52 Dante, Alighieri, *The Divine Comedy*, 138 (Oxford University Press, 1977): "Here the Evil Counselors move about endlessly, hidden from view inside great flames. Their sin was to abuse the gifts of the Almighty, to steal His virtues for low purposes. And as they stole from God in their lives and worked by hidden ways, so are they stolen from sight and hidden in the great flames which are their own guilty consciences. And as, in most instances at least, they sinned by glibness of tongue, so are the flames made into a fiery travesty of tongues."

under SEC Rule of Practice 102(e) pursuant to which attorneys may be censored, suspended or barred from practicing before the SEC.[53]

Improper Influence on Conduct of Audits

The SOA requires the SEC to adopt rules that would make it unlawful for any officer or director of an issuer to fraudulently influence, coerce, manipulate or mislead any independent public or certified accountant engaged in the performance of an audit of the financial statements of the issuer for the purpose of rendering the financial statements materially misleading.[54] This provision is intended to strengthen the auditor's position in receiving truthful information and to prevent the issuer's officers and directors from providing misleading information to the auditor to cover up adverse financial problems of the issuer. The SEC has the exclusive authority to enforce this provision and any rule or regulation against the officer or director, that is, there is no private right of action for civil damages.

Financial Statements and Material Correcting Adjustments

The SOA amended Section 13 of the Securities Exchange Act of 1934 to provide that each financial report that contains financial statements must reflect "all material correcting adjustments" that have been identified by a registered public accounting firm in accordance with GAAPs and SEC rules.[55] There is no definition of "correcting adjustments", but the term would appear to include all reclassified journal entries made during the performance of the audit. This provision was effective immediately upon the enactment of the SOA on 30 July 2002.

---

53 Securities and Exchange Commission Rule of Practice 102(e), 17 C.F.R. 201.102(e). The Sarbanes-Oxley Act codified part of Rule 102(e) in Section 602 in order to clarify that the Securities and Exchange Commission has authority to discipline professionals who appear and practice before it. Rule 102(e) and its predecessor Rule 2(e) have been seldom used by the Securities and Exchange Commission to discipline attorneys since *In re Carter* [81 Binder] Fed.Sec.L.Rep. (CCH) Paragraph 82,847 (SEC 1981) (attorneys learning of substantial and continuing disclosure violations to take prompt steps to effect compliance) (separate opinion of Commissioner Evans); *In re Kern*, [89 Binder] Fed.Sec.L.Rep. (CCH) Paragraph 84,342 (SEC 1988) (Section 15(c)(4) administrative proceeding).

54 Sarbanes-Oxley Act, Section 303.

55 Sarbanes-Oxley Act, Section 401.

Material Off-Balance Sheet Transactions Section 401

The SOA requires the SEC to adopt rules to provide that each annual and quarterly report shall disclose:

> ". . . all material off-balance sheet transactions, arrangements, obligations (including contingent obligations) and other relationships of the issuer with unconsolidated entities or other persons that may have a material current or future effect on financial condition, changes in financial condition, results of operations, liquidity, capital expenditures, capital resources or significant components of revenues or expenses".[56]

The provision requires the SEC to codify the interpretive guidance that the SEC issued in January 2002 in which the SEC advised issuers to augment their disclosure of off-balance sheet transactions in the section of management discussion and analysis in their periodic reports.[57] The provision responds primarily to the Raptor, Chewco and other special purpose entities of Enron Corporation.

Reconciliation of *Pro Forma* Presentation

The SOA requires the SEC to promulgate rules to require that *pro forma* information included in any periodic or other report filed with the SEC or in any public disclosure or press release or other release must be presented in a manner that does not contain an untrue statement on material fact or omission.[58] The rules must also require reconciliation of any *pro forma* information with the financial condition and results of operations of the issuer as required under GAAPs. This requirement will result in earnings being presented consistent with GAAPs any time that *pro forma* earnings are presented. This presentation is intended to allow investors to compare the differences between the *pro forma* and GAAPs presentations.

---

56 Sarbanes-Oxley Act, Section 401.

57 "Commission Statement About Management's Discussion and Analysis of Financial Condition and Results of Operations", Exchange Act Release Number 45321 [01–02 Binder] Fed.Sec.L.Rep. (CCH) Paragraph 86,617 (22 January 2002).

58 Sarbanes-Oxley Act, Section 401.

Disclosure of Insider Transactions

The SOA amended Section 16(a) of the Securities Exchange Act of 1934 to require that directors, executive officers and more than ten per cent beneficial shareholders disclose any change in their ownership of the issuer's equity securities "before the end of the second business day following the day upon which the subject transaction has been executed, or at such other times as the Commission shall establish, by rule, in any case in which the Commission determines that such two-day period is not feasible".[59] Currently, the insider reports on Form 4. Anything that reflects changes in insider beneficial ownership is filed ten days after the end of the month in which the insiders' transactions occur, which can result in a delay in the filing up to forty days after the transaction. The new filing requirement is intended to make insider trading readily transparent to the trading markets within two business days.[60] These rule changes include revisions to the Form 4 filing requirements and amendments to Rule 16a-3(f) to require transactions between directors and officers and the issuer that were being reported annually on annual Form 5 to now be reported on Form 4 within two business days. The SEC also encouraged issuers to file their Section 16(a) reports electronically, and indicated that rulemaking and system programming would be undertaken expeditiously to assure electronic filing within the required one-year period.

The two business day deadline is fairly short because at least one day will be required for courier delivery. Commencing not later than one year after the enactment of the SOA, on approximately 30 July 2003, the Section 16(a) forms must be filed electronically with the SEC, and the SEC is required to publish such statements on an Internet site no later than the end of the business day on which the filing is received. The issuer is required to publish the filing on its website if it has a corporate website.[61] Other filing provisions and

59 Sarbanes-Oxley Act, Section 403.

60 Exchange Act Release Number 46313 (6 August 2002), http://www.sec.gov/rules/other/34–46313.htm; "Form 8-K Disclosure of Certain Management Transactions", Exchange Act Release Number 45742 [01–02 Binder] Fed.Sec.L.Rep. (CCH) Paragraph 86,625 (12 April 2002) (rule proposal to require disclosure pursuant to Form 8-K of director and officer transactions in issuer's equity securities and loans to directors and officers).

61 On 27 August 2002, the Securities and Exchange Commission adopted revisions consistent with the two business day requirement of the Sarbanes-Oxley Act: http://www.sec.gov/rules/final/33-8124.htm; Williams, Krissah, "SEC Tightens Deadlines on Corporate Disclosure", *The Washington Post* (28 August 2002).

changes affecting insider trading are effective from approximately 30 July 2003, although the time period for filing an initial Form 3 may remain the same — ten days after the person becomes subject to the reporting requirements under Section 16(a).

Internal Control Report and Form 10-K

The SOA requires the SEC to promulgate rules requiring each filed annual report to include an "internal control report".[62] This report will describe the responsibility of management for establishing and maintaining an internal control structure and financial reporting procedures. The report must contain an assessment, as of the end of the most recent fiscal year, of the effectiveness of the internal control structure and financial reporting procedures of the issuer for recording its financial results.

Each registered public accounting firm that prepares the audit report for an issuer must attest to, and report on, the internal control assessment made by management. This attestation shall not be a separate engagement, but should be deemed part of the audit engagement. The SEC has not yet offered any guidance in this area, particularly with respect to any disagreements between management and the registered public accounting firm regarding the effectiveness of the internal controls.[63]

Identification of Audit Committee Financial Expert

The SOA requires the SEC to promulgate rules that will require each issuer to disclose whether or not, and if not, the reason why not, the audit committee of the issuer does not have at least one member who is a "financial expert".[64] The definition of a "financial expert" is to be developed by the SEC considering whether a person has:

(1) An understanding of GAAPs and financial statements through education and experience as an accountant or CFO, CAO or controller;
(2) Experience in preparing or auditing financial statements of generally comparable issuers;
(3) Experience with internal accounting controls and the accounting principles for the setting of estimates, accruals and reserves; and

---

62 Sarbanes-Oxley Act, Section 404.

63 http://www.sec.gov/rules/final/33–8124.htm.

64 Sarbanes-Oxley Act, Section 407.

(4) An understanding of audit committee functions.[65]

Enhanced Review of Periodic Reports

The SOA requires the SEC to review the periodic disclosures made by issuers on a "regular and systematic basis".[66] The SOA provides that the filed reports of issuers be reviewed at least once every three years, and that such review includes the issuers' financial statements. The SEC must consider for review purposes, *inter alia,* whether issuers:

(1) Have made material restatements of financial results;
(2) Have experienced significant volatility in their stock prices;
(3) Have large market capitalizations;
(4) Are emerging companies with disparities in price to earnings ratios;
(5) Have operations that significantly affect any material sector of the economy; and
(6) Any other factors that the SEC considers relevant.[67]

This provision became effective upon the enactment of the SOA on 30 July 2002.

Real Time Issuer Disclosures

The SOA amends Section 13 of the Securities Exchange Act of 1934 to require each issuer to disclose:

> "...on a rapid and current basis, such additional information concerning material changes in the financial condition or operations of the issuer, in plain English, which may include trend and qualitative information and graphic presentations, as the Commission determines, by rule, is necessary or useful for the protection of investors and in the public interest".[68]

---

65 Hilzenrath, David S., "Some Audit Panels Admit Ignorance of Accounting", *The Washington Post* (10 May 2002) (quoting audit committee from annual report of Goldman Sachs Group: "The members of the Audit Committee are not professionally engaged in the practice of auditing or accounting and are not experts in the fields of accounting or auditing.").

66 Sarbanes-Oxley Act, Section 408.

67 The House version of the legislation would have required the Securities and Exchange Commission to give each issuer a risk rating (which would be confidential), based on these factors, that would also affect the frequency of a review. However, this rating system was not included in the Sarbanes-Oxley Act.

68 Sarbanes-Oxley Act, Section 409.

The significance of this disclosure requirement will depend on the SEC rulemaking. The SEC has already proposed rules which address this provision to some extent. On 17 June 2002, the SEC proposed modifications to Form 8-K which would require disclosure of thirteen additional events on Form 8-K and would require all Form 8-Ks to be filed within two business days of the triggering event (as opposed to the current requirement of five business days or fifteen calendar days, depending on the nature of the event). The SEC may expand these proposals under Form 8-K in response to the real time disclosure requirements of the SOA.

The SOA did not set any deadline for the SEC to complete its rulemaking in this area, but the SEC adopted a thirty-five-day filing deadline for Form 10-Q and a sixty-day filing deadline for Form 10-K with a phase-in period over three years.[69]

Analyst Conflicts of Interest

Title V of the SOA requires the SEC and self-regulatory bodies to adopt rules reasonably designed to address conflicts of interest between research analysts, investment banking divisions and issuers, as well as rules governing disclosures to be made by research analysts. On 10 May 2002, the SEC approved rules of the New York Stock Exchange (NYSE) and NASD that addressed these issues. These rules became effective on 9 July 2002, although some rules did not become effective until 9 September or 6 November 2002. While the Senate Report notes that the SOA is not intended to negate or visciate regulations already enacted, the SOA does require the SEC and the self-regulatory bodies to go further than the NYSE and NASD

69 Final rules at http://www.sec.gov/rules/final/33-8124.htm; Williams, Krissah, "SEC Tightens Deadlines on Corporate Disclosure", *The Washington Post* (28 August 2002). A large number of issuers had commented negatively on the proposed shorter filing deadlines. *See also* "Additional Form 8-K Disclosure Requirements and Acceleration of Filing Date", Exchange Act Release Number 46084, [Current Binder] Fed.Sec.L.Rep. (CCH) Paragraph 86,703 (17 June 2002). The Securities and Exchange Commission stated that it was proposing "these amendments in order to provide investors with better and faster disclosure of important corporate events". *See also* "Acceleration of Periodic Report Filing Dates and Disclosure Concerning Website Access to Reports", Exchange Act Release Number 45741 [01–02 Binder] Fed.Sec.L.Rep. (CCH) Paragraph 86,626 (12 April 2002) (rule proposal to file Form 10-Q within thirty days (instead of forty-five days) and Form 10-K within forty-five days (instead of ninety days).

regulations that have already been promulgated.[70] The SOA requires that the SEC adopt the regulations under Title V within one year of the enactment of the SOA, that is, by approximately 30 July 2003.

Investment Banking to Be Separated from Research

The SOA requires the SEC to adopt rules to provide that only non-investment banking personnel can supervise and determine the compensation of research analysts.[71] This regulation is intended to prevent investment bankers from controlling or influencing the work of research analysts. The SOA also requires rules to be adopted to prevent investment banking personnel from clearing or approving the research reports to be issued. The SOA also requires the SEC to adopt rules to establish structural safeguards ("Chinese walls") to separate the research analyst from any other pressures of review or oversight by investment banking personnel.[72]

---

70 "Order Approving Rule Changes By The [NASD] and [NYSE]", Exchange Act Release Number 45908 [01–02 Binder] Fed.Sec.L.Rep. (CCH) Paragraph 86,639 (10 May 2002); Labaton, Stephen, "SEC Adopts New Rules for Analysts", *The New York Times* (9 May 2002); O'Harrow Jr., Robert, "The Era of the Superstar Analyst May Be Over", *The Washington Post* (22 May 2002).

71 Sarbanes-Oxley Act, Section 501.

72 Those issues arise from the perception that the investment banking (underwriting) division of full service broker-dealer firms control and direct the research personnel and arrange for research that bolsters and supports, if not manipulates, the market prices of securities underwritten by the investment bankers. This was a basic concern of the SEC in issuing an "investor alert" in July 2001 that highlighted the conflicts between the investment banking and research departments: www.sec.bov/investor/pubs/analysts.htm; Lauricella, Tom, "Analyst Reports Pressure of Employer's Trading", *The Wall Street Journal* (4 September 2001). In addition, there is the perception that investment bankers use positive research to source new companies for underwriting or merger and acquisition purposes: O'Harrow Jr., Robert, "Analysts Accused of Touting 'Junk' to Boost Profits", *The Washington Post* (19 April 2002). There is also a perception that a research analyst is never able to issue a negative recommendation because that might jeopardize the investment banking relationship with the issuer. In response to these concerns, on 24 July 2002, the Securities and Exchange Commission proposed Regulation AC for comment that would require securities analysts to certify that the recommendations in their research reports represent their actual views. The certification would also indicate whether the research report or recommendation related to the analyst's compensation in any manner: "Regulation Analyst Certification", Exchange Act Release Number 46301 [Current Binder] Fed.Sec.L.Rep. (CCH) Paragraph 86,716 (2 August 2002); "SEC Proposal Would Require Analysts to Certify Belief in Recommendations", 34 BNA *Securities*

Retaliation by Investment Banking

The SOA requires the SEC to adopt rules to prohibit the investment banking department from retaliating against or threatening to retaliate against any security analyst who has issued an adverse, negative or otherwise unfavorable research report.[73] Investment bankers usually perceive an unfavorable research report as harming the investment banking relationship with the issuer that is the subject of the unfavorable report. The Senate Report commented that the rules should also cover the situation where the retaliation is conducted under a false pretense in order to avoid appearing as retaliation for a negative research report. The Senate Report suggested that the rules address this problem by shifting the burden of proof or imposing punitive damages for such conduct.

Quiet Periods for Research Reports

The SOA requires the SEC to adopt rules to define periods during which underwriters that have participated or are about to participate as underwriters or dealers in a public offering shall not publish or distribute research reports relating to the securities to be publicly offered.[74] The Senate Report suggested that the rules should also consider prohibiting so-called "booster shots" or research reports issued just before the expiration of the six-month lock-up period following a public offering. These booster shots are perceived as bolstering or

---

Regulation and Law Report 1226 (29 July 2002); White, Ben, "Ebbers Got Early IPO Shares", *The Washington Post* (28 August 2002); McGeehan, Patrick, "Merrill Lynch to Pay $100 Million to Settle Analyst Charges", *The New York Times* (22 May 2002); Michaely, Roni and Womack, Kent L., "Conflict of Interest and the Credibility of Underwriter Analyst Recommendations", 12 *The Review of Financial Studies* 653 (1999); Burns, Judith, "SEC Says Analysts Deceived Investors About Its Results", *The Wall Street Journal* (12 October 2001); Miller, Sam S. and Boyd, Bradford Q., "Analysts under Fire", 15 *Insights* 8 (December 2001).

73 Sarbanes-Oxley Act, Section 501. The Act defines a research report to include: "a written or electronic communication that includes an analysis of equity securities of individual companies or industries, and that provides information reasonably sufficient upon which to base an investment decision".

74 Sarbanes-Oxley Act, Section 501.

manipulating the stock price at the time that insiders are first permitted to sell their shares following the public offering.[75]

Conflict of Interest Disclosures by Analysts

The SOA requires the SEC to adopt rules reasonably designed to require each analyst to disclose in public appearances, and each broker-dealer to disclose in each equity research report, existing conflicts of interest that are known or should have been known to exist by the analyst or the broker-dealer.[76] The Rules should require disclosure of:

(1) The extent to which analysts have debt or equity investments in the issuer that is the subject of any public appearance or research report;
(2) Whether any compensation has been received by the broker-dealer, or any affiliate, from the issuer that is the subject of the public appearance or report;
(3) Whether the issuer has been a client of the broker-dealer;
(4) The types of services that the broker-dealer has provided to the issuer;
(5) Whether the analyst receives compensation with respect to a research report based on the investment banking revenues of the broker-dealer; and
(6) Any other disclosures of conflicts of interest material to investors, research analysts or broker-dealers.

The recently adopted regulations already require some of the disclosures that the SOA identified. The SEC will likely adjust these regulations through rulemaking to conform with the SOA requirements.[77]

---

75 The new rules of the NASD and the New York Stock Exchange impose quiet periods of fifty days after an initial public offering and ten days after a secondary offering. *See also* Securities Act of 1933, Rules 139 and 174 and Securities Exchange Act of 1934, Rule 15c2–8, which require quiet periods in the context of a registered public offering, and Securities Act Release Number 5130 (16 August 1971), which addresses the limitations on publication of analyst reports during the registration and post-effective periods.

76 Sarbanes-Oxley Act, Section 501.

77 Miller, Sam S., "Chaperoning Analysts: Procedures to Manage, Minimize and Disclose Conflicts", 34 BNA *Securities Regulation and Law Report* 879 (3 June 2002); Jenkins Jr., Holman W., "Don't Shoot the Analysts, Spin 'em Off", *The Wall Street Journal* (6 March 2001); White, Ben., "Grubman Quits As Salomon Analyst", *The Washington Post* (16 August 2002).

Other Analyst-Related Rulemaking

The SOA requires that the SEC and self-regulatory bodies consider other issues and regulations appropriate for analysts.[78] The Senate Report identified the following considerations for such rulemaking:

(1) Whether analysts should participate in road shows or in the selling process;
(2) Whether broker-dealers should be liable for recommendations that do not have a reasonable basis;
(3) Whether additional disclosures should be made of the investment positions of analysts and their families, as well as the positions of the firm's management and the firm itself;
(4) Whether disclosure should be made of gifts received from a subject company by the analyst or the firm's investment banking division;
(5) Whether additional explanation of a firm's rating system is necessary;
(6) Whether ratings should be more regularly updated or confirmed, particularly in times of volatility in the stock market;
(7) Whether the issuance of final reports should be required when research coverage is discontinued; and
(8) Whether rules are necessary to prohibit issuer intimidation of analysts, such as telephone calls to the firm's senior management, litigation against the analyst and the firm, not returning telephone calls or not answering questions on analysts' calls.

Federal Crimes and Penalties for Corporate Fraud[79]

Destruction of Records in Federal Investigations

The SOA established a new federal crime for the destruction of records involved in any federal government investigation or

---

78 Sarbanes-Oxley Act, Section 501.

79 On 9 July 2002, President Bush appointed Larry D. Thompson, the deputy attorney general, to head a newly organized corporate fraud task force — "a financial crimes swat team" — to fight corporate crime: Carney, Dan, "Corporate Crime's New Top Cop", *Business Week* 32 (22 July 2002).

bankruptcy.[80] The SOA provides that "whoever knowingly alters, destroys, mutilates, conceals, covers up, falsifies or makes a false entry in any record, document or tangible object with an intent to impede, obstruct or influence the investigation or proper administration of any matter within the jurisdiction of any department or agency of the United States or any case filed under Title 11 [the bankruptcy code]" will be fined, imprisoned for not more than twenty years, or both.[81]

Senator Patrick Leahy (D-Vt.), the Chairman of the Senate Judiciary Committee, commented on this provision in the Congressional Record on 25 July 2002:

> "This statute is specifically meant not to include any technical requirement, which some courts have read into other obstruction of justice statutes, to tie the obstructive conduct to a pending or imminent proceeding or matter by intent or otherwise. It is also sufficient that the act is done "in contemplation" of or in relation to a matter or investigation. It is also meant to do away with distinctions, which some courts have read into obstruction statutes, between court proceedings, investigations, regulatory or administrative proceedings (whether formal or not) and less formal government inquiries, regardless of their title. Destroying or falsifying documents to obstruct any of these types of matters or investigations, which in fact are proved to be within the jurisdiction of any federal agency, are covered by this statute."

Destruction of Corporate Audit Records

The SOA establishes a new federal crime for the willful failure to retain audit and review work papers.[82] The SOA provides that any accountant who audits an issuer of securities must maintain all audit or review work papers for a period of five years from the end of the physical period in which the audit review was concluded. The SOA provides that any person who "knowingly and willfully" does not

---

80 This provision amends 18 U.S.C. Section 1519 which is entitled "Destruction, Alteration or Falsification of Records in Federal Investigations and Bankruptcy". It was proposed by Senator Leahy.

81 Sarbanes-Oxley Act, Section 802.

82 Sarbanes-Oxley Act, Section 802. This provision amends 18 U.S.C. Section 1520, which is entitled "Destruction of Corporate Audit Records". It was proposed by Senator Leahy.

maintain workpapers for five years, or violates any SEC rule relating to maintaining audit workpapers, will be fined, imprisoned for not more than ten years, or both.

Senator Patrick Leahy stated in the Congressional Record on 25 July 2002:

> "The regulations are intended to cover the retention of all such substantive material, whether or not the conclusions, opinions, analyses or data in such records support the final conclusions reached by the auditor or expressed in the final audit or review so that state and federal law enforcement officials and regulators and victims can conduct more effective inquiries into the decisions and determinations made by accountants in auditing public corporations. Non-substantive materials, however, such as administrative records which are not relevant to the conclusions or opinions expressed (or not expressed), need not be included in such retention regulations."

Securities Fraud Involving a Public Company

The SOA establishes a new federal crime for securities fraud involving a public company that whoever knowingly executes, or attempts to execute, a scheme or artifice to defraud any person in connection with any security of an issuer filing periodic reports by means of false or fraudulent pretenses or representations or promises any money or property in connection with the purchase or sale of any security of an issuer will be fined under this title, or imprisoned for not more than twenty-five years, or both.[83]

Senator Leahy explained on 25 July 2002, in the Congressional Record, that this provision is intended broadly to "cover any scheme or artifice to defraud any person in connection with a publicly traded company". This broad provision is designed to be a flexible tool for prosecutors to address "a wide array" of fraud and misconduct that can occur in a publicly traded issuer.

83 Sarbanes-Oxley Act, Section 807. This provision amends 18 U.S.C. Section 1348 which is entitled "Securities Fraud". It was proposed by Senator Leahy.

Tampering with a Record or Impeding an Investigation

The SOA establishes a new federal crime for tampering with documents to be used in an official proceeding.[84] The SOA provides that any person who corruptly alters, destroys, mutilates or conceals a record document or other object, or attempts to do so, with the intent to impair the object's integrity or availability for use in an official proceeding or otherwise obstructs, influences or impedes any official proceeding, or attempts to do so, shall be fined or imprisoned for up to twenty years, or both.

Longer Statute of Limitations for Securities Fraud

The SOA provides that private rights of action that involve claims of fraud, deceit or manipulation in contravention of a regulatory requirement concerning the securities laws may be brought no later than the earlier of two years after discovery of the facts constituting the violation or within five years after the violation.[85] The new statute of limitations applies to all proceedings commenced on or after the effective date of the SOA — 30 July 2002. This statute of limitations, which was proposed by Senator Leahy, does not create any new private right of action.

Whistleblower Protection for Employees of Public Issuers

The SOA creates a new civil action in Section 806 for employees of public issuers who believe they have been discharged due to their actions as a whistleblower.[86] The SOA provides that an issuer, as well as any officer, employee, contractor, subcontractor or agent, may not discharge, demote, suspend, threaten, harass or in any manner discriminate against an employee because the employee has provided information, caused information to be provided or otherwise assisted in an investigation regarding any conduct which the employee reasonably believes constitutes a violation of the federal mail fraud,

---

84 Sarbanes-Oxley Act, Section 1102. This provision amends 18 U.S.C. Section 1512 which is entitled "Tampering With a Record or Otherwise Impeding an Official Proceeding". It was proposed by Senator Leahy.

85 Sarbanes-Oxley Act, Section 804.

86 This provision amends 18 U.S.C, Section 1514A which is entitled "Civil Action to Protect Against Retaliation in Fraud Cases". It was proposed by Senator Leahy.

wire fraud or securities fraud statutes, any SEC rule or any provision of federal law relating to fraud against shareholders. The information or assistance must be provided to, and the investigation must be conducted by, a federal regulatory or law enforcement agent, any member of Congress or any Congressional Committee, or a person with supervisory authority over the employee.

The applicable statute of limitations provides that any action under Section 806 must be commenced with the Secretary of Labor no later than ninety days after the date upon which the violation occurs. The person must first file a complaint with the Secretary of Labor and, if no action is taken within 180 days, the person can bring the action in the appropriate federal district court.

On 31 July 2002, Senator Leahy and Senator Charles Grassley (R-Iowa) sent a letter to the White House that expressed the view that Section 806 applies broadly to any information or assistance provided to a "member of Congress" or "any Committee of Congress". The letter emphasized that it is unnecessary for a formal investigation to have been authorized under the rules of the Senate or House in order for the person to be protected in providing the information. The White House had suggested that a formal investigation had to be in place in order for the whistleblower protection to apply.[87]

The SOA creates, in Section 1107, a new federal criminal action that whoever knowingly, with the intent to retaliate, takes any action harmful to any person, including interference with the lawful employment of any person, for providing to a law enforcement officer any truthful information relating to the commission or possible commission of a federal offense, will be fined or imprisoned for up to ten years, or both.[88]

These provisions were effective immediately upon the enactment of the SOA on 30 July 2002.

---

87 "Lawmakers Decry Bush's Interpretation of Whistleblower Protections in New Law", 34 BNA *Securities Regulation and Law Report* 1326 (12 August 2002); "Grassley Protests Portion of Fraud Law", *The Washington Post* (31 August 2002). Senator Grassley assisted Senator Leahy in drafting and sponsoring the whistleblower protections.

88 This provision amends 18 U.S.C. Section 1513 which is entitled "Retaliation Against Informants".

Increased Criminal Penalties

Section 903 of the SOA increases the penalty for each incident of mail fraud and wire fraud from a maximum of five years' imprisonment to a maximum of twenty years' imprisonment.[89] The SOA provides that any person who attempts or conspires to commit an offense such as wire fraud, mail fraud and securities fraud shall be subject to the same penalties as those prescribed for the primary offense.

Section 904 of the SOA increases the penalty for violations of ERISA from one year to ten years' imprisonment and a fine from US $100,000 to US $500,000.

Section 1106 of the SOA amends the Securities Exchange Act of 1934 to increase the penalty for a "willful" violation of that Act by an individual from a fine of up to US $1-million to a fine of up to US $5-million and from imprisonment for up to ten years to imprisonment for up to twenty years. The penalty for a "willful" violation by a corporation is increased to US $25-million.

Broader Securities and Exchange Commission Enforcement Powers

Temporary Freeze Authority

The SOA amends the Securities Exchange Act of 1934 to provide the SEC with new temporary freeze authority that can be applied during the course of an investigation whenever it appears likely to the SEC that the issuer will make extraordinary payments to its directors, officers, agents or employees.[90] The SEC may petition a federal court for a temporary order to escrow the payments in an interest bearing account for a period of forty-five days, which period can be extended up to ninety days if necessary and appropriate. The temporary order requires notice and an opportunity for a hearing unless the court determines that notice and a hearing would be impracticable or contrary to public interests. If the issuer or other person is charged with a securities law violation, the freeze order will remain in effect until the conclusion of the legal proceedings. This provision became

89 This provision amends 18 U.S.C. Sections 1341 and 1343, which are the mail and wire fraud statutes. It was proposed by Senator Biden.

90 Sarbanes-Oxley Act, Section 1103.

effective upon the enactment of the SOA on 30 July 2002. It was proposed by Senator Trent Lott (R-Miss.).

Temporary or Permanent Director and Officer Bars

The SEC did not have authority to bar an individual from serving as an officer or director of a public company in its administrative proceedings, although it had such authority to obtain this remedy in an order of the federal court.[91] The SOA grants to the SEC the authority in administrative cease and desist proceedings to bar a person from being an officer or director of any issuer that files periodic reports with the SEC. The advantage to the SEC under this new authority is that it can obtain the bar faster in its own proceedings than in a federal court. The SEC carries the burden of establishing that the conduct of the person "demonstrates unfitness" to serve as an officer or director of a public issuer.

Standard for Court Ordered Officer and Director Bars

Prior to the SOA, the SEC had to establish that a person demonstrated "substantial unfitness" to serve as an officer or director of a corporation.[92] The SEC commented that this was a high standard that impeded its remedial efforts. As a result, the SOA changed the "substantial unfitness" standard to an "unfitness" standard.[93]

Authority to Discipline Professionals

Over the years, there had been an issue raised as to whether the SEC had authority, under its Rule of Practice 102(e), to discipline professionals, such as accountants and lawyers, who practiced before the

91 Section 1105 of the Sarbanes-Oxley Act was proposed by Senator Lott. The authority to bar officers and directors from public companies in a court order, typically in an injunctive enforcement action, was first provided to the Securities and Exchange Commission under the Securities Enforcement Remedies Act of 1990.

92 This was the statutory standard under Section 21(d)(2) of the Securities Exchange Act of 1934 and Section 8A of the Securities Act of 1933 that had been incorporated into the Securities Enforcement Remedies Act of 1990.

93 Sarbanes-Oxley Act, Section 1105.

SEC.[94] The SOA clarifies that issue by codifying the SEC's authority to censor or temporarily or permanently bar any person from appearing before the SEC if such person is found, after a notice and opportunity for a hearing, not to possess the requisite qualifications to represent others, or lacks character or integrity or has engaged in unethical or improper professional conduct, or has willfully violated or willfully aided and abetted the violation of any provision of the federal securities laws and the regulations thereunder.[95] This provision of the SOA became effective upon the date of its enactment on 30 July 2002.

Authority to Bar Individuals Sanctioned by Other Regulators

The SOA authorizes the SEC to bar individuals from joining the securities industry if they have already been barred by a states securities, banking or insurance regulator.[96] This authority is intended to prevent persons who have disciplinary problems in the financial services area from exploiting gaps in the regulatory system by rotating among the various sectors in the financial industry. Under this authority, the SEC can prevent "fraud artist" persons from migrating to and entering the securities industry if they have already been barred or suspended by a state securities, banking or insurance regulator because of fraudulent, manipulative or deceptive conduct. This provision became effective upon the enactment of the SOA on 30 July 2002.

---

94 This was one of the first rules adopted by the Securities and Exchange Commission. It was adopted as Rule II and became effective on 13 September 1935. Pickholz, Marvin G. and Ziffer, Adam S., "A Brief History of SEC Rule 2(e)", *Section of Business Law of the American Bar Association* (22 November 2995); *Touche Ross & Co.* v. *Securities and Exchange Commission*, 609 F.2d 570, 582 (2d Cir. 1979) (rule was reasonable attempt by the Securities and Exchange Commission to protect the integrity of its own processes "to ensure that those professionals, upon whom the commission relies heavily in the performance of its statutory duties, perform their tasks with a reasonable degree of competence"); *Davy* v. *Securities and Exchange Commission*, 792 F.2d 1418, 1421 (9th Cir. 1986).

95 Sarbanes-Oxley Act, Section 602.

96 Sarbanes-Oxley Act, Section 604.

Studies and Reports

The SOA requires that nine separate studies be conducted. Six of these studies must be prepared by the SEC, and three studies must be prepared by the Comptroller General and its General Accounting Office.

Adoption of Principles-Based Accounting

The SEC must study the adoption in the United States of a principles-based accounting regimen.[97] There was considerable discussion before the Senate Committee on Banking, Housing and Urban Affairs during the hearings regarding the differences between an accounting system that contains detailed rules for treatment of transactions and a system that contains general principles to be applied to transactions. The discussion also focused on the issue that, in the detailed rule system, there is a delay of the standard setting bodies in providing necessary updated rules for the treatment of new developments and new types of transactions. The study should include an examination of the two systems of accounting, the length of time required for changes in rules in the rule-based system and how feasible it is to move to a principles-based system, as well as an economic analysis of moving to such a system.[98] The SEC must submit its report no later than one year following the enactment of the SOA, on approximately 30 July 2003, to the Senate Committee on Banking, Housing and Urban Affairs and the House Committee on Financial Services.

Mandatory Rotation of Registered Public Accounting Firms

The Comptroller General and its General Accounting Office must conduct a study and review the potential effects of requiring mandatory rotation of accounting firms.[99] The study must analyze the potential

97 Sarbanes-Oxley Act, Section 108.

98 Blustein, Paul, "Accounting's Rival Rules: With U.S. System on Defensive, Europe's Gets Another Look", *The Washington Post* (10 March 2002) ("GAAPs . . . are too laden with long, specific prescriptions that end up giving corporate financial wizards . . . the opportunity to circumvent them. By contrast, international standards are unquestionably more 'principles-based', relying more on general guidelines than on precise rules").

99 Sarbanes-Oxley Act, Section 207.

effects of a requirement that registered public accounting firms must be rotated among issuer clients within a set period of years. The Comptroller General must submit a report no later than one year after the enactment of the SOA, by approximately 30 July 2003, to the Senate Committee on Banking, Housing and Urban Affairs and the House Committee on Financial Services.

More Effective Restitution for Injured Investors

The SEC must review and analyze its enforcement actions over the last five years in order to identify instances where restitution for injured investors can be provided on a more effective and fair basis.[100] The study should also consider what improvements can be taken in the collection rates for civil penalties and disgorgements.

Utilization and Economics of Special Purpose Entities

The SEC must study filings by issuers to determine the extent to which off-balance sheet transactions are being utilized and whether GAAPs rules result in financial statements that reflect the economics of such transactions.[101] The SEC's report should include the amount or estimate of the off-balance sheet transactions, and whether GAAPs or SEC rules result in financial statements that adequately report such transactions. The report must also include recommendations for improving the transparency and quality of reporting off-balance sheet transactions in the financial statements and disclosures filed with the SEC. The SEC must complete its study no later than one year after the enactment of the SOA, on approximately 30 July 2003, and no later than six months thereafter, on approximately 30 January 2004, submit a report to the President,[102] the Senate Committee on Banking, Housing and Urban Affairs and the House Committee on Financial Services.

---

100 Sarbanes-Oxley Act, Section 308.

101 Sarbanes-Oxley Act, Section 401.

102 This study was proposed by Senator Schumer. This study on special purpose entities and the study on credit rating agencies in Section 702 are the only studies to be delivered to the President.

Consolidation of Public Accounting Firms

The Comptroller General and its General Accounting Office must conduct a study to identify the factors that have led to the consolidation of the public accounting firms since 1989.[103] The study must evaluate the impact of this consolidation on capital formation and the impact of providing audit services to large national and multi-national businesses. The study must consider any problems that have resulted from limited competition, including higher costs, lower qualify of services, impairment of independence and the lack of choice in light of the consolidation. The Comptroller General must submit a report on this topic no later than one year following the enactment of the SOA, on approximately 30 July 2003, to the Senate Committee on Banking, Housing and Urban Affairs and the House Committee on Financial Services.

Role and Function of Credit Rating Agencies

The SEC had to conduct a study of the role and function of credit rating agencies in the operation of the securities market and submit its report no later than six months following the enactment of the SOA, on approximately 30 January 2003, to the President, the Senate Committee on Banking, Housing and Urban Affairs and the House Committee on Financial Services.[104]

Aiding and Abetting Conduct by Securities Professionals

The SEC must study[105] securities law violations by securities professionals during a four-year period and consider the number of professionals who have been found to have aided and abetted a violation of the federal securities laws, but who were not named or penalized as a

103 Sarbanes-Oxley Act, Section 701.

104 Sarbanes-Oxley Act, Section 702.

105 Sarbanes-Oxley Act, Section 703. This study was proposed by Senator Richard Shelby (R-Ala.): Johnson, Carre, "New Fight Brewing Over Limits on Investor Suits", *The Washington Post* (10 May 2002) ("Surveying the post-Enron wreckage, [Senator Shelby] says Congress needs to take some blame, noting that seven years ago lawmakers passed a measure that made it more difficult for investors to sue corporations and accounting firms involved in fraud" referring to the Private Securities Litigation Reform Act of 1995).

primary violator in any proceeding.[106] The study should describe the kind of sanctions that have been imposed on the violators and be submitted to the Senate Committee on Banking, Housing and Urban Affairs and the House Committee on Financial Services.

Reporting and Disclosure Violations in Enforcement Actions — Section 704

The SEC must analyze its enforcement actions over a five-year period and identify areas of reporting that have been most susceptible to fraud, inappropriate manipulation or inappropriate earnings management, such as revenue recognition and the accounting treatment of off-balance sheet special purpose entities.[107] The SEC was to submit a report no later than 180 days after the enactment of the SOA to the Senate Committee on Banking, Housing and Urban Affairs and the House Committee on Financial Services.

Role of Investment Banks

The Comptroller General and its General Accounting Office must conduct a study on whether investment banks and financial advisers assisted issuers in manipulating their earnings and obfuscating their true financial condition.[108] The study should address the role of investment banks and financial advisers in the collapse of Enron Corporation and Global Crossing LLC, particularly whether they created market transactions that were designed solely to enable these and other companies to manipulate revenue streams, obtain loans or move liabilities off balance sheets or utilize other mechanisms to obscure the issuers' financial conditions. With respect to Enron Corporation, the study should include the use of derivatives transactions, special purpose entities and other arrangements that altered and obscured the financial condition of Enron Corporation in its financial statements. The Comptroller General was to submit its report to Congress no later than 180 days after the enactment of the SOA with recommendations for regulatory or legislative action.

---

106 The Sarbanes-Oxley Act specifies that the four-year period is to be from 1 January 1998 to 31 December 2001.

107 Sarbanes-Oxley Act, Section 704.

108 Sarbanes-Oxley Act, Section 705.

The War against Corruption Goes International

Sesto E. Vecchi and Kevin C. Chua
Russin & Vecchi
Ho Chi Minh City, Vietnam

Introduction

American companies operating through foreign subsidiaries and foreign agents are not insulated from liability under America's anti-bribery laws. The United States' presence is felt beyond its borders through the overwhelming number of American multinational corporations which operate in virtually every country. Corporations based in the United States, and their overseas subsidiaries and agents, are subject to the Foreign Corrupt Practices Act, Congress' answer to the problem of transnational bribery of foreign officials.

The Foreign Corrupt Practices Act of 1977 (FCPA) makes it a criminal offense for American companies and foreign companies subject to American law to pay bribes to foreign government officials. The FCPA has been criticized by some American businessmen who argue that the law makes it difficult to compete because other countries impose no such sanctions. Foreign competitors of American companies, it is argued, secure commercial advantages through the payment of bribes in a way that American companies cannot. To the extent that this may once have been true, however, the situation began to change in late 1997. The OECD Convention on Combating Bribery of Foreign Public Officials in International Business Transactions (the OECD Convention), adopted on 21 November 1997, is a step initiated by the twenty-nine members of the Organization for Economic Cooperation and Development (OECD) countries and five non-member (Argentina, Brazil, Bulgaria, Chile and Slovenia) signatories, and is intended to eliminate corruption as an accepted practice. As will be seen, however, the Convention has itself spawned major changes to the FCPA. Among other changes, the reach of the FCPA now extends to any United States national anywhere in the world.

D.Campbell and S.Woodley (eds.), The Comparative Law Yearbook of International Business 2003, 163-177

The Problem with Corruption

Corruption undermines the decision-making process and rewards the under-qualified. It debilitates and weakens fragile institutions, especially in developing countries. Against this background, a consensus has developed within industrial countries that corruption practiced by their citizens abroad is no less repugnant than when practiced at home.

Perceived Disadvantages of American Firms under the FCPA

Moral considerations alone would probably not have been a sufficient motivation for the industrialized countries to have taken such a revolutionary step. The FCPA has the potential to erode American commercial competitiveness, and studies have shown that American competitiveness has indeed suffered as a result of the FCPA. It is said that there are no legal constraints on American companies' foreign competitors; they are free to bribe officials, and thereby obtain a commercial advantage. There is no accurate measurement, but in a study authorized by the United States Government, it was concluded that from 1994 to April 1998, bribes had influenced the outcome of 239 international contract competitions. Moreover, the report showed that, in competitions with known outcomes, with only a few exceptions, a company that paid a bribe was awarded the contract.[1] An international effort to combat corruption on a worldwide scale became inevitable. Several victories have been achieved. They include the Inter-American Convention Against Corruption signed by the Organization of American States on 29 March 1996, the International Chamber of Commerce's new rules against corruption, the World Bank's strategy to battle bribery, the policy of the International Monetary Fund (IMF) of denying loans to countries where corruption is rampant and, most recently, the OECD Convention to combat bribery.

The concept and implementation of the OECD Convention did not occur in a vacuum, but drew much of its inspiration from the FCPA. Of similar importance, the United States amended the FCPA to achieve a mirror-like symmetry with the OECD Convention. When it was first signed, the OECD Convention was only a commitment and

---

1 Glenn R. Simpson, "Foreign Deals Rely on Bribes, US Says," Asian WSJ, 24 February 1999, at p. 6.

statement of purpose but, as of June 2003, implementing legislation has been in force in all thirty-four signatory countries to arm the OECD Convention with legal force in their respective countries. Since the FCPA is the most extensive and detailed statute that exists on the subject among the industrialized countries, the United States has had considerable experience implementing this statute and the OECD Convention framework follows the FCPA framework, it would be instructive to examine the development of the FCPA and its application to American companies.

The Foreign Corrupt Practices Act: An Overview

The FCPA consists of two substantive parts: accounting requirements and bribery prohibitions. These two parts are relatively distinct and can be considered separately. Throughout this chapter, discussion of these two areas will be delineated, although in practice they do overlap.

Accounting

Public companies must keep accurate accounts and put in place strict accounting controls aimed at uncovering and deterring corruption.

Bribery Prohibitions

American companies, citizens and residents are forbidden from making illicit payments to foreign officials to procure a commercial benefit.

Historical Overview

The FCPA had its genesis in investigations conducted by the Securities and Exchange Commission (SEC) from 1973 to 1976. The investigations uncovered more than 270 cases of bribes paid to foreign officials. One of the more notorious cases was the US $22-million which Lockheed paid in bribes to foreign government officials. The Congressional view was that these corrupt practices were not only immoral but that they destabilized American foreign policy, as the practice eroded international confidence in the United States. The media took up the cause and was firmly in favor of reform.

Scope

The jurisdiction of the FCPA is far-reaching. It applies to all companies, citizens and residents subject to American law. In specific terms, the FCPA applies to what the Act defines[2] as:

(1) "Issuers" — defined as any issuer of a security registered according to the Securities and Exchange Act;

(2) "Domestic concerns", which includes any citizen, national or resident of the United States, as well as virtually any commercial organization organized under American law or which is resident in the United States;

(3) Any "officer, director, employee, agent or stockholder" — American citizens employed by foreign subsidiaries or foreign companies are included[3] and, as will be discussed below, American firms can be liable, albeit indirectly, for the actions of their foreign subsidiaries, though it should be noted that the accounting provisions only apply to issuers — a specific subset of "domestic concerns";[4] and

(4) Persons other than issuers and domestic concerns — in November 1998, in a far-reaching amendment to the FCPA,[5] foreigners and commercial entities organized under foreign laws are now also subject to the FCPA.

"Corrupt Practices" under the Foreign Corrupt Practices Act

By Whom?

For a business or commercial entity to be liable under the FCPA,[6] it must be any "issuer" or "domestic concern", a test which is easily satisfied. The question of its foreign subsidiaries is far more uncertain and will be discussed in greater detail below.

2 15 U.S.C. Sections 78dd-1(a), 78dd-2(a), (h)(1).

3 H.R. Conf. Rep. No. 95–831, pt. 1st Sess., at p. 14 (1977).

4 15 U.S.C. Section 78dd-2(h)(1).

5 15 U.S.C. Section 18dd-3.

6 15 U.S.C. Section 78dd-1(a), 78dd-2(a).

To Whom?

The FPCA prohibits a bribe paid to any foreign government official. The definition of a "foreign government official" probably includes employees of quasi-government institutions and members of the legislature. The amendments of November 1998 expanded the definition by introducing the concept of a "public international organization", which is any international organization designated by executive order.[7]

What Kind of Payment?

The payment or a gift of "anything of value" is not statutorily defined in the FCPA and, thus, interpretation given in other criminal statutes and judicial decisions have been applied. Anything of value could be the promise of a benefit, assistance in obtaining contracts or even an offer of sexual favors. It is clearly not restricted to monetary payments.

Intent and Purpose

The payment must be made to a foreign official "while knowing" that it is for a corrupt purpose.[8] Prior to 1988, the knowledge requirement was particularly onerous because, on the basis of "having reason to know", an American company could be liable for any payment made to another party which was subsequently given to a foreign official for a corrupt purpose. This strict standard imposed a duty of strict liability on American companies to be meticulous in their business dealings. The knowledge requirement was significantly modified in amendments passed in 1988, called the Omnibus Trade and Competitiveness Act.[9] Instead of "having reason to know", companies became liable only if they made payments "while knowing" that the money would go to a foreign official.

Unlike the previous more onerous standard, the amendment does not impose an affirmative obligation to make inquiries, but neither does it permit the domestic concern to turn a blind eye to a suspicious

---

7 15 U.S.C. Sections 78dd-1(f)(1), 78dd-2(h)(2).

8 15 U.S.C. Sections 78dd-1(f)(2), 78dd-2(h)(3).

9 Omnibus Trade and Competitiveness Act, Pub. L. No. 100-418, 102 Stat. 1107, 1415–25 (1988) (codified as amended at 15 U.S.C.).

situation. Stated differently, relaxation of the duty does not permit a covered entity to act recklessly. Companies will more likely than not be liable if they fail to make inquiries which a reasonably prudent person would make. Thus, American firms must be particularly alert to the actions of their subsidiaries and agents.

Previously, to constitute a corrupt purpose, the payment must have been intended to "influence an official to do or omit to do an act . . . in order to [obtain] or [retain] business". Judicial decisions explicitly state that this does not pertain only to contracts but also, for example, to favorable but illegal tax treatment or customs duties. Recent amendments after the signing of the OECD Convention have significantly broadened even this interpretation.[10] In addition to obtaining or retaining business, the mere act of influencing any foreign official to do or omit to do any act in violation of his lawful duty or in securing any improper advantage is now also prohibited. Thus, even acts wholly unrelated to a contract may give rise to prosecution under the FCPA. Incidentally, these changes allow the FCPA to achieve harmony with the equivalent provisions in the OECD Convention which impose liability for "undue advantages". These points are discussed in more detail below in the sub-section entitled "Brief Comparison of the FCPA and the OECD Convention".

The bribe need not be a direct payment by a domestic concern to a foreign official; authorizing a representative or subsidiary to make such a payment makes the domestic concern liable. The legislative history of the FCPA makes it clear that an attempt to bribe a foreign official is, in itself, a violation of the Act.[11]

Illustration

Company A, an issuer incorporated in the United States, wishes to obtain a contract abroad. Its representative in the country approaches a low-level government employee and requests him to "persuade" his superior to grant the contract to Company A. In consideration, Company A will, upon obtaining the contract, offer the government employee a job in its representative office. Company A has violated the FCPA.

---

10 15 U.S.C. Sections 78dd-1(a)(2), 78dd-2(a)(2), 78dd-3(a)(3).

11 H.R. Rep. No. 95–640, 1st Sess., at p. 18 (1977).

Exceptions and Defenses: The 1988 Amendments

In its early form, the FCPA placed comprehensive restrictions on American companies, because it introduced a blanket prohibition on most forms of payment to foreign officials. As a result, companies lobbied for some differentiation between conduct which is allowed and conduct which is actionable. The 1988 amendments made some payments clearly acceptable.[12]

Travel and lodging expenditure spent on foreign officials became permissible after the 1988 amendments. An affirmative defense applies where the expenditure is incurred by a foreign official and is related to "the promotion, demonstration or explanation of products or services; or where payments relate to the execution or performance of a contract with a foreign government".[13] Such expenditure must still be reasonable and free from corrupt intent. Excessive expenditure will rebut any reasonable presumption that the expenditure was for a *bona fide* purpose.

Another affirmative defense removes liability for any payment made to a foreign official that is "lawful under the written laws and regulations"[14] of that country. The principal purpose of this defense was probably political, in that it addresses the prior anomaly of possibly making illegal a practice that may be legal in another country. However, the utility of such a defense is probably marginal as mere silence in local law is an insufficient defense.

Facilitating payments for routine government actions[15] are now allowed, and remain something of an anomaly in the Act. The 1988 amendments changed the focus of payments for routine government actions from the status of the recipient to the purpose of the payment. Routine government actions are actions that the official is already obliged to perform, and a facilitating payment is merely intended to expedite that performance. An obvious example is a payment to speed up the legitimate release of goods held by customs officials.

---

12 These exceptions and also the affirmative defenses have not been affected by the 1998 amendments.

13 15 U.S.C. Sections 78dd-1(c)(2), 78dd-2(c)(2).

14 15 U.S.C. Sections 78dd-1(c)(1), 78dd-2(c)(1).

15 15 U.S.C. Sections 78dd-1(b), 78dd-2(b).

Sub-Contractors

Generally, if an American company is the sub-contractor of a foreign prime contractor that makes illegal payments to officials, the American sub-contractor will not be liable. There are, however, exceptions to this rule. One exception is when the American sub-contractor knows of the prime contractor's illegal payments, but nevertheless enters into a contract with the prime contractor. Even when the American sub-contractor only finds out about the bribes after it signs the sub-contract, suspicion may be cast on it if it continues a long-term relationship with that prime contractor.

Effect of the 1998 Amendments on Foreign Subsidiaries

The reach of the FCPA has been considerably lengthened. The OECD Convention and the subsequent International Anti-Bribery and Fair Competition Act of 1998 (International Bribery Act) remove the need for the use of any "instrumentality of interstate commerce" in order to hold a United States national or issuer liable under the FCPA.[16] Instead, the very act of a corrupt payment by a United States national or issuer abroad is sufficient cause for prosecution. Also, although the amended FCPA does not prohibit payments made by foreign nationals, whether foreign employees or agents, in foreign countries on behalf of the United States company, United States companies may still be liable for the acts of their foreign subsidiaries under traditional principles of vicarious liability and agency.[17] American companies thus have a duty to be aware of the activities and particularly the accounts of their subsidiaries and agents.

Furthermore, foreign nationals may still be prosecuted under the FCPA if they attempt to commit corrupt practices within Omnibus Trade and Competitiveness Act[18] territory.[19] To a limited extent, the FCPA now also extends to non-United States nationals.

---

16 15 U.S.C. Section 78dd-1(c)(1)(g) (1998).

17 Bruce Yannett and Leigh Schachter, "The Foreign Corrupt Practices Act Goes Global", *International Financial Law Review*, February 1999, at p. 22; Omnibus Trade and Competitiveness Act, Pub. L. No. 100–418, 102 Stat. 1107, 1415–25 (1988).

18 Pub. L. No. 100–418, 102 Stat. 1107, 1415–25 (1988).

19 15 U.S.C. Section 78dd-3.

Accounting Issues

American companies have generally paid greater attention to the criminal nature of the anti-bribery provisions than to the equally important accounting provisions. The corporate scandals in the United States that began to surface in late 2001 have changed the landscape. Investigations of Enron, WorldCom, Xerox and Tyco, among others, have put a spotlight on accounting abuses. In addition, two American laws, the Patriot Act and the Sarbanes-Oxley Act, have increased scrutiny of companies' accounting practices. This is very likely to raise the awareness of the accounting aspects of the FCPA. A company can be free from criminal liability under the provisions on corrupt practices, but can be liable under the accounting provisions. Issuers are now required to keep accounts "which, in reasonable detail, accurately and fairly reflect the transaction and dispositions of the assets of the issuer".[20] The issuer need not record with unrealistic precision every single transaction in which it is involved, but the records must not conceal any payment of bribes.

After the 1988 amendments, criminal liability for violating the accounting provisions was imposed on any "person" who "knowingly circumvent[s] or knowingly fail[s] to implement a system of internal accounting controls, or knowingly falsif[ies] any book . . .".[21] A "person" includes both an individual and a company. Thus, if a low-level employee falsifies the accounts without the knowledge of his superiors, the company (as well as that employee) will be liable if the company has failed to put in place effective controls to deter falsification. For the purposes of the accounting provisions, which have been unaffected by the 1998 amendments, the definition of "person" remains unchanged.

As indicated earlier, potential liability can be much wider under the accounting requirements. A company may have found out about a bribe made by its foreign subsidiary only after the bribe was paid but, if the company fails to disclose the payment in its books of account, it would have falsified its accounts. This is so despite the fact that no authorization whatsoever was given for the bribe and despite the fact that the company was unaware of the bribe before it took place. This is to say that, even if the company is not liable under the anti-bribery provisions, it must still record a bribe paid without its authorization if it later finds out about the bribe.

20 15 U.S.C. Section 78m(b)(2)(A) (1996).
21 15 U.S.C. Section 78m(b)(5) (1996).

Before the 1988 amendments, an American parent was also responsible for the internal accounting controls of its foreign subsidiaries. The amendments brought a welcome and realistic clarification of the issuer-foreign subsidiary relationship.[22] Now, the issuer is liable for the accounts of its foreign subsidiary only if it owns more than fifty per cent of that subsidiary's shares. In cases where the issuer owns less than fifty per cent of the shares, it is only obliged to "proceed in good faith to use its influence" to persuade the subsidiary to comply with FCPA requirements. However, genuine good faith efforts are required.

Even so, an American company is responsible for the activities of its subsidiaries. A striking example is the criminal prosecution of the Italian company, Montedison SPA Montedison, which, although Italian in origin, had shares registered under the Securities and Exchange Act, and was, therefore, subject to SEC jurisdiction. Montedison was alleged to have paid off Italian politicians. Because of a technicality, Montedison was not liable under the anti-bribery provisions[23] but, as the bribes were not recorded in the company books, the company violated the books and records provisions of the FCPA.

Enforcement Agencies and Penalties

The SEC is empowered to investigate violations of accounting provisions by issuers, and the Department of Justice is responsible for prosecuting violations by both domestic concerns and issuers. Both agencies can bring civil actions against violators.

Penalties are significant.[24] For bribery offenses, maximum criminal penalties can reach US $2-million. Specific fines vary for individual offenders. Within the limitations of the statutory maximum, the amount of the fine is governed by the Federal Sentencing

---

22 15 U.S.C. Section 78m(b)(6).

23 Previously, under the FCPA anti-bribery provisions, a domestic concern was required to use an "instrumentality" of interstate commerce such as a phone call, fax or telex to communicate its approval or authorization of a bribe. In the Montedison case, no instrumentalities were used. This loophole has been abolished by Sections 78dd-1(g) and 78dd-2(i), which provide that a person subject to the Act who operates outside the United States is liable even if he does not make use of an instrumentality of interstate commerce to make a bribe.

24 *See* generally 15 U.S.C. Sections 78dd-2(g), 78ff.

Guidelines.[25] Individuals are also subject to prison sentences of up to five years. When an individual is the employee of an American domestic concern, the employer may not pay the fine for the employee. The SEC or the Attorney General is also empowered to bring a civil action against offenders for an amount of up to US $10,000. Injunctive relief in the form of a permanent injunction or a temporary restraining order is also available. For accounting violations, a fine not exceeding US $2.5-million may be imposed on organizations, while individuals can be fined up to US $1-million and imprisoned for up to ten years.

The amendments make a distinction between natural persons and domestic concerns that are not natural persons.[26] Before the amendments, individuals and corporations were lumped together under the definition of "domestic concerns", which may have resulted in some confusion when trying to determine the penalties for an FCPA offense.

Multinational Efforts against Corruption

Notable success was achieved in globalizing the war against corruption with the adoption of the OECD Convention on Combating Bribery of Foreign Public Officials in International Business Transactions. As of August 2003, the thirty-four signatories of the Convention have deposited their instruments of ratification with the OCED Secretariat, including the non-OCED members. All signatories to the OCED Convention have also implemented the requisite domestic legislation, in some cases — such as Norway and Hungary — via amendments to existing penal statutes. Others, like Korea and Chile, have enacted new laws to implement the OCED Convention.

Essentially, the OECD Convention requires the signatories to:

(1) "Take such measures as may be necessary to establish [that] it is a criminal offense" to offer bribes to foreign officials (Article 1);

(2) Prescribe "effective, proportionate and dissuasive criminal penalties" which are comparable to the signatories' own laws against bribery of their officials (Article 3);

25 Don Zarin, "Doing Business under the Foreign Corrupt Practices Act", *Practicing Law Institute* (1998) at p. 8–5.

26 15 U.S.C. 78dd-2(g).

(3) "Take such measures as may be necessary" to establish an effective accounting procedure to expose bribery of foreign officials or the cover-up of such bribery (Article 8); and
(4) Render assistance to other signatories in order to enforce the OECD Convention, including extradition (Articles 9 and 10).

Brief Comparison of the FCPA and the OECD Convention

The footprint of the FCPA is clearly visible in the provisions of the OECD Convention. Equally, since ratifying the Convention, the United States has substantially amended the FCPA to achieve a closer symmetry with the Convention. The net effect of these amendments, together with the 1988 amendments, is to expand the jurisdiction of the FCPA.

By Whom?

It is in this area that the OECD Convention may be wider in scope. "Any person" who gives a bribe is liable, and this presumably includes even foreign subsidiaries, as long as they are within the jurisdiction of the signatory state (Article 1.1). However, after the November 1998 amendments, the FCPA now covers "any natural person other than a national of the United States or any commercial organization".[27] Also, as discussed above, United States companies can be vicariously liable for bribery payments made by their foreign subsidiaries if it can be established that they had failed to make necessary and reasonable inquiries.

To Whom?

Like the amended FCPA, foreign officials include all government officials, including officials in state-owned enterprises and international public bodies, such as the IMF (Article 1.4). As mentioned earlier, the 1998 amendments appear to have widened the scope to include officials of quasi-government organizations, bringing it in line with the

27 15 U.S.C. Section 18dd-3.

OECD Convention. The OECD Convention, following the FCPA, does not cover officials of political parties or political candidates.

What Kind of Payment?

"Any undue pecuniary or other advantage" constitutes a bribe under the OECD Convention (Article 1.1). The examples in American case law which refer to "anything of value" should be relevant here as well.

Intent and Purpose

To attempt to obtain any improper advantage or to attempt to "obtain or retain business" establishes a corrupt purpose (Article 1.1). The OECD Convention, however, does not prescribe a standard of knowledge. That may be dealt with in the implementing legislation of the signatories.

The OECD Convention is a milestone in the fight against corruption. The effects of the OECD Convention are not yet fully evident. A committee called the OECD Working Group on Combating Bribery is responsible for guiding the progress of post-Convention activities on implementation. In addition, the International Bar Association, which straddles 183 countries, has set up an informal group.[28] While these groups are not enforcement organs, they will be vital in raising awareness about the importance of effective implementing laws and can be expected to provide ideas and create momentum.

Having pressed for a level playing field for decades, it is not surprising that the Unites States is now aggressively monitoring compliance with the OCED Convention. Every year, as required by the International Anti-Bribery and Fair Competition Act of 1998, the Unites States Secretary of Commerce must deliver a report to the United States Congress setting out the progress made by the United States and the OECD signatories in both the enactment of legislation to implement the Convention and the enforcement of such legislation. The annual reports are comprehensive and contain significant detail. They are prepared with input from the United States Departments of Justice, State, Treasury and Commerce. However, the reports, objective as they may be, are written from the perspective of

28 *International Bar News*, Volume 52, Number 2, August 1998.

the United States Government. As the reports repeatedly make clear, the views contained in the reports reflect the views of those United States Government agencies, and not necessarily those of the OECD Working Group on Combating Bribery.

The test of the OECD Convention is not only in the efforts of the respective signatories to enact domestic legislation. Enacting the law is only the first, and arguably the easiest, step. Since ratifying the Convention, the United States has commenced at least nine enforcement actions under the FCPA. By contrast, none of the other signatories have brought charges under their amended domestic legislation against any offender.

In order to succeed, OECD Convention signatories need a robust implementation program. In the United States, enforcement is handled by the SEC and the Department of Justice.[29] Similar agencies in each country should be tasked with investigation and prosecution of corruption cases. Examples of single-purpose anti-corruption bodies are Hong Kong's Independent Commission Against Corruption (ICAC) and Singapore's Corrupt Practices Investigation Bureau (CPIB), both law-enforcement agencies with powers similar to those of a police force. Similar independent agencies with the requisite expertise and enforcement authority will have a role to play.

The concept of the OECD Convention is alien to many countries, especially to countries where bribes to foreign officials are even tax deductible. In some countries, the law does not recognize corporate crime. Although the OECD signatories have all agreed, where applicable, to amend their domestic legislation and thereby to outlaw the tax deductibility of bribes, this remains unfamiliar ground for the tax authorities of many countries which routinely allow such deductions. It will be a challenge for tax authorities to distinguish valid payments from bribes, since their domestic laws may not contain the same strict accounting provisions found in the FCPA that might otherwise raise a red flag. It is crucial, therefore, that the United States renders assistance and advice, and that its experience with the FCPA be shared. For many of the OECD countries, the OECD Convention may require a new cultural conditioning. The United States has an existing legal framework and experience in the war against corruption. Because

29 Interestingly, although Singapore is not a signatory to the Convention, the Singapore Prevention of Corruption Act, like the Foreign Corrupt Practices Act, is extra-territorial in nature, and holds offenders criminally liable for acts of corruption committed outside the country.

there are moral implications in respect of the FCPA, it is important that the United States acts with great sensitivity in order that it be effective in promoting this important objective.

Conspicuously absent, to date, from the list of signatories to the OECD Convention are the Asian countries, except for Japan and South Korea. A quick perusal of statistics on investment activities will reveal that Asian countries consistently rank among the top ten investors.[30] The American firms' most formidable competitors, in this part of the world at least, may be from the Asian economies, not the OECD countries. It is, therefore, imperative for the United States to take steps to persuade more Asian countries to sign and implement the OECD Convention, so that there is a recognized world standard.

Conclusion

It is essential that American companies adopt measures to prevent their foreign employees from paying bribes to foreign officials, since the parent United States company can be liable for their wrongdoing either under the anti-bribery provisions or, more likely, under the accounting requirements. This highlights the need for a company to be aware of its overseas activities. The OECD Convention has prompted extensive changes to the FCPA and, in so doing, has made its scope far broader than when it was first conceived. American firms with international business interests should tread warily in the midst of the new legal framework which has thus been created.

It is also clear from the series of recent prosecutions in the United States, and with the impetus of the new Patriot and Sarbanes-Oxley Acts, that the United States will aggressively enforce the FCPA. It will do so not only for its own purposes, but to set an example with the hope that other countries will prosecute their own violators.

Note: The law in this chapter is current as at August 2003.

30 *Vietnam Economic Times*, January 2000.

Investment and Taxation

Preferential Tax Regimes from a Perspective of the Island of Madeira

Rodrigo Cesar Caldas de Sa
Trigueiro Fontes Advogados
Recife, Brazil

Organization for Economic Cooperation and Development and Tax Competition

Background

After World War II, the Organization for European Economic Cooperation (OEEC) was created in Paris to help manage the Marshall Plan, with the main target and scope of reconstructing the economy of the European Continent. In recognition of the success of the program, this Organization, created in 1948, was later turned into the Organization for Economic Cooperation and Development (OECD) in 1961. The objective of the OECD was to strengthen the economies of its members and implement free market policies in both developed and so-called developing countries. Those were the times of Bretton Woods, the General Agreement on Tariffs and Trade (GATT) and the International Monetary Fund (IMF).

The crisis of the entering into war years had led countries to increase protection of their internal markets, which raised more tension in a shattered world. From then on, it was recognized that it would be important to set some guidelines and rules to improve international trade and make it more efficient through open market policies. Better means of communication between nations would strengthen commerce but, perhaps most importantly, prevent crises that would lead to the pre-World War II scenario.[1]

1 For a good background on the Organization for Economic Cooperation and Development and the Bretton Woods systems, *see* Rosa M. Lastra, "The Bretton Woods Institutions in the XXIst Century: The Reform of International Financial Architecture".

D.Campbell and S.Woodley (eds.), The Comparative Law Yearbook of International Business 2003, 181-201

The OECD thus came into being under an environment of restructuring world commercial links and economic concepts. Today, it plays an important and much broader role in the improvement of both member and non-member countries. It extracts statistics, produces documents, reviews and makes decisions and recommendations, all to help the development of a global economy. It might not have the legitimacy of the United Nations nor the World Trade Organization (WTO), but it does have the force of thirty member countries that represent most of the richest nations in the world.

Tax Competition

Taxation used to be a process by which states levied money to subsidize their activities. History has shown, however, that it can also be used to close or open internal markets, change decisions on expenditure and prevent or encourage commerce. Potential investors in a foreign country are influenced in their choice by considerations such as the existence of an extensive infra-structure, an educated labor force, available technology and tax benefits. Countries deficient in some of these features may use tax incentives as their main attraction.[2] Taxpayers from other countries start to move their capital and tax liabilities to, and sometimes through, jurisdictions with preferential tax regimes in order to enjoy such "facilities". This has been named tax competition.

However, most countries cannot extend benefits without threatening their essential revenue. Also, not uncommonly, tax advantages are accompanied by the warm blanket of bank and legal secrecy, guaranteed by tight internal legislation, which has been considered an open door to money laundering, tax fraud and the protection of assets of criminal organizations.[3] For these reasons, some aspects of tax competition have been considered harmful. The OECD has decided

2 "In some countries, tax incentives represent the major legislative effort yet undertaken to hasten development; in many others, they represent only one among a variety of measures which have been undertaken for this purpose. These tax subsidies may be cast in a variety of forms. The most common are partial or complete exemptions, ordinarily for a limited period of time, from one or several taxes, and special allowances under the individual and corporation income taxes for accelerated depreciation or reinvestment": Heller and Kauffman, *Tax Incentives for Industry in Less Developed Countries* (Law School of Harvard University, Cambridge, 1963) at p. 2.

3 The Organization for Economic Cooperation and Development has recently published its report, "Behind the Corporate Veil: Using Corporate Entities for Illicit Purposes", on the secrecy of pseudo-corporations used for criminal purposes.

to coordinate an initiative to tackle such practices, with the help of its Committee on Fiscal Affairs (CFA).

Reports on Harmful Tax Competition

In 1998, the OECD made public its work on harmful tax competition by releasing its report "Harmful Tax Competition: An Emerging Global Issue". The project has, as its object, the identification of harmful tax practices in countries (or their dependencies) defined as tax havens and countries (or their dependencies) with preferential tax regimes. It is concerned with easily "movable" investments, such as financial and other service activities, and does not consider trading activities.

This first report, approved by the OECD Council with the abstention of Luxembourg and Switzerland, warns about the effects of harmful tax competition, sets criteria to define and differentiate tax havens and preferential tax regimes and urges member countries to:

(1) Identify and eliminate or modify possible preferential tax regimes within their territories or dependencies;
(2) Adopt recommendations to tackle harmful tax practices; and
(3) Act as much as possible in a coordinated manner.

Non-member countries were invited to become familiar with the project, by means of a forum led by the CFA, particularly those having specific contact with jurisdictions that allegedly promoted harmful tax competition. Their commitment to join the project was welcomed. A list of tax havens and preferential tax regimes would be produced in due time, and countries should remove any harmful features of their tax systems within five years from the approval of the Guidelines by the Council. Taxpayers enjoying tax benefits until December 2001 would have their benefits removed not later than 31 December 2005.

Following the project, the CFA presented to the 2000 Ministerial Council Meeting its report, "Towards Global Tax Cooperation". It reinforces the intention of the project and lists groups of jurisdictions or dependencies as being tax havens or having preferential tax regimes. It also suggests counter measures to tackle harmful tax regimes and provides for the creation of a list of uncooperative havens, to include jurisdictions that keep their harmful practices. The 2001 Progress Report updates the progress of both member and non-member countries' work and jurisdictions' commitments to join in the recommendations set by the Committee.

Madeira's Tax System

Among the member jurisdictions with potentially harmful "preferential regimes", the 2000 Progress Report lists the tax system of the Portuguese Island of Madeira. It is said to be potentially harmful in areas such as insurance, fund management, banking, headquarter regimes and shipping. The benefits had already been considered illegal by the European Commission when preparing its Code of Conduct on Business.[4] The Commission's work has resulted in some principles and guidelines for European Community (EC) countries to avoid harmful tax competition. The Portuguese Parliament has set a schedule, from January 2001 to December 2011, to extinguish these practices. This does not mean, however, the end of the *Madeira* v. *Commission* affair.

Tax Havens and Preferential Tax Regimes

Definition

In very broad terms, tax havens could be defined as countries or dependencies which offer their legal systems to cover the activities of taxpayers wishing to avoid or evade tax liabilities from other countries, leading to the erosion of the tax basis of the latter. In other words, a tax haven would be a country or dependency where:

(1) Little or no tax is charged on business profits, so that taxpayers from other countries pay little or no tax on the income derived from their business;

(2) Commercial and civil law have special structures for businesses and entities so that shareholders and beneficial owners will not be identified and the structures can be managed from outside the country;

(3) Banking law is guarded by tight secrecy legislation, providing heavy penalties for entities and persons who disclose information on investors and business;

(4) There is no cross-border financial control so that money can flow out of and into the country without any effective supervision;

4 Actually, several features of the Portuguese tax system have been considered illegal by the Primaloro Report, such as depreciation schemes, fund managers and reinsurance companies. The full Report can be viewed at http://www.uv.es/cde/TEXTOS/primaloro_en.pdf.

(5) The country does not have treaties or administrative legislation to exchange information with other countries regarding tax matters, even if they have agreements to exchange information on money laundering from crimes such as financial fraud, drug dealing and terrorism; and

(6) The country advertises itself as an attractive place for business, for the reasons mentioned above.[5]

However practical these concepts might appear, they are far from serving as perfect guides to countries that want to defend their tax base from the reach of tax havens. What might for some countries be a tax haven might not be so for others.[6] Furthermore, some jurisdictions do not offer their juridical system to attract business, but are still considered tax havens for specific sorts of activities. Therefore, attention should be turned to any preferential tax regime, the definition of which can prove much more relative.

One could say that they would be jurisdictions which, though they did not meet all the criteria listed above, could be used as means for tax avoidance or evasion through the use of preferential tax schemes. Differentiating tax havens and countries with potentially harmful tax regimes would be a matter of the perspective of those making the assessment and the extent to which the allocation of capital would be distorted. For these reasons, the use of a "designated jurisdiction" approach for the application of controlled foreign corporation (CFC)[7] legislation is not efficient. The use of international tax schemes is, therefore, beyond the reach of lists, whatever their range.

Bearing this in mind, some countries have set CFC rules that take tax rates as a base to establish whether the income derived from

---

5 Other characteristics of tax havens are usually listed as, for instance, the existence of a disproportionate financial sector, good communications services and the assurance of economic and political stability. These would be side-effects or ancillary, and would be important to qualify a tax haven as a good haven or not: Moerman, Sebastien, "The Main Characteristics of Tax Havens", *Intertax*, Number 27 (Kluwer Law International, 1999) at p. 368.

6 ". . . Venezuela, which levies tax on a territorial basis but does not promote itself aggressively as a base for foreign operations, is included in the French, German and Japanese lists as a tax haven and also in the United Kingdom list as a non-tax haven country": Arnold, Brian J., "The Taxation of Controlled Foreign Corporations: Defining and Designating Tax Havens II", *British Tax Review*, 1986, at p. 363.

7 Rules applied by a country to income, or some types of income, derived from abroad, to which little or no tax abroad has been paid and whose beneficiaries are resident taxpayers.

abroad should be subject to taxation. This has been named the "transactional" approach.[8] Many countries that apply CFC rules keep the use of lists as a guide for both tax authorities and taxpayers. This combination not only avoids the problems of identifying tax havens, but also does not need to define preferential tax regimes and sets a certain level of fairness between those taxpayers who will and those who will not use international schemes in order to avoid tax, keeping the burden of taxation the same for everyone.

Tax Havens

The OECD recognizes the difficulties of defining tax havens. It sets as the first and main factor in determining whether a jurisdiction is a tax haven the no tax or nominal tax criterion, among other features, such as lack of transparency and exchange of information and the absence of substantial activity.[9] The 2000 Progress Report resumes this approach, stating that the key point for identifying a tax haven is to check whether the country has no or nominal taxation on financial and related service activities and whether it offers itself as a means of evasion of other countries' tax. Again, other key factors are used to identify tax havens, notably the absence of exchange of information and lack of transparency.

The 2001 Report describes a tax haven as a jurisdiction where no or nominal taxation is charged, though "the no or nominal tax criterion is not sufficient, by itself, to result in characterization as a tax haven".[10] Other key factors also have to be considered. The OECD view on defining tax havens is, therefore, as follows:

(1) The jurisdiction has no or nominal tax on relevant income and offers itself to taxpayers who wish to escape taxation in their home countries;

(2) There is no effective exchange of information regarding tax matters with other countries' tax authorities;

---

8 In France, Article 209B of the *Code Général des Impôts* states that, when a company established in a foreign jurisdiction or territory is subject to privileged taxation within the meaning of Article 238A, the company will be subject to French corporate tax.

9 Harmful Tax Competition Report 1998, at p. 23.

10 It goes on, stating that "the OECD recognizes that every jurisdiction has a right to determine whether to impose direct taxes and, if so, to determine the appropriate tax rate": 2001 Progress Report, at p. 9.

(3) The jurisdiction's regime lacks transparency, that is, there are no clear public rules to determine the amount of tax to be paid by whom to whom; and

(4) The jurisdiction facilitates the establishment of foreign entities without the need for substantial activity, for example, a taxpayer can be considered a resident even if it has no physical presence within the country.

The CFA has shown a slight change in its attitude towards classifying tax havens. The initial concern has changed from a "no or nominal taxation" approach to that of the problem of exchange of information.[11] Uncooperative havens would be subject to coordinated measures, suggested by the OECD, from other countries wishing to protect their tax base from such regimes. It would be an alternative "global" way of applying CFC legislation, by means of using a black list of (uncooperative) tax havens, largely announced and published by the OECD.

Besides the "designated jurisdiction" and the "transactional" approaches, this could be defined as "the name and shame" approach. The project provides for the adoption of soft, but later to be hardened, law.[12] On the one hand, it is impossible to achieve broad international agreement on the issue of a multilateral treaty; on the other hand, the resolve to gather adherence to the initiative has been reflected in the retaliation proposed by the OECD against uncooperative havens. The jurisdictions so far named and shamed as uncooperative are Andorra, Liechtenstein, Liberia, Marshall Islands, Monaco, Nauru and Vanuatu.[13]

---

11 The Committee might have recognized that the sole fact that a country applied little taxation was not the main problem with tax havens, and also a legitimate feature of a country's legal framework very difficult to tackle: 2001 Progress Report, Paragraphs 27 and 28.

12 "Soft law is a device that can be deliberately used by non-State acts to influence State behavior when there is little prospect of successfully concluding a treaty. Lack of *opinio juris* prevents comity becoming merged with custom, but failure to comply may lead to acts of retortion against the non-complying entity — indeed, acknowledgement that retortion is applicable against actions not contrary to international law testifies to the weight accorded to non-legal norms": Chinkin, Christine, "Normative Development in the International Legal System" in *Commitment and Compliance — The Role of Non-Binding Norms in the International Legal System* (Dinah Shelton (ed.), Oxford University Press).

13 http://www.oecd.org/EN/document/0,EN-document-22-nodirectorate-no-12-28534-22,00.html.

Preferential Tax Regimes

The concept of a preferential tax regime as a regime used to avoid tax is far too broad to be sustained. The OECD took the view that the focus should be directed towards preferential tax regimes strong enough to be potentially harmful to the natural flow of the economy, though not strong enough to be a tax haven. The 1998 Report sets out "key factors" for considering a country or its dependency as a place with potentially harmful preferential tax regimes in the following manner:[14]

(1) There is no or little taxation on the relevant income of a business;
(2) The system is "ring fenced", that is, residents of the country are excluded from tax advantages, and companies are explicitly or implicitly prohibited from doing business within the country;
(3) The regime is designed and/or administered in a non-transparent way; and
(4) There is no effective exchange of information regarding tax matters with foreign tax authorities.

The Report does not give a satisfactory definition of a preferential regime located in a country that is not a tax haven.[15] Instead, it sets out other factors that might be considered to qualify a regime as potentially harmful, including an artificial definition of the tax base and the distortion of internationally acceptable transfer pricing principles and a willingness to negotiate the tax rate and/or the tax base. However, they could be considered tools of the categories above, especially items (1), (2) and (4). The use of a wide range of tax treaties, especially when foreign income is exempt, might be considered another accessory feature.

Finally, the forty-seven regimes included in the 2000 Report do not include holding companies. The work focused on activities such as insurance, offshore banking, shipping registries and portfolio investment companies. The Report states that the Forum believed that the complexities of analyzing these features did not allow the Committee to actually come to any conclusion on the matter. This

---

14 Harmful Tax Competition Report 1998, at p. 27.

15 Apparently, the main difference would be the "ring fencing" features. However, if a tax haven might be a country or its dependency, a "ring fenced" tax regime could be considered a dependency and, in this sense, a tax haven.

might appear to be just a detail, but signals an important tendency of the project. The preferential schemes of countries with a wide range of tax treaties, such as Portugal or the Netherlands, provides great support for holding company regimes.

Conclusions

The definition and differentiation of tax havens and countries with potentially harmful preferential tax regimes do not contain major details, except perhaps for the "ring fencing" features of the latter. Both have harmful effects on the allocation of investment and encourage the evasion and avoidance of other countries' tax revenues. The main preferential schemes of Madeira are analyzed below. This analysis might raise interesting insights on why a country decides to establish a preferential tax regime and how. Moreover, it intends to highlight how this regime can be potentially harmful to the economy and to other countries' tax revenues, and whether there would be a practical reason for establishing a difference between tax havens and preferential tax regimes.

Madeira and Its Preferential Tax Regimes

History and Legal Regime

Finding stable economic activities for Madeira has always been a difficult issue for Portugal.[16] The archipelago, Madeira being the biggest island, was initially an important center for navigation. However, the time soon came when the growing population demanded a more active economy. The first major industry was the production and export of sugar, followed by the production of grains, export of wood (madeira) and the production of wine, still its finest export. These alternatives have always been linked to heavy international investment, due not only to eventual "outflows" of the Portuguese

---

16 "Madeira suffers from the socio-economic problems facing ultra-peripheral islands: traditional products in decline, cheap competition and a dire need for diversification and restructuring": Corkill, David, *The Development of the Portuguese Economy — A Case of Europeanization* (Routledge, London and New York, 1999) at p. 131.

Central Government and to military and political instability in Europe at that time, but also to the country's difficulties in managing Madeira's affairs.[17]

No relevant records of independence claims have been reported, even during the unsuccessful "Revolution of 1931", caused by unpopular economic measures adopted by the dictator António de Oliveira Salazar in the aftermath of the American crisis of 1929. In fact, despite the criticisms, Madeira has sought integration with the major political concerns of the Continent. It has followed, in alignment and influence, the last centuries of Portugal's history. The fall of the dictatorship on 25 April 1974, with the bloodless *Revolucao dos Cravos*, gave a new perspective of effective autonomy to Madeira.[18]

The Constitution of 2 April 1976 granted Madeira the power to manage local affairs under the auspices of the national sovereignty exercised by the central government,[19] which keeps a Minister on the Island.[20] It has the power to create new taxes and adapt national taxes to its regional demands.[21] In order to encourage necessary foreign investment to stand beside the tourism, agriculture and wine industries, the Portuguese Government decided to create the Madeira Free Zone.[22] The Regional Government of Madeira decided in 1986[23] to attract financial and offshore banking activities, with the rise of the International Business Center.[24]

Preferential Regimes of Madeira

The framework created within the free zone, adapted lately to work also as an International Business Center, comprises tax incentives,

17 After the revolution of 1 December 1620 and so that Portugal could manage to assure its independence against a powerful Spain, it was obliged to make damaging agreements with England, which started to open up its economy and wealth to British mercantilism, especially after the Treaty of Methuen.

18 "The political-administrative regime of the islands of Azores and Madeira is based on their geographic, economic, social and cultural characteristics, as well as on the historical autonomy aspiration of islanders": Constitution of Portugal, Article 225(1).

19 Constitution of Portugal, Article 225(3).

20 Constitution of Portugal, Article 230.

21 Constitution of Portugal, Article 227(1)(i).

22 Decrees 53 and 54/82.

23 Decree Law Number 163 of 26 June 1986.

24 Diamond, Dorothy B., "Madeira" in *Tax Havens of the World*, Volume 2 (LexisNexis, 2001) at p. 1.

special forms of entities and administrative regulations that seek to ensure a less costly atmosphere for business and property management. Considering the nature and depth of such structures, the OECD has qualified them as harmful.

"Ring Fenced" Schemes

Portuguese Decree Law Number 215/89 is the country's Statute on Tax Incentives (*Estatuto de Beneficios Fiscais* — STI). The new legislation has modified Articles 33 and 34 of the Statute, relating to Madeira's incentives. The scenario is, therefore, different from the one presented by the OECD in its 1998 and 2000 Reports. Entities registered in the International Business Center will enjoy exemption from personal income tax (*Imposto sobre o Rendimento de Pessoas Singulares* — IRS) and corporate tax (*Imposto sobre o Rendimento de Pessoas Coletivas* — IRC), under certain terms and conditions, up to 31 December 2011. As the OECD work is related to "movable" activities and the focus in Madeira has been directed at shipping, insurance, fund managers and banking and headquarter regimes, tax treatment of activities such as manufacturing and commerce will not be discussed here.

Shipping Qualified shipping entities are exempt from IRC on the income derived from the transport of passengers and cargo, since they do not involve activities between Portuguese ports.[25] Other forms of income, for instance, the sale of shares in ships, are also exempt from any corporate tax.[26] Finally, officers and crews of ships registered under the International Shipping Registry, approved by Decree Law Number 96/69, amended in 1993 by Decree Law Number 393, are exempt from IRS.[27] As opposed to other activities that began to have their tax incentives restricted from January 2001, the shipping industry will enjoy its preferential schemes up to 31 December 2011, with no restrictions announced so far.[28]

The International Shipping Registry has followed the framework by which ships can have dual flags. Article 8(1) of the OECD Model

25 Statute on Tax Incentives, Article 33(1)(b).

26 Statute on Tax Incentives, Articles 33(2)(b) and 33(2)(c).

27 Statute on Tax Incentives, Article 8.

28 Statute on Tax Incentives, Article 34(4).

Convention on Income and Capital gives priority to the place of effective management to define where business from shipping and aircraft activities should be taxed. Profits are deemed to be paid to the country of residence if the place of effective management is on board.[29] However, the commentary to Article 8 states that contracting states are free to choose the place of residence of the company in order to define the place where profits should be taxed.[30] Shipping companies with a dual flag scheme from Madeira can benefit from Portugal's wide range of tax treaties. The Portugal–United Kingdom tax treaty, for example, establishes the place of residence to define where profits of the company should be taxed in these cases.[31]

Banking Financial and credit institutions also benefit from the exemption from IRC related to the revenue of the respective activity. However, they do not involve operations with a Portuguese resident, with a non-resident's permanent establishment located in Portugal nor with an entity linked by a controlling interest within Portuguese territory but not in the free zone.[32] A permanent establishment in Portugal is a fixed installation through which a commercial, industrial or agricultural activity is carried on.[33] The benefits will apply until December 2011 to entities registered before 1 January 2001. Companies registered from then on will follow the schedule set by Article 34(2) of the STI: those licensed in 2001/2002 will be subject to a 7.5 per cent rate of IRC; those registered in 2003/2004 will be taxed at ten per cent; and those registered in 2005/2006 will be taxed at 12.5 per cent.

Fund Management Entities that carry out activities of fund investment are exempt from tax, provided that units are acquired by non-residents of Portuguese territory. It does not, however, include permanent establishments which operate exclusively with

---

29 Model Convention on Income and Capital, Article 8(3). The Portugal–France Tax Treaty adopts this approach.

30 Commentary update of 29 April 2000 to Article 8 of the Model Convention, at p. C(8)-1.

31 Article 8 of the Portugal–United Kingdom Tax Treaty on shipping and air transport states that "Profits which a resident of a Contracting State derives from the operation of ships or aircraft in international traffic shall be taxable only in that Contracting State".

32 Statute on Tax Incentives, Articles 33(c)(1) and 33(c)(2).

33 Sousa da Camara, Francisco and Caballero, Miguel-Angelo, "Portugal" chapter in *The Taxation of Companies in Europe: Guides to European Taxation*, Volume II, at p. 131.

non-residents or in other jurisdictions situated outside Portuguese territory.[34] Entities registered before 1 January 2001 will enjoy the benefits up to December 2011. Those registered after this date will be taxed according to the schedule set in Article 34(1) of the amended STI: entities licensed in 2001/2002 will be subject to a one per cent tax rate; entities licensed in 2003/2004 will be subject to a two per cent rate; and entities licensed between 2005/2006 will be taxed at a three per cent rate.

Insurance and Reinsurance Insurance and reinsurance companies and pensions managers also enjoy the benefits of exemption, provided that the beneficiary with whom the company contracts is a non-resident of Portugal. The exemption will not include income derived from a permanent establishment within Portuguese territory.[35] Actually, the European Commission considered benefits for companies in mainland Portugal illegal in relation to special deduction provisions.[36] Following the same pattern of fund investments, these entities will benefit from such exemptions until 31 December 2011 if they were registered before 1 January 2001. Those registered in 2001/2002 will be taxed at a rate of one per cent; those registered between 2003/2004 will be charged at a rate of two per cent; and those registered in 2005/2006 will pay a three per cent rate of IRC.

Headquarter Regimes — Holding Companies Madeira has several types of entities that can be used as headquarters to manage businesses abroad. These entities include limited liability companies (*sociedades limitadas*), share companies (*sociedades anonimas*), trusts and holding companies (*sociedades gestoras de participacoes sociais* — SGPS). Entities with their headquarters within the free zone enjoy not only the exemptions granted by the STI, but the option of being effectively managed abroad. In the case of companies, shareholders do not need to reside in Madeira, nor even come to the island for obligatory meetings; they can appoint representatives for this purpose.[37]

---

34 Statute on Tax Incentives, Article 33(d). The net global value of the fund must contain a minimum of ten per cent cash, bank deposits, deposit certificates or investments in interbank markets.

35 Statute on Tax Incentives, Articles 33(e) and 33(f).

36 Primaloro Report, at p. 48.

37 The provision is contrary to Article 5 of the Model Convention on Income and Capital, which fixes the center of management and control as the tie-breaker rule for defining a permanent establishment.

With the help of European Community Parent-Subsidiary Directive 90/435, which restrains Member States from taxing distributions between European Union (EU) parent and subsidiary companies, a Portuguese SGPS can be used to avoid tax.[38] Portugal taxes SGPSs at a rate of thirty-two per cent,[39] but they can deduct a full 100 per cent on their income derived from abroad, which means no taxation at all.[40] In this sense, a Madeiran SGPS could be used as a link to non-EU investors who derive income from their EU companies without substantial taxation. Some countries use the option of Article 1(2) of the EU Parent-Subsidiary Directive for the prevention of fraud or abuse[41] but, even so, Madeiran SGPSs apparently benefit from prohibited state aid from Portugal.[42]

Lack of Transparency — Exchange of Information

Portuguese Tax Statute Decree Law Number 398 of 17 December 1998 ensured legal and bank secrecy, except in special cases where a judicial order was required to disclose information. However, the Tax Reform Act of December 2000[43] brought significant modifications with the new draft of Article 63(2). Tax authorities no longer require a judicial order to disclose information. Under certain terms and conditions, information can be demanded directly from financial institutions. The changes might be of relevance for entities registered in Madeira, especially if interpreted in the light of EC Directive 77/799/EEC of 19 December 1977.

---

38 "The Directive has two main effects: first, payments of dividends are not to be subjected to withholding tax in the country of the subsidiary (Article 5); second, relief from double taxation must be given in the country of the parent, either by exempting dividends received from tax or by granting a foreign tax credit (Article 4)." Easson, A.J., *Taxation in the European Community* (The Athlone Press, London and Atlantic Highlands, N.J. 1993) at p. 6.

39 Following a progressive schedule up to December 2011.

40 Statute on Tax Incentives, Article 31; Corporate Tax Statute, Articles 47(1) and 47(5). The income is exempt up to December 2011 if it comes from a non-European Union subsidiary: Statute on Tax Incentives, Article 33(g).

41 Terra, Ben and Wattel, Peter, *European Tax Law*, 3rd ed. (Kluwer Law International, 2001) at pp. 364 and 365.

42 European Community Treaty, Article 87.

43 The Organization for Economic Cooperation and Development Report of 2000 is, therefore, prior to new measures regarding transparency and the exchange of information.

Albeit the Directive dates back to 1977, its Article 7(3) could bring serious restrictions upon the effective exchange of information in schemes such as the Portuguese ones cited above. This Article states that Member States do not need to produce or exchange information if that means breaching their internal legislation.[44] Countries must exchange information regarding fiscal matters within the limits of their own legislation. Portugal has followed the same attitude when concluding tax treaties.[45] With the new legislation, a new procedure for the exchange of information might bring effects yet difficult to foresee.

Madeiran trusts have a confidentiality clause regarding the settlor and the beneficiaries, which supposedly continues to guarantee their secrecy. Under Decree Law Number 149/94, trusts having a duration of more than one year must be registered with the Commercial Registry, giving information on the settlor, beneficiaries and trustees.

Offshore banks are exempt from tax on income derived from transactions with non-Portuguese residents. Nevertheless, they must keep records and accounts for annual inspections that check whether there were, and to what extent there were, taxable transactions.

Conclusion

Luxembourg and Switzerland abstained from voting on the 1998 OECD Report and consider themselves not bound by the document or its recommendations. According to Luxembourg, by focusing on movable activities, the report had adopted "a partial and unbalanced approach".[46] Switzerland took the same view, and claimed that the report had selected criteria to define tax havens that dealt with the sovereignty of states.[47] The United States had initially criticized the project, its reasons having turned on the legitimacy of the initiative

44 *See* Richard Burke, Member of the European Commission, at the 2nd European Tax Consultants Congress, published by Kluwer Law on behalf of the Confederation Fiscal Europeene, 1982, at p. 97.

45 Portugal–United Kingdom Tax Treaty, Article 25(2)(b) and Portugal–France Tax Treaty, Article 27(2)(b) state that there should be no exchange of information in cases where the information could not be gathered under domestic law.

46 Luxembourg's statement in the Harmful Tax Competition Report 1998, at p. 74.

47 Switzerland's statement in the Harmful Tax Competition Report 1998, at p. 77.

compared with the power of states to legislate on fiscal matters.[48] Later on, as the OECD demonstrated a slight deviation in the path of the project, now more focused on the exchange of information, the Treasury Secretary, Paul O'Neil, showed support for the initiative.[49]

Most countries cannot offer tax incentives as attractive as those of many other countries without threatening their own tax base, which is eroded by the migration of their residents' liabilities to low-tax jurisdictions. Moreover, taxpayers not using international schemes to minimize their tax obligations subsidize most of the activities of these states.[50] This affects confidence and compliance within tax systems. In some jurisdictions, banking and legal secrecy are also a clear opportunity for the evasion of other countries' taxes, not to mention the use of such schemes for money laundering and other illegal activities. In the case of Madeira, the schemes to attract business artificially interfere with the normal flow of capital in the EC, where its schedules violate provisions such as Article 10 (duty of loyalty) and Article 87 (State aid) of the EC Treaty.

If it is right to affirm, on one hand, that countries have the right to legislate on their legal and fiscal matters,[51] it does not seem wrong to say, on the other hand, that practices largely recognized as harmful might be fought by other jurisdictions that feel damaged by them.[52] Countries' individual measures to defend their tax bases from harmful tax competition have proved of little success.[53] The possible schemes

---

48 The 2001 Report clearly states that it is not about "dictating to any country what should be the appropriate level of tax rates". On the other hand, the United States Treasury Secretary under the Bush Administration, Mr. Paul O'Neil, says that "the United States does not support efforts to dictate to any country what its own tax rates should be".

49 http://www.ecommercetax.com/doc/072901.htm.

50 "Though society is not founded on a contract, and though no good purpose is answered by inventing a contract to deduce social obligations from it, everyone who receives the protection of society owes a return for the benefit . . .": Mill, John Stuart, *On Liberty*, Elizabeth Rapaport (ed.) (Hackett Pulishing Company Inc., Cambridge) at p. 73.

51 Kureshi, A.H., "The Freedom of a State to Legislate in Fiscal Matters under General International Law", *Bulletin of the IBFD*, 1987, at p. 14.

52 Article 38(1)(c) of the Statute of the International Court of Justice recognizes, though it does not list, the existence of the general principles of law recognized by civilized nations.

53 ". . . it is likely that the main effect of CFC legislation has been to induce firms to reorganize their offshore subsidiary structures. This may have resulted in the repatriation of a higher proportion of retained foreign earnings; but to a significant extent, companies have been able to avoid the CFC rules": Picciotto, Sol, *Taxation of International Business: A Study in the Internationalization of Business Regulation* (George Weidenfeld and Nicolson Ltd., 1993) at pp. 149 and 150.

to avoid or evade tax and the intentional aid of jurisdictions' sovereignty are enemies very difficult to fight.[54] For these reasons, the OECD has decided to use its expertise and political force to help curb tax competition, aiming to achieve a comprehensive view of how harmful tax practices affect the location of investments and undermine countries' tax bases. The initiative seems, therefore, legitimate insofar as the work with Member States achieves reasonable results compared to the work with non-members.

The work on preferential tax regimes has its critics. Firstly, the difference between tax schemes that would be "potentially harmful" and tax havens is not defined, except for the "ring fencing" feature. The geographical area "inside the ring" can be classed as a separate dependency of the country and, therefore, be called a tax haven. It has been claimed that the difference set by the OECD would not go beyond the fact that preferential tax regimes are found in OECD member countries and that tax havens are mostly non-member jurisdictions. Besides, one could take as rather cautious and euphemistic the definition of a preferential tax regime contained in the 2000 Progress Report.[55]

A country like Panama, for example, has special rules of taxation that can enable investors to pay no or very little tax. It also has tight rules guaranteeing secrecy of operations and no effective exchange of information on tax matters. Moreover, as in Madeira, doing business from Panama does not necessarily mean doing business while in Panama, as the country's legal framework permits investors to carry out their activities anywhere in the world. Also, as in Madeira, in order to enjoy most of the beneficial regimes of the Colón Free Zone in Panama, one cannot do business with Panamanian residents. According to the guidelines set by the OECD, Panama is a tax haven. Madeira, however, has a preferential regime, even though it has other characteristics of offshore centers, such as good communications and an over-developed financial sector.

54 "Harmful tax competition could never exist without the State's participation in the avoidance or evasion of revenue committed by non-residents in their territory": Rosembuj, Tulio, *Intertax*, Volume 27 (Kluwer Law International, 1999) at p. 316.

55 Progress Report 2000, at p. 12.

It could be argued that, since both tax havens and preferential tax regimes are targeted as harmful, the distinction would be mere rhetoric. However, the OECD proposes different attitudes towards (uncooperative) tax havens and preferential tax regimes — retaliation to the former and self-assessment for the latter. Moreover, the fact that the country isolates the geographic or economic area of such regimes suggests that the country is aware of the economic damage of the schemes in such a way that it prevents any harmful effects to its own economy. If one talks about fairness in international commerce, these two issues are quite peculiar.

The path followed by Madeira is not unique. As soon as the island got its desired autonomy, with the support of the Central Government, it decided to offer itself as an attractive place for offshore business. This has been the path followed by several jurisdictions and dependencies with difficulties in developing their local economy. Albeit economic policies, taxation included, can create a desirable artificial environment for business, it has been decided for decades that the market should follow, as far as possible, rules of efficiency in supply and demand to allow the creation and circulation of wealth.[56]

On the other hand, though the use of tax incentives to develop certain areas might help to cope with problems of employment and minimum economic activity, it prevents the region itself from raising as much revenue as it would have done had it chosen other alternatives of economic growth.[57] The table below shows relevant data regarding the IRC in Portugal's four major taxable centers in 1996. The list includes Funchal, the capital of Madeira, wherein most of the IBC companies are registered.

---

56 "Were the Americans, either by combination or by any other sort of violence, to stop the importation of European manufactures . . . they would retard instead of accelerating the further increase in the value of their annual produce, and would obstruct instead of promoting the progress of their country towards real wealth and greatness": Smith, Adam, *The Wealth of Nations* (Penguin Books) at p. 466.

57 "Although the stimulus of tax incentives may be desirable in economically less developed countries, the costs of such incentives in terms of government revenue sacrifices are generally of considerable importance": Heller and Kauffman, *Tax Incentives for Industry in Less Developed Countries* (Law School of Harvard University, Cambridge, 1963) at p. 178.

District	Companies	Amount of Business	Taxable Income	Actual Corporation Tax
Setubal	13,775	1,849,095,723,173	51,321,320,316	15,482,179,165
Funchal	5,047	973,533,091,350	124,140,856,686	3,154,474,764
Porto	39,268	6,051,138,427,925	131,917,558,325	39,580,725,085
Lisboa	75,095	17,593,444,958,150	874,881,325,281	295,659,847,167

Source: Diretoria Geral de Impostos, Minister of Finance, Portugal, 1996.
All values are in Escudos, the former Portuguese currency.

The table shows that, though Setubal has got more than two and a half times the number of companies as Funchal, it has half the taxable income, but its IRC contribution is almost five times the revenue raised by Funchal. Porto has a taxable income slightly bigger than that of Funchal, but its IRC contribution is over ten times that of Madeira's capital. After a brief look at the table, interpreted according to what has been shown so far, as to the tax system of Madeira, one could affirm that:

(1) The volume of business carried out in Madeira is disproportionate to the IRC it collects;

(2) Some people are not contributing to the burden of taxation with the rest of the country at a time when Portugal has been raising its value added tax (VAT) rates and demanding fiscal austerity;[58] and

(3) The island and the country might not benefit sufficiently from the tax incentives granted to investors, even if the level of employment has been significantly raised by such tax incentives.

Despite the new legislation adopted by Portugal diminishing Madeira's tax incentives and improving the system of disclosure of information, the *Madeira* v. *Commission* affair is not yet settled. The island's tax system is still under investigation by the Commissioners, and the schedule prepared by the Portuguese Government has not received any formal approval from the EC.[59]

In the meantime, some countries have taken legislative measures they consider valid to defend their tax bases from EU preferential

58 *The Economist*, Volume 363, Number 8273, 18–24 May 2002, at pp. 48–49.

59 "The conflict between Madeira and the EU was supposed to end with a compromise on 29 December 2000 when the Portuguese Parliament passed a schedule of tax rate changes effective in the Free Zone of Madeira from 1 January until 31 December 2011."

regimes like Madeira. Regarding the Parent-Subsidiary Directive, for example, France withholds tax if the final link is not to an EU shareholder. On inbound flows, it does not grant relief when a French company establishes an EU subsidiary to convert taxable income, such as royalties and interest, into non-taxable income, that is, distribution of profits.[60] In both situations, a Madeiran SGPS could be used for tax avoidance if French measures are not applied. However, applied in a broad formula, they might undermine the intent of the Parent-Subsidiary Directive[61] and be contrary to the free movement of establishment, as has been held in *Commission* v. *France and St. Gobain*.[62] In these cases, different treatment granted to EU parents, subsidiaries and shareholders was considered contrary to the freedom of establishment.[63]

Problems of residence might also arise with Madeiran entities, since the effective management and control tests can bring different interpretations, especially within the EC. In order to apply CFC legislation, for example, the United Kingdom makes reference to entities controlled by United Kingdom residents.[64] The transfer of management and control to modify residence status, which is one of the advantages offered by Madeira, could also bring problems within the EC, such as those raised in *Daily Mail*.[65] In this situation, however, the problem would not be to take the place of management and control from the island, but to install it in another EC country under the principle of the free movement of establishment.

While the Code of Conduct of Business Transactions is only a proposed set of principles and guidelines according to EC Law,[66] Member States can rely on the work of the European Commission and other

60 Survey of the Implementation of the EC Corporate Tax Directives, coordinated by Wijnen, W.F.G. (IBFD Publications, 1995) at pp. 414 and 426.

61 Survey of the Implementation of the EC Corporate Tax Directives, coordinated by Wijnen, W.F.G. (IBFD Publications, 1995) at pp. 429 and 430.

62 EC Cases 270/83 and 307/97.

63 EC Treaty, Articles 43 and 48.

64 Income and Corporate Taxes Act 1988, Section 747(1).

65 EC Case Number 81/1987.

66 "The Code of Conduct is a political commitment (gentlemen's agreement) . . . It defines harmful tax measures as 'measures (including administrative practices) which affect or may affect in a significant way the location of business activity in the Community' and which provide for a significantly lower effective level of taxation than the general level of taxation in the Member State concerned . . .": Terra, Ben and Wattel, Peter, *European Tax Law*, 3rd ed. (Kluwer Law International, 2001) at p. 193.

remedies available to avoid the use of schemes for tax avoidance within the EC. While Community Law develops, the struggle between the four freedoms, Community loyalty and State aid will remain in the hands of the European Court of Justice (ECJ). Meanwhile, jurisdictions such as Madeira can assess the benefits they have been taking from their preferential schemes, bearing in mind that the revenues not collected from their investors could perhaps be EC revenue used to improve its infrastructures and facilities.

Foreign Investment in E-Commerce in China

Anthony W. Y. Chan, Padraig Walsh and Wynne Mok
Barlow Lyde & Gilbert
Hong Kong, China

Introduction

This chapter examines the road China is taking to regulate its e-commerce industry and surveys some of the key legislative measures involved in this process. Long before China acceded to the World Trade Organization (WTO), numerous commercial opportunities existed in the Chinese e-commerce industry due to the density of population and relative affluence of its major urban centers. However, many sectors were highly regulated, and there were often insurmountable obstacles to foreign investment. China's recent accession to the WTO has heralded a new impetus towards liberalizing the e-commerce and associated communications sectors, despite a current downturn in both sectors.

The recent troubled global history of e-commerce has underlined that e-commerce does not revolutionize the basic precepts of commerce, but is simply a new business delivery system that can be markedly more efficient depending on the market sector. Perhaps more troubling from the perspective of a foreign investor seeking to apply e-commerce precepts to his business in China is that the advent of e-commerce, rather than eliminating regulatory barriers, has hitherto increased the need to be extra careful about legal and regulatory requirements in China.

Past Restrictions

Much of the regulation of e-commerce is covered under the aegis of legislation applicable to the telecommunications sector. Various telecommunications-related markets (such as mobile telephony services,

D.Campbell and S.Woodley (eds.), The Comparative Law Yearbook of International Business 2003, 203-231

local VSAT communications services, telephone information services, computer information services and e-mail services) have ostensibly been open to private investment since 1993. This openness has been more apparent than real, however, given the circumspect and prohibitive policy on foreign investment that the Chinese Government has from time to time followed in these sectors. This restrictive approach was expressly set out, in the first instance, in the Opinion of the Ministry for Post and Telecommunications on Further Strengthening the Administration of Telecommunications Services Market of 3 August 1993,[1] and subsequently reiterated in the Tentative Regulations for the Administration of the Liberalized Telecommunications Services Markets promulgated by the Ministry of Post and Telecommunications on 10 November 1995. Lest there was any shadow of a doubt on government policy, the Interim Rules on Guiding Foreign Investment Orientation and the Catalogue for Guiding Foreign Investment issued in mid-1995[2] contained a blanket prohibition on foreign investment in telecommunications businesses.

Not all foreign investors were willing to subordinate their "gold rush" plan to rules and regulations. A number of investors adopted the "Chinese-Chinese-Foreign" investment model to make investments in the telecommunications and e-commerce industry. However, the prospects of this investment model have turned out to be false, just as the hopes of any prospectors in any "gold rush", with the subsequent disapproval by the Chinese Government of such investment model.

China's Accession to the World Trade Organization

As China's industries open up following China's accession to the WTO, the first question a foreign investor in e-commerce projects needs to address is whether such investment is permitted. The answer usually lies in the Rules on Guiding Foreign Investment Orientation[3]

1 The Ministry of Post and Telecommunications is now the Ministry for the Information Industry. Article 5 of the Opinion states that "Foreign entities shall not operate or participate in the operation of telecommunications services in China".

2 The State Development Planning Commission, State Economic and Trade Commission and the Ministry of Foreign Trade and Economic Cooperation promulgated the Interim Rules on Guiding Foreign Investment Orientation and the Catalogue for Guiding Foreign Investment on 20 June 1995.

3 These Regulations were promulgated by the State Council on 11 February 2002.

(the Foreign Investment Rules) and the Catalogue of Encouraged Foreign Investments Industries[4] (the Catalogue). The Foreign Investment Regulations and the Catalogue replaced the earlier Foreign Investment Rules and Catalogue of 1995. Under the Foreign Investment Rules, foreign investment projects invested in by foreign-invested enterprises (FIEs) are divided into four categories, namely, encouraged, permitted, restricted and prohibited projects. (Projects that are not encouraged, restricted and prohibited projects are deemed to be permitted projects under the Foreign Investment Rules).[5]

That being said, specific legislative measures will also need examining for every project. A key piece of legislation is the Administration of Foreign-Invested Telecommunications Enterprises Regulations (the FITE Regulations).[6] The FITE Regulations are the first of a number of significant steps showing China's commitment to the gradual opening of its telecommunications and the e-commerce markets to foreign investment. However, stringent requirements and vaguely worded procedures still abound.

Under the FITE Regulations, foreign-invested telecommunications enterprises (FITEs) are required to be sino-foreign equity joint ventures, as opposed to co-operative joint ventures. Among other things, this means that a foreign investor's profits and losses as a joint venture party are shared proportionately in accordance with its joint venture interest and cannot be adjusted freely. The registered capital of a FITE providing basic telecommunications services (BTS)[7] cannot be

4 The Foreign Investment Industrial Guidance Catalogue was jointly promulgated by the State Development Planning Commission, the State Economic and Trade Commission and the Ministry of Foreign Trade and Economic Cooperation on 11 March 2002.

5 Foreign Investment Rules, Article 4.

6 The Administration of Foreign-Funded Telecommunications Enterprises Provisions were promulgated by the State Council on 11 December 2001 and came into effect on 1 January 2002.

7 Basic telecommunications services and value added telecommunications services are defined in the Telecoms Regulations. Basic telecommunications services refers to the business of providing public network infrastructure, public data transmission and basic voice communications services, while value added telecommunications services are defined as telecommunications and information services provided through the public network infrastructure. A detailed classification of telecommunications services is attached to the Telecoms Regulations, according to which, value added telecommunications services include Internet access services and Internet information services.

not less than RMB2-billion. For a foreign investor involved in an e-commerce project involving value added telecommunications services (VATS), a FITE providing such services must have registered capital of RMB10-million.

Foreign capital contribution to a FITE engaging in the provision of BTS is limited to forty-nine per cent of the total capital in the FITE,[8] whereas foreign investors in FITEs providing VATS may hold up to fifty per cent of the total equity.[9] As explained later, such restrictions on foreign capital contribution will be loosened gradually. Territorial restrictions were imposed at the initial stage of liberalization of the telecommunications market.[10] However, foreign investors may now establish joint venture enterprises engaging in telecommunications services businesses in seventeen cities, with the understanding that all territorial restrictions will be removed in time.

Investors, whether Chinese or foreign enterprises, must satisfy certain stringent qualitative requirements before establishing a FITE in China. These qualitative requirements are stated in Articles 8 and 9 of the FITE Regulations, and are summarized in Appendix A. Cumulatively, these restrictions and requirements amount to a significant hurdle (if not a barrier) to entry into the Chinese market.

The establishment of a FITE, whether engaging in BTS or VATS, nonetheless remains a highly regulated process. Application must be made to the Ministry for the Information Industry (the MII) or the relevant provincial or municipal telecommunications administrative authority where the FITE proposes to do VATS business. Documents, such as articles of association, a feasibility report, the project proposal and documents proving compliance with Articles 8, 9 and/or 10

8 Administration of Foreign-Invested Telecommunications Enterprises Regulations, Article 6.

9 Administration of Foreign-Invested Telecommunications Enterprises Regulations, Article 7.

10 Article 4 of the Administration of Foreign-Funded Telecommunications Enterprises Provisions states that, "The territory within which a Foreign-Funded Telecommunications Enterprise may provide its services shall be determined by the State Council's department in charge of the information industry in accordance with relevant regulations". This shall be read together with the Schedule of Specific Commitments on Services annexed to the World Trade Organization's Protocol of Accession of China, which provides that foreign investment shall be firstly allowed in Beijing, Shanghai and Guangzhou and then gradually extended to other cities in China, including Chengdu, Chongqing, Dailian, Fuzhou, Hangzhou, Nanjing, Ningbo, Qingdao, Shenyang, Shenzhen, Xiamen, Xian, Taiyuan and Wuhan.

of the FITE Regulations[11] must be submitted for examination. The procedures for obtaining a business license to engage in BTS or VATS business are often subject to regulatory and administrative delay, which is a risk frequently associated with doing business in China.

The timetable regarding the gradual opening up of e-commerce and associated related telecommunications markets is summarized in Appendix B. The pace of change is frustrated by the uncertainty that remains concerning when, or if, foreign investors will be able to establish wholly foreign-owned enterprises providing VATS and domestic and international telecommunications services. On the other hand, foreign investors engaging in on-line wholesaling and retailing business will be much better off, as wholly foreign-owned enterprises will be permitted by 11 December 2004.

It is not uncommon for many foreign investors to put their chips on the table and accommodate their aspirations and business plans around the current restrictions in the hope of more favorable regulatory change in the future. For instance, while some telecommunications and e-commerce services are in the restricted category, technology development is encouraged by the Chinese Government. Some foreign investors who cannot wait for the full liberalization of the market have risked adopting legally questionable techniques as a lever to position themselves to become future players in a fully liberalized market.

Legal Overview

Prior to surveying various areas of the e-commerce industry, it is essential to note a number of frequently raised issues associated with e-commerce in China.

11 In the case of a foreign-invested enterprise engaging in value added telecommunications services within a province, autonomous region or municipality, a project proposal is not required. Article 14 of the Administration of Foreign-Invested Telecommunications Enterprises Regulations lays down the requisite contents of a feasibility report and project proposal. Further, where a feasibility report is required, the law allows the applicant to defer the submission of the feasibility report for one year.

Foreign Trade, Joint Venture, Tax and Exchange Laws

As the importation of foreign goods or services is likely to be involved, the provisions in the Foreign Trade Law, and other relevant licensing requirements and quotas, must be complied with. China also has a relatively well-developed body of joint venture laws relating to sino-foreign equity and cooperative joint ventures, and for wholly foreign-owned investment enterprises. These laws further complement China's strict foreign exchange regulations relating to the use, exchange and repatriation of foreign currency and tax regime.

Intellectual Property Rights

Foreign investors are entitled to protection of the intellectual property rights in their products to be sold and distributed via the Internet under applicable intellectual property legislation in China. Under the Copyright Law,[12] copyright confers on its owner various moral and economic rights, including the right of publication, the right of reproduction and the right to protect the copyright work against misrepresentation and distortion. While there is a formal registration procedure for copyright in China, registration of copyright does not confer additional rights upon the copyright owner. Copyright registration can be defeated by providing the relevant proof to the court.

The Copyright Law makes clear that certain acts constitute copyright infringement which will lead to civil liability. Such infringing acts include the publication of a copyright work without permission from the copyright owner and plagiarism. The court has the discretion to order the cessation of infringing acts and the payment of damages based on the actual losses of the copyright owner. In addition, the court may order that the unlawful income of the infringing party be confiscated. Infringing acts, such as reproducing and distributing to the public via an information network without permission from the copyright owner, also have criminal implications.

Provided that an invention, a utility model or a design is patentable under the Patent Law,[13] its owner may apply for registration to the

12 The Copyright Law and its Implementing Rules came into effect on 1 June 1991 and were revised on 27 October 2001.

13 The revised Patent Law and the revised Implementing Rules came into force in July 2001.

State Intellectual Property Office (the SIPO). The term of patent protection is twenty years for inventions and ten years for utility models and designs. Any exploitation of a patent without the patent holder's authorization constitutes an infringement of the patent right. Negotiation is the obligatory first port of call for a patent holder and, thereafter, he may commence proceedings in the people's court. Interim injunctive measures are available to immediately stop any infringing acts prior to the full trial.

A common trap for foreign investors occurs where an infringing party has filed for patent protection before the proper patent holder has marketed the relevant product in China. In such circumstances, the rightful owner of the patent may request the Patent Re-examination Board to declare the registered patent invalid. There is a right of appeal to the people's court.

China, being a signatory to the Trade-Related Aspects of Intellectual Property Rights (TRIPS) Agreement, accords protection of international standards to trademark owners within its territory. Trademark applications are reviewed by examiners of the Chinese Trademark Office. Upon submission of the application for registration of a trademark, the applicant must wait for a period of three months. After the expiry of this period, the application may proceed to registration if no opposition to the application has been filed. A successful registration is valid for ten years. Unsuccessful applicants may appeal to the Trademark Review and Adjudication Board within fifteen days of the notification of rejection.

The Trademark Law[14] provides a list of acts which constitute trademark infringement. As in the context of patent infringement, amicable forms of dispute resolution must be sought before resorting to the courts.

Domain Name and Website Name Registration

In China, protection of an enterprise's domain name, whether in Chinese or otherwise, is as important as protection of its trade name. Registration of domain names is governed by the China Internet Domain Name Regulations[15] (the Internet Domain Name Regulations) and the

14 The Trademark Law was promulgated on 2 August 1982, revised on 27 October 2001 and came into force on 1 December 2001.

15 The China Internet Domain Name Regulations were promulgated by the Information Office of the State Council on 1 August 2002.

China Internet Network Information Center (CNNIC) Implementing Rules of Domain Name Registration.[16] The CNNIC is the organization responsible for handling the registration of domain names.[17] To provide an opposition mechanism, the CNNIC has adopted the CNNIC Domain Name Dispute Resolution Policy and the Rules for CNNIC Domain Name Dispute Resolution Policy[18] (the Dispute Resolution Measures).

Domain name owners are required to register their website names with the Beijing Administrative Bureau for Industry and Commerce (the Beijing AIC).[19] This registration system works in favor of the website owners. Analogous to trademark owners, a website owner enjoys exclusive rights over its registered website name.[20] Applicants for registration of a website name are required to apply on-line.[21] This website is managed by the Beijing AIC. The examination of website names is governed by the "first-to-file" rule.[22]

Owners of profit-making websites[23] must record and register the websites with the Beijing AIC and obtain recording and registration certificates for profit-making websites in accordance with the Interim Measures on the Administration of Recording and Registration of Profit-Making Websites.[24]

---

16 These Rules came into effect on 1 December 2002.

17 The website of the CNNIC is www.cnnic.net.cn.

18 These came into effect on 30 September 2002.

19 Interim Measures on Administration of Registration of Website Names and their Implementing Rules, both promulgated on 15 August 2000 by the Administrative Department for Industry and Commerce of Beijing Municipality. Article 4 defines "owner of website" as the owner of the domain name of a website.

20 Website Names Registration Interim Measures, Article 7.

21 At www.hd315.gov.cn: Website Names Registration Interim Measures, Article 12; Implementing Rules, Article 2.

22 Article 19 of the Website Names Registration Interim Measures provides that where two or more applicants apply for registration of the same website name, the Department of Registration of the Beijing Administrative Bureau for Industry and Commerce shall carry out a preliminary examination of the website name applied for.

23 Article 2 of the Profit-Making Website Registration Interim Measures defines "profit-making website" as an electro-platform established by means of Internet technology and granted an independent domain name applied for with the administrative department for domain names for the purpose of issuing information, advertising, setting up e-mail boxes, developing business affairs on the Internet or providing others with Internet space for conducting these acts.

24 These Interim Measures were promulgated by the Beijing Administrative Bureau for Industry and Commerce on 15 August 2000, together with their Implementing Rules.

Advertisements

Enterprises engaging in on-line sales invariably publish advertisements to promote their products on their respective websites. Such enterprises must comply with the provisions of the Advertisement Law.[25]

The rule of thumb is that all advertisements must be truthful, lawful and comply with the requirements of socialist cultural and ideological development.[26] Advertisements for pharmaceuticals, medical apparatus and instruments, agricultural pesticides and veterinary drugs are subject to specific provisions and approval systems.[27] No advertisements are allowed for tobacco under Article 18 of the Advertisement Law.

The activities of advertising agents and advertisement publishers are also regulated by the Advertisement Law. In particular, advertising agents and advertisement publishers are under the somewhat burdensome obligation to verify the contents of advertisements in accordance with the provisions in the Advertisement Law,[28] including establishing and maintaining a registration, examination and verification system.[29] The Advertisement Examination Authority has the authority to stop the publication of any advertisement which fails to comply with the provisions of the Advertisement Law. A fine based on the amount of advertising expenses or charges, not exceeding five times such expenses or charges, may be imposed on any entity for non-compliance.[30]

Consumer Protection

Business operators manufacturing and selling products or providing services to the public must comply with the Law on the Protection of

---

25 An "advertiser" is defined in the Advertisement Law as any legal person, economic organization or individual that, for the purpose of promoting the sale of goods or providing services, designs, produces and publishes advertisements either by itself or by commissioning others to do so. Apart from advertisers, the activities of advertising agents and publishers are also governed by the Advertisement Law.

26 Advertisement Law, Article 3.

27 Advertisement Law, Articles 14–17. Under Article 34, such advertisements shall be subject to examination prior to their publication in accordance with the provisions in the Advertisement Law.

28 Advertisement Law, Article 27.

29 Advertisement Law, Article 28.

30 Advertisement Law, Chapter 5.

Consumers' Rights and Interests (the Consumer Protection Law).[31] Various rights are conferred on consumers by the Consumer Protection Law, which include:

(1) The right to be assured of personal and property safety;
(2) The right to be entitled to true information concerning products supplied or services provided;
(3) The right to a fair deal, which includes the right to a quality guarantee and the right to reasonable prices for products or services; and
(4) The right to be compensated for personal injury or property damage resulting from purchase and consumption of the products or services.

Such consumers' rights give rise to corresponding obligations on business operators, such as:

(1) An obligation to guarantee that the products supplied or services provided meet the personal and property safety requirements, including giving accurate instructions and warnings, information on correct ways of usage and methods to prevent damage;
(2) An obligation to provide true information about products or services and advertising information, including answering inquiries;
(3) Obligations to guarantee the quality, function, usage and life expectancy of products under normal situations, and not to impose unfair or unreasonable terms on consumers through standard contracts, notices or announcements or reduce or escape liability for infringement of consumers' rights;
(4) An obligation to compensate consumers for their personal injury, death or property loss as a result of defective or non-conforming products, deliberate delay or unreasonable refusal to repair, remanufacture or replace a defective or non-conforming product upon a consumer's request, in accordance with the law; and
(5) An obligation to listen to consumers' opinions on products or services.

---

31 The Consumer Protection Law was promulgated by the National People's Congress on 31 October 1993 and came into effect on 1 January 1994.

Given that the Consumer Protection Law was promulgated at a time when on-line business was not popular, it was hardly within the contemplation of the draftsmen that it should cover business operators selling their products or services on-line. However, there is no reason why the Consumer Protection Law should not apply to business operators who choose to sell their products or services on-line instead of in more conventional ways.

Local legislation also plays a key role in implementing country-wide legislation. For instance, the Beijing AIC promulgated the Protection of the Lawful Rights and Interests of Consumers in On-line Economic Activities Notice[32] (the Notice) to specifically apply existing consumer protection measures to on-line business conducted within the territory of Beijing. On-line auctions, however, remain outside the scope of the Notice. The Notice is based on and mirrors the Consumer Protection Law. It is significant in that it also regulates website owners, including those providing electronic platforms for business operators to sell products and services. It explicitly provides that these website owners must comply with the obligations imposed on business operators by the Consumer Protection Law, and are further obliged to:

(1) Clearly indicate prices of products or services on their websites;
(2) Clearly indicate a product's place of origin, producer, specifications, grade and quality;
(3) Respond to consumers' inquiries regarding, *inter alia*, quality, performance, main ingredients and production date;
(4) Prevent false publicity about the products or services; and
(5) Meet personal and property safety requirements.

In addition, the Notice provides that website owners must manage their businesses, and require business operators who use their websites to operate their businesses, in a lawful manner and in good faith. The Notice does not provide any details as to how website owners should comply with this requirement, nor does it prescribe any penalty if website owners fail to monitor the activities of business operators. Foreign investors must wait and see how the Municipal AIC will implement the Notice. This is, however, a shot across the boughs for on-line businesses, and is indicative of possible similar national legislation in the future.

32 The Notice was promulgated and came into effect on 28 June 2000.

Selected Industry Areas

It must be said that, despite regulatory and procedural uncertainties, the gradual liberalization of e-commerce-related markets holds out the possibility of more opportunities available for foreign investors, particularly in such areas as:

(1) On-line transactions;
(2) On-line banking;
(3) On-line auctions;
(4) The provision of certain e-commerce services;
(5) Technology transfer; and
(6) Venture capital.

On-Line Transactions Generally

In early 1999, the National People's Congress passed the Unified Contract Law,[33] which recognizes the validity of a contract in any form. Article 11 specifically defines "written form" as any form which renders the information contained in a contract capable of being reproduced in tangible form, such as a written agreement, letter or electronic text, including telegram, telex, facsimile, electronic data interchange and e-mail. Accordingly, all principles of contract law applicable to conventional contracts are applicable to electronic contracts.

To promote international commerce, the Electronic Commerce Administrative Department (the ECAD) of the Ministry of Foreign Trade and Economic Cooperation (MOFTEC) has implemented a promotion scheme under which promotional activities are to be organized to promote international e-commerce operators (IEOs) approved by the ECAD. IEOs covered by the scheme include:

(1) Enterprises which operate e-commerce via their own websites or websites established by others;
(2) Enterprises which provide information consultancy services to the above enterprises, including the setting up of databases and websites; and
(3) Enterprises which provide software necessary for logistics, customer services and electronic transactions.

33 The Unified Contract Law was adopted by the National People's Congress on 15 March 1999.

On-Line Banking

The Chinese Government has put much emphasis on the development and promotion of on-line banking. On 29 June 2001, the People's Bank of China (the PBOC) issued the Administration of On-line Banking Services Tentative Procedures, which are applicable to all types of banking institutions subject to PBOC approval and supervision, that is, including equity joint venture banks and wholly foreign-owned banks. Under the On-line Banking Services Tentative Procedures, the provision of on-line banking services is subject to examination and approval by the PBOC. Banks offering on-line services must fulfil certain qualitative requirements, including possession of internal risk management systems, uniform computer systems, effective computer networks and qualified management and technical personnel. Once approved, such banks are under the obligation to ensure network and information security stated in the Internet Information Services Procedures. The PBOC has since promulgated implementing rules setting out factors to be considered by the PBOC in approving the provision of on-line banking services.[34]

As in many other jurisdictions, security aspects of on-line banking services in China remain high on the PBOC's agenda. To ensure the necessary security for on-line financial transactions and thus facilitate the development of on-line banking, led by the PBOC, the China Financial Certification Group was established in August 2001.[35] The Group seeks to provide security services for the entire financial sector in China.

On-Line Auctions

On-line auctions are increasingly popular in China as much as anywhere else. Foreign investors with plans to establish on-line auction

34 Provisions Relevant to the Implementation of the Administration of On-line Banking Services Tentative Procedures promulgated by the People's Bank of China on 10 April 2002. Factors to be considered include risk management capabilities, security assessment, contingency plans and internal monitoring capabilities of the banking institution concerned.

35 www.entrust.com/news, 30 August 2001. The China Financial Certification Group is a joint venture of thirteen banking institutions, including Industrial and Commercial Bank, China Construction Bank and Agricultural Bank of China.

sites should be mindful of the Auction Law,[36] which standardizes auction activities conducted in China. Enterprises engaged in conducting on-line auctions must comply with key requirements on registered capital and employees.[37] Under the Auction Law, both tangible and intangible property, such as property rights, can be made available for auction. The auction of certain items, such as cultural relics, may be subject to examination and approval by the relevant supervisory authority. As auctioneers, auction enterprises must disclose any defect in an object to potential bidders, necessitating cautious document verification and object examination processes. Auctioneers must obtain the prior agreement of their clients as to the amount of commission as, in the absence of such agreement, the Auction Law provides that the auctioneer's commission is capped at five per cent of the transaction price.[38]

Provision of Certain E-Commerce Services

The MII promulgated the Measures on the Administration of Licenses for the Operation of Telecommunications (the Licensing Measures) on 26 December 2001, which came into effect on 1 January 2002. Under the Licensing Measures, there are three types of telecommunications service operation licenses having an impact on e-commerce providers:

(1) BTS operation license;
(2) Inter-provincial VATS operation license; and
(3) Intra-provincial VATS operation license.

The definitions and classifications of telecommunications services stated in the Telecoms Regulations are also relevant in this regard. The respective requirements for obtaining each of the above telecommunications service operation licenses are set out in Appendix C.

More than a year before the promulgation of the Licensing Measures, the State Council had already created a licensing regime in respect of "Internet information service providers" (ISPs). Under the

---

36 The Auction Law was promulgated on 5 July 1996 and came into effect on 1 January 1997.

37 Auction Law, Articles 12 and 15.

38 Auction Law, Articles 56 and 57. Article 58 provides that, should the transaction fall through, the auction enterprise will be entitled to reimbursement of reasonable expenses.

Administration of Internet Information Service Procedures (the Internet Procedures),[39] Internet information services (IIS) are divided into commercial and non-commercial IIS. Commercial ISPs must obtain an Internet information services value added telecommunications services operation license[40] from the MII (or the relevant provincial telecommunications administration authorities), while non-commercial ISPs only need to be registered.

Internet information services are defined as the activities of providing information services via the Internet. As such, mere purveyors of content are not regarded as ISPs for the purposes of the Internet Procedures and do not need a license, even if they provide information to be put on websites for profit. However, it is unclear whether website operators who publish on their websites content provided by others for profit fall within the licensing regime. This, however, seems to be the case as, firstly, the MII has adopted a sweeping approach in respect of Internet activities and, secondly, the Internet Procedures contain provisions seemingly applicable to entities other than ISPs as generally understood. For instance, Article 16 provides that ISPs, upon discovering any information transmitted via their websites which is prohibited, are obliged to stop such transmission. In addition, it is provided that anyone who produces, copies, publishes or spreads any prohibited information may risk the shutting down of its website. It is clear that draftsmen had in mind website operators who provide platforms for disseminating information. In these circumstances, until clear written guidelines are given, foreign investors who intend to launch websites and publish materials provided by others, whether for profit or not, must be mindful of the provisions in the Internet Procedures.

The purpose underpinned by the Internet Information Services Procedures, namely, to ensure network and information security, is manifested in the qualitative requirements and obligations imposed upon licensees. Among other things, license applicants must show that they will implement effective procedures to ensure the security

39 The Internet Procedures were promulgated by the State Council on 25 September 2000.

40 Article 5 of the Internet Information Services Procedures provides that if the information to be provided is about news, education, medical treatment, health, pharmaceuticals or medical apparatus, the prior consent of the relevant authorities must be obtained before applying for an Internet information services value added telecommunications services operation license.

of the network and information transmitted via the Internet.[41] Such procedures must include mechanisms for website security, information confidentiality and security of subscribers' personal information.

More importantly, ISPs must comply with certain stipulated obligations or face immediate shutting down of their websites. These stipulated obligations are:

(1) To ensure the high quality of services to on-line subscribers and lawfulness of the information provided;
(2) To keep a record of the information provided, time of dissemination and the URLs or domain names where the operator engages in services, such as on-line news, publishing or electronic bulletin boards — such information must be kept by the operator for sixty days;[42]
(3) Not to produce, reproduce or disseminate any information which:
    (a) contradicts the fundamental principles stated in the Constitution;
    (b) divulges state secrets or otherwise damages national security;
    (c) affects the interests of the State;
    (d) constitutes racial or ethnic discrimination;
    (e) propagates heretical teachings or feudal superstitions;
    (f) spreads rumors or disrupts social stability;
    (g) is obscene, violent or about gambling;
    (h) is insulting and slanderous; or
    (i) includes such other content as is prohibited under law; and
(4) Upon discovery, to stop the transmission of any information with the above content.

In reality, the Chinese Government may, for its own reasons, block access to websites, as shown in the recent blockage of access to Google.[43] China's strict views towards the divulgence of state secrets and the dissemination of information affecting the interests of the State and the flexibility with which such views are interpreted need to be taken seriously by foreign investors, especially during any period

41 Internet Information Services Procedures, Article 6.

42 Internet service providers are under a similar obligation under the Internet Information Services Procedures, namely, that they must keep records of such information as on-line traffic, on-line subscribers' account numbers and telephone numbers and the URLs or domain names for sixty days.

43 Jay Lyman, "Google Responds to China Ban", 3 September 2002, www.newsFactor.com.

of political uncertainty and sensitivity. Positive steps, such as direct liaison with the relevant authorities and good relationships (*guanxi*), may be an effective way to prevent any liability arising.

Certain on-line information service activities are more specifically regulated. The following are examples.

Internet Publication Services

Any ISP intending to publish selected and edited works created by themselves or others on websites, or to disseminate such works via the Internet to end users for browsing, reading, using or downloading, must seek the prior approval of the General Administration of Press and Public of the MII under the Interim Provisions on the Administration of Internet Publication.[44] Information similar to the prohibited information under the Internet Procedures is also prohibited under the Internet Publication Interim Provisions.

Internet News Publication Services

All websites engaging in news publication require the approval of the Press Office of the State Council and must abide by the Interim Provisions on the Administration of Websites Engaging in News Publication Business.[45] To publish news on a website, a private non-press entity must fulfil certain requirements, including the requirement that news to be published should come from the central press units, press work units under the central government or a press work unit directly subordinate to a province, autonomous region or municipality directly under the central government. News published must not

44 The Internet Publication Interim Provisions were promulgated by the State Press and Publication Administration and the MII on 27 June 2002. Approval by the State Press and Publication Administration or the relevant provincial press and publication administrative bureau is required. Stringent obligations are imposed on operators, such as the obligation to implement an editor responsibility system, whereby specialized editors shall be responsible for censoring contents of the publications to guarantee the integrity of Internet publications.

45 The News Publication Interim Provisions were promulgated by the Press Office of the State Council and the MII on 7 November 2000. Approval by the Press Office is required for the release or republication of Chinese news or foreign news. Only the source of Chinese news specified in the News Publication Interim Provisions is allowed. Non-compliance with the provisions may risk closure of the websites and revocation of the operators' telecommunications service operation licenses.

contain any information stated in Article 13 of the News Publication Interim Provisions, including content that harms State reputation or interests or that damages national unity. Separate approval is necessary for linking Chinese news websites to overseas websites.

Internet Pharmaceutical Information Services

To provide on-line pharmaceutical information, including information on medical instruments, health materials and pharmaceutical packaging materials for profit, an entity needs to undergo an examination and verification process by the State Drug Administration under the Interim Provisions on the Administration of Internet Pharmaceutical Information Services.[46] Separate application for approval must be made if it intends to sell pharmaceutical products on-line.

Apart from the obligations under the Licensing Measures, the MII has also imposed control over the quality of services provided by the telecommunications services operation licensees. Under the Interim Measures on the Administration of Quality Control of Telecommunications Services promulgated on 11 January 2001, the telecommunications department in charge of quality control of telecommunications services is empowered to make inquiries and conduct on-site inspections and random inspections to ensure that the telecommunications services providers comply with the quality standards. Telecommunications services operators are also required to comply with other obligations, including the payment of a quality service security deposit to telecommunications subscribers' complaint centers and the provision of complaint hotlines.

Technology Transfer

An e-commerce-related investment project usually involves some element of technology transfer. China encourages the import of advanced and applied technologies which are to be utilized and adapted for national development, as enshrined in the Regulations on the Control of Import and Export of Technologies.[47]

---

46 The Pharmaceutical Information Services Interim Provisions were promulgated by the State Drug Administration on 11 January 2001.

47 The Technology Import and Export Regulations were promulgated by the State Council on 10 December 2001 and came into effect on 1 January 2002.

The Technology Import and Export Regulations divide technology imports into three categories: prohibited, restricted and permitted. References must be made to the Foreign Trade Law,[48] under which the import or export of certain technologies are prohibited or restricted. The import of restricted technologies is subject to licensing control. Article 16 of the Foreign Trade Law restricts the importation of technologies where such restriction is required for:

(1) Safeguarding national security or public interests;
(2) Developing a particular domestic market;
(3) Control over any form of agricultural, animal husbandry or fishery products;
(4) Safeguarding the State's international financial position and ensuring trade balance; or
(5) Compliance with the requirements under international treaties or agreements signed or acceded to by China.

The import of technologies which will endanger national security, health or the environment are prohibited.[49]

As far as restricted technologies are concerned, the importer must first seek the approval of MOFTEC.[50] Once MOFTEC is satisfied with the contents of the technological import contract[51] submitted by the importer, it will then issue a technological import license. The technological import contract is then registered with MOFTEC. The importation of permitted technologies, however, is subject only to an on-line record filing system.[52]

---

48 The Foreign Trade Law was promulgated on 12 May 1994 and came into effect on 1 July 1994.

49 Foreign Trade Law, Article 17.

50 The Ministry of Foreign Trade and Economic Cooperation was replaced by the Ministry of Commerce on 25 March 2003. The Ministry of Commerce inherited all the functions of the Ministry of Foreign Trade and Economic Cooperation and, old habits dying hard, "MOFTEC" is currently the anacronym of choice.

51 Under the Administration of Registration of Technology Import and Export Contracts Procedures, promulgated by the Ministry of Foreign Trade and Economic Cooperation on 30 December 2001 and effective as of 1 January 2002, technology import and export contracts shall include patent right assignment contracts, patent application right assignment contracts, patent licensing contracts, know-how licensing contracts, technical services contracts and other contracts containing provisions regarding the import or export of technology.

52 Technology Import and Export Regulations, Article 18; Contracts Registration Procedures, Article 3. Registration shall be done on-line at http://info.ec.com.cn.

It is common for technology transfer to form part of the rationale for setting up a joint venture business. Typically, foreign investors transferring their technology to the joint venture will tend to impose restrictions on the joint venture and their Chinese partners to regulate their use of the technology transferred. However, the Technology Import and Export Regulations prohibit contractual arrangements which have the following effects:

(1) The transferee (usually the Chinese entity) being required to accept dispensable conditions incidental to the technological import, including the purchase of dispensable technologies, raw materials, products, equipment or services;
(2) Improvement of the imported technology and the use of such improved technology by the transferee being restricted;
(3) The transferee being restricted in acquiring technology which is identical to or similar to, or which competes with, the imported technology;
(4) The transferee's sources of raw material, parts, components or equipment being unreasonably restricted;
(5) Quantities, varieties and sale prices of the finished products being unreasonably restricted; and
(6) Export channels for the finished products being unreasonably restricted.

The first batch of restricted and prohibited technologies stated in the Catalogue of Technology Prohibited or Restricted from Import into China issued in December 2001 did not appear to include any technologies necessary for the development of the telecommunications and Internet sectors. Therefore, until the promulgation of the next batch, foreign investors can freely enter into contracts for the transfer of telecoms or Internet-related technologies.

Venture Capital

The Chinese Government has, since 1999, recognized the country's potential in converting science and technology (including e-commerce-related technologies) into the establishment of a viable local technology industry, and realized the importance of private equity and venture capital in its technological development. Venture investment mechanisms were given a nod of approval specifically for the then fledgling high-tech industries under the Several Opinions on Establishing a Venture Investment Mechanism (the 1999 Opinions).[53] The prevailing venture investment entities discussed under the 1999 Opinions are the venture capital company (VCC) and the venture capital fund (VCF).

VCCs are described under the 1999 Opinions as non-financial investment companies investing directly in new and high technology companies and mid to small-scale technology-related companies. Investment can be in the form of the provision of services for mid to small-scale technology-related companies. Private enterprises and individuals, including foreign investors, can become shareholders of VCCs. On the other hand, a VCF is described in the 1999 Opinions as a kind of investment fund the specific role of which is to invest in small and medium-sized science and technology enterprises. Exit strategies permitted under the 1999 Opinions include enterprise acquisitions and mergers, equity buy-backs and listing on domestic and overseas stock markets. The 1999 Opinions were brief and offered no more than a framework for further legal development.

It was not until March 2003 that the Provisions on the Administration of Foreign-Invested Venture Capital Enterprises, which offered more legal substance, came into effect.[54] The Foreign-Invested Venture Capital Enterprises Provisions basically mirror the principles under the 1999 Opinions. Under the Foreign-Invested Venture Capital Enterprises Provisions, foreign investors may independently, or together with Chinese parties, establish VCCs, which can be in the form of limited liability equity joint ventures, cooperative joint ventures in the form of limited liability companies or cooperative joint ventures without legal personality. An approval certificate for an FIE issued by MOFTEC is necessary for the establishment of a foreign-invested venture investment enterprise.

Various qualifying conditions must be satisfied. The essential foreign investor in a VCC must be a venture capital business with funds under management in the previous three years of not less than

---

53 The 1999 Opinions were promulgated by the Ministry of Science and Technology, SDPC, State Economic and Trade Commission, Ministry of Finance, People's Bank of China, State Administration of Taxation and China Securities Regulatory Commission on 30 December 1999.

54 The Provisions on the Administration of Foreign-Invested Venture Capital Enterprises were promulgated jointly by the Ministry of Foreign Trade and Economic Cooperation, the MST, the SIAC, the State Tax Administration and SAFE on 30 January 2003.

US $100-million, of which at least US $50-million must have been used for venture capital.[55] Each non-essential Chinese party is required to contribute not less than US $1-million, which must be paid up as registered capital. Given the requirements on Chinese investors, foreign investors may find it difficult to find appropriate Chinese parties with whom they can team up. It has been suggested that a wholly foreign-owned VCC can be formed by an offshore venture investment fund and its manager. However, even if the offshore fund has the requisite investment amount, it is unclear whether MOFTEC would check with the actual investors in the offshore fund to determine whether the requirement on the investment amount is satisfied by any of these investors.[56]

Under the Foreign-Invested Venture Capital Enterprises Provisions, if a foreign-invested VCC acquires not less than twenty-five per cent of the registered capital of the invested enterprise, it will then be treated as an FIE.[57] Foreign-invested VCCs must not invest in businesses in the prohibited category under the Foreign Investment Regulations and Catalogue.

Apart from making investments in encouraged or permitted high technology fields under the Foreign Investment Regulations and Catalogue, foreign-invested VCCs may also provide consultation services to the invested enterprises.[58] Foreign-invested VCCs are prohibited from investing in securities, options, futures or any financial derivatives, directly or indirectly, and in immovable property which is not for the use of the invested enterprise, and they are generally prohibited from providing loans or guarantees.[59]

Similar to that provided in the 1999 Opinions, the Foreign-Invested Venture Capital Enterprises Provisions contemplate disposal by means of a sale, a share buy-back by the invested enterprise or listing as possible exit strategies for the investors. All exit strategies require regulatory approval.[60]

---

55 Foreign-Invested Venture Capital Enterprises Provisions, Article 7.

56 "China's Foreign Venture Capital Law: How Far from Customary International Fund Practice" at www.chinalawandpractice.com.

57 Foreign-Invested Venture Capital Enterprises Provisions, Article 46.

58 Foreign-Invested Venture Capital Enterprises Provisions, Article 31.

59 Foreign-Invested Venture Capital Enterprises Provisions, Article 32.

60 Foreign-Invested Venture Capital Enterprises Provisions, Article 34.

The Road Ahead

According to a recent survey conducted by the CNNIC, the total Internet users in China surged from 26.5-million in July 2001 to 45.8-million in July 2002[61] and is continuing to increase. This sounds very encouraging for potential investors who wish to cash in on the opportunities in the growing e-commerce market. It is foreseeable that, as in the past, foreign investors will innovate to come up with ideas to get around existing restrictions on foreign investment by such means as complicated structuring. At the same time, China expects a mass of new legislation to be implemented to upgrade its legal infrastructure in light of WTO accession. There is no doubt that legislative measures in the area of e-commerce are becoming more sophisticated with time. Despite this, foreign investors will still face the interesting challenge of accurate risk assessment and implementing a successful business strategy for their Chinese e-commerce investment.

61 Website of the CNNIC at www.cnnic.net.cn.

Appendix A

Qualitative Requirements for Investing in a Foreign-Invested Enterprise

Type of Business	Type of Investor	Qualitative Requirements
BTS	Main Chinese investor[62]	(1) Lawfully established company; (2) Adequate funds and suitable professional personnel for the business to be engaged in; (3) Complying with the due diligence and specific requirements laid down by the MII, including the requirements stated in the Telecoms Business Permit Regulations.
	Main foreign investor[63]	(1) Enterprise with legal personality; (2) Adequate funds and suitable personnel suitable for the business to be engaged in; (3) Possessing BTS permit in the country or region in which it is incorporated; and (4) Good performance and experiences in the provision of BTS.
VATS	Main Chinese investor	Nil
	Main foreign investor	Good performance and experience in provision of VATS.

62 Article 8 defines "main Chinese investor" as the Chinese investor who makes the largest capital investment of all the Chinese investors in the foreign-invested enterprise and whose capital contribution amounts to not less than thirty per cent of the total contributions of all the Chinese investors.

63 Article 9 defines "main foreign investor" as the foreign investor who makes the largest investment among all the foreign investors in the foreign-invested enterprise and whose capital contribution accounts for not less than thirty per cent of the total contributions of all the foreign investors.

Appendix B

Timetable for Opening of Telecommunications and E-Commerce Services Markets

Sector	Deadline	Maximum capital contribution of the foreign party
Telecommunications services markets		
VATS/Paging	11 December 2001	Not exceeding thirty per cent
	11 December 2002	Not exceeding forty-nine per cent
	11 December 2003	Not exceeding fifty per cent
Mobile Voice/Data Services	11 December 2001	Not exceeding twenty-five per cent
	11 December 2002	Not exceeding thirty-five per cent
	11 December 2004	Not exceeding forty-nine per cent
	11 December 2006	Wholly foreign-owned enterprises permitted
Domestic/ international services	11 December 2004	Not exceeding twenty-five per cent
	11 December 2006	Not exceeding thirty-five per cent
	11 December 2007	Not exceeding forty-nine per cent
E-commerce-related markets		
Commission agency/ wholesale (including on-line sale)	11 December 2002	Not exceeding fifty per cent, but not permitted to deal in books, newspapers, magazines, pharmaceutical products, agrochemicals, mulching films, chemical fertilizers, processed oils and crude oil.
	11 December 2003	Controlling interest permitted.
	11 December 2004	Wholly foreign-owned enterprise permitted and foreign-invested enterprises generally permitted to deal in books, newspapers, magazines, pharmaceutical products, agrochemicals and mulching films.
	11 December 2006	Foreign-invested enterprises generally permitted to deal in chemical fertilizers, processed oil and crude oil.

Sector	Deadline	Maximum capital contribution of the foreign party
Retail (excluding tobacco)	11 December 2001	Foreign investment permitted, but prohibited from dealing in books, newspapers, magazines, pharmaceutical products, agrochemicals, mulching films, chemical fertilizers and processed oil. Foreign investors shall not hold any controlling interests in enterprises operating chain stores with more than thirty outlets and dealing in motor cars, books, newspapers, magazines, pharmaceutical products, agrochemicals, mulching films, processed oil, chemical fertilizers, cereals, vegetable oils, edible sugars, tobacco or cotton.
	11 December 2002	Not exceeding fifty per cent and allowed to deal in books, newspapers and magazines.
	11 December 2003	Controlling interest permitted.
	11 December 2004	Wholly foreign-owned enterprises allowed. Foreign-invested enterprises generally allowed to deal in pharmaceutical products, agrochemicals, mulching films and processed oil.
	11 December 2006	Foreign-invested enterprises generally permitted to deal in chemical fertilizers.

Appendix C

Requirements for Telecommunications Operation Licenses

	BTS	Inter-provincial VATS	VATS
Qualitative requirements	(1) Legally established enterprise specializing in BTS; (2) Adequate funds and suitable personnel for the business; (3) A business site and corresponding resources; (4) Good reputation; (5) Having not committed any criminal acts for three years prior to the date of application.	(1) A site and corresponding resources for the business (2) Having not committed any criminal acts for three years prior to the date of application.	
Registered capital	For intra-provincial BTS, RMB200-million; For inter-provincial BTS, RMB2.2-billion.	RMB10-million.	RMB1-million.
Share ratio	Fifty-one per cent of total capital shall be State capital	N/A	N/A

	BTS	Inter-provincial VATS	VATS
Documents to be submitted	(1) Feasibility study; (2) Technical plan for formation of the network; (3) Written application; (4) Business license (if available); (5) General situation of the enterprise; (6) Annual financial and accounting statements or capital assessment; (7) Articles of association, corporate structure and information on shareholders; (8) Measures for providing long-term services to customers and quality control; (9) Information security measures; (10) Credit proof; (11) Proof of enterprise's reputation (if available); (12) The undertaking by the enterprise's representative in respect of due compliance with the law.	(1) Feasibility study; (2) Technical plan; (3) Written application; (4) Business license (if available); (5) General situation of the enterprise; (6) Annual financial and accounting statements or capital assessment; (7) Articles of association, corporate structure and information on shareholders; (8) Measures for providing long-term services to customers and quality control; (9) Information security measures; (10) Credit proof; (11) Proof of enterprise's reputation (if available); (12) The undertaking by the enterprise's representative in respect of due compliance with the law.	(1) Feasibility study; (2) Technical plan; (3) Written application; (4) Business license (if available); (5) General situation of the enterprise; (6) Annual financial and accounting statements or capital assessment; (7) Articles of association, corporate structure and information on shareholders; (8) Measures for providing long-term services to customers and quality control; (9) Information security measures; (10) Credit proof; (11) Proof of enterprise's reputation (if available); (12) The undertaking by the enterprise's representative in respect of due compliance with the law.

	BTS	**Inter-provincial VATS**	**VATS**
Government authority in charge	MII	MII	Provincial MII
Term	Five or ten years	Five years	Five years

Note: The authors wish to thank Anna Zhang and Cathleen Sun for their assistance in preparing this chapter.

Agreement on Trade-Related Investment Measures: A Five-Year Review

Catherine Curtiss
Hughes Hubbard & Reed LLP
Washington, D.C., United States

Introduction

The Agreement on Trade-Related Investment Measures (TRIMs Agreement), the first multilateral effort to discipline government-imposed investment restrictions, is now five years old. It is part of the Marrakesh Agreement establishing the World Trade Organization (WTO) and took effect on 1 January 1995.[1] At its birth, the prospects for the TRIMS Agreement were unclear. It is short and oblique. It does not directly regulate foreign investment and it does not govern whether or how foreign investment may enter a country or how it is treated there. Rather, it centers on the narrower issue of government measures in the area of investment that are deemed to have restrictive and distorting effects on trade in goods (hence the phrase "trade-related investment measures").

Further, the TRIMs Agreement does not prohibit all of the means by which governments can regulate investment in the production of goods. It focuses on discriminatory treatment of imported and exported products related to local production and, in particular, on two related concerns of investors: the ability to operate free from "local content" requirements and the ability to use imported parts and materials. Many areas related to the liberalization and protection of investment remain outside the disciplines of the TRIMs Agreement.

1 The Agreement on Trade-Related Investment Measures is included in Annex 1A: Multilateral Agreements on Trade in Goods, of the Marrakesh Agreement Establishing the World Trade Organization. *See* GATT Secretariat, *The Results of the Uruguay Round of Multilateral Trade Negotiations, The Legal Texts* (1994) at p. 365.

D.Campbell and S.Woodley (eds.), The Comparative Law Yearbook of International Business 2003, 233-255

Nonetheless, the TRIMs Agreement has proven to have teeth. It creates specific obligations that have started to shape global investment decisions that have already been enforced in significant WTO panel rulings, and that provide a basis for any further negotiation of multilateral disciplines on government regulation of investment.[2]

This chapter assesses the operation of the TRIMs Agreement in its first five years. Part I reviews the definition of a TRIM, and Part II identifies those subject to the Agreement. Part II also discusses the other provisions that surround the Agreement's heart, that is, its prohibitions. Part III reviews the background leading up to the TRIMs Agreement, Part IV discusses WTO panel decisions and other disputes involving the TRIMs Agreement and Part V touches on the relationships between the TRIMS Agreement and the investment-related provisions in the General Agreement on Trade in Services (GATS) and Agreement on Subsidies and Countervailing Measures (SCM Agreement). Part VI concludes with a look forward to possible future expansion of the Agreement from further investment negotiations.

Definition of a Trade-Related Investment Measure

Although the TRIMs Agreement is short, it does not lend itself to ready interpretation. A threshold source of confusion is its lack of a generic definition of "trade-related investment measure". Trade-related investment measures in general can take as many forms as government ingenuity and necessity can devise. Such measures can include, among others:[3]

(1) Local content requirements, which require that a given percentage of the value of the final output be either of local origin or purchased from local sources;

---

2 P. Sauve, "A First Look at Investment in the Final Act of the Uruguay Round", *Journal of World Trade*, Volume 28, Number 5, at p. 5 (October 1994) (discussing the limitations and contributions of the Agreement on Trade-Related Investment Measures and comparing those provisions to the investment-related provisions of the General Agreement on Trade in Services).

3 T. Stewart (ed.), *The GATT Uruguay Round: A Negotiating History (1986-1992)* Volume II at pp. 2086–87 (list of trade-related investment measures as defined in a European Communities submission) and pp. 2114–2116 (discussing means by which investment measures can further social and economic growth); *The EIU Guide to the New GATT* (1994) at pp. 32–33 (summarizing studies on the impact of trade-related investment measures on investment and trade).

(2) Trade balancing requirements, which require a company to export an amount equivalent to a certain proportion of imports, or tie the import of certain products or components to exports of other products;
(3) Exchange restrictions, which limit the investor's access to foreign currency and thereby the capacity to import products or components used or sold by the enterprise, or link access to foreign currency to the enterprise's export earnings;
(4) Domestic sales requirements, which stipulate that a specified proportion of the output or a specific minimum quantity or value of the goods produced are sold on the market of the host country;
(5) Export performance requirements, which require that a specified proportion of the output or a specific minimum quantity or value of the goods produced are exported;
(6) Investment incentives, which are benefits granted in conjunction with an investment, such as a tax holiday;
(7) Licensing requirements, which compel the investor to allow the production, use or sale of a specific product or technology by other companies in the host country;
(8) Local equity requirements, which specify a certain percentage of the equity of a company that must be held or controlled by local investors or a ceiling on foreign equity;
(9) Manufacturing limitations, which prohibit an enterprise from producing certain goods;
(10) Manufacturing requirements, which require the company to manufacture locally certain products or components used or sold by it;
(11) Remittance restrictions, which place limits on the ability of the foreign investor to remit profits, capital and other funds associated with the investment; and
(12) Technology transfer requirements, which require the foreign investor to adopt production or processing techniques that incorporate specific technology into the product or to conduct a specific minimum amount of research and development in the host country.

Any given investment scheme can incorporate one or more of these elements. Certain elements may also be combined, such as by tying a tax holiday, duty reduction or other benefit to local content requirements, or staging content requirements according to the level of exports.

Unraveling the elements of a TRIM and assessing its conformity with the TRIMs Agreement can, therefore, pose challenging factual and legal issues.

Provisions of the Agreement on Trade-Related Investment Measures

Rather than defining TRIMs, the Agreement highlights the principles of national treatment (under Article III of the General Agreement on Tariffs and Trade (GATT))[4] and the elimination of quantitative restrictions (under Article XI of GATT) as applied to government regulation of investment in production. It includes an Illustrative List of measures that are deemed to be inconsistent with those principles, principally local content and trade-balancing restrictions. The list is not exclusive, however. In theory, under Article 2 of the Agreement, any government measure related to investment in production that has elements inconsistent with either of those two principles is potentially in violation of the TRIMs Agreement.[5]

Other key TRIMs Agreement provisions require notification and the phasing out of inconsistent measures,[6] require the publication of TRIMs and other steps to improve transparency,[7] allow for flexibility in developing country implementation and permit exceptions,[8] confirm the availability of consultation and dispute settlement through GATT 1994 and the Dispute Settlement Understanding[9] and establish administrative arrangements.[10]

4 General Agreement on Tariffs and Trade 1994, Annex 1A: "Multilateral Agreements on Trade in Goods", Marrakesh Agreement Establishing the World Trade Organization, reprinted in GATT Secretariat, *The Results of the Uruguay Round of Multilateral Trade Negotiations, The Legal Texts* (1994) at pp. 21 and 486.

5 Agreement on Trade-Related Investment Measures, Article 2 and Illustrations List in the Annex.

6 Agreement on Trade-Related Investment Measures, Article 5.

7 Agreement on Trade-Related Investment Measures, Article 6.

8 Agreement on Trade-Related Investment Measures, Articles 1, 3 and 4.

9 Agreement on Trade-Related Investment Measures, Article 8.

10 Agreement on Trade-Related Investment Measures, Articles 7 and 9.

National Treatment and Elimination of Quantitative Restrictions

The key substantive provisions of the TRIMs Agreement are in Article 2 and the Illustrative List in the Annex. These provisions must be read with Articles III and XI of GATT 1994, which the TRIMs Agreement incorporates by reference. In particular, Article 2 states that WTO members may not "apply any TRIM that is inconsistent with the provisions of Article III or Article XI of GATT 1994", and refers to the Annex for an "Illustrative List" of TRIMs that are inconsistent with GATT Articles III(4) and XI(1). Article 2 thus, obliquely, introduces the concept of national treatment (the subject of Article III of GATT) and quantitative restrictions (the subject of Article XI of GATT).

National Treatment

Article III of GATT 1994 requires national treatment in internal taxation and regulation of imported goods. Paragraph 4, which is explicitly identified in the TRIMS Agreement, requires that imported goods be "accorded treatment no less favorable than that accorded to like products of national origin in respect of all laws, regulations and requirements affecting their internal sale, offering for sale, purchase, transportation, distribution or use". The TRIMs Agreement in effect moves this prohibition to the investment stage, prohibiting certain investment restrictions in the form of preferences for domestic over imported goods used in local production.

The portion of the Illustrative List of the TRIMs Agreement that describes measures inconsistent with Article III(4) is more explicit. It reads:

> "1. TRIMs that are inconsistent with the obligation of national treatment provided for in Paragraph 4 of Article III of GATT 1994 include those which are mandatory or enforceable under domestic law or under administrative rulings, or compliance with which is necessary to obtain an advantage, and which require:
>
> "(a) the purchase or use by an enterprise of products of domestic origin or from any domestic source, whether specified in terms of particular products, in terms of volume or

> value of products, or in terms of a proportion of volume or value of its local production; or
>
> "(b) that an enterprise's purchases or use of imported products be limited to an amount related to the volume or value of local products that it exports."[11]

By its terms, Paragraph 1 deals with internal measures affecting the purchase or use of products after importation. Subparagraph 1(a) prohibits local content requirements — the requirement to "purchase or use" products of domestic origin when manufacturing or assembling a product. That type of requirement can be inconsistent with the TRIMs Agreement even if it is imposed in a non-discriminatory manner on domestic and foreign enterprises, the inconsistency with the Agreement arising in part from the discriminatory treatment of imported products in favor of domestic products. Subparagraph 1(b) prohibits an internal "trade balancing" requirement — the obligation imposed by a host country on an enterprise to limit the purchase or use of imported goods according to the quantity or value of the enterprise's exports.

In combination, these subparagraphs protect the ability of investors in a manufacturing plant to use parts and materials that have been produced outside the host territory. Whether a given measure imposes prohibited local content on trade balancing requirements, however, can be disputed; it may be that the requirements do not stem from a government "measure", do not relate to investment, are not "mandatory" or "necessary to obtain an advantage" or have some other factual complication that takes them out of the purview of the TRIMs Agreement.

Quantitative Restrictions

Article XI of GATT 1994 eliminates quantitative restrictions on imported and exported goods. Paragraph 1, which is explicitly identified in the TRIMs Agreement, states that "[n]o prohibitions or restrictions other than duties, taxes or other charges" may be "instituted or maintained" on the importation or exportation of products. As with the national treatment obligation, the TRIMs Agreement in effect moves this prohibition to the investment stage, prohibiting certain

11 Agreement on Trade-Related Investment Measures, Annex, Illustrative List, Paragraph 1.

investment restrictions in the form of quantitative limits on imports for or exports from local production.

The Illustrative List again makes this prohibition explicit. Paragraph 2 of the Illustrative List to the TRIMs Agreement describes measures inconsistent with Article XI(1) and reads:

> "2. TRIMs that are inconsistent with the obligation of general elimination of quantitative restrictions provided for in Paragraph 1 of Article XI of GATT 1994 include those which are mandatory or enforceable under domestic law or under administrative rulings, or compliance with which is necessary to obtain an advantage, and which restrict:
>
> "(a) the importation by an enterprise of products used in or related to its local production, generally or to an amount related to the volume or value of local production that it exports;
>
> "(b) the importation by an enterprise of products used in or related to its local production by restricting its access to foreign exchange to an amount related to the foreign exchange inflows attributable to the enterprise; or
>
> "(c) the exportation or sale for export by an enterprise of products, whether specified in terms of particular products, in terms of volume or value of products, or in terms of a proportion of volume or value of its local production."[12]

Where Paragraph 1 addresses the purchase or use of products by an enterprise, Paragraph 2 deals with border measures affecting an enterprise's importation or exportation of products. Subparagraph 2(a) prohibits restrictions on imports for use in local production. It also specifically prohibits trade-balancing requirements akin to those addressed in subparagraph 1(a), but relating directly to border restrictions rather than to what may be internally purchased or used.

Subparagraph 2(b) addresses foreign exchange balance. It prohibits host governments from restricting imports to be used in local production through restrictions on access to foreign exchange, in particular, restrictions in the form of balancing foreign exchange

---

12 Agreement on Trade-Related Investment Measures, Annex, Illustrative List, Paragraph 2.

access with foreign exchange inflows. Finally, subparagraph 2(c) prohibits host country investment measures that restrict the exports of the local production in which the investment is made.

Mandatory and Non-Mandatory Measures

The common introductory language to each paragraph of the Illustrative List refers to "mandatory or enforceable" host country requirements, and of measures for which compliance "is necessary to obtain an advantage". The effect is to require WTO members to refrain from applying the specified measures, whether the measures are a mandatory condition of investment or operation of an enterprise, or whether they are framed as a non-mandatory benefit or "advantage".

For example, a flat requirement that all manufacturing operations use a specified minimum percentage of domestically produced materials would constitute a mandatory condition of investment or operation. By contrast, basing import duty preferences on compliance with local content requirements would not technically constitute a mandatory condition of investment or operation; an investor could choose not to comply with local content requirements, although the cost of doing so would be higher duties. However, that type of restriction could still be prohibited, as a TRIM that must be complied with to obtain an "advantage" — import duty reductions.[13]

Summary of Substantive Provisions

The TRIMs Agreement requires WTO members to refrain from applying certain measures related to investment in production that are inconsistent with the GATT Article III national treatment obligation or the GATT Article XI elimination of quantitative restrictions. Explicitly prohibited are certain types of:

(1) Local content requirements;
(2) Trade balancing requirements;
(3) Foreign exchange balancing;
(4) Restrictions that limit an enterprise's exports; and
(5) Restrictions that limit an enterprise's imports.

---

13 The World Trade Organization panel in *Indonesian Autos* confirmed this point.

These types of measures may run foul of the TRIMs Agreement if they are imposed by the government as a mandatory condition or as part of an incentive package.

Notification and Phase-Out of Existing Inconsistent Measures

The TRIMs Agreement provided a novel approach to WTO rules, in that notification of inconsistent measures before a certain date was a condition for transitional phase-out rather than immediate elimination of those measures. In particular, under Article 5 of the TRIMs Agreement, WTO members were to notify and phase out existing measures not in conformity with the Agreement. Under Article 5.1, members were required to notify to the Council for Trade in Goods any TRIMs that were not in conformity with the Agreement within ninety days of the date of entry into force of the WTO Agreement (which was 1 January 1995).[14] The notified measures were then to be eliminated within a defined period after 1 January 1995, according to the stage of development of the WTO member: two years for developed countries, five years for developing countries and seven years for least-developed country members, with an extension permitted for developing countries demonstrating "particular difficulties" in implementing the Agreement.[15]

As of 1 January 1997, developed countries should have eliminated their notified inconsistent measures, and as of 1 January 2000, developing and least-developed countries should have done the same. At this point, the only remaining inconsistent measures that are permitted are of least developed countries, or developing countries that have obtained an extension of the phase-out period.

As of 31 July 1998, notifications of existing inconsistent measures had been received from twenty-five countries. These were: Argentina, Barbados, Bolivia, Chile, Colombia, Costa Rica, Cuba, Cyprus, the Dominican Republic, Ecuador, Egypt, Indonesia, India, Malaysia, Mexico, Nigeria, Pakistan, Peru, Philippines, Romania, South

14 By a decision adopted in April 1995, the World Trade Organization General Council decided that governments that were not members of the World Trade Organization on 1 January 1995 but that were entitled to become original members within a period of two years after that time should make Article 5.1 notifications within ninety days of their acceptance of the World Trade Organization Agreement: World Trade Organization Annual Report 1998, at p. 96.

15 Agreement on Trade-Related Investment Measures, Articles 5.2 and 5.3.

Africa, Thailand, Uganda, Uruguay and Venezuela.[16] Many of these notifications relate to high-profile sectors, principally automobiles.

In addition, a number of developing and least-developed countries have requested extensions of their phase-out periods under Article 5.3. Lack of Agreement clarity concerning the approval process, however, has led to issues of whether extensions had to have been granted before the end of the transition period in order to be valid. These transitional provisions, however, protected only existing measures. Under Article 5.4, TRIMs introduced within six months of 1 January 1995 "shall not benefit from the transitional arrangements" related to the phase-out period. Any such new measure would therefore be vulnerable to challenge by another WTO member without regard to the transition period for existing notified measures.

The TRIMs Agreement also has "standstill" provisions under which members agreed not to modify the measures notified under Article 5.1 to make them more trade restrictive.[17] Some flexibility existed for extending the application of notified TRIMs to new investments; a country could apply a notified TRIM to a new investment producing "like products" to those of an established enterprise in order to avoid a distortion of competition.[18] However, no member had notified such measures as of 31 July 1998.[19]

The Agreement does not specifically require countries to notify TRIMs adopted after 1 January 1995 that may be inconsistent with the Agreement. However, the obligation to notify existing non-conforming measures would seem to extend automatically to any TRIM added to the Illustrative List in the future.[20] In addition, as discussed in the next section, undertakings on transparency call for the notifications of measures that could constitute elements of a TRIM and could be read as requiring notification of prohibited TRIMS.

---

16 World Trade Organization Annual Report 1998, at p. 96.

17 Agreement on Trade-Related Investment Measures, Article 5.4.

18 Agreement on Trade-Related Investment Measures, Article 5.5.

19 World Trade Organization Annual Report 1998, at p. 96.

20 Agreement on Trade-Related Investment Measures, Articles 5.1 and 6; Ministerial Decision on Notification Procedures adopted on 15 April 1994 (agreeing to notify measures covered by an annexed list, which includes all measures covered by the Multilateral Trade Agreements in Annex 1A to the World Trade Organization Agreement, which, in turn, includes the Agreement on Trade-Related Investment Measures.

Transparency

Article 6 contains provisions that improve the transparency of TRIMs. Article 6.2 calls for notification to the WTO of the publications in which TRIMs may be found, including those applied by regional and local governments and authorities. In September 1996, the TRIMs Committee adopted a procedure for the implementation of this provision. As of 31 July 1998, information on publications containing TRIMs had been provided by thirty-three countries: Argentina, Australia, Brunei Darussalam, Bulgaria, Chile, China, Costa Rica, Cuba, the European Community, Fiji, Hong Kong, Iceland, India, Indonesia, Israel, Jamaica, Japan, Liechtenstein, Mauritius, Nicaragua, Norway, Paraguay, Peru, Philippines, Romania, Singapore, Switzerland, Thailand, Tunisia, Uganda, the United States, Uruguay and Venezuela.[21]

In Article 6.1, the members also reaffirmed their "commitment to obligations on transparency and notification" contained in three sources: Article X of GATT 1994; the undertaking on "Notification" contained in the Understanding Regarding Notification, Consultation, Dispute Settlement and Surveillance, adopted on 28 November 1997 (the 1997 Understanding),[22] and the Ministerial Decision on Notification Procedures adopted on 15 April 1994 (the 1994 Decision).[23] Collectively, these commitments call for the notification of measures that could constitute elements of a TRIM, if not TRIMs themselves.

GATT Article X(1) calls for members to publish promptly any:

> "[l]aws, regulations, judicial decisions and administrative rulings of general application . . . pertaining to . . . requirements, restrictions or prohibitions on imports or exports or on the transfer of payments therefor, or affecting their sale, distribution . . . mixing or other use".

Article X(2) requires prior publication of a "measure of general application . . . imposing a new or more burdensome requirement,

---

21 World Trade Organization Annual Report 1998, at p. 96. Some of the notifications are also listed in G/TRIMS/N/2/Rev.2.

22 BISD 26S/210, reprinted in GATT, *The Texts of the Tokyo Round Agreements* (1986) at p. 200.

23 Reprinted in GATT Secretariat, *The Results of the Uruguay Round of Multilateral Trade Negotiations, The Legal Texts* (1994) at p. 444.

restriction or prohibition on imports, or on the transfer of payments therefor". To the extent that a TRIM involves restrictions on imports, exports or foreign exchange, therefore, Article X would seem to require its publication.

In the 1997 Understanding, at Paragraph 3, members undertake "to the maximum extent possible, to notify" the members of "their adoption of trade measures affecting the operation of" the GATT. The 1994 Decision extends that general undertaking to an annexed list of measures. That Annex, called the "Indicative List of Notifiable Measures", includes measures relating to quantitative restrictions, export restrictions and foreign exchange controls related to imports and exports — all potentially elements of a TRIM. In addition, the Indicative List specifies "[a]ny other measure covered by the Multilateral Trade Agreements in Annex 1A to the WTO Agreement". Since Annex 1A includes the TRIMs Agreement, the 1994 Decision can reasonably be read as calling for the notification of any prohibited TRIMs, namely, investment measures that are inconsistent with Articles III or XI of GATT.

The notifications vary to some extent in the comprehensiveness of detail. However, all are made to the same format. Collectively, these notifications — with those of inconsistent measures under Article 5.1 — form an unprecedented body of information on worldwide investment practices related to the production of goods. This information has helped to generate informal government-to-government questions and discussions, formal requests for consultation and disputes, and ideas for further multilateral negotiation.

Limitations and Exceptions

The principal limitations of the TRIMs Agreement are that it pertains to "investment measures related to trade in goods only" (Article 1) and that it prohibits only measures that are inconsistent with national treatment or the elimination of quantitative restrictions (Article 2). Restrictions on foreign investment *per se* are not the subject of the TRIMs Agreement. The Agreement also does not prohibit a myriad of other forms of investment, although other WTO agreements discipline some of these measures.

In addition, the TRIMs Agreement embodies exceptions for developing countries, including a longer (but now expired) transition period in which to phase-out existing inconsistent measures (Article 5.2), and flexibility to extend that period based on difficulties in implementation (Article 5.3). Developing countries are also permitted to deviate temporarily from the prohibitions of Article 2 for balance-of-payments reasons (Article 4).

Finally, Article 3 of the TRIMs Agreement incorporates "[a]ll exceptions under GATT 1994 . . . as appropriate". Although not further specified, national security,[24] health and safety,[25] government procurement,[26] balance of payments[27] and export control exceptions[28] would apply to the imposition of TRIMs by a WTO member.[29] Presumably, regional content requirements that relate to trade within a free trade area or customs union permitted under Article XXIV of GATT would also be permissible, as the purpose of such areas is to eliminate barriers on trade in products "originating" in such territories.[30] The full extent of these and other potential exceptions to the TRIMs Agreement obligations have not yet been tested.

Consultation and Dispute Settlement

As part of the commitments related to transparency, Article 6.3 calls for each WTO member to "accord sympathetic consideration to requests for information, and afford adequate opportunity for consultation, on any matter arising from" the TRIMs Agreement. Under Article 8, the WTO dispute settlement procedure, as described in the Dispute Settlement Understanding, also applies to disputes arising under the TRIMs Agreement. The disputes that have arisen to date under the TRIMs Agreement are discussed below.

---

24 General Agreement on Tariffs and Trade, Article XXI.

25 General Agreement on Tariffs and Trade, Article XX(b).

26 General Agreement on Tariffs and Trade, Article III(8).

27 General Agreement on Tariffs and Trade, Articles XII(1) and XVIII.

28 General Agreement on Tariffs and Trade, Articles XI(2) and XX(i).

29 Statement of Administrative Action, Uruguay Round Trade Agreements Act, at p. 135 (United States Government view of exceptions embodied in Article 3 of the Agreement on Trade-Related Investment Measures), reprinted in H. Doc. 103–316, Volume 1, Uruguay Round Trade Agreements, Texts of Agreements, Implementing Bill, Statement of Administrative Action and Required Supporting Statements (27 September 1994) at p. 805.

30 General Agreement on Tariffs and Trade, Article XXIV(8).

Administration and Institutional Structure

The TRIMs Agreement, finally, also establishes an institutional structure in the form of a Committee on TRIMs. Article 7 establishes this Committee as a forum for examining the implementation and operation of the Agreement. It is required by Article 7.1 to meet at least once each year, although in practice it has usually met twice annually. Meetings are open to all WTO members and governments with observer status; inter-governmental organizations (for example, the International Monetary Fund, the Organization for Economic Cooperation and Development and the United Nations Commission on Trade and Development) may also attend as observers. Minutes of the TRIMs Committee meetings are available on the WTO website (in the G/TRIMS/M series).

The Committee is required by Article 7.3 to report annually to the Council for Trade in Goods. Its annual reports are also available on the WTO website. The Council for Trade in Goods in turn reports to the General Council, which is the WTO governing body. The operations of the WTO, including those related to the TRIMs Agreement and Committee, are described each year in the WTO Annual Report.

In its first year, 1995, the Committee established its own procedures and notification formats. Much of its work since then has focused on the notifications received under Article 5.1. The Committee examines and discusses the notifications, including taking questions and answers on their factual content.[31] Questions on auto-related schemes have dominated the question-and-answer sessions, although meetings have discussed other notifications-related issues, such as the consequences of the many late Article 5.1 filings, the overlap between the investment and subsidy notification provisions and the distinguishing features of a TRIM. The TRIMs Committee has, though, disclaimed any obligation to undertake a collective evaluation of the legal validity of the notifications.

Article 9 of the TRIMs Agreement calls for a five-year review of the operation of the Agreement. The review is to consider whether the Agreement should be "complemented with provisions on investment policy and competition policy". In part, in order to implement this "built-in agenda", the Singapore Ministerial Declaration of 13 December 1996 established a Working Group on the Relationship between Trade and Investment and a Working Group on the

31 Written questions and responses are circulated in documents in the G/TRIMS/W series.

Interaction between Trade and Competition Policy. The Working Groups have submitted annual reports on their activities to the General Council, most recently in 1999.[32]

Background to the Agreement

Although the TRIMs Agreement is often referred to as a new subject for GATT, to some extent, trade-related investment measures are covered by GATT articles existing before the Uruguay Round.[33] Prior to the TRIMs Agreement, however, the linkage between trade and investment received little attention. The most significant development was a GATT panel ruling in Canada — Administration of the Foreign Investment Review Act (FIRA Panel Report),[34] which simultaneously demonstrated the potential application of GATT obligations to investment affecting trade in goods, and the limitation of those obligations in the investment context.

Foreign Investment Review Act Panel

The Canadian Parliament enacted FIRA in 1973 to ensure that businesses in Canada established or acquired by foreigners would be of "significant benefit" to Canada. The dispute, on the complaint of the United States, centered on the practice of allowing certain investments subject to FIRA, conditional upon written undertakings by the investors. The undertakings were varied, but in essence called on the investors to purchase goods of Canadian origin (local content requirements), to manufacture certain products in Canada (manufacturing requirements) or to export a certain amount or percentage of output (export performance requirements).[35]

---

32 World Trade Organization Annual Report 1998, at pp. 76–77 and 78; 1999 Annual Report of the Working Group on the Interaction between Trade and Competition Policy, WT/WGTI/3; 1999 Annual Report of the Working Group on Trade and Competition Policy, WT/WGTCP/3.

33 T. Stewart (ed.), *The GATT Uruguay Round: A Negotiating History (1986–1992)* Volume II at pp. 2073 and 2131–36 (listing GATT articles with some connection to trade-restrictive effects of investment measures).

34 Canada — Administration of the Foreign Investment Review Act, Report of the Panel, BISD 30S/140, (7 February 1984).

35 Report of the Foreign Investment Review Act Panel, at Paragraphs 2.2–2.7.

The Panel did not rule on the manufacturing requirements, finding that examination to be outside its terms of reference. With respect to the two other types of undertakings, it found the local content but not the export performance requirements to be inconsistent with GATT obligations.[36] The Panel emphasized that it was examining the consistency with GATT of trade-related measures taken by Canada under its foreign investment legislation, and not Canada's right to regulate foreign investment, since GATT "does not prevent Canada from exercising its sovereign right to regulate foreign direct investments".[37]

With that qualification, the Panel viewed the local content requirements as inconsistent with the national treatment obligation of Article III(4) of GATT. The Panel found that the undertakings to purchase goods of Canadian origin "without any qualification exclude the possibility of purchasing available imported products so that the latter are clearly treated less favorably than domestic products". Such requirements were, therefore, not consistent with Article III(4), which obliges governments to accord imports "treatment no less favorable than that accorded" to like domestic products.[38] These undertakings did not, though, violate the elimination of quantitative restraints provisions of Article XI(1), for they did not prevent the importation of goods; the undertakings only discriminated against imported goods after importation.[39]

The Panel did not find the export performance requirements to be inconsistent with GATT obligations. The United States had argued that those requirements were inconsistent with Article XVII(1), which it viewed as establishing an obligation to allow enterprises to act in accordance with commercial considerations. The Panel concluded that Article XVII(1)(b) did not establish the asserted obligation and did not apply here. It further concluded that no provision of GATT forbids requirements to sell goods in foreign markets in preference to the domestic market. Accordingly, the Panel concluded that, in accepting investment proposals upon the condition that the investor export a certain quantity or proportion of his product, Canada had not acted inconsistently with any of the general principles of non-discriminatory treatment prescribed in GATT.[40]

---

36 Report of the Foreign Investment Review Act Panel, at Paragraphs 5.3, 6.1 and 6.2.

37 Report of the Foreign Investment Review Act Panel, at Paragraph 5.1.

38 Report of the Foreign Investment Review Act Panel, at Paragraphs 5.8–5.11 and 6.1.

39 Report of the Foreign Investment Review Act Panel, at Paragraph 5.14.

40 Report of the Foreign Investment Review Act Panel, at Paragraphs 3.1 and 5.18.

Negotiation of the Agreement on Trade-Related Investment Measures

The timing of the FIRA Panel ruling suggests that it may have been a precipitating factor for the inclusion of TRIMs issues in the Uruguay Round of multilateral trade negotiations. The Panel decision was issued in 1984, and the agenda for what became the Uruguay Round was formed in 1985. Certainly, as with other "new" issues, the focus under GATT on customs tariffs and border measures had started to shift to internal, non-tariff measures that affected global trade, and the FIRA Panel ruling highlighted the limitations of the existing GATT framework with respect to disciplines on investment restrictions.

However, a focus on trade policy issues related to economic development pre-dated the FIRA Panel decision. Economic problems of several developing nations and economic crises of the 1970s prompted a broad policy consensus on the advantages of a more outward-looking trade policy, in which direct foreign investment played a key role. With the increased importance of direct foreign investment came support for the notion that oversight of investment policy should be brought within the auspices of GATT.[41]

Under the GATT Ministerial Declaration of 1982, trade policy issues related to economic development were incorporated into the "work program and priorities for the 1980s". In 1985, when a Preparatory Committee was formed to develop an agenda for a new round of multilateral trade negotiations under GATT, a proposal for separate discussion of TRIMs was introduced. The *Punta del Este* Ministerial Declaration, which launched the Uruguay Round in 1987, included the subject of trade-related investment measures as a subject for the new round, with the following mandate for the Negotiating Group on TRIMs:[42]

> "Following an examination of the operation of GATT articles related to the trade restrictive and distorting effects of investment measures, negotiations should elaborate, as appropriate, further provisions that may be necessary to avoid such adverse effects on trade."

41 T. Stewart (ed.), *The GATT Uruguay Round: A Negotiating History (1986–1992)* Volume II at pp. 2051–52.

42 T. Stewart (ed.), *The GATT Uruguay Round: A Negotiating History (1986–1992)* Volume I at pp. 102–103.

The emphasis on "adverse effects on trade" made clear that the negotiations were not to deal with the regulation of investment as such. Nonetheless, within that limited mandate, TRIMs became an agenda item.

In the ensuing seven years, the Negotiating Group on TRIMs met formally and informally. The formal record of negotiations includes twenty-three meetings with minutes recorded and twenty-seven formal submissions by various parties. Different aspects of these submissions were developed into "Chairman's Drafts", the last of which was the "Dunkel Draft". This text, released in December 1991, represented a compromise on issues that had not been resolved by the negotiations.[43]

The fundamental split was between developed countries — such as the United States, Japan, Switzerland, the European Community and the Nordic countries — and the developing nations from Asia, Africa and the Americas. In general, the developed countries supported the need for an expansion of the disciplines covered by existing GATT articles, including prohibitions against certain investment policies. By contrast, a group of developing countries advocated that only the "effects" of investment measures and not the investment measures themselves should be brought under GATT disciplines. These countries further asserted that these effects should be considered on a case-by-case basis through empirical evidence and that, if adverse effects were demonstrated, "ways and means" be found to deal with them.[44]

The Dunkel compromise was just that — a compromise. The substantive portion of what became the TRIMs Agreement is essentially limited to interpreting and clarifying the application to trade-related investment measures of the GATT provisions on national treatment for imported goods (Article III) and on quantitative restrictions on imports or exports (Article XI). Elements of the positions favored by developed countries can be seen in the presence of some prohibited TRIMs and the notification and transparency requirements. Elements of the positions favored by some of the developing countries can be seen in the shortness of the list of prohibited TRIMs, the increased

43 T. Stewart (ed.), *The GATT Uruguay Round: A Negotiating History (1986–1992)* Volume I at p. 103 and Volume II at pp. 2074-75 (chronology of TRIMs meetings and formal submissions).

44 T. Stewart (ed.), *The GATT Uruguay Round: A Negotiating History (1986–1992)* Volume I at p. 105.

flexibility in implementation for developing countries and the availability of all GATT exceptions.[45] Thus, at the conclusion of negotiations, an Agreement existed with some prohibitions, but it did not cover many of the measures that had been discussed and proposed, including export performance requirements and transfer of technology requirements.

Trade-Related Investment Measures and the World Trade Organization

In the five years of operation of the TRIMs Agreement, its provisions have been the basis of one published panel ruling and considered in two other published panel rulings, although neither of the latter contained a specific finding on the consistency of the challenged measures with the TRIMs Agreement. They have also prompted several requests for consultations. All but one of these disputes have involved the automobile industry.

Indonesian Autos

The first WTO panel to interpret and apply the TRIMs Agreement concerned measures applied by Indonesia in the automotive sector. On 23 July 1998, the WTO Dispute Settlement Body adopted the Panel Report in Indonesia — Certain Measures Affecting the Automobile Industry (Indonesian Autos).[46] The principal findings of that report were that Indonesia's 1993 and 1996 car programs violated Article 2 of the TRIMs Agreement and Article III(2) of GATT 1994.

In essence, the 1993 program consisted of duty relief on imports of automotive parts and accessories based in part on the local content of the finished motor vehicle in which the parts were used. Similar duty relief applied to imports of subparts, depending on the local content of the completed part or accessory. The principal element of the 1996 car program was "pioneer" or National Car company status, under

---

45 T. Stewart (ed.), *The GATT Uruguay Round: A Negotiating History (1986–1992)* Volume I at p. 106.

46 "Indonesia — Certain Measures Affecting the Automobile Industry", Report of the Panel, WT/DS54/R, WT/DS55/R, WT/DS59/R, WT/DS64/R (2 July 1998).

which car companies enjoyed certain duty and tax exemptions if they met increasing local content requirements over a three-year period.[47]

The Panel decided that the tax and tariff benefits contingent upon meeting local content requirements violated Article 2.1 of the TRIMs Agreement. In reaching that conclusion, the Panel applied a four-step analysis. First, it decided that the Indonesian measures at issue were "investment measures". Although the Panel disclaimed an intent to provide an "overall definition of what constitutes an investment measure" and the Indonesian Government had argued that it did not consider or administer the programs as investment measures, the Panel found that the 1993 and 1996 car programs had "investment objectives and investment features".[48]

Second, the Panel determined that the measures were "trade-related". In its view, local content requirements "by definition, always favor the use of domestic products over imported products, and, therefore, affect trade".[49] Third, the Panel decided that the measures were in violation of Article 2.1 of the TRIMs Agreement because "compliance with the provisions for the purchase and use of particular products of domestic origin is necessary to obtain the tax and customs benefits on these car programs, as referred to in Item 1(a) of the Illustrative List of TRIMs".[50] Fourth, the Panel found that the lower duty rates were "clearly 'advantages' within the meaning of the chapeau of the Illustrative List to the TRIMs Agreement". The Panel noted that "a simple advantage conditional upon the use of domestic goods is considered to be a violation of Article 2 of the TRIMs Agreement even if the local content requirement is not binding as such".[51]

Along the way, the Panel discussed the relationship of the TRIMs Agreement to the SCM Agreement and to Article III of GATT. On the former topic, the Panel concluded that the two agreements "may have overlapping coverage in that they may both apply to a single legislative act, but they have different foci, and they impose different types

47 "Indonesia — Certain Measures Affecting the Automobile Industry", Report of the Panel, Paragraphs 2.15–2.17 and 2.3–2.4.

48 "Indonesia — Certain Measures Affecting the Automobile Industry", Report of the Panel, Paragraph 14.80.

49 "Indonesia — Certain Measures Affecting the Automobile Industry", Report of the Panel, Paragraph 14.82.

50 "Indonesia — Certain Measures Affecting the Automobile Industry", Report of the Panel, Paragraph 14.88.

51 "Indonesia — Certain Measures Affecting the Automobile Industry", Report of the Panel, Paragraphs 14.89 and 14.90.

of obligations".[52] With respect to local content requirements, for example, the SCM Agreement prohibits the grant of a subsidy contingent upon use of domestic over imported goods (an "import substitution" subsidy),[53] while the TRIMs Agreement prohibits the requirement to use domestic goods as such.[54]

As to Article III, the Panel concluded that "the TRIMs Agreement has an autonomous legal existence, independent from that of Article III". Consequently, "even if either of the two sets of provisions were not applicable, the other one would remain applicable".[55]

European Community Bananas and Canadian Autos

The interplay between Article III of GATT and Article 2 of the TRIMs Agreement was revisited by WTO panels in European Community — Regime for the Importation, Sale and Distribution of Bananas (EC Bananas) and Canada — Certain Measures Affecting the Automotive Industry (Canadian Autos).

Although the disputes relating to the European Community's import licensing procedures for bananas raised TRIMs issues, the Panel established in those disputes did not make findings under that Agreement. Instead, it considered the claims under Article 2.1 of the TRIMs Agreement and those under Article III(4) of GATT together.[56] Finding that the EC measures were inconsistent with the latter, the Panel did not find it necessary to rule on the measures' consistency with the TRIMs Agreement.[57]

The panel established to examine the complaints of Japan and the European Community concerning Canada's application of the United

52 "Indonesia — Certain Measures Affecting the Automobile Industry", Report of the Panel, Paragraph 14.52.

53 Agreement on Subsidies and Countervailing Measures, Article 3.1(b).

54 "Indonesia — Certain Measures Affecting the Automobile Industry", Report of the Panel, Paragraph 14.50.

55 "Indonesia — Certain Measures Affecting the Automobile Industry", Report of the Panel, Paragraph 14.62.

56 European Community — Regime for the Importation, Sale and Distribution of Bananas, Panel Reports, WT/DS27/R/ECU, WT/DS27/R/GTM, WT/DS27/R/HND, WT/DS27/R/MEX, WT/DS27/R/USA (25 September 1997).

57 European Community — Regime for the Importation, Sale and Distribution of Bananas, Panel Reports, WT/DS27/R/ECU, WT/DS27/R/GTM, WT/DS27/R/HND, WT/DS27/R/MEX, WT/DS27/R/USA, Paragraphs 7.185–7.187.

States–Canada Auto Pact adopted a similar approach.[58] Noting the difference between EC Bananas and Indonesian Autos, the Panel in Canadian Autos found the measures to be inconsistent with Article III(4) of GATT and a specific ruling on the consistency of the Canadian measures with Article 2.1 of the TRIMs Agreement to be unnecessary.[59]

Other Disputes on Trade-Related Investment Measures

Measures of Brazil, India and the Philippines have been the subject of bilateral consultations pursuant to the TRIMs Agreement, although panels have not been requested in those disputes. The Brazilian dispute centered on domestic content requirements and trade balancing in that country's automotive scheme.[60] The Indian dispute also concerned local content and export balancing requirements in measures affecting the automotive industry.[61]

The first Philippines dispute related to measures affecting pork and poultry. The United States requested consultations in part on the grounds that the implementation of Philippine tariff-rate quotas on those commodities appeared to be inconsistent with Articles 2 and 5 of the TRIMs Agreement.[62] The second Philippines dispute related to measures affecting the motor vehicles industry. Among other grounds, the United States requested consultations pursuant to Article 8 of the TRIMs Agreement ("to the extent it incorporates by

---

58 Canada — Certain Measures Affecting the Automotive Industry, Report of the Panel, WT/DS139/R, WT/DS142/R (11 February 2000). Under the applicable Canadian rules, manufacturers had to meet, among other things, two requirements to qualify for an import duty exemption: a production-to-sales ratio requirement and a Canadian value added requirement. The European Community challenged these requirements under Article III(4) of the General Agreement on Tariffs and Trade and Article 2.1 of the Agreement on Trade-Related Investment Measures (Japan presented identical claims except for the challenge to the ratio requirement under Article 2.1 of the Agreement on Trade-Related Investment Measures).

59 Canada — Certain Measures Affecting the Automotive Industry, Report of the Panel, Paragraphs 10.63 and 10.90–10.91.

60 Brazil — Certain Automotive Investment Measures, Request for Consultations by Japan, WT/DS51/1, G/L/98, G/TRIMS/D/1 (6 August 1996).

61 India — Measures Affecting the Automotive Sector, Request for Consultations, WT/DS146/1, G/L/261, G/TRIMS/D/14 (12 October 1998).

62 Philippines — Measures Affecting Pork and Poultry, Request for Consultations by the United States, WT/DS102/1, G/L/191, G/AG/GEN/11, G/LIC/D/12, G/TRIMS/D/9 (9 October 1997).

reference Article XXIII [Nullification or Impairment] of GATT 1994") regarding the Philippine measures which made tariff advantages for motor vehicle manufacturers conditional upon domestic content requirements and foreign exchange requirements (balancing imported parts and components with exported finished vehicles).[63]

Conclusion

Despite its limited terms, the TRIMs Agreement has had a significant effect. It has led many WTO members to identify and describe their investment measures, prompted consultations and generated formal disputes. There is also no doubt that the Agreement has precipitated governments to reassess and start to modify their investment regimes, although those efforts are not public until the new regimes are unveiled. As government measures continue to come within the WTO dispute settlement mechanism, a better definition of a TRIM and of prohibited measures will follow. The collapse of the MAI and a broader round of WTO negotiations at Seattle suggest that it will be some time before the TRIMs Agreement expands by negotiation. Over time, however, multilateral agreement to discipline additional forms of investment measures seems inevitable.

63 Philippines — Measures Affecting Trade and Investment in the Motor Vehicle Sector, Request for Consultations by the United States, WT/DS195/1, G/L/380, G/TRIMS/D/16, G/SCM/D35/1 (31 May 2000).

Pension Funds in Nigeria

J.U.K. Igwe
Law Development, Research, Publications and Consulting Limited
Lagos, Nigeria

Introduction

In most countries of the world, the central importance of upholding, protecting and projecting the rights of the investor is now acknowledged. The Ombudsman for the investments and securities industry and the Securities and Exchange Commission (SEC) have a responsibility to protect investors and all other participants in order to maintain confidence in the system and uphold integrity, stability and professionalism. In Nigeria, the realization of this need has led to the promulgation of the Securities and Exchange Commission Act 1979 and its regulations.[1] However, with the passage of time, it was necessary to consolidate the approach and introduce new market infrastructures and a wide-ranging system of regulation of investment and securities business in Nigeria, all designed or intended to protect investors; hence, the promulgation of the Investment and Securities Act 1999,[2] which came into force on 26 May 1999.

An analogy of this development in Nigeria can be drawn from the rationale behind the United States Securities Act 1933. President Franklin D. Roosevelt stated, *inter alia*:

> "The purpose of the Legislation is to protect with the least possible interference to honest business. This is one broad purpose of protecting investors and depositors. It should be followed by legislation relating to better supervision of the purchase and sale of all property dealt in an exchange, and by legislation to correct the unethical and unsafe practices on the part of officers . . . what we seek is a clear

1 Originally promulgated as Act Number 29 of 1978, re-enacted in 1979 and later reproduced as Cap. 406, Laws of the Federation, 1990.

2 Act Number 45 of 1999.

D.Campbell and S.Woodley (eds.), The Comparative Law Yearbook of International Business 2003, 257-283

> understanding of the ancient truth that those who manage banks, corporations, and other people's money, are trustees for others."[3]

A similar passage appeared in the Kimber Report, which stated the objectives of securities legislation in Canada in the following words:

> "1.17 The committee believes that changes in the province of Ontario should be devised in recognition of two basic propositions. To the extent that Securities Legislation is improved upon in the interests of investors, the securities industry will benefit from increased public confidence. To the extent that the industry becomes a more effective and efficient part of the economy, the general public will benefit. Both objectives will be achieved by raising the standards governing the industry to the level presently maintained by the responsible members of the securities industry and what should be maintained, as a requirement of law in the public interest. In this context, the Committee points out that the substantial majority of the recommendations contained in the Report deal directly or indirectly with the disclosure of information to investors, that is to say, with the factor of public confidence."[4]

Although, in the United States and Canada, pension funds are regulated by specific regulations, the above illustrate in a general context the seriousness with which the question of protecting investors and maintaining the confidence of investors and beneficiaries has been taken. In the case of Nigeria, meeting the needs of public confidence and protecting all market operators engendered the need for comprehensive legislation, which turned out to be the Investment and Securities Act 1999. However, the focus in this chapter shall be centered primarily on one aspect of an investment scheme recognized by the Act, that is, pension funds. Consequently, the following questions invariably arise:

(1) What are the laws and regulations that govern the management, control, administration and investment of pension funds in

---

3 I.L. Loss at p. 127; also cited in *Proposals for a Securities Market Law for Canada*, Volume 3, April 1978, at p. 228.

4 Kimber Report 1.17, *Proposals for a Securities Market Law for Canada*, Volume 3, April 1978, at pp. 228–229.

Nigeria, and what is the importance of the regulations to the Nigerian economy and to the capital market?

(2) Which organization, agency or authority is recognized by law as the institutional regulator for the management and control of pension funds in Nigeria?

(3) What are the statutory powers of the SEC of Nigeria to regulate investments and securities, particularly pension schemes?

(4) What is the intention of the legislature in enacting the provisions on pension funds?

(5) Are the provisions in conflict with any other law and how shall any such conflict be resolved?

(6) What is the legal position of the SEC Rules and Regulations enacted by the SEC pursuant to the powers conferred upon it by the Investments and Securities Act 1999, particularly those aspects touching and concerning the regulation of pension funds?

(7) Are there adequate provisions on the investment in pension funds in Nigeria, and is there any need to amend this aspect of the law?

(8) What is the position of insurance law *vis-à-vis* the regulation of pension funds, and should insurance of certain pension funds be a reason for exclusion from regulations presently established in Nigeria?

(9) What are the roles of managers, trustees and operators of pension funds as required by the law?

(10) Are pension funds protected by the Nigerian Constitution, or are they restricted by it?

(11) What is the position of the Nigerian Social Insurance Trust Fund regarding pension funds in Nigeria?

(12) What is the role of the Joint Tax Board regarding pension schemes in Nigeria?

(13) What is the registration procedure for pension funds, and are such procedures onerous?

(14) What is the attitude of the law in dealing with conflict of interest situations in the regulation of collective investment schemes, and how are such conflicts usually resolved? and

(15) What are the problems under Nigerian law and the institutional framework for handling complaints regarding pension funds?

This chapter examines all of the above issues as well as others that arise in the course of dealing with the problems identified. In order to effectively get to the root of each matter, comparative illustrations from other jurisdictions shall be used.

Regulation of Pension Funds in Nigeria

Importance of Regulation

In the United States, the Employee Retirement and Income Security Act 1974 (ERISA) was essentially enacted to eliminate several of the major differences and abuses associated with the management of pension funds. With this legislation, the importance of pension funds to the American economy and to the capital market increased tremendously. Statistics[5] show that, as at December 1983, the assets of all public and private pension and retirement funds in America totaled approximately US $1,280-billion. Pension funds today constitute the largest pool of investable capital in the world.[6] As at the end of 1989, the capital from pension funds stood at US $2.6-trillion in assets, which is half the gross national product (GNP) of the United States and equal to the GNP of Japan.[7] This astonishing growth compelled investment experts in the United States to conclude that pension funds fueled the economic surge of the 1980s and made the stock market boom in America possible.

By 2000, pension funds owned at least forty per cent of all the corporate stock in America — a success mostly traceable to the adoption and effective monitoring of the legal standards applied to pension operators, stating what they can and cannot do with pension funds. For example, one of the key obligations created by ERISA which ensured the success of pension funds in America is the "prudent man" rule. The rule states that pension fund sponsors, trustees, investment advisors, investment brokers, consultants to the plan, bond managers, asset allocators, lawyers, accountants or actuaries, among others, must carry out their pension-related duties with "care, skill, prudence and diligence". Moreover, assets in the plan are to be used exclusively for the benefit of the plan participants in order to provide retirement benefits for the participants.

---

5 Dougal, Herbert E. and Gaumnitz, Jack E., *Pension and Retirement Plans*, at p. 134.
6 Charafes, Dimitris N., *The Globalization of Money and Securities*, at p. 183.
7 Charafes, Dimitris N., *The Globalization of Money and Securities*, at p. 183.

The above illustration demonstrates how properly regulated and managed pension schemes have been major stimulants to the economic progress of America. Thus, the importance of laws and institutional frameworks over pension funds cannot be over-emphasized. This is because, if properly regulated and managed, pension fund schemes will no doubt be a major tool of investment and economic growth in Nigeria.

Laws Regulating Pension Funds in Nigeria

The following laws apply to pension funds in Nigeria:

(1) Pensions Act;[8]
(2) Pension Rights of Judges Act;[9]
(3) Pensions (Transfer of Responsibility — United Kingdom Agreement) Act;[10]
(4) Investments and Securities Act 1999[11] and Rules and Regulations made by the Securities and Exchange Commission pursuant to the Act;
(5) Trustee Investments Act;[12]
(6) Personal Income Tax Decree 1993;[13]
(7) Constitution of the Federal Republic of Nigeria;
(8) Nigeria Social Insurance Trust Fund Decree 1993;
(9) National Insurance Commission Act (Number 1) 1997; and
(10) Insurance Act (Number 2) 1997.

Pensions Act

The Pensions Act came into force in Nigeria on 1 April 1974. It consolidated all enactments dealing with pensions, war pensions and disability benefits and gratuities for civilian employees of the government. It made provision for matters such as the computation of pensions and gratuities,[14] the fact that sums paid as pension payments shall be charged on the Consolidated Revenue Fund of the

8 Cap. 346, Laws of the Federation, 1990.
9 Act Number 5 of 1985, Cap. 347, Laws of the Federation, 1990.
10 Number 29 of 1979, Cap. 348, Laws of the Federation, 1990.
11 Act Number 45 of 1999.
12 Reproduced as Cap. 449, Laws of the Federation, 1990.
13 Decree Number 104 of 1993.
14 Pensions Act, Section 1.

Federation[15] and the circumstances in which pensions and gratuities may be granted.[16] Unfortunately, this Act was silent on the issues of registration, regulation, management and dissolution of pension funds.

Pension Rights of Judges Act

The Pension Rights of Judges Act also merely amended the relevant provisions of the Constitution to alter retirement benefits for judges. Again, this legislation is silent on the issues of registration, regulation, management and dissolution of pension funds.

Pension (Transfer of Responsibility — United Kingdom Agreement) Act

Aptly referred to as the Public Officers' Pension (Nigeria) Agreement 1979, the above legislation implemented the agreement concluded between the Governments of Nigeria and the United Kingdom transferring from the Government of Nigeria to the British Government responsibility for the administration and payment of pensions to certain British subjects who were retired government or local authority employees before 1 July 1979 and those retiring after that date. Again, this legislation made no contribution to the vital issues of registration, regulation, administration and dissolution of pension funds in Nigeria.

Investments and Securities Act

General The Investment and Securities Act came into force on 26 May 1999. This legislation, for the first time in Nigeria's history, went beyond the traditional tools of registration, surveillance, investigation and internal enforcement as a means of investor protection. It introduced the concepts of an investors' protection fund and the Investment and Securities Tribunal. The Act also extended the powers and responsibilities of the SEC.[17] Section 8(a) of the Act grants to the Commission the power to regulate investment and securities business in Nigeria "as defined in this Act".

---

15 Pensions Act, Section 2.

16 Pensions Act, Section 3.

17 Investments and Securities Act, Section 8.

Also, under Section 8(g) of the Act, the SEC is vested with the responsibility of registering and regulating the workings of venture capital funds and collective investment schemes, including mutual funds. In addition, the SEC has the power under the law to:

> "(n) Act as a regulatory apex organization for the Nigerian capital market, including the promotion and registration of self-regulatory organizations and capital market trade associations to which it may delegate its powers;
>
> "Note: This will include associations such as the Association of Pension Fund Managers if they wish to become self-regulatory organizations.
>
> "(s) Levy fees or other charges on any person for carrying out investment and securities business in Nigeria;
>
> "(u) Prevent fraudulent and unfair trade practices relating to the securities industry;
>
> "(w) Disqualify unfit individuals from being employed anywhere in the Securities industry; and
>
> "(y) Perform such other functions and exercise such other powers not inconsistent with the Act as are necessary or expedient for giving full effect to the provisions of the Act."

Also, prior to the promulgation of the Act, by virtue of Sections 575 to 589 (Chapter 3) of the Companies and Allied Matters Act (now replaced by Sections 124 to 148 of the Investment and Securities Act 1999), a unit trust scheme was the only legally recognized form of collective investment scheme in Nigeria.

Accepting without doubt that the Act extended the functions and responsibilities of the SEC, the following questions invariably arise:

(1) Can it be asserted with confidence that the regulation of pension funds also fall within the regulatory mechanism vested in the SEC by the enabling law, that is, the ISA 1999?

(2) Do pension funds qualify under the enabling law as investment and securities business as defined in the Act?

(3) Can pension funds be rightly regarded as a form of collective investment scheme under the enabling law?

(4) What was the intention of the legislature in enacting the provisions?
(5) Can it be said that the enabling law contains detailed provisions on pension funds or is there a legislative lacuna in the law? and
(6) What is the effect in law of the rules and regulations made by the SEC pursuant to the provisions of the Act, particularly as a form of delegated legislation?

Section 9 of the ISA 1999 provides in clear terms that the SEC shall establish specialized departments for the purposes of regulating "(c) Collective investments, including all collective investment schemes, such as unit trusts, the Esusu Scheme, Pension Funds and such other schemes". Under Part I of the Second Schedule to the Act, one of the types of investments constituting investments and investment business are "Units in a collective investment scheme . . .". Also, under Part II of the said Schedule, establishing, operating or winding up a collective investment scheme is listed as one of the activities constituting investment business in Nigeria. Thus, it is clear that the Act regards pension funds as one of the forms of collective investment schemes in Nigeria. It is also clear that the Act regards collective investment schemes as a form of investment business in Nigeria and vests in the SEC powers over the regulation of collective investment schemes.

However, another problem arises: should pension funds really be regarded as a form of collective investment scheme in view of Section 123(3) of the same Act? In the alternative, is there a conflict between the sections and the schedules to the Act discussed above with Section 123(3) of the Act? As another alternative, should Section 123(1) be interpreted to exclude pension funds, or should Section 123(3) be interpreted to include pension funds in Nigeria? The answer to this problem lies in a proper understanding or conceptualization of the meanings of "collective investment scheme" and "pension fund". Under Section 123(1) of the Act, "collective investment scheme" means:

"(a) any arrangement with respect to property of any description, including money, the purpose or effect of which is to enable persons taking part in the arrangements (whether by becoming owners of the property or any part of it or likewise) to participate in or receive profits or income arising from the acquisition, holding, management or disposal of the property or sums paid out of such profits or income;

"(b) any arrangement described in paragraph (a) of this subsection in which the participants do not have day-to-day control over the management of the property underlying the arrangement notwithstanding that they have a right to be consulted or to give directions;

"(c) any arrangement as set out in paragraphs (a) and (b) of this subsection in which participants pool their contributions for the purpose of sharing the profits or income arising from the management of their money or property solely from the benefit of a third party."

Under Subsection (3), the following are not collective investment schemes:

"(a) arrangements operated by a person otherwise than by way of business;

"(b) arrangements where each of the participants carries on a business other than investment business and enters into the arrangements for commercial purposes related to that business;

"(c) arrangements where each of the participants is a body corporate in the same group as the operator."

The next step is to "x-ray" the definition of "pension fund" and to juxtapose the said definition with the definition of collective investment scheme under the enabling law. Although "pension fund" is not defined in the ISA 1999, Rule 250 of the Rules and Regulations made by the SEC pursuant to the Act contains a definition *in pari materia* with Section 1 of the Fourth Schedule to the Personal Income Tax Decree 1993.[18] Rule 250 states as follows:

> "Pension fund for the purposes of these Rules and Regulations shall be any society fund or scheme the assets of which are held under irrevocable trusts the main objects of which are the provision of non-assignable and non-commutable retirement pensions or annuities for an individual or his dependants after his death or for any group or class of such individuals and their dependants."

18 Act Number 45 of 1999.

Another question is are company managed funds or self-administered pension schemes a form of collective investment scheme? No doubt the above definitions are very clear on this point: collective investment schemes include pension funds. Can it, therefore, be rightly argued that company-managed funds or self-administered schemes are not collective investment schemes under Nigerian law because they are not operated by way of business, but as a welfare scheme, and also because the investment of the fund so accumulated (by contributions) is a derived function of the funds and not an original purpose for setting up the scheme?

It is not correct to say that pension funds are not operated by way of business. As earlier identified, Section 9(c) of the Act classified pension funds as a form of collective investment scheme. One of the activities listed as constituting an investment business in Nigeria by Part II of the Second Schedule to the Act is the establishment and operation of a collective investment scheme.

Apart from the above, Rule 250 clearly states that the assets of pension schemes shall be held under "irrevocable trust". The implication in law is that the operation of a pension scheme becomes analogous to an investment or business trust, offering a pragmatic demonstration of the collective investment function of the law of trusts. It becomes, more or less by virtue of Rule 250, an adaptation of the objective of carrying on investment business by trustees and/or managers of pension funds for the benefit of pensioners or beneficiaries. Thus, as applicable to other forms of investment trusts, the principles of equity jurisprudence applicable to trust estates generally will constitute the foundation stone upon which the business trust plan is founded.[19]

This will include, among other things, the duty imposed by law on trustees to exercise their powers in the best interests of the pensioners and beneficiaries. In the case of *Cowan & Ors.* v. *Scargill & Ors.*,[20] Megarry, V.C. held, *inter alia*, that:

> "I can see no reason for holding that different principles apply to pension fund trusts from those which apply to other trusts. Of course, there are many provisions in pension schemes which are not to be found in private trusts, and to

19 "Business Trusts", 150 A.L.R. Anno, at p. 30; Decision of the U.S. Supreme Court in *Hecht* v. *Halley* (1924) 265 U.S. 144, 68, Led 949, 445 at 462.

20 [1984] 2 All E.R. 751.

> these the general law of trusts will be subordinated. But subject to that, . . . the trusts of pension funds are subject to the same rules as other trusts. The large size of pension funds emphasizes the need for diversification rather than lessening it, and the fact that much of the fund has been contributed by members of the scheme seems to me . . . to make it even more important that the trustees should exercise their powers in the best interests of the beneficiaries."[21]

The above sound, equitable principles common to England and most jurisdictions in the United States[22] are intended, by the wording of Rule 250, to be applicable to Nigeria. Thus, the intention of Rule 250 must be to treat pension schemes as irrevocable investment trusts and the powers of investment of trustees of pension funds must be exercised in the best interests of their beneficiaries. Rule 254 deals directly with the point by stipulating that "the pension fund must be operated in a way that is connected with the carrying on of a trade, business, profession or vocation".

Apart from the above-settled position of the law, English courts have confirmed that company-managed funds or self-administered schemes are collective investment schemes. The recent English case of *Bus Employees Pension Trustees Ltd. & Anor.* v. *Harrod & Ors.*[23] was based on a company pension scheme. In that case, NCBPT was the corporate trustee of the pension funds for employees of subsidiaries of NCB, a statutory corporation whose subsidiaries were sold to the private sector between 1986 and 1988 and which was itself dissolved in 1991. During the privatization process in England, the pension funds were wound up and their members paid off. The court had to decide, *inter alia*, whether the schemes remained occupational pension schemes. Sir Richard Scott V.C. held that, before the schemes were wound up, there was no doubt that they were occupational pension schemes.

The unique importance of this case is that the interpretation of "occupational pension scheme" in Section 1 of the English Pension Schemes Act 1993 is on all fours with the description of a collective

---

21 [1984] 2 All E.R. 751, 763 (lines c–e).

22 For American cases on the point, *see Blankenship* v. *Boyle* (1971) 329 F. Supp. 1089; *Wither* v. *Teachers' Retirement System of the City of New York* (1978) 447 F. Supp. 1248.

23 [1999] 2 All E.R. 993.

investment scheme under Section 123(1) of Nigeria's ISA 1999. It is submitted, therefore, that company-managed pension funds are also a form of collective investment scheme. It is incorrect to suggest that they are not operated by way of business, but as a mere welfare scheme. This submission is also in accord with other decisions of American and English courts on the point.

For example, *Blankenship* v. *Boyle*[24] was an American case heard in the District of Columbia. The trustees of a pension fund allowed large sums of money to remain in bank accounts bearing no interest at a bank controlled by the Union. Over an eighteen-year period, varying sums between US $14-million and US $75-million, representing fourteen per cent and forty-four per cent of the fund's total resources, had been left in this way. The fund was established for the benefit of the employees of coal operators, their families and dependents. The court reaffirmed the duty of undivided loyalty that a trustee owes to the beneficiaries in handling an investment by way of business. In an English case, *Butler* v. *Saunders*,[25] Whym-Parry J. said that trustees "have an overriding duty to obtain the best price which they can for their beneficiaries".[26]

Furthermore, it is difficult to accept that company-managed funds are excluded from collective investment schemes because the investment of the fund so accumulated (by contributions) is a derived function of the funds and not an original purpose of setting up the scheme. That argument may not, however, be tenable in the light of Rules 251 and 261 of the SEC Rules and Regulations and on the face of practical realities and the essence of operation of pension funds as a form of investment trust. In stating the purpose of pension funds, Rule 251 recognizes as one of the purposes of pension funds ". . . accumulation of sums payable to an employee in leaving the service of an employer".

Rule 261 requires that at least fifty per cent of the funds of a pension scheme shall be invested in securities issued by or under the authority of any government in Nigeria and other capital market instruments. In effect, the investment of accumulated funds is not a derived function, but constitutes an original purpose of setting up a pension fund in Nigeria. The intention of the law must be to ensure certainty and to formally establish a pension fund as an investment

24 (1971) 329 F. Supp. 1089.
25 [1950] 2 All E.R. 193.
26 [1950] 2 All E.R. 193, 195.

portfolio where beneficiaries pull resources together with a view to receiving future benefits, income or profit from the arrangement.

Intention of the Legislature It is submitted that a formidable approach towards avoiding the problem of interpretation of the provisions of the ISA 1999 *vis-à-vis* the control and management of pension funds in Nigeria is to read the entire legislation as a whole and to consolidate this approach by examining the legislative purpose of the Act on Pension Funds, otherwise referred to as "legislative intention". In an English case, Attorney General's Reference (Number 1 of 1988),[27] the English Court of Appeal settled the problem of interpretation of Section 1 of the English Securities (Insider Dealing) Act 1985 by upholding the contention of the prosecution that, looking at the Act as a whole, it was aimed at those who took unfair advantage of a privileged advantage. The government white paper on the subject[28] showed that the intention was to stop cheating by insiders who profit from their dealings with others. The court construed the word "obtained" in the light of the purpose behind the Act.[29]

Thus, it is often tempting to look at the section that seems immediately applicable to the problems at hand, but this is as likely to lead to a misconception of the total effect of the provision as is the reading of a passage of a novel out of context.[30]

In *Metropolitan Gas Company* v. *The Federated Gas Employees' Industrial Union*,[31] the Australian courts held that ". . . every passage in a document must be read, not as if it were entirely divorced from its context, but as part of the whole instrument".[32] Also, American courts agree that the primary purpose of statutory construction is to:

> ". . . ascertain the intention of the legislature, not only from the language used, but also from the reason and necessity for

27 *The Times*, 19 October 1988.

28 "Conduct of Company Directors", Cmnd. 7037 of 1977.

29 *Johnson* v. *Moreton* [1978] 3 All E.R. 37; *Fothergill* v. *Monarch Airlines Ltd.* [1980] 3 W.L.R. 209.

30 Pearce, D.C., *Statutory Interpretation in Australia* (Butterworths, 1974) at p. 25.

31 [1924] 35 C.L.R. 449; *See also Scott* v. *Commissioner of Taxation of the Commonwealth* (1996) C.L.R. 514.

32 *Metropolitan Gas Company* v. *The Federated Gas Employees' Industrial Union* [1924] 35 C.L.R. 449, at p. 455.

> the Act, the evil sought to be remedied and the objects and purpose sought to be obtained by it".[33]

Applied to pension funds under Nigeria's ISA 1999, the Act must be read in its entirety, bearing in mind the manifest intention of protecting innocent pensioners and beneficiaries through proper and adequate regulation of the duties of operators of the schemes. In this way, doubts as to the responsibilities vested in the SEC under the Act need not arise. Moreover, legislation on pension provisions is classified under the law (along with provisions on workmen's compensation and family maintenance) as remedial or beneficial provisions. A remedial or beneficial provision is one that gives some benefit to a person and thereby remedies some injustice. The position of the law is that such remedial provisions ought to be interpreted liberally. In *Bull* v. *The Attorney General for New South Wales*,[34] an Australian court identified:

> "In the first place, this is a remedial Act and, therefore, if any ambiguity existed, like all such Acts, should be construed beneficially. This means, of course, not that the true signification of the provisions should be strained or exceeded, but that it should be construed so as to give the fullest relief which the fair meaning of its language will allow".[35]

Applied to the problem of interpretation of provisions on pension funds under the ISA 1999, assuming an ambiguity exists as to the interpretation of Section 123 of the ISA or any other provision on pension funds, it must be construed beneficially without stretching the interpretation beyond the fair meaning. An example of stretching the interpretation beyond its fair meaning is the contention that a company managed fund does not qualify as a collective investment scheme.

---

33 *Tallios* v. *Tallios*, 350 Ill. App. 299, 112 N.E. 2d 723 (Appellate Court of Illinois); *Boyd* v. *Cress*, 26 Cal. 2d 164, 293 P.2d 37 (Supreme Court of California, 1956); *United States* v. *Ninety-Nine Diamonds*, 139 F. 961 (United States Circuit Court of Appeal, Eighth Circuit, 1905); *Schneller* v. *Schneller*, 356 Ill.89, 190 N.E. 121, 92 A.L.R. 838; *Barnes* v. *City of Chicago*, 323 Ill.203 153 N.E. 821, 52 A.L.R. 560.

34 (1913) 17 C.L.R. 370.

35 Per Isaacs J, at p. 384. *See* further, *Holmes* v. *Permanent Trustee Company of New South Wales Ltd.* (1932) 47 C.L.R. 113; *Reid Murray Dev. Queensland (Pty) Ltd.* v. *Lynwood Holdings Pty Ltd.* [1964] Q.W.N.I. 32; *Matthews* v. *Foggit Jones Ltd.* [1925] 37 C.L.R. 455.

However, would the beneficial interpretation of provisions on pension funds in Nigeria be valid under the law in view of the fact that Rule 271 of the SEC Rules and Regulations contains provisions on penalties for failure to authorize and register pension funds in Nigeria? The effect of Rule 271 on the problem of interpretation is that the provisions on pension funds cannot be regarded solely as remedial or beneficial provisions, but as a combination of both remedial and penal law. Thus, in order to achieve its beneficial purpose, the SEC Rules penalize certain types of conduct. Is there a conflict between the approach of interpreting beneficial legislation liberally to achieve its purpose and the approach of not extending the operation of a penal provision beyond its actual wording?

A close examination of Rule 271 of the SEC Rules shows a glaring absence of conflict. The words are very clear and seek to make effective the remedy sought to be introduced. In another Australian case,[36] Isaacs J. cited the dictum of Lord Shaw in *Butler* (*or Black*) v. *Fife Coal Co.* to the effect that ". . . Consistently with the actual language employed, the Act shall be interpreted in the sense favorable to making the remedy effective and the protection secure".[37]

It may be contended that there is a legislative gap in the ISA 1999 since there are no detailed provisions on pension funds in the ISA. However, Section 258(1) of the Act provides:

> "The commission may make regulations -
>
> "(a) providing for anything requiring to be prescribed under this Decree; and
>
> "(b) generally for carrying out the principles and objectives of this Decree."

Also, Section 262(1) of the Act provides:

> "The commission may, from time to time, make rules and regulations for the purpose of giving effect to the provisions of this Decree and may, in particular, without prejudice to the generality of the foregoing provisions, make regulations -

---

36 *Matthews* v. *Foggit Jones Ltd.* [1912] AC 178–179.

37 [1912] AC 178–179.

"(m) providing for anything requiring to be prescribed under this Decree; and

"(n) generally for carrying out the principles and objectives of this Decree."

Pursuant to the above powers, the SEC prescribed the Rules and Regulations now in force. Rules 250 to 272 deal with pension funds.

Securities and Exchange Commission Rules and Regulations It is submitted that the SEC has taken the proper steps in prescribing the Rules and Regulations now in force pursuant to the powers conferred on the Commission by the ISA 1999. Although, it shall be submitted later in this review that some provisions in the Rules and Regulations may need amendment.

The above submission is based on the accepted legal position that an Act may authorize the making of other forms of legislation. This is collectively known as delegated legislation. Legally, it should not be regarded as some inferior form of legislation, but carries out its maker's commands as does an Act of the National Assembly.[38] In effect, the argument as to a legislative gap in the ISA 1999 need no longer arise. However, it is observed that some aspects of the Rules and Regulations may have to be reviewed, amended or repealed.

Suggestions for Reform Since it is accepted that the whole essence of effective regulation and management of pension funds is to sanitize the system and protect innocent investors, that is, the pensioners, it is imperative that there ought to be in the enabling law or in the Rules a provision on the procedure for effective consideration and adjudication of complaints of aggrieved pensioners. The object of the provision will be to deal with complaints by Nigerian pensioners (who at the moment have nobody to complain to) in a procedurally fair, economical and expeditious manner.

In South Africa, complaints by aggrieved pensioners are handled by the Pension Funds Adjudicator appointed pursuant to Section 30c of the Pension Funds Act 1956 (as amended).[39] Ample provisions are made in the enabling legislation on issues such as submission and

38 Pearce, D.C., *Statutory Interpretation in Australia* (Butterworths, 1974) at pp. 1–2.
39 Act Number 24 of 1956.

consideration of complaints by aggrieved pensioners, resolution of complaints, parties to the complaints, legal representation, recording of proceedings and enforceability of any determination made.

In England, the Pensions Ombudsman has a statutory function of adjudicating complaints of mal-administration of pension funds that may be made to him. Consequently, it was possible for a pensioner to lodge a complaint before the Pensions Ombudsman recently in *Bus Employees Pension Trustees Ltd. & Anor.* v. *Harrod & Ors*.[40] The aspect of that case concerning the submission above is that a Mr. Wheler, a pensioner, was outraged by the diversion of the fund surplus from the members and pensioners. He challenged the validity of a 1986 deed of variation. He did so by making a complaint to the Pensions Ombudsman, who held that the deed of variation was invalid.

Absence of a provision on procedure for the handling of complaints of aggrieved pensioners is a serious oversight or omission in Nigeria's SEC Rules and Regulations. Unfortunately, the Investment and Securities Tribunal introduced pursuant to Section 224 of the ISA 1999 has yet to be formally established. However, assuming that the Tribunal has been formally established, would the scope of jurisdiction of the Tribunal cover cases of complaints by pensioners? Section 234(1) of the Act provides:

> "The Tribunal shall have power to adjudicate on disputes and controversies arising under this Decree and the Rules and Regulations made thereunder."

Since the issue of complaints of aggrieved pensioners are neither provided for under the Act nor under the Rules and Regulations made pursuant to the Act, it is safe to conclude that complaints by aggrieved pensioners, who ought to be protected by the law, may not fall within the scope of jurisdiction of the Investments and Securities Tribunal. It is, therefore, submitted that a detailed provision on the handling of complaints of aggrieved pensioners be inserted into the Rules and Regulations, bringing the provision within the scope of the jurisdiction of the Tribunal.

Assuming (which is not the case) that the issue of complaints by aggrieved pensioners does fall within the Tribunal's jurisdiction, there are some sections of the ISA on the authority and procedure of the Tribunal that need to be expunged from the statute book. This

40 [1999] 2 All E.R. 993, 998.

submission is proffered with the objective intention of avoiding situations where the Tribunal may be clogged by disputes and unnecessary litigation.

Section 231 of the Act contains an outer clause which provides as follows:

> "The question as to the validity of the appointment of any person as a capital market assessor shall not be the cause of litigation in any court or tribunal and no act or proceedings before the Tribunal shall be called into question in any manner on the ground merely of any defect in the constitution of the Tribunal."

The following questions arise:

(1) Is any form of grievance procedure or remedy provided in the enabling Act for cases where unqualified capital market assessors are appointed and where the Tribunal hears and determines a matter without being properly constituted?

(2) Would it not conflict with the cherished principles of law that such cases should be allowed to stand? and

(3) Would it not be taken up before the Court of Appeal or Supreme Court against the Investment and Securities Tribunal that the Tribunal lacked the requisite jurisdiction when it heard or determined a case without being properly constituted or its members (capital market assessors) were not qualified?

It is submitted that Section 231 of the ISA must be seen as being in conflict with the rule of law and should be expunged from the Act. The growth and well-being of the law and the country's citizens depends on the existence of an independent and virile judiciary unhindered by any statutory provision from inquiring into the acts of government officials. In Nigeria's nascent democracy, the rule of law is not only a policy of the State, but also a veritable instrument of social engineering and integration. The absolute supremacy, unquestionability and validity of the appointment of any person as a capital market assessor in Nigeria by the Minister of Finance may amount to arbitrariness. It may amount to an erroneous acceptance that what is officially done by the Minister with respect to capital market assessors is law. As succinctly articulated by Sir Jon Latham, a former Chief Justice of Australia in *Arthur Yates & Company*

Limited v. *Vegetable Seeds Committee*,[41] "It is not the English view of law that whatever is officially done is law . . .".[42]

Also, it is now accepted in democratic governments that judicial review, that is, the power of the law courts to examine executive and legislative actions in order to ascertain whether such actions conform with the enabling law or the Constitution, is a corollary of the doctrine of the rule of law.[43]

Apart from the above, it is submitted that cases where the Investments and Securities Tribunal determines matters without being properly constituted or where the capital market assessors are not competent to act may be challenged before the appellate courts on the basis of lack of jurisdiction. As provided by Section 243(1) of this Act, a person dissatisfied with a decision of the Tribunal constituted under the Act may appeal against such decision on points of law to the Court of Appeal upon giving notice in writing to the Secretary to the Tribunal within thirty days after the date upon which such decision was given. This is fundamental because Nigerian courts agree that where a court or tribunal has no jurisdiction to entertain an action, anything done in respect thereof will be futile.[44] In *Gabriel Madukolu & Ors.* v. *Johnson Nkemdilim*,[45] the Federal Supreme Court of Nigeria held that a court or a tribunal is competent to adjudicate on a matter when:

(1) It is properly constituted with respect to the number and qualifications of its members;
(2) The subject matter of the action is within its jurisdiction;
(3) The action is initiated by due process of law; and
(4) Any condition precedent to the exercise of its jurisdiction has been fulfilled.

It is, therefore, suggested that Section 231 of the ISA 1999 ought to be repealed in order to preserve the principles of the rule of law and to

41 [1945] 72 C.L.R. 37.

42 *Arthur Yates & Company Limited* v. *Vegetable Seeds Committee* [1945] 72 C.L.R. 37, at p. 66; *See also Entwick* v. *Carprington* (1965) 19 St. Tr. 1030; *Wolf Tone Case* (1798) 29 St. Tr. 614.

43 Pronouncement of Chief Justice Marshall in *Marbury* v. *Madison*, 5 U.S. (1 Crach) 137 (1803) U.S. Supreme Court; Judgment of Uche Omo J.S.C. in *Attorney-General of Anambra State* v. *Okafor* [1992] 2 N.W.L.R. (Part 224) 396.

44 *A.G. Anambra State & Ors.* v. *A-G of the Federation & Ors.* [1993] 6 N.W.L.R. (Part 301) 570.

45 (1962) 2 A.N.L.R. 581.

meet the requirements of justice. Section 237(3) makes this argument more compelling, providing that any proceeding before the Tribunal shall be deemed to be a judicial proceeding and that the Tribunal shall be deemed to be a civil court for all purposes.

Section 242 of the ISA 1999 provides:

> "Save as provided elsewhere in this Act, no civil court shall have jurisdiction to entertain any suit or proceeding in respect of any matter which the Tribunal constituted under this Act is empowered by or under this Act to determine and no injunction shall be granted by any court or other authority in respect of any action taken or to be taken in pursuance of any power conferred on the Tribunal by or under this Act."

The arguments and submissions proffered against Section 231 apply equally to Section 232 of the Act.

Section 255(1) of the Decree should be expunged from the ISA 1999. It provides:

> "If the Minister is of the opinion that is necessary or expedient so to do in the public interest, he may exempt any person buying or selling securities or otherwise dealing in the securities market from the operation of the provisions of this Act."

On the other hand, it ought to be in the public interest and that of the investors that all persons or class of persons buying or selling securities or otherwise dealing in the securities market should comply with the provisions of the Act essentially enacted to protect the public and investors.

Section 251 of the Act presently provides:

> "No suit, prosecution or other legal proceedings shall lie against the Federal Government or any officer or any member, officer or other employee of the Commission for anything which is done in good faith or intended to be done under this Act or rules or regulations made thereunder."

It is submitted that any conduct may be justified under Section 251 of the Act as having been done in good faith, since no grievance procedure has been provided against possible abuse in isolated cases. Moreover, if the Federal Government and officials perform their responsibilities without fear, favor or properly in the interests of corporate Nigeria, they will have nothing to fear in relation to legal proceedings against their conduct. In any event, the fact that improper conduct is likely to attract a lawsuit ought to be a formidable instrument for checking the activities of officials. Section 251 is also in conflict with the principles of the rule of law and ought to be expunged from the statute book. These provisions, as they presently stand, may discourage local and foreign investors. The majority of leaders of industry are of the view that the ISA will stand as the most innovative legislation of the time without the above provisions and an amendment to some onerous registration procedures.

In relation to the setting up and registration of pension funds, Rule 265 provides that "All applications for authorization for pension funds shall comply with the requirements of the Trustee Investment Act and all other rules of the Commission". On 23 May 1957, the Government and Other Securities (Local Trustee Investment) Ordinance was promulgated in Nigeria. It was simply titled as an ordinance to facilitate the investment of trusts and other funds in Nigeria in locally issued securities and was divided into four sections. However, on 12 May 1962, the Trustee Investment Act 1962 came into force with the objective of extending the powers of trustees. The Act was reproduced in 1990 as Chapter 449 of the Laws of the Federation without amendments to the law of 1962 and has remained the law to date.

Why should an application for authorization of a pension fund have to comply with the requirements of the Trustee Investment Act as prescribed by Rule 265 of the SEC Rules and Regulations when the issues of form of securities to which the Trustee Investment Act apply and the securities in which a trustee may invest are not matters to be concerned with prior to the authorization of a pension fund and its registration? As these are issues which arise after authorization, it is submitted that such issues ought to be amended.

In view of the economic realities of modern Nigeria, there remains the urgent need to review the provisions of the Trustee Investment Act in order to enhance investment by trustees in several other viable areas of investment outside the companies quoted on the Stock Exchange. Rule 261 of the SEC Rules and Regulations, in an effort to reduce the harsh effects of the limitations contained in the Trustee Investment Act, provides that at least fifty per cent of the funds of pension schemes in Nigeria shall be invested in securities issued by or under the authority of any government in Nigeria and other capital market instruments.

Interestingly, it is noted that there is no provision in the SEC Rules and Regulations applicable to pension funds requiring trustees of pension schemes to carry out their responsibilities pursuant to the provisions of the Trustee Investment Act, except Rule 265, discussed earlier, on applications for authorization. Even if it is intended to apply to investments by trustees of pension funds (which is not conceded), it will be interpreted to conflict with Rule 265 of the SEC Rules and Regulations. In that case, Section 261 of the ISA 1999 will apply. This Section provides:

> "(1) Notwithstanding the provisions of this Act, the relevant provisions of all existing enactments, including the following -
>
> "(a) the Trustee Investment Act etc. . . . Shall be read with such modification as to bring them into conformity with the provisions of this Act."

If the SEC wants the Trustee Investment Act to apply to investment by trustees of pension schemes, then it should be expressly provided under the Rules and Regulations. However, this must be done with great caution in view of the inherent criticisms and limitations contained in the Trustee Investment Act which need urgent review to ensure greater industrialization and the attraction of investors.

For example, in an era where Nigeria's democratic government encourages trade liberalization and has done so much to encourage privatization and commercialization, one wonders why only four corporations should remain scheduled to the Act.[46] This might only be appreciated prior to Nigerian independence and shortly after independence in 1960, when the Government battled to get a hold on the foundations of the Nigerian economy.

Another example is found in the severe limitations contained in Sections 2 and 3 of the Act, which are major sources of disincentives to investors. Also, reference to the Lagos Stock Exchange in the Act should be amended to refer to stock exchanges generally. Moreover, the discretion of the trustee provided under Section 3(2) is not very helpful, since that discretion is restricted by the limits in terms of securities provided by the Act and is subject to any consent or direction required by the instrument, if any, creating the trust.

---

46 Cap. 449, Laws of the Federation of Nigeria, Section 2(1)(c).

Although an interesting provision touching on breach of trust and cessation of authorization of investment is reproduced in Section 4 of the Act, the Section raises a number of questions without answers. That Section provides:

> "A trustee shall not be liable for breach of trust by reason of his continuing to hold an investment which has at any time ceased to be an investment authorized by the provisions of this Act."

What are the remedies provided by the Act to beneficiaries whose trustees deliberately continue to hold an investment which ceases to be an investment under the Act? Would a trustee be justified in continuing to hold an investment without legal backing or exempted from liability for breach of trust in such circumstances, that is, when the structures of the law conferring on him the authority to act in respect of an investment are dismantled? At least, what would be the fate of those investors?

One gropes in darkness to find the answer to the above problems from the Act. It is, therefore, suggested that the Trustee Investment Act be amended. The result at the moment would be that a trustee who holds back an investment which the law no longer authorizes can continue to do so without liability or accountability. The Act should at least stipulate what would happen to such investments and the fate of the beneficiaries who invested legally while the investments were authorized by the Act. This would foster more confidence in investors.

Authorization Fee

The SEC's recent requirement indicates that the authorization fee for the regulation of pension funds is presently calculated by working out a percentage of the net income as follows:

(1) Registration of fund up to N1-million — one per cent;
(2) Registration of fund over N1-million but below N250-million — 0.75 per cent;
(3) Registration of fund over N250-million but below N500-million — 0.5 per cent;
(4) Registration of fund over N500-million — 0.25 per cent;
(5) Annual renewal of the fund — one per cent of gross income, minimum of N10,000, or where there is no income;

(6) Registration of pension fund manager — N20,000;
(7) Registration of two principal officers — N1,000; and
(8) Renewal of pension fund managers — N10,000.

While there may not be problems with items (6) to (8) above, there may be serious problems with items (1) to (5). Since the major aim of the entire regulatory mechanism taken as a whole is to protect investors, in this case innocent pensioners, it may be safe to adopt a system of calculation of authorization fees which may not be interpreted as depleting the net asset value or base of pension funds in Nigeria. Perhaps this may be calculated on the profits derived from the investments of these funds and shall entail effective monitoring and control so that returns are duly made and profits duly ascertained and verified.

Benefit under Pension Schemes

Rule 256 of the SEC Rules provides:

> "No person entitled to benefit under the scheme shall lose his benefit except upon dismissal based on fraud or misconduct constituting a criminal offence."

The implication of this provision is that a person dismissed by his employer on grounds of fraud or misconduct regarded as a criminal offence shall lose his benefit under a pension scheme in Nigeria. It is submitted that this provision should be amended to provide that such a person shall be entitled to a pension based on the contribution he has made up to the time of his dismissal. In *Bold* v. *Brough, Nicholson & Hall Ltd.*,[47] the plaintiff was held to be entitled to receive a pension based on the contributions he had made although dismissed from service on 27 July 1962.

Apart from the above, it is wrong to relate problems arising between a master and his servant to contributions made by an employee, particularly where such dismissal, based on fraud or misconduct regarded as constituting a criminal offence, is not supported by a decision of a court or by the rules of natural justice. Cases exist where courts have set aside the wrongful dismissal of employees

47 (1963) Q.B.D. 849.

based on non-observance of the rules of natural justice.[48] Rule 256 should, therefore, be amended in the light of the above suggestions.

Rule 262(1) of the SEC Rules and Regulations prescribes that managers of pension funds shall file with the SEC, not later than the fifteenth day of the next month, monthly and quarterly returns. Also, Rule 262(iii) requires that the penalty of N1,000 per day be paid out of the fund where the manager is liable in cases of non-compliance.

While it is appreciated that the management of pension funds needs to be closely monitored, hence the need for regular returns by managers, it is submitted that the dual requirement of monthly and quarterly returns may be cumbersome. This may be made annual or twice a year, but it must be made in order to ensure a close monitoring of the management of pension funds in Nigeria.

It is difficult to understand why the penalty in Rule 262(iii), under which a manager of a fund is liable to pay due to his failure to perform his paid responsibility, should be borne by the fund. It is submitted that this should be borne by the manager, which would serve to ensure that the manager strives to comply with the requirements of the law.

Constitutional Provisions on Pension Funds

Sections 173 and 210 of the 1999 Constitution of Nigeria protect the right of government and local authority employees to receive a pension or gratuity. The provisions are silent on the right of persons other than government and local authority employees to receive a pension, although Sections 173(4) and 214(4) provide that pensions in respect of service with the government or local authorities shall not be taxed.

The express mention of the protection of pension rights for government and local authority employees may be interpreted as excluding all others. Instead of subjecting this constitutional protection to interpretation, therefore, it might be appropriate to amend that section of the Constitution to also provide express protection of pension rights to persons in companies and other organizations. There may then be the need to expressly state which pensions should be taxed under the law and which should not.

48 *U.N.N. & Anor.* v. *Hope Chinyelu Nnoli* [1994] 8 N.W.L.R. (Part 303) 376; *Edward Aiyetan* v. *N10PR* [1987] 3 N.W.L.R. (Part 59) 48.

Joint Tax Board and Pension Funds

Section 85 of the Personal Income Tax Act 1993 established the Joint Tax Board. The powers of the Board are clearly spelt out under the enabling law. They are limited to approval of pension funds only for the purpose of ascertaining employees' contributions under their retirement benefits which may be exempted from tax and from the profit or loss of a company.

Social Insurance Trust Fund and Pension Funds

The Nigerian Social Insurance Trust Fund was established by the Nigerian Social Insurance Trust Fund Decree 1993 and applies in respect of every person listed in Sections 10(1)(a)–10(1)(c) of the Law. Section 10(3) of the Law provides that the existence of a private pension scheme in respect of workers to whom the Act applies shall not exempt an employer or employees referred to in Section 10(1) from the provisions of the Act. Again, the functions of the Nigerian Social Insurance Trust Fund do not include the regulation of pension funds.

National Insurance Commission Act and Insurance Act

Based on the definitions of "insurance business" and "group life insurance fund" contained in Sections 2(2) and 97 of the Insurance Act 1997, insurance companies in Nigeria manage underwritten funds relating to life insurance business on a group of lives, including staff retirement schemes. Regulation of the insurance industry is vested in the National Insurance Commission established by the National Insurance Commission Act 1997. To the extent that the National Insurance Commission regulates all insurance companies and the conduct of all classes of insurance business, the Commission can be regarded as a regulator of pension funds emanating from those classes of insurance business only.

Conclusion

It is apparent that controversy exists concerning aspects of the legal and institutional framework presently regulating pension funds in

Nigeria. A few suggestions have been proffered in this chapter, particularly on the legal implication or interpretation of several aspects of the subject. Despite the criticisms, it must be realized that the provisions of the ISA 1999 and the Rules and Regulations made pursuant to it remain law and should be obeyed except where a court rules *per contra* or if the laws and regulations are repealed.

In the course of this review, it was recognized that pension funds are a form of collective investment scheme under Nigerian law. Whatever suggestions that are adopted at the end of the exercise, the best are those that protect the interests of investors (pensioners), that monitor closely the activities of the operators and ensure sound and safe regulatory mechanisms. A situation where anyone having a role to play in investing a pension plan's assets is regarded as a fiduciary is recommended for adoption in Nigeria. It is important that pension funds be given their rightful place in Nigeria's economic and social development.

Note: The writer served as a member of the National Committee on Private Pension Fund Management in Nigeria and headed the Legal Subcommittee.

United States Securities Law Implications of Employee Stock Purchase and Option Plans

Joseph G. Krassy
Thelen Reid & Priest LLP
New York, United States

Introduction

The era of globalization has generally been identified with overseas expansion of business activities by international entities. Countless entities organized and headquartered in the United States have established subsidiaries abroad or developed foreign operations by merging with or acquiring companies located in such jurisdictions. Not surprisingly, overseas expansion has also meant that non-United States international entities are increasingly likely to establish subsidiaries or operations in the United States by merging with or acquiring companies located in the United States. Like their American counterparts, such companies often find it convenient to structure compensation arrangements for employees in the United States around the issuance of securities.

When purchase plans or option plans and similar employee benefit plans or agreements provide for the issuance of securities to employees of such entities or of their subsidiaries located in the United States,[1] the issuing entity will need to be aware of and to comply with applicable securities laws in the United States.

The most obvious of such securities laws is the Securities Act of 1933, as amended. The Securities Act generally requires registration of securities "offered" and "sold" to United States citizens (wherever located) and to non-United States persons residing in the United

1 Such compensatory arrangements are frequently structured to qualify as employee stock purchase plans under Section 423 of the United States Internal Revenue Code of 1986, as amended, or as incentive stock options within the meaning of Section 422. This chapter does not address issues that may arise under the Internal Revenue Code.

D.Campbell and S.Woodley (eds.), The Comparative Law Yearbook of International Business 2003, 285-312

States.[2] The Securities Act is administered by the Securities and Exchange Commission (SEC).

In addition, the Securities Exchange Act of 1934, as amended (the Exchange Act), generally regulates securities markets and market participants (such as broker-dealers), but also imposes periodic reporting requirements on companies with publicly traded securities that are subject to registration.[3] The Exchange Act is also administered by the SEC.

Finally, each of the States of the United States (including the District of Columbia) has its own securities law to regulate the offer and sale of securities to a person within such jurisdiction. Such state securities laws[4] and the state agencies charged with their administration function independently of the Securities Act, the Exchange Act and the SEC.

Federal Implications — Rule 701

General

Although there are several exemptions under the Securities Act whereby an "offer" and "sale" of securities may be made in the United States without registration,[5] Rule 701 (attached hereto as Appendix A) was specifically promulgated as an exemptive rule to cover securities issued as employment compensation.

Generally, Rule 701 allows an issuer that is not a registered and full United States reporting company under the Exchange Act to sell securities issued by the company, its parent or majority-owned

2 One of the constituent elements for jurisdiction under the Securities Act is that the "offer" and "sale" of securities in the United States involve the use of "means of interstate commerce", such as mail or telephone.

3 Companies with more than US $10-million in assets whose securities are held by more than 500 owners must file annual and other periodic reports.

4 State securities laws generally predated the Securities Act and the Exchange Act. They are often identified by the sobriquet "Blue Sky" laws in a colloquial reference to an early United States Supreme Court case upholding the exercise by states of parallel but equal jurisdiction.

5 Section 4(2) of the Securities Act exempts sales that are "not to the public", Rule 504 of Regulation D exempts small offerings that may be to the public and Rule 506 of Regulation D exempts offerings to a limited number of purchasers and private placements under a "safe harbor" promulgated by the SEC pursuant to Section 4(2).

subsidiaries to employees, directors, general partners, trustees (where the issuer is a business trust), officers or consultants and advisors, and their family members who acquire such securities from such persons through gifts or domestic relations orders, pursuant to a written compensatory benefit plan (or written compensation contract) without filing a Securities Act registration statement. A "compensatory benefit plan" is any purchase, savings, option, bonus, stock appreciation, profit sharing, thrift, incentive, deferred compensation, pension or similar plan. Under Rule 701, the issuer must provide such employees with a copy of the compensatory benefit plan or contract.

Rule 701 does not limit the amount of securities offered in reliance upon the rule. However, Rule 701 does limit the aggregate sales price or amount of shares sold in reliance upon the rule. During any consecutive twelve-month period, the aggregate sales price or amount of securities that may be sold in reliance upon Rule 701 may not exceed the greatest of the following:

(1) US $1-million;
(2) Fifteen per cent of the total assets of the issuer to be measured as of the most recent balance sheet date; or
(3) Fifteen per cent of the outstanding amount of the class of securities being offered or sold in reliance upon Rule 701, measured as of the most recent balance sheet date.

In calculating the aggregate sales price, options are to be valued based on the exercise price of the option. The value of the options is counted towards the aggregate sales price when an option grant is made without regard to when the option becomes exercisable. For the purposes of calculating fifteen per cent of the total outstanding amount of securities, securities underlying all currently exercisable options are considered outstanding securities. Because the aggregate sales price will be calculated based on the options granted rather than the options exercised, an issuer can avoid the possibility of inadvertently exceeding the limit since it has no control over the timing of exercises of the options.[6]

---

6 If an issuer determines to issue stock options to or engage in other "sale" transactions with United States-based employees in reliance upon Rule 701 at any time, it must monitor the aggregate amount of its securities sold during the immediately preceding twelve-month period so as to avoid exceeding the limit on the aggregate sales price of such securities.

If the aggregate sales price or amount of securities sold during any consecutive twelve-month period exceeds US $5-million, each of the United States beneficiaries (and not just those in excess of the limit) must receive, within a reasonable period before the exercise of any options or purchase of any securities, among other items of disclosure, the following:

(1) A summary of the material terms of the compensatory benefit plans;

(2) Information about the risks associated with investment in the securities sold pursuant to the benefit plans;

(3) Financial statements as of a date no more than 180 days before the sale of the securities in reliance upon Rule 701 — financial statements that are not prepared in accordance with United States generally accepted accounting principles (United States GAAP) must be accompanied by a reconciliation to United States GAAP; and

(4) Disclosure of the options a reasonable period of time before the date of exercise of the options.

Securities issued in reliance upon Rule 701 are deemed to be "restricted securities" as defined in Rule 144 under the Securities Act. The Rule permits the public sale in ordinary transactions of limited amounts of securities owned by persons controlling, controlled by or under common control with the issuer and by persons who have acquired restricted securities of the issuer in transactions that were not otherwise subject to registration.[7] As a result, such securities will need to bear a restrictive legend and cannot be freely resold in the United States, although such limitations will not be particularly onerous to United States beneficiaries where no market currently exists for securities in the United States.[8]

Because Rule 701 is self-executing, there is no requirement to file reports or notifications with the SEC under Rule 701. An issuer does,

---

7 Rule 144 generally emphasizes the need for adequate current public information regarding an issuer and imposes a holding period prior to the resale of restricted securities to assure that those persons who buy securities under claim of an exemption are not acting as conduits (underwriters) for sale to the public of unregistered securities on behalf of an issuer.

8 If the issuer does become subject to the reporting requirements of the Exchange Act, Rule 701 provides a resale exemption to United States beneficiaries for securities underlying options beginning ninety days after the issuer becomes a full reporting company subject to the United States reporting requirements of the Exchange Act.

however, need to provide United States beneficiaries with a copy of the plan, and to monitor actively and restrict the amount of securities sold in reliance upon Rule 701 to a level within the allowed limit.

Rule 506 of Regulation D

As noted above, Rule 701 is not the sole exemption from Securities Act registration requirements. Reliance on one exemption does not preclude reliance on others that may be available for the same transaction or series of transactions. Rule 506 of Regulation D is one such exemption that may exist side-by-side with Rule 701 as a non-exclusive election, in whole or in part, to apply to recipients of options who meet certain criteria as "accredited investors".[9]

Rule 506 exempts the sale by an issuer of its securities without registration under the Securities Act in an offering that is limited to not more than thirty-five non-accredited investors. There is no limit on the number of accredited investors or the aggregate dollar amount of securities that may be sold under this exemption, but its conditions include both a prohibition on public solicitation or advertising and the imposition of restrictions on resale or transferability of such securities. No specific disclosure or offering document is required by Rule 506 when sales are limited to accredited investors. A Report of Sale on Form D is required to be filed with the SEC within fifteen days after the first sale of securities sold in reliance upon Rule 506.

The amount of securities sold in reliance upon the Rule 506 exemption will not be counted towards the US $5-million limit under Rule 701. Thus, in circumstances where an issuer's sale of securities or grant of options pursuant to Rule 701 approaches the US $5-million limit, the issuer may elect to count all sales or grants to such accredited investors as exempt under Rule 506, with only the remaining United States beneficiaries (non-accredited investors) counted under Rule 701.

---

9 The term accredited investor, within the meaning of Rule 501(a) of Regulation D, includes: (1) Any director or executive officer of the issuer; (2) A natural person whose individual net worth or joint net worth with his spouse exceeds US $1-million at the time of purchase; or (3) A natural person who had an individual income in excess of US $200,000 in each of the two most recent years or joint income with his spouse in excess of US $300,000 in each such year and has a reasonable expectation of reaching the same income level in the current year.

Exemption from Exchange Act Periodic Reporting Requirements

In recognition of the hesitancy of foreign companies to become full United States reporting companies and the burdens such status would impose, the SEC's Rule 12g3-2(b) under the Exchange Act provides an "information supplying" exemption for foreign private issuers.[10] With Rule 12g3-2(b), the SEC has adopted an easy procedure to allow foreign private issuers to issue securities in the United States without becoming full United States reporting companies. In short, the exemption is available to any foreign company that undertakes to furnish the SEC on an ongoing basis with all information that the company publicly releases, files with a stock exchange or distributes to its shareholders. If an issuer has obtained a Rule 12g3-2(b) exemption from the SEC, no further action need be taken with respect to Rule 12g3-2(b) other than normal monitoring of compliance with the rule.

State Law Implications

Each state of the United States has its own securities laws under which the sale of securities in the respective jurisdiction is regulated. An issuer must make a determination on a state-by-state basis whether exemptions are available or registration requirements apply under the securities law of each state in which participating employees reside.

With some variations, the securities, or "Blue Sky", laws of most states exempt from their registration requirements "securities issued in connection with an employees' stock purchase, savings, pension,

10 Rule 3b-4 under the Exchange Act defines a "foreign private issuer" as any foreign issuer (other than a foreign government) except an issuer meeting both of the following conditions: (1) More than fifty per cent of the outstanding voting securities of such issuer are held on record either directly or through voting trust certificates or depositary receipts by residents of the United States; and (2) Any of the following: (a) the majority of the executive officers or directors are United States citizens or residents; (b) more than fifty per cent of the assets of the issuer are located in the United States; or (c) the business of the issuer is administered principally in the United States. For the purpose of the definition, the term "resident" means any person whose address appears on the records of the issuer, the voting trustee or the depositary as being located in the United States.

profit-sharing or similar benefit plan".[11] The variations, as summarized below, fall into three categories: those states that impose no conditions upon the broad language of the exemption; those states that require a filing prior to issuance of securities under a plan;[12] and those states that require compliance with specific, and occasionally substantive, conditions set forth by statute or in corresponding regulations.

States That Impose No Conditions

The following states impose no conditions upon the exemption:
(1) Alabama;
(2) Alaska;
(3) Colorado;
(4) Connecticut;
(5) District of Columbia;
(6) Florida;
(7) Hawaii;
(8) Idaho;
(9) Illinois;
(10) Iowa;
(11) Kansas;
(12) Kentucky;
(13) Maine;
(14) Massachusetts;
(15) Michigan;
(16) Minnesota;
(17) Mississippi;
(18) Montana;
(19) Nebraska;
(20) Nevada;
(21) New Hampshire;
(22) New Jersey;
(23) New Mexico;
(24) North Carolina;

---

11 Unlike Rule 701, which is available for transactions with consultants and advisors, certain states expressly restrict their exemption to *bona fide* employees.

12 However, certain states make exemption conditional upon a filing prior to the inception of a plan. The term "inception" is generally not defined. For this purpose, inception may reasonably be deemed to occur at the time that participating employees first submit payment. A more restrictive construction could arguably find that "inception" occurs when a plan is adopted by the issuer's board of directors.

(25) North Dakota;
(26) Ohio;
(27) Oklahoma;
(28) Pennsylvania;
(29) Rhode Island;
(30) Texas;
(31) Utah;
(32) Vermont;
(33) Virginia; and
(34) Wisconsin.

States That Impose Filing Conditions

The following states require a filing prior to the issuance of securities:
(1) Delaware;
(2) Maryland;
(3) New York;
(4) Oregon;
(5) South Carolina;
(6) South Dakota;
(7) Tennessee;
(8) Washington;
(9) West Virginia; and
(10) Wyoming.

States That Require Specific Compliance

The following states require compliance with specific conditions:
(1) Arizona requires that a plan either meet certain requirements for qualification under the Internal Revenue Code of 1986 (the Tax Code) or, for plans that satisfy the requirements of SEC Rule 701, that certain disqualifiers (attached as Appendix B) are not triggered;
(2) Arkansas requires that a plan either meet certain requirements for qualification under the Tax Code or that a notice of the transaction is filed before sales occur;
(3) California requires:
    (a) compliance with SEC Rule 701;
    (b) a notice of the transaction to be filed within thirty days after the initial issuance of a security; and

(c) compliance with regulations (attached as Appendix C) that impose substantive conditions, for example, plan termination date of not more than ten years, shareholder approval, a purchase price (exercise price in the case of option plans) of not less than eighty-five per cent of the fair value of the stock at the time of grant or annual financial statements to be provided to participants;

(4) Georgia has different rules for purchase plans and option plans — purchase plans must either meet certain requirements for qualification under the Tax Code, or those that satisfy the requirements of SEC Rule 701 must ensure that certain disqualifiers (attached as Appendix D) are not triggered and that a notice of the transaction is filed before sales occur;

(5) Indiana requires that a plan either meet certain requirements for qualification under the Tax Code or that a notice of the transaction be filed before sales occur;

(6) Louisiana has different rules for purchase plans and option plans; and

(7) Missouri requires that a plan either meet certain requirements for qualification under the Tax Code or that a notice of the transaction be filed before sales occur.

Alternative State Law Exemptions

As noted in the above discussion of Rule 506 of Regulation D, more than one exemption may be available for the same transaction or series of transactions in most states. As with federal law, the issuer need not generally make an exclusive election between applicable exemptions in one state's securities laws or between similar provisions of different states' securities laws.

Where an issuer elects compliance with the requirements of Rule 506 as to securities sold or options granted to accredited investors, such securities would be "covered" securities in accordance with the pre-emptive provisions of Section 18 of the Securities Act. The states are not authorized to regulate "covered" securities as such, but nevertheless may require certain notice filings (the same Report of Sale on Form D as is filed with the SEC), consents to service of process and fees. For this purpose, however, an issuer may not rely on Rule 506 of Regulation D for exemption under state securities laws unless all of the sales or grants in that state are to accredited investors.

In this context, most of the enumerated states do have a useful alternative analogous to Rule 506. Transactions involving the sale of securities to a limited number of persons (usually not more than ten persons in incremental periods of twelve months) are generally exempt. The principal restriction is that there be no public solicitation or advertising or payment of commission, sometimes with the further requirement that a purchaser must represent to the issuer that he is purchasing for investment and not with a view to resale. An issuer may thereby be able to grant options under an employee plan to a limited number of people in states where the filing requirement for an employee benefit plan exemption may be inconvenient or burdensome.

Appendix A

Rule 701 — Exemption for Offers and Sales of Securities Pursuant to Certain Compensatory Benefit Plans and Contracts Relating to Compensation

Preliminary Notes

1. This section relates to transactions exempted from the registration requirements of Section 5 of the Act. These transactions are not exempt from the anti-fraud, civil liability or other provisions of the federal securities laws. Issuers and persons acting on their behalf have an obligation to provide investors with disclosure adequate to satisfy the anti-fraud provisions of the federal securities laws.
2. In addition to complying with this section, the issuer also must comply with any applicable state law relating to the offer and sale of securities.
3. An issuer that attempts to comply with this section, but fails to do so, may claim any other exemption that is available.
4. This section is available only to the issuer of the securities. Affiliates of the issuer may not use this section to offer or sell securities. This section also does not cover resales of securities by any person. This section provides an exemption only for the transactions in which the securities are offered or sold by the issuer, not for the securities themselves.
5. The purpose of this section is to provide an exemption from the registration requirements of the Act for securities issued in compensatory circumstances. This section is not available for plans or schemes to circumvent this purpose, such as to raise capital. This section also is not available to exempt any transaction that is in technical compliance with this section but is part of a plan or scheme to evade the registration provisions of the Act. In any of these cases, registration under the Act is required unless another exemption is available.

a. Exemption. Offers and sales made in compliance with all of the conditions of this section are exempt from Section 5 of the Act.

b. Issuers eligible to use this section.

   1. General. This section is available to any issuer that is not subject to the reporting requirements of Section 13 or 15(d) of the Securities Exchange Act of 1934 (the "Exchange Act") and is not an investment company registered or required to be registered under the Investment Company Act of 1940.

   2. Issuers that become subject to reporting. If an issuer becomes subject to the reporting requirements of Section 13 or 15 (d) of the Exchange Act after it has made offers complying with this section, the issuer may nevertheless rely on this section to sell the securities previously offered to the persons to whom those offers were made.

   3. Guarantees by reporting companies. An issuer subject to the reporting requirements of Section 13 or 15(d) of the Exchange Act may rely on this section if it is merely guaranteeing the payment of a subsidiary's securities that are sold under this section.

c. Transactions exempted by this section. This section exempts offers and sales of securities (including plan interests and guarantees pursuant to paragraph (d)(2)(ii) of this section) under a written compensatory benefit plan (or written compensation contract) established by the issuer, its parents, its majority-owned subsidiaries or majority-owned subsidiaries of the issuer's parent, for the participation of their employees, directors, general partners, trustees (where the issuer is a business trust), officers or consultants and advisors, and their family members who acquire such securities from such persons through gifts or domestic relations orders. This section exempts offers and sales to former employees, directors, general partners, trustees, officers, consultants and advisors only if such persons were employed by or providing services to the issuer at the time the securities were offered. In addition, the term "employee" includes insurance agents who are exclusive agents of the issuer, its subsidiaries or parents, are or derive more than fifty per cent of their annual income from those entities.

   1. Special requirements for consultants and advisors. This section is available to consultants and advisors only if:

      i. They are natural persons;

   ii. They provide *bona fide* services to the issuer, its parents, its majority-owned subsidiaries or majority-owned subsidiaries of the issuer's parent; and
   iii. The services are not in connection with the offer or sale of securities in a capital-raising transaction, and do not directly or indirectly promote or maintain a market for the issuer's securities.
2. Definition of "Compensatory Benefit Plan". For the purposes of this section, a compensatory benefit plan is any purchase, savings, option, bonus, stock appreciation, profit sharing, thrift, incentive, deferred compensation, pension or similar plan.
3. Definition of "Family Member". For the purposes of this section, family member includes any child, stepchild, grandchild, parent, stepparent, grandparent, spouse, former spouse, sibling, niece, nephew, mother-in-law, father-in-law, son-in-law, daughter-in-law, brother-in-law or sister-in-law, including adoptive relationships, any person sharing the employee's household (other than a tenant or employee), a trust in which these persons have more than fifty per cent of the beneficial interest, a foundation in which these persons (or the employee) control the management of assets and any other entity in which these persons (or the employee) own more than fifty per cent of the voting interests.

d. Amounts that may be sold.
   1. Offers. Any amount of securities may be offered in reliance upon this section. However, for the purposes of this section, sales of securities underlying options must be counted as sales on the date of the option grant.
   2. Sales. The aggregate sales price or amount of securities sold in reliance upon this section during any consecutive twelve-month period must not exceed the greatest of the following:
      i. US $1-million;
      ii. fifteen per cent of the total assets of the issuer (or of the issuer's parent if the issuer is a wholly owned subsidiary and the securities represent obligations that the parent fully and unconditionally guarantees), measured at the issuer's most recent annual balance sheet date (if no older than its last fiscal year end); or

iii. fifteen per cent of the outstanding amount of the class of securities being offered and sold in reliance upon this section, measured at the issuer's most recent annual balance sheet date (if not older than its last fiscal year end).

3. Rules for calculating prices and amounts.

i. Aggregate sales price. The term aggregate sales price means the sum of all cash, property, notes, cancellation of debt or other consideration received or to be received by the issuer for the sale of the securities. Non-cash consideration must be valued by reference to *bona fide* sales of that consideration made within a reasonable time or, in the absence of such sales, on the fair value as determined by an accepted standard. The value of services exchanged for securities issued must be measured by reference to the value of the securities issued. Options must be valued based on the exercise price of the option.

ii. Time of the calculation. With respect to options to purchase securities, the aggregate sales price is determined when an option grant is made (without regard to when the option becomes exercisable). With respect to other securities, the calculation is made on the date of sale. With respect to deferred compensation or similar plans, the calculation is made when the irrevocable election to defer is made.

iii. Derivative securities. In calculating outstanding securities for the purposes of paragraph (d)(2)(iii) of this section, treat the securities underlying all currently exercisable or convertible options, warrants, rights or other securities, other than those issued under this exemption, as outstanding. In calculating the amount of securities sold for other purposes of paragraph (d)(2) of this section, count the amount of securities that would be acquired upon exercise or conversion in connection with sales of options, warrants, rights or other exercisable or convertible securities, including those to be issued under this exemption.

iv. Other exemptions. Amounts of securities sold in reliance upon this section do not affect "aggregate offering prices" in other exemptions, and amounts of securities sold in reliance upon other exemptions do not affect the amount that may be sold in reliance upon this section.

e. Disclosure that must be provided. The issuer must deliver to investors a copy of the compensatory benefit plan or the contract, as applicable. In addition, if the aggregate sales price or amount of securities sold during any consecutive twelve-month period exceeds US $5-million, the issuer must deliver the following disclosure to investors within a reasonable period of time before the date of sale:

1. If the plan is subject to the Employee Retirement Income Security Act of 1974 (ERISA) (29 U.S.C. 1104-1107), a copy of the summary plan description required by ERISA;
2. If the plan is not subject to ERISA, a summary of the material terms of the plan;
3. Information about the risks associated with investment in the securities sold pursuant to the compensatory benefit plan or compensation contract; and
4. Financial statements required to be furnished by Part F/S of Form 1-A (Regulation A Offering Statement) under Regulation A. Foreign private issuers as defined in Rule 405 must provide a reconciliation to generally accepted accounting principles in the United States (United States GAAP) if their financial statements are not prepared in accordance with United States GAAP (Item 17 of Form 20-F). The financial statements required by this section must be as of a date no more than 180 days before the sale of securities in reliance upon this exemption.
5. If the issuer is relying upon paragraph (d)(2)(ii) of this section to use its parent's total assets to determine the amount of securities that may be sold, the parent's financial statements must be delivered. If the parent is subject to the reporting requirements of Section 13 or 15(d) of the Exchange Act, the financial statements of the parent required by Rule 10-01 of Regulation S-X and Item 310 of Regulation S-B, as applicable, must be delivered.
6. If the sale involves a stock option or other derivative security, the issuer must deliver disclosure within a reasonable period of time before the date of exercise or conversion. For deferred compensation or similar plans, the issuer

must deliver disclosure to investors within a reasonable period of time before the date that the irrevocable election to defer is made.

f. No integration with other offerings. Offers and sales exempt under this section are deemed to be a part of a single discrete offering and are not subject to integration with any other offers or sales, whether registered under the Act or otherwise exempt from the registration requirements of the Act.

g. Resale limitations.
   1. Securities issued under this section are deemed to be "restricted securities" as defined in Rule 144.
   2. Resales of securities issued pursuant to this section must be in compliance with the registration requirements of the Act or an exemption from those requirements.

Ninety days after the issuer becomes subject to the reporting requirements of Section 13 or 15(d) of the Exchange Act, securities issued under this section may be resold by persons who are not affiliates (as defined in Rule 144) in reliance upon Rule 144, without compliance with paragraphs (c), (d), (e) and (h) of Rule 144, and by affiliates without compliance with paragraph (d) of Rule 144.

Appendix B

Regulations under the Arizona Securities Act

Section R14-4-136. Exemption Disqualification

B. Except as provided in subsection (c), an exemption pursuant to this Section is not available for the securities of an issuer if the issuer or any of its predecessors, affiliates, directors, officers, general partners or beneficial owners of ten per cent or more of any class of its equity securities:
   1. Has been convicted of a misdemeanor or felony involving racketeering or a transaction in securities of which fraud is an essential element.
   2. Has been convicted within the ten years before any issuance of securities under this Section, or at any time thereafter, of a misdemeanor involving racketeering or a transaction in securities of which fraud or dishonesty is an essential element.
   3. Is subject to an order, judgment or decree of a court of competent jurisdiction entered within ten years of the date of any issuance of securities under this Section enjoining or restraining it from engaging in or continuing any conduct or practice in connection with the sale or purchase of securities or involving fraud, deceit, racketeering or consumer protection laws.
   4. Has been subject to any state or federal administrative order or judgment in connection with the purchase or sale of securities entered within five years before any issuance of securities under this Section or at any time thereafter.
   5. Is subject to an order of an administrative tribunal, self-regulatory organization or the Securities and Exchange Commission denying, suspending or revoking membership or registration as a broker/dealer in securities or as an investment adviser or investment adviser representative for a period of six months or more.

C. A disqualification under subsection (B) ceases to exist if any of the following occurs:
   1. The basis for the disqualification has been removed by the jurisdiction creating it.

2. The jurisdiction in which the disqualifying event occurred issues a written waiver of the disqualification.
3. The jurisdiction in which the disqualifying event occurred declines in writing to enforce the disqualification.

Appendix C

Regulations Relating to Exemption under Section 25102(o) of the California Corporate Securities Law of 1968

Rule 260.140.41. Employee, director, manager and consultant options.

Options granted to employees, directors, managers or consultants of the issuer or any of its affiliates shall be pursuant to a plan or agreement that provides for all of the following:

(a) The total number, or percentage as calculated in accordance with Section 260.140.45, of securities which may be issued and the persons eligible to receive options to purchase these securities.

(b) An exercise price which is not less than eighty-five per cent of the fair value (Section 260.140.50) of the underlying security at the time the option is granted, except that the price shall not be less than 110 per cent of the fair value in the case of any person who owns securities possessing more than ten per cent of the total combined voting power (as defined in Section 194.5 of the Corporations Code in the case of a corporate issuer) of all classes of securities of the issuer or its parent or subsidiaries possessing voting power.

(c) An exercise period of not more than 120 months from the date the option is granted.

(d) The non-transferability of the option, provided that the plan or agreement may permit transferability by will, by the laws of descent and distribution or as permitted by Rule 701 of the Securities Act of 1933, as amended (17 CFR 230.701).

(e) The proportionate adjustment of the number of securities purchasable and the exercise price thereof under the option in the event of a stock split, reverse stock split, stock dividend, recapitalization, combination, reclassification or other distribution of the issuer's equity securities without the receipt of consideration by the issuer, of or on the issuer's class or series of securities underlying the option.

(f) The right to exercise at the rate of at least twenty per cent per year over five years from the date the option is granted, subject to reasonable conditions such as continued employment. However, in the case of an option granted to officers, directors, managers or consultants of the issuer of the option or the issuer of the underlying security or any of its affiliates, the option may become fully exercisable, subject to reasonable conditions such as continued employment, at any time or during any period established by the issuer of the option or the issuer of the underlying security or any of its affiliates.

(g) Unless employment is terminated for cause as defined by applicable law, the terms of the plan or option grant or a contract of employment, the right to exercise in the event of termination of employment, to the extent that the optionee is entitled to exercise on the date employment terminates, is as follows:
   (1) At least six months from the date of termination if termination was caused by death or disability.
   (2) At least thirty days from the date of termination if termination was caused by other than death or disability.

(h) A plan termination date of not more than ten years from the date the plan is adopted or the date the plan is approved by the security holders, whichever is earlier, and an agreement termination date of not more than ten years from the date the agreement is entered into or the date the agreement is approved by the security holders, whichever is earlier.

(i) The plan or agreement must be approved by a majority of the outstanding securities entitled to vote within twelve months before or after the date the plan is adopted or the date the agreement is entered into. Any option exercised before security holder approval is obtained must be rescinded if security holder approval is not obtained within twelve months before or after the plan is adopted or the agreement is entered into. Such securities shall not be counted in determining whether such approval is obtained.

(j) Compliance with Section 260.140.46 of these rules regarding the information required to be received by security holders.

(k) If provisions give an issuer the right to repurchase securities upon termination of employment, the repurchase price will be presumptively reasonable if:
   (1) It is not less than the fair market value of the securities to be repurchased on the date of termination of employment, and the right to repurchase must be exercised for cash or cancellation of purchase money indebtedness for the securities within ninety days of termination of employment (or in the case of securities issued on exercise of options after the date of termination, within ninety days after the date of

the exercise), and the right terminates when the issuer's securities become publicly traded; or

(2) It is at the original purchase price, provided that the right to repurchase at the original purchase price lapses at the rate of at least twenty per cent of the securities per year over five years from the date the option is granted (without respect to the date the option was exercised or became exercisable) and the right to repurchase must be exercised for cash or cancellation of purchase money indebtedness for the securities within ninety days of termination of employment (or in the case of securities issued upon exercise of options after the date of termination, within ninety days after the date of the exercise). In addition to the restrictions set forth in clauses (1) and (2), the securities held by an officer, director, manager or consultant of the issuer or an affiliate of the issuer may be subject to additional or greater restrictions.

(l) Compliance with Section 260.140.1 of these rules regarding the voting rights of common stock and similar equity securities.

Rule 260.140.42. Employee, director and consultant purchases.

Shares sold to employees, directors or consultants of the issuing corporation or any of its affiliates shall be pursuant to a plan that provides for all of the following:

(a) The total number of shares which may be issued and the persons eligible to purchase shares under the plan.

(b) A purchase price of:

(1) At least eighty-five per cent of the fair value (Section 260.140.50) of the stock at the time the person is granted the right to purchase shares under the plan, or at the time the purchase is consummated; or

(2) 100 per cent of the fair value (Section 260.140.50) of the stock either at the time the person is granted the right to purchase shares under the plan, or at the time the purchase is consummated, in the case of any person who owns stock possessing more than ten per cent of the total combined voting power or value of all classes of stock of the issuing corporation or its parent or subsidiary corporations.

(c) The non-transferability of the employee's, director's or consultant's rights to purchase shares under the plan other than by will or the laws of descent and distribution.

(d) The adjustment of the number of shares allocated to an employee, director or consultant under the plan in the event of a stock split, reverse stock split, stock dividend, recapitalization, combination or reclassification of the issuing corporation's stock;

(e) A plan termination date of not more than ten years from the date the plan is adopted or the date the plan is approved by the shareholders, whichever is earlier.

(f) Shareholder approval of the plan within twelve months before or after the plan is adopted. Any shares purchased before shareholder approval is obtained must be rescinded if shareholder approval is not obtained within twelve months before or after the plan is adopted. Such shares shall not be counted in determining whether such approval is obtained.

(g) Compliance with Section 260.140.46 of these rules regarding the information required to be received by employees.

(h) If provisions give an issuer the right to repurchase securities upon termination of employment, the repurchase price will be presumptively reasonable if: (1) it is not less than the fair market value of the securities to be repurchased on the date of termination of employment, and the right to repurchase must be exercised for cash or cancellation of purchase money indebtedness for the shares within ninety days of termination of employment, and the right terminates when the issuer's securities become publicly traded; or (2) it is at the original purchase price, provided that the right to repurchase at the original purchase price lapses at the rate of at least twenty per cent of the shares per year over five years from the date the option is granted (without respect to the date the option was exercised or became exercisable) and the right to repurchase must be exercised for cash or cancellation of purchase money indebtedness for the shares within ninety days of termination of employment.

(i) Compliance with Section 260.140.1 of these rules regarding the voting rights of common stock.

Rule 260.140.45 Limitation on number of shares.

The total number of shares issuable upon exercise of all outstanding options [exclusive of rights described in Section 260.140.40 and warrants described in Sections 260.140.43 and 260.140.44 of these rules, and any stock purchase plan as described in Section 260.140.42 of these rules, provided that the stock purchase plan provides that all shares will have a purchase price of 100 per cent of the fair value (Section 260.140.50) of the stock either at the time the person is granted the right to purchase shares under the plan or at the time the purchase is consummated], and the total number of shares called for under any stock bonus or similar plan shall not exceed a number of shares which is equal to thirty per cent of the then outstanding shares of the issuer (convertible preferred or convertible senior common shares will be counted on an as if converted basis), exclusive of shares subject to promotional waivers under Section 260.141, unless a percentage higher than thirty per cent is approved by at least two-thirds of the outstanding shares entitled to vote. The thirty per cent limitation set forth in this Rule, or such other percentage limitation as may be approved pursuant to this Rule, shall be deemed satisfied if the plan provides that at no time shall the total number of shares issuable upon exercise of all outstanding options and the total number of shares provided for under any stock bonus or similar plan of the issuer exceed the applicable percentage as calculated in accordance with the conditions and exclusions of this Rule, based on the shares of the issuer which are outstanding at the time the calculation is made.

Rule 260.140.46. Information to employees.

Plans pursuant to which securities are to be issued to employees, consultants and directors (including stock option, stock purchase and stock bonus plans) shall provide that the security holder(s) will receive financial statements at least annually. This section does not require the use of financial statements in accordance with Section 260.613 of these rules. This section shall not apply when issuance is limited to key employees whose duties in connection with the issuer assure them access to equivalent information.

Rule 260.140.1. Voting rights of common stock.

Common shares and similar equity securities should normally carry equal voting rights on all matters where such vote is permitted by applicable law.

Appendix D

Regulations under the Georgia Securities Act

Rule 590-4-5-.03 Exemption Disqualification

(b) No exemption under this Rule shall be available for the securities of any issuer if the issuer or any of its affiliates:

1. is subject to any order, judgment or decree of any court of competent jurisdiction temporarily or preliminarily restraining or enjoining or is subject to any order, judgment or decree of any court of competent jurisdiction, entered within five years prior to commencement of the offering, permanently restraining or enjoining such person from engaging in or continuing any conduct or practice in connection with the purchase or sale of any security or involving the making of any false filing with any state;
2. has been convicted within five years prior to commencement of the offering of any felony or misdemeanor in connection with the purchase or sale of any security or any felony involving fraud or deceit including but not limited to forgery, embezzlement, obtaining money under false pretenses, theft by conversion, theft by deception, larceny or conspiracy to defraud;
3. is subject to any order, judgment or decree issued by any state securities administrator, the United States Commodities Futures Trading Commission or the United States Postal Service in which fraud, deceit or registration violations were found, after notice and opportunity for hearing, if the order was entered within five years prior to the commencement of the offering in reliance upon this exemption; or
4. is subject to any order barring or suspending membership in any self-regulatory organization registered pursuant to the Securities Exchange Act of 1934, if the order was entered within five years prior to the commencement of the offering in reliance upon this exemption.

(c) The disqualification referred to in subparagraph (b) above shall not apply:

1. if the issuer or its affiliate subject to the disqualification is currently registered or licensed to conduct securities-related business in the jurisdiction where the administrative order or judgment was entered against such issuer or affiliate;
2. if the jurisdiction which created the basis for disqualification determines on a showing of good cause that it is not necessary under the circumstances that the exemption be denied; or
3. if the Commissioner, in his discretion, waives the disqualification.

Appendix E

Regulations under the Oregon Securities Act

Rule 441-65-270. Registration for Compensatory benefit plans and contracts.

An issuer of a compensatory benefit plan offering that is exempt under SEC Rule 701 (17 C.F.R. 230.701) may use this registration rule. The issuer shall submit:

- (a) A completed Form U-1 (Application to Register Securities), except documents required under Section 8 of Form U-1;
- (b) A registration fee in accordance with ORS 59.065;
- (c) At least one completed Application to License a Salesperson on Form U-4 and license fee of US $15 per application in accordance with ORS 59.165. The salesperson must be a *bona fide* affiliate of the issuer, its parent or majority-owned subsidiary, and must either:
  - (A) Be an officer, director, general partner or trustee of the issuer, its parent or majority-owned subsidiary; or
  - (B) Have significant involvement in the administration of the benefit plan or contract.
- (d) The following information:
  - (A) Type of business organization;
  - (B) Full title of plan or description of contracts;
  - (C) Type of plan;
  - (D) Affirmation that the offering is exempt from federal registration pursuant to SEC Rule 701; and
  - (E) Aggregate offering price of securities to be offered or sold pursuant to this application.
- (e) An election regarding the expiration date of an Order of Registration pursuant to Section 5 of this rule; and
- (f) Any supplementary materials requested by the Director.

(5) Order of registration. Renewal. An initial Order of Registration, if issued, shall, at the election of the registrant, expire thirty days following the end of the issuer's fiscal year, otherwise, one year after the date of issuance. The election must be made at the time application is made pursuant to Section 3 of this rule. An application may be submitted for renewal. An Order of Renewal, if issued, shall expire one year after the date of issuance.

[Note that the Rule requires the issuer, its parent or majority-owned subsidiary to provide each participant in a compensatory benefit plan with a copy of such plan, and a copy of a written contract relating to compensation shall be provided to the parties.]

General Commercial Issues

Likelihood of Association under the Influence of European Community Law

Sara Delbecque and Alex Schmitt
Bonn Schmitt Steichen
Luxembourg

Introduction

The protection of trademarks[1] has become a highly sensitive issue within the framework of the establishment of the Single Market and the development of European Community (EC) law. In the absence of any Directive relating to trademarks, Member States ultimately decided the extent of trademark protection within their boundaries.

In order to assess trademark infringement (unlawful use of a trademark), most of the Member States referred to the criterion of likelihood of confusion. However, Benelux countries applied another criterion, which was likelihood of association. These different criteria directly affect the extent of trademark protection. Likelihood of confusion tends to protect a trademark against direct[2] and indirect[3] confusion, whereas likelihood of association tends to protect trademarks in the event that the second sign is of a nature to arouse an unjustified feeling of having already seen it, without any confusion. As a result, these differences in assessing trademark infringements could have thwarted the setting up of the Single Market and the free movement of goods.

It became necessary to approximate national legislation in respect of trademarks by the adoption of an EC Directive to define a harmonized criterion to apply in the event of trademark infringement in the

1 Trademarks are typically used to distinguish the products and services of one undertaking from those of other undertakings.

2 Where the public confuses the sign and the mark in question.

3 Where the public makes a connection between the proprietors of the sign and those of the mark and confuses them as a result.

D.Campbell and S.Woodley (eds.), The Comparative Law Yearbook of International Business 2003, 315-325

EC. It is interesting to assess the development of the Benelux concept of likelihood of association through contact with EC law.

Concept of Likelihood of Association

Creation of the Concept

In the sixties, the Belgium, Netherlands and Luxembourg Governments agreed to create an economic union between their countries. To achieve that goal, it was necessary to adopt uniform laws enforceable in the three countries. In that context, they adopted a uniform law in the area of trademark law: the Uniform Trademark Act (UTA) on 19 March 1962, which entered into force in the Benelux countries in 1971.

In order to assess a trademark infringement, Article 13(A)(1) of the UTA referred to the notion of similarity between the signs. Similarity was thus sufficient. The notion of similarity between the signs was first seen as an implicit reference to the notion of likelihood of confusion, which was, prior to the adoption of the UTA, the criterion for determining trademark infringement in the three countries. It was not interpreted as a new concept, since the parliamentary works did not mention any novelty in the adoption of the notion. However, one commentator, Mr. S.K. Martens, considered that the notion of similarity, introduced in Benelux law by the UTA, was a new concept, and he considered that the notion should be interpreted as allowing the protection of a trademark against the likelihood of association.

This association criterion is characterized by the fact that there is an assimilation to the trademarks of others by reminding or by awakening a memory but without producing any confusion in the consumer's mind. Although the public is aware that the signs are different, the association helps the second mark to sell better in making it more attractive. Pouillet estimated that, to assess the existence of a likelihood of association, it is necessary to consider at least two trademarks, placing them side by side, watching them successively and asking whether the impression given by the latter reminds one of the impression given by the former.[4] The classic example

4 Pouillet, Eugène, "Traité des marques de fabrique et de la concurrence déloyale", *Paris Marchal et Billard*, 6th ed., 1912, Number 189.

of likelihood of association is usually taken to be the case of *Monopoly* v. *Antimonopoly.*[5]

S.K. Martens explained that the function of a trademark should not be limited to the simple indication of the origin of the product, but that it also has an advertising function. The goodwill attached to a mark and the image connected with it, which derive from considerable marketing efforts, must be taken seriously and protected by a broad scope of exclusivity for the mark.

While Martens was a judge at the Benelux Court of Justice, the concept of likelihood of association was formally introduced into Benelux law. In 1983, the Benelux Court of Justice, which is empowered to interpret the UTA, specified that the notion of similarity required a likelihood of association. Thus, the Benelux Court, in the *Union* v. *Union Soleure* case,[6] held that:

> ". . . there was similarity between a mark and a sign when taking account of the particular circumstances of the case, including the distinctive power of the mark . . . a similarity such as to establish an association between the sign and the mark".

By this wording, the Benelux Court of Justice established a precedent which was followed by the Benelux jurisdictions. In adopting this new criterion of likelihood of association, Benelux countries reversed case law that existed in all Member States that the criterion to apply in the event of trademark infringement is likelihood of confusion. It was in that context that the Trademarks Directive was adopted.

Trademarks Directive

The aim of Council Directive 89/104 of 21 December 1988 to approximate laws of the Members States relating to trademarks[7] was not to undertake full-scale approximation of the trademark laws of the

5 Judgment of the Netherlands Supreme Court (*Hoge Raad*) of 24 June 1977, Ingénieur-Conseil 1977, at p. 294.

6 Judgment of 20 May 1983, *Henri Jullien* v. *Verschuere*, Ingénieur-Conseil, Numbers 8–9, August–September 1983, at pp. 191–194.

7 Council Directive 89/104 of 21 December 1988, ECJ L40, 11 February 1989.

Member States, but simply to approximate "those national provisions of law which most directly affect the functioning of the internal market".[8]

During the Council meeting, the Benelux countries initially endeavored to adopt the concept of similarity of both signs in assessing trademark infringement. However, this was not approved by their opponents, who insisted on the traditional importance of a likelihood of confusion. The Benelux delegation then attempted to introduce at least the concept of the risk of association as an alternative to the risk of confusion. This was rejected as well. Finally, they accepted the compromise stated in Article 5(1)(b) of the Directive:

> "The proprietor shall be entitled to prevent all third parties not having his consent from using in the course of trade: any sign where, because of its identity with, or similarity to, the trademark and the identity or similarity of the goods or services covered by the trademark and the sign, there exists a likelihood of confusion on the part of the public, which includes the likelihood of association between the sign and the trademark."

Some commentators held that Article 5 of the Trademark Directive implemented the Benelux concept of likelihood of association into EC Law.[9] They argued that the minutes of the Council meeting contained the following statement: "the Council and the Commission note that likelihood of association is a concept which, in particular, has been developed by Benelux case law".[10]

As a result, Benelux countries implemented the Directive in amending the UTA[11] without any mention of the concept of likelihood

8 Fourth Recital of the Directive.

9 Van Innis, Th., *Les signes distinctifs*, at pp. 393–406; Gielen, Ch., "De beschermingsomvang van het merk, in Algemene problemen van merkenrecht", CIR Bruylant, 1994, pp. 140–142; Wichers Hoet, L. *(bewerkt door Gielen en anderen)*, *Kortbegrip van het intellectuele eigendomsrecht*, 7th ed., 1993, at pp. 145–148.

10 Wagner, Annett, "Infringing Trademarks: Function, Association and Confusion of Signs According to the E.C. Trademarks Directive" [1999] EIPR 3, at p. 127.

11 Protocol of 2 December 1992.

of confusion, noticing that the concept of likelihood of association[12] had become an EC concept. The amended Article 13(A)(1) provides that:

> "... the exclusive right of a trademark entitles the proprietor to oppose any commercial use of the mark or a similar sign in respect of the products for which the mark is registered or similar products when there exists, in the mind of the public, a risk of association between the sign and the mark".

Furthermore, it should be underlined that Benelux case law and, more particularly, Belgian case law, refused to interpret the EC Directive relating to trademarks as imposing on Benelux countries an obligation to adopt the criterion of likelihood of confusion.

The Brussels Court of Appeal, on 27 May 1993,[13] stated that "the first Directive approximating the laws of the Member States did not have the purpose of ruling out the likelihood of association criterion as developed by the Benelux Court of Justice". The Court rejected the defendant's allegation that, under the Directive, the only criterion to apply was the likelihood of confusion. The Antwerp Court of Appeal, on 1 June 1993,[14] even held that:

> "... however, the convergence existing between the Directive wording and the protocol wording relating to the amendment of the Uniform Benelux Trademark Law confirms, without any doubt, that the term of similarity, as interpreted by the Benelux Court of Justice as regards the likelihood of association criterion, is now considered to be an EC standard. There is then no need to ask for an interpretation from the Benelux Court of Justice or the ECJ".

Benelux countries were, as a result, persuaded that the concept of likelihood of association had become part of EC law. However, this interpretation has not been followed by other Member States. In an English case, known as the *Wagamama* case,[15] the judge, Mr. Justice Laddie, formally rejected the possibility that the Directive aimed to

---

12 Gielen, Ch., "Likelihood of Association, What does it mean?", *Trademark World*, February 1996, at p. 20.

13 *Intellectuele Eigendom en Reclamerecht* (Netherlands) 1993, at p. 112.

14 *Isover* v. *Isoglass*, Ingénieur Conseil 1993, at p. 206.

15 *Wagamama Ltd.* v. *City Centres plc* [1995] FSR 713.

adopt the criteria of likelihood of association to assess trademark infringement. The judge argued that this criterion would have significantly extended trademark rights and would thereby have significantly restricted the freedom of traders to compete. It would be expected that any such expansion would "have been stated in clear and unambiguous words so that traders throughout the European Union would be able to appreciate that their legislators had created a new broad monopoly".

As the wording of Article 5(1)(b) was very unclear and led to contradictory interpretation, many voices called for clarification from the ECJ.

Likelihood of Association and European Community Law

European Court of Justice's Rejection of Concept

The European Court of Justice (ECJ) has had several opportunities to interpret the Trademarks Directive. The ECJ has progressively created comprehensive case law giving national jurisdictions objective and unambiguous criteria for assessing trademark infringements under Article 5(1)(b) of the Directive.

By an order of 29 June 1995, the German Federal Court of Justice (*Bundesgerichtshof*) first asked the ECJ to give an interpretation of the ambiguous wording of Article 4(1)(b)[16] of the Directive: "a likelihood of confusion . . . which includes the likelihood of association with the earlier trademark". In the *Sabel* v. *Puma* case of 11 November 1997,[17] the ECJ held that:

> ". . . it follows from that wording that the concept of likelihood of association is not an alternative to that of likelihood of confusion, but serves to define its scope. The terms of the provision itself exclude its application, where there is no likelihood of confusion on the part of the public".[18]

---

16 Article 4(1)(b) relating to the conditions of registration of a trademark has the same wording as Article 5(1)(b) relating to trademark infringement.

17 Case C-251/95, ECR 1997, at p. I-6191.

18 Case C-251/95, ECR 1997, at p. I-6191, Section 18.

In support of this interpretation, the ECJ went on to cite the Tenth Recital in the Preamble to the Directive, according to which the likelihood of confusion concept constitutes the specific condition for the protection of trademarks under the Directive.

The ECJ did not approve the Benelux concept of likelihood of association. The ECJ rejected the possibility of protecting a trademark where the public considers the sign to be similar to the mark and perception of the sign calls to the mind of the consumer the memory of the mark, although the two cannot be confused. The ECJ formally stressed that the likelihood of confusion is the overall requirement which must necessarily be fulfilled. However, the ECJ did not expand on the concept of likelihood of confusion.

There exist two types of confusion: direct confusion, where the public confuses the sign and the mark in question, and indirect confusion, where the public makes a connection between the owners of the sign and those of the mark and thus confuses them. The interpretation given to the term of confusion may affect the extent of the trademark protection.

Therefore, in a second case, on 2 April 1998, *Canon Kabushiki Kaisha* v. *Metro-Goldwyn-Mayer Inc.* (*Canon* case),[19] the ECJ explained the meaning of likelihood of confusion in stating that:

> ". . . the risk that the public might believe that the goods or services in question come from the same undertaking or, as the case may be, from economically-linked undertakings, constitutes a likelihood of confusion within the meaning of Article 4(1)(b) of the Directive".[20]

As a result, the ECJ has adopted a stance on the middle ground between direct confusion (very restrictive trademark protection), on the one hand, and the likelihood of association (very broad trademark protection), on the other hand.

In a third case, the *Lloyd Schuhfabrik Meyer & Co.* v. *Klijsen Handel BV* case,[21] the ECJ characterized the average consumer that must be taken into consideration in assessing trademark infringement. Although Benelux case law considered the consumer as not alert, the ECJ underlines that "for the purposes of that global appreciation, the

19 Case C-39/97, ECR 1998, at p. I-5507.

20 Case C-39/97, ECR 1998, at p. I-5507, Section 29.

21 Case C-342/97, ECR 1999, at p. I-3819.

average consumer of the category of products concerned is deemed to be reasonably well-informed and reasonably observant and circumspect".[22] The ECJ seems to have taken into consideration the fact that the modern consumer is observant and aware of the tight competition existing between the manufacturers of products and knows that leading trademarks very often inspire others to follow.

The Supreme Court of the Netherlands (*Hoge Raad*) referred an interpretation question to the ECJ to ascertain whether Article 5(1)(b) of the Directive must be interpreted as meaning that the owner of the mark may prevent a third party from using the sign if the distinctive character of the mark is such that the possibility of an association made by the public between the sign and the mark giving rise to confusion cannot be ruled out. By asking this question, the *Hoge Raad*, in effect, asked the Court to reverse the terms of the Directive. The ECJ, in the *Marca Mode CV* v. *Adidas AG and Adidas Benelux BV* case of 22 June 2000,[23] rejected that possibility in recalling its previous statement in *Sabel* v. *Puma* that the only criterion to be applied is the likelihood of confusion.

Likelihood of Association: Inappropriate Criterion

Advocate General Jacobs, in his opinion delivered on 27 January 2000 in the *Marca* case,[24] noted a number of reasons of principle that make it undesirable to adopt the concept of likelihood of association in EC law. First, a broad interpretation of the concept of confusion (by the adoption of the concept of association) would hinder the internal market. In the *Hag* case,[25] on 3 July 1974, the ECJ observed that the exercise of trademarks tends to contribute to the partitioning off of markets and thus to affect the free movement of goods. Therefore, the ECJ has developed case law striking a balance between the free movement of goods and the protection of trademarks leading to justified restrictions on the free movement of goods and services.

It should also be pointed out that the requirement of confusion as a condition of protection of trademarks was not a novel concept introduced by the Directive. The concept of likelihood of confusion was

22 Case C-342/97, ECR 1999, at p. I-3819, Section 26.

23 Case C-425/98, ECR 2000, at p. I-4861.

24 Opinion delivered in the case *Marca Mode CV* v. *Adidas AG and Adidas Benelux BV*, Case C-425/98, Sections 33–35.

25 *Van Zuylen Frères* v. *Hag AG*, Case C-192/73, ECR 1974, at p. I-0731.

established by case law of the Court on the scope of trademark owners' rights in light of Articles 28 and 30 of the amended EC Treaty. In determining the essential function of the trademark, the ECJ pointed out that the scope of the trademark is to not be confused with the trademarks of others.[26]

Three functions of trademarks may be distinguished:[27]

(1) Origin function — trademarks deserve protection so that they may operate as indicators of the trade source from which goods or services come, or are in some other way connected;

(2) Quality or guarantee function — trademarks deserve protection because they symbolize qualities associated by consumers with certain goods or services and guarantee that the goods or services measure up to expectations; and

(3) Investment or advertising function — trademarks are ciphers around which investment in the promotion of a product is built, and that investment is a value which deserves protection as such, even when there is no abuse arising from misrepresentations either as to origin or quality.

On the one hand, Benelux case law considered that the origin function, but also the economic and the identification or advertising function, of the trademark should be protected and implemented, therefore, the likelihood of association criterion. On the other hand, the ECJ has stated, since the *Terrapin* case,[28] that the essential function of the trademark is to guarantee to the consumer or end user the identity of the trademarked product's origin by enabling him to distinguish it without any risk of confusion from products of different origin. Moreover, it should be underlined that the Tenth Recital points out that the function of the trademark is, in particular, to guarantee the trademark as an indication of origin.

The adoption of the likelihood of association concept would lead to a reversal of the ECJ case law and EC law in recognizing that the advertising function of the trademark should also be protected by trademark laws. Moreover, the Advocate General also noted that a

---

26 *Société Terrapin (Overseas) Ltd.* v. *Société Terranova Industrie CA Kapferer & Co.*, judgment of 22 June 1976, Case 119/75, ECR, at p. 1039, Section 4.

27 Cornish, W.R., *Intellectual Property*, Third Edition (Sweet and Maxwell, 1996) 15–21, at p. 527.

28 *Société Terrapin (Overseas) Ltd.* v. *Société Terranova Industrie CA Kapferer & Co.*, judgment of 22 June 1976, Case 119/75, ECR, at p. 1039.

broad interpretation of the notion of confusion would seriously hinder the effective application of the Community Trademark Regulation.[29] This Regulation, which provides for the establishment of a Community Trademark, contains provisions relating to confusion between marks which are virtually identical to those in the Directive. Therefore, the provisions of the Directive should be interpreted in the same way as the corresponding provisions of the Regulation. An EC trademark can be granted only for the entire territory of the European Union and, thus, a conflict with just one trademark in one Member State is sufficient to prevent registration of a sign as an EC trademark.

An application to register an EC trademark may be opposed on the basis of an already existing EC trademark, a national trademark registered in any Member State or, under certain circumstances, an unregistered right recognized in a Member State. Too broad a protection for trademarks on the basis of a risk of "association" with other marks would accordingly make it very difficult for many marks to be registered at Community level and could preclude the efficiency of the EC trademark system.[30]

Furthermore, the international conventions to which the Community and/or Member States are party provide no support for the view that trademark protection may be based on mere association. Although the final recital of the Directive stresses that its provisions must be "entirely consistent with those of the Paris Convention", that Convention makes express reference only to confusion. The Agreement on Trade-Related Aspects of Intellectual Property Rights (TRIPS) similarly links the protection of marks with use which would result in a likelihood of confusion. At the very least, it should be remarked that the concept of likelihood of association is simply far too broad and inconvenient. The Vice-President of the Appeal Court of The Hague also underlined that:

> ". . . the criterion of likelihood of association was not so easy to employ; particularly in plain cases with plain trademarks, I had often a feeling that that criterion favored a protection of the right holder that went too far".[31]

---

29 Council Regulation Number 40/94 of 20 December 1993 on the Community Trademark.

30 Opinion of Advocate General Jacobs delivered on 27 January 2000, Case C-425/98, *Marca Mode CV* v. *Adidas AG and Adidas Benelux BV*, Section 35.

31 Brinkhof, J-J, "Het begrip overeenstemming: terugblikken en vooruitkijken", *Livre jubilaire Benelux*, 1996, at pp. 50–51.

Furthermore, as an author, Peter Prescott[32] explained:

> ". . . widening the monopoly makes it more difficult for the trader to choose a safe trademark to use in the first place. In real life, corporations do not spend too much time worrying about association without confusion, but they spend an awful lot of their time selecting marks which can be used without conflicting with other registrations".

As a result, the adoption of the criterion of likelihood of association may lead to unjustified restrictions in the choice of a trademark.

Conclusion

The rejection of the likelihood of association concept leads Benelux jurisdictions to reverse their case law and to go back to the criterion of likelihood of confusion that existed in Benelux countries before the Union case judgment. As Mr. Charles Gielen pointed out, the ECJ case law stating that:

> ". . . the likelihood of confusion must be appreciated globally, thus it must be all-embracing, taking into account all factors relevant to the circumstances of the case . . . does sound familiar to Benelux practitioners".[33]

Furthermore, it can be observed that there is, actually, no kind of opposition from Benelux jurisdictions to refer to the criterion of confusion as established by the ECJ. The Benelux countries have even decided to amend the UTA in order to comply with the requirements of Trademark Directive 89/104 of 21 December 1988 and case law developed by the ECJ as regards the interpretation to be given to Article 5(1)(b). In a Protocol signed in Brussels on 11 December 2001, the Benelux countries agreed to reproduce in the UTA the exact wording of Article 5(1)(b) of Trademark Directive 89/104. This amended version of the UTA has not yet entered into force in the Benelux countries, however, as the amending Protocol has not been ratified.

32 Peter Prescott, "Think Before You Waga Finger" [1996] 1 EIPR 3.

33 Gielen, Charles, "A Benelux Perspective, *Sabel* v. *Puma*" [1998] 3 EIPR, 109.

Merger Provisions of the Nigerian Federal Competition Bill

Nnamdi Dimgba
Faculty of Law
University of West of England
Bristol, United Kingdom

Introduction

Towards the end of 2002, the National Council on Privatization (NCP) announced proposals to introduce an antitrust regime in Nigeria as part of the Government's reform of several sectors of the economy. Specifically, the antitrust regime is to complement the privatization program of the Government and ensure that private monopolization initiatives do not come to replace the public monopolies that the Government has sought to dismantle through privatization. To this end, the Government has commissioned draft antitrust legislation entitled "the Federal Competition Bill" (the Bill), which is presently before the National Assembly.[1] While it is clearly not impossible to carry out a comprehensive and yet thorough critique of such lengthy legislation in a single chapter, the purpose of this discussion is to attempt an evaluation of the provisions of the Bill that seek to regulate mergers.

Indubitably, while the overall good intention of the Government in seeking to get things up to speed is saluted,[2] it is argued that, without prejudice to the motivation of the consultants who advised the Government and drafted the law, the provisions on merger appear to have been structured without sufficient consideration being given to the real antitrust consequences of a merger. Consequently, the Bill appears to proceed

1 The Bill was drafted and placed on the Internet by a Washington, United States-based firm, with an invitation for comments from Nigerians.

2 Not to mention the opportunity afforded (at least potentially) for some Nigerians who have been engaged in the study of antitrust abroad to ply their trade in their home country.

D.Campbell and S.Woodley (eds.), The Comparative Law Yearbook of International Business 2003, 327-339

from the premise that a merger is of the same malign status and on equal antitrust footing with cartel agreements and abuses of dominant position. Perhaps, for this reason, it makes provision for penalties following a merger that appear quite misconceived and bear no relation whatsoever to the harm that is caused.

The Bill contains other provisions on mergers which, taken together, fail to provide a coherent body of policy and, therefore, fail to indicate any clear direction for business undertakings and their advisers contemplating a merger; they have the tendency to confuse even the most astute and brilliant. Given the unquantifiable harm that could be done to an economy from the enactment of seemingly innocuous but latently defective provisions in highly specialized legislation such as an antitrust law, especially for a developing economy like Nigeria, it could be argued that a redraft of the entire provisions of the Bill relating to mergers may be advisable so as to make it clear that at least some consideration has been given to the real antitrust effect of a merger, and to assure undertakings, as is the case in jurisdictions where antitrust has been practiced for decades, that what is being punished is not the act of merging *per se*, but rather the wrong way of doing it.

Purpose of Merger Control

Broadly, a merger occurs where two or more formerly independent entities unite. The purpose of merger control is to enable competition authorities to regulate changes in market structure by deciding whether two or more commercial companies may merge, combine or consolidate their business into one.[3] Since competition authorities are hostile to anti-competitive agreements concluded between independent companies, especially horizontal ones, it is not surprising, therefore, that they are also suspicious of mergers, since they do tend to create a more permanent and lasting change to the market than agreements. It might be expected, therefore, that many mergers, especially horizontal ones, would be forbidden:

> "Because the horizontal merger involves two firms in the same market, it produces two consequences that do not flow

---

3 For merger control to be effective, it is necessary to control both amicable agreements to merge and hostile takeovers.

> from vertical or conglomerate mergers: 1) after the merger, the relevant market has one firm less than before; 2) the post-merger firm ordinarily has a larger market share than either of the partners had before the merger."[4]

Mergers thus raise severe competition concerns. In particular, they may result in the undertakings acquiring or strengthening a position of market power and, consequently, in an increase in the market price of the products or services on the relevant market. A merger between two or more previously independent undertakings which does not lead to the creation of an individual dominant position may nonetheless lead to a substantial increase in the concentration of a particular industry. This may lead to the creation or strengthening of a collective dominant position on an oligopolistic market and may consequently facilitate collusion, explicit or tacit, between the undertakings operating on the relevant market. As a commentator put it:

> "These structural changes raise two potential competitive concerns. First, by eliminating the competitive constraints which currently exist between the parties, the merger may weaken to a significant degree the strength of the overall competitive constraints acting on one or both of the two parties. As a result, the prices charged by the merged entity may increase relative to their pre-merger level. A merger which has these characteristics is said to give rise to a situation of single dominance [the unilateral effect of the merger] . . . Secondly, the merger may lead to a reduction in the effectiveness of competition if the change in market structure creates a competitive environment more favorable to sustainable tacit collusion."[5]

Many competition authorities, therefore, adopt a merger policy which seeks to prevent undertakings from merging to create or strengthen a collective dominant position. In the United States, Hovenkamp states that one of the principal concerns of United States

---

4 H. Hovenkamp, *Federal Antitrust Policy: The Law of Competition and its Practice* (West Publishing, 1994) at p. 445.

5 S. Bishop and M. Walker, *The Economics of EC Competition Law: Concepts, Application and Measurement* (Sweet & Maxwell, London, 1999) at 6.08.

merger policy has been that "horizontal mergers may facilitate express or tacit collusion or Cournot-style oligopoly behavior". In his words:

> "Merger policy is the most powerful weapon available in the American antitrust arsenal for combating tacit collusion or Cournot-style oligopoly. Since we cannot go after oligopoly directly under Section 1 of the Sherman Act, we do the next best thing. We try to prevent (taking efficiencies and other factors into account) the creation of market structures that tend to facilitate Cournot or collusion-like outcomes."[6]

However, for all their drawbacks, mergers also generate certain advantages which, in the long run, are conducive to the overall good structure of the economy and, therefore, enhance competition and market efficiency. For instance, mergers give the owner of a business the opportunity to sell it. Without this possibility, entrepreneurs might be reluctant to start businesses. A merger may provide an escape route for a company facing an otherwise inevitable liquidation. In a case such as this, the possibility of selling the business to another may mean that productive assets are kept in production and that creditors, owners and employees are protected from the adverse consequences of the undertaking's failure. As one commentator stated:

> "A policy of free transferability of capital assets tends to put them in the hands of those who will use them to their utmost economic advantage, thus tending to maximize society's total output of goods and services . . . Entry by merger may stimulate improved economic performance in an industry characterized by oligopolistic lethargy and inefficiency."[7]

Further, mergers provide many other efficiency opportunities. The entity may be able to exploit economies of scale in production.[8] Such economies will be of particular importance in a market in which the

---

6 H. Hovenkamp, *Federal Antitrust Policy: The Law of Competition and its Practice* (West Publishing, 1994) at pp. 445 and 447.

7 D. Turner, "Conglomerate Mergers and Section 7 of the Clayton Act" (1965) 78 *Harvard Law Review* 1313, at p. 1317.

8 This argument will be strongest in the context of horizontal or, sometimes, vertical mergers where related operations are combined.

cost of production of a product is high in comparison to the size, or anticipated size, of the market or where there is a minimum efficient scale of production. The merger may also give rise to other operating efficiencies[9] or the ability to pool research development skills, giving rise to the opportunity for greater innovation. Management efficiency is also encouraged, since mergers often bring new and superior management to the business.[10] All these advantages would be difficult to attain through internal growth.

It is precisely because of the above beneficial effects of a merger that, generally, antitrust bodies the world over are reluctant to make mergers unlawful *per se*, unlike price fixing, market division and other cartel agreements and abuses of dominant position, or anything that comes anywhere near such a rule. The task of the competition authorities is to identify and prohibit those mergers which have such an adverse impact on competition or society that any benefits resulting from them are outweighed or should be ignored. Although the motives for, and benefits of, mergers are important, the key to effective merger control is to identify why and when a merger should be prohibited.

Merger Provisions of the Federal Competition Bill

The merger provisions of the Bill are contained in Part V of the Bill, and also some sections of Part VII relating to authorizations and clearances. Specifically, Section 29(1) provides that:

> "No person shall acquire assets of a business or shares of a company or any of the company's undertakings if, as a result of the acquisition (a) that person, or another person associated or affiliated with that person, will likely be in a dominant position in a market; or (b) that person's or an associated person's dominant position in a market will likely be strengthened."

9 Arising, for example, from broader product lines, streamlining of the sales force and the use of popular advertising.

10 Indeed, the simple threat of a take-over may encourage the incumbent management of a company to strive for efficiency (rigid control of mergers will remove or greatly reduce this perceived threat). However, over-confident entrepreneurs may overestimate their ability to manage more complex undertakings or businesses in an unfamiliar field or market.

The following subsections and sections go on to define when two or more persons would be deemed to be in a dominant position or affiliated, and also spell out the criteria to be taken into account in establishing dominance. The other provisions of this Part are quite pedestrian as they recommend to the proposed Federal Competition Commission a need to publish guidelines from time to time for the control of mergers and acquisitions.[11] What is quite startling is Section 30 dealing with offences relating to Part V. Specifically, it provides that:

> "Any person who violates any provision of Part V of this Bill shall be guilty of an offence and liable on conviction, in the case of an individual, to imprisonment for three years or a fine of N3, 00,000, or to both; and, in the case of an enterprise, to a fine not exceeding twenty per cent of the average sales turnover of the enterprise for the three financial years immediately preceding the date of the commission of the offence."[12]

Also:

> "Where an enterprise violates any provision of Part V of this Bill, every director or officer who knowingly participates in or fails to prevent such violation shall be guilty of an offence and punishable on conviction to imprisonment for three years or a fine of N3 million, or to both."[13]

In addition, in Part VII, dealing with authorizations and clearances, two sections contain provisions that deal specifically with authorizations and clearances for mergers. Section 46 provides that:

> "A person who proposes to acquire assets of a business or shares of a company may give the Commission a notice seeking clearance for the acquisition . . . within twenty-one days after the date of registration of the notice, the Commission shall either grant the clearance or decline to grant the

11 Federal Competition Bill, Sections 29(2)–29(4).
12 Federal Competition Bill, Section 30(1).
13 Federal Competition Bill, Section 30(2).

clearance depending on whether it perceives that the effects described in Section 29 will result or not from the merger."[14]

Also, Section 47 provides that:

"A person who proposes to acquire assets of a business or shares of a company may give the Commission notice seeking authorization for the acquisition . . . within sixty days after the date of registration of the notice, the Commission shall either grant the authorization because the effect described in Section 29 would not result or, in any case, the merger would benefit the public, or decline to grant the authorization if the merger would either result in the effect described in Section 29 or would not benefit the public."[15]

A Critique of the Provisions

As stated above, a merger has never been a crime in itself. What is offensive and, therefore, unacceptable is the wrong way of merging. By insisting that merger parties should go through the proper route in their quest to merge, the entities afford the competition authority an opportunity to make an *a priori* examination of the impact of the proposed merger on the structure of the relevant market after its consummation.[16] If the impact would be deleterious, the merger would be prohibited. Where the impact would be positive or at least neutral from a competition perspective, the merger would be allowed to proceed. It becomes self-evident that what is key in any effective merger control regime is a mandatory prior notification system, not draconian and undefined penalties, since mergers are never unlawful *per se*, or even malign. This is precisely where it appears that the drafters of the Bill got it wrong.

Apart from other provisions that are considered below, the Bill imposes very large penalties for mergers without defining appropriately the basis on which liability would attach. These huge fines for mergers contained in the Bill have no equivalents in any other antitrust jurisdiction known to the author. One wonders if they are

---

14 This is the author's summary of Section 46 and its subsections.

15 This is the author's summary of Section 47 and its subsections.

16 Decision of the European Commission on the concentration (merger) between Nestle and Perrier, Case IV/M190, *Nestle/Perrier* [1992] OJ L356/1, [1993] 4 CMLR M17.

necessary in a jurisdiction such as Nigeria, which is suffering from poor industrial performance and where mergers are clearly desirable. Also, the draftsman has ended up confusing corporate undertakings and their advisers. What exactly is "clearance", as used in Section 46, and "authorization" within Section 47? What is the difference between the respective deadlines for the decisions of the Federal Competition Commission?[17]

Considering that the decision that could be reached on an application for clearance could also be made on an application for authorization,[18] are two distinct provisions really needed? Given that neither the duty to seek clearance nor the duty to seek authorization is mandatory (both are choices open to the firms), when exactly should a firm seek clearance instead of authorization? Precisely when will liability to pay the huge penalties attach? Is it after a merger is consummated without seeking either clearance or authorization? If this were to be the case, then it would clearly go against logic and legal reasoning, since the law never imposes such mandatory duties upon entities contemplating mergers. Alternatively, is it whenever a merger lessens competition regardless of whether or not clearance or authorization is sought? This may be the intent of the draftsman, as can be seen from Section 30. This Section attaches a heavy fine to a merger in breach of Part V. Yet the Part mentions nothing about clearance or authorization.

In effect, the provisions, wittingly or unwittingly, make mergers illegal *per se*, and, for that reason, put all undertakings contemplating a merger into a quandary. This would restrict the freedom of undertakings in embracing a merger as a viable business option in order to turn their ailing entities around and ultimately become more

---

17 Twenty-one days for clearance and sixty days for authorization.

18 Compare Section 46(3)(a), which provides that: "within twenty-one days after the date of registration of the notice, or such longer period as the Commission and the person who gave the notice may agree, the Commission shall either: a) if it is satisfied that the acquisition will not result in an effect described in paragraph (a) or paragraph (b) of Section 29(1) of this Bill, by notice in writing to the person by whom or on whose behalf the notice was given, give clearance for the acquisition" and Section 47(3)(a), which provides that: "within sixty days after the date of registration of the notice, or such longer period as the Commission and the person who gave the notice may agree, the Commission shall either: a) if it is satisfied that the acquisition will not result in an effect described in paragraph (a) or paragraph (b) of Section 29(1) of this Bill, by notice in writing to the person by whom or on whose behalf the notice was given, give clearance for the acquisition".

competitive. They do not know when the antitrust enforcer may come calling with fines of up to twenty per cent of their turnover for the preceding three years, and do not understand the basis for this liability.

The provisions also impose upon undertakings the additional burden of having to seek legal advice whenever they are making preliminary internal consultations regarding the option of a merger. This amounts to an unjustifiable increment in transaction costs which would otherwise be avoided were the provisions as a whole simpler and less confusing than they are at present. This last opinion is predicated on the understanding that the aim of the proposed antitrust regime is not to generate more revenue for legal specialists (even if it may be an incident of it), but to promote the overall competitive structure of the economy, of which legal transparency is an integral part.

On the issue of authorization, what is the interpretation to be drawn from Section 47(3)(b), which permits the Federal Competition Commission to grant authorization for a merger or acquisition if it is satisfied that the acquisition will result in such a benefit to the public that it should be permitted? Does it mean that "even though this acquisition will be anti-competitive, we still approve it because we know it would result in a benefit to the public"? If this is the intent, it is really not clear from the way the provision is couched. Is there going to be a competition analysis at all?

Furthermore, Section 48 provides that clearance or authorization given expires twelve months after the date upon which it was granted. If the clearance or authorization expires, does it mean that an unconsummated merger is frozen and abandoned or that a merger that is already consummated should demerge? Mergers are normally complex corporate arrangements that involve so many factors, including legal and non-legal matters. They often take some time to be completed, even after being approved. If, in the process of consummating a merger, twelve months elapse, would it then mean that the parties must freeze in their tracks and go back to the Commission for fresh clearance or authorization, otherwise they will be liable to heavy penalties?

Section 38(2) provides that:

> "A person who wishes to engage in the practice of resale price maintenance to which Section 26 of this Bill may pertain, or to perform an act to which Section 29 of this Bill may pertain, may apply to the Commission for authorization to do so."

The question to be asked is: Which section of the Bill actually regulates the authorization of a merger? Is it Section 47 or Section 38(2)? Clearly, a provision such as in Section 38(2) is unnecessary and sows a seed of confusion that needs to be uprooted, more so when Section 47 is the main provision intended to govern authorizations.

Finally, Section 48(3) provides that:

> "Notwithstanding Section 46 or Section 47 of this Bill, where the Commission is of the opinion that a proposed acquisition is, for reasons other than those arising from the application of any provision of this Bill, unlikely to be proceeded with, the Commission may, in its discretion, decline to give clearance or grant authorization in respect of that acquisition."

This provision appears quite disagreeable in its entirety because of the enormous danger it could pose in the future, and also its potential to destroy transparency in the process. It is likely to be nothing short of a blackmail tool in the hands of the antitrust enforcer, and might be used to settle political scores. Any other legitimate concerns that could arise from a proposed merger, such as corporate governance issues, should be dealt with by other regulators and should not be the business of the antitrust enforcer, especially as there are already too many legal and regulatory hurdles that merging parties must encounter in Nigeria apart from the proposed Federal Competition Commission. It is only when a merger would lessen competition because of the creation of a single or oligopolistic dominance in the relevant market post merger (ascertained through a thorough economic analysis using relevant econometric tools) that it should interest the Federal Competition Commission. Nigerian society is already awash with insinuations that the powers conferred by certain laws on some public bodies have been used to achieve aims that border on the political.[19]

The conclusion to be drawn from the above appears to be that the draftsman wittingly or unwittingly places a merger on the same footing as an abuse of dominant position. After all, Part V, dealing with

19 Many Nigerians are already familiar with the battle going on between the Senate President and the Independent Corrupt Practices Commission. They would also have heard the insinuations made regarding the withdrawal of the operating license of Savannah Bank and the ongoing court battle.

mergers and acquisitions, comes after Part III, dealing with abuses of dominant position, and the language of the penalties are the same. This arises precisely because sufficient consideration does not appear to have been given to the true antitrust effect of a merger and how it should be controlled.

Moving Forward

There is something to be said for clarity and simplicity in drafting specialized legislation such as the Bill. Therefore, it is desirable that all the issues raised above are considered and the merger provisions redrafted in a way that would lend them to easier understanding. The disagreeable provisions need to be jettisoned or at least revised. Clearly, as argued above, what is really necessary for effective merger control is not draconian penalties *per se*, otherwise firms would be dissuaded from embracing needed corporate restructuring initiatives. This may have adverse effects on the economy both in the short and the long term, and inevitably defeat the underlying object of the proposed antitrust regime to promote overall industrial growth through a virile competitive process.

What should be the fulcrum of the merger regime is a mandatory prior notification system. Any fines should be predicated on the obligation to notify. In this respect, there is something to recommend the European merger control regime. Under the European system, pursuant to the European Merger Regulation,[20] concentrations (mergers) with a Community dimension must be notified to the Commission not more than one week after the conclusion of the agreement or the announcement of the public bid or the acquisition of a controlling interest.[21] Upon notification, the Commission is obliged to assess, within a period of one month,[22] whether or not that concentration falls within the scope of the Merger Regulation and, if so, whether it raises

20 Council Regulation (EEC) Number 4064/89 of 21 December 1989 on the control of concentrations between undertakings (OJ 1990, Number L257/13), as amended by Council Regulation (EC) Number 1310/97 of 30 June 1997 (OJ 1997, Number L180/1).

21 European Merger Regulation, Article 4.

22 European Merger Regulation, Article 10.

serious doubts about its compatibility with the common market.[23] Broadly, this means that the Commission must determine whether:

(1) The concentration creates or strengthens a dominant position; and
(2) As a result of which, effective competition in the common market would be significantly impeded.[24]

Approximately ninety to ninety-five per cent of Community merger cases are dealt with at this stage and, therefore, within a period of one month. Where the Commission believes that the concentration raises serious doubts about its compatibility with the common market, a second phase investigation will be launched to analyze whether or not this is the case.

The second investigation must normally be concluded within a period of four months from its initiation.[25] In general, the concentration shall not be put into effect either before its notification or until it has been declared compatible with the common market by the Commission.[26] As for the issue of fines, these only arise where a party fails to notify a concentration or where it supplies incorrect or misleading information in a notification.[27] Such fines are normally between €1,000 and €50,000, and are likely to be greater the more serious the impact the non-notified concentration has on competition. Undertakings which intentionally or negligently breach the suspensory provisions of the Regulation by going ahead with the implementation of a merger without first waiting for a decision from the Commission as to its likely effect and whether it should proceed may be liable to pay fines of up to ten per cent of their turnover in the preceding year.[28] Clearly, this liability arises simply because the duty to notify is mandatory, and whoever does not notify as required by law is already in breach of the Regulation. At least, however, the basis is very clear to firms.

In Nigeria, where the Bill imposes no mandatory duty to notify in advance, it becomes somewhat misconceived to impose such harsh and unprecedented penalties as highlighted above. Undertakings in

---

23 These are the Phase I investigations.
24 European Merger Regulation, Article 2.
25 European Merger Regulation, Article 10.
26 European Merger Regulation, Article 7.
27 European Merger Regulation, Article 14.
28 European Merger Regulation, Article 14(2).

Europe which do not notify a concentration to the Commission or which do not comply with the suspensory period risk having to reverse their concentration if the Commission later finds that the concentration is not compatible with the common market.

Under the United Kingdom regime, there is no provision for fines. Under the Fair Trading Act,[29] which regulates mergers, mergers made without notification and which raise serious competition concerns are simply required to break up and revert to the *status quo ante*. The imposing of heavy fines may send the wrong signal that what is disapproved of is the merger itself, and not just the method of merging. This false impression does not help the economy or long-term competition.

29 Mergers are governed by Sections 63–75 of the Fair Trading Act 1973. Newspaper mergers are subject to a more rigorous regime under Sections 52–62.

Mexico–European Community Economic Association

Omar Guerrero R. and Juan Francisco Torres Landa R.
Barrera, Siqueiros y Torres Landa, S.C.
Mexico City, Federal District, Mexico

Mexico's Network of International Trade Agreements

Mexico has always had a culture of staying behind its borders. However, in the late 1980s, that all changed and, since then, Mexico has played an active role in the execution of international trade and bilateral investment agreements. For over forty years, Mexico followed a traditional protectionist model of import substitution to foster internal growth. This strategy seemed sufficient until its drawbacks and limitations were revealed. In particular, the reduction in competition provided prime ground for monopolies (with no effective antitrust policy until the 1993 enactment of the Federal Law on Economic Competition). Repeated financial crises that began in 1976 have slowed Mexico's economic expansion. Mexico had grown heavily dependent on oil exports, and was thus forced to default on foreign loans. The country had no option but to restructure its trade and industrial policies to allow a full liberalization of its economy. These hard decisions have succeeded, however, as recent economic achievements show, and have resulted in Mexico becoming the nation with the single largest network of international trade agreements in the world. This economic redirection has also involved economic deregulation, liberalization policies and a new competition framework.

One significant event in the change being discussed was Mexico signing of the General Agreement on Tariffs and Trade (GATT) in 1985 to take advantage of the benefits of trade liberalization and gradual decrease in tariffs. In 1990, Mexico became a founding member of the European Bank for Reconstruction and Development (EBRD). This path was further followed in 1991 by the commencement of negotiations leading to the execution in 1993 of the North American Free Trade Agreement (NAFTA) between Mexico, the United States of America and Canada. In 1991, Mexico and Chile

D.Campbell and S.Woodley (eds.), The Comparative Law Yearbook of International Business 2003, 341-359

executed a Complementary Commercial Agreement which was further replaced by a Free Trade Agreement in 1999. Mexico became, in 1993, the first Latin American member of the Asia-Pacific Economic Cooperation Forum (APEC), which seeks to establish a free trade area by the year 2010 for APEC's developed members' economies and 2020 for its developing members. In January 1994, NAFTA came into effect and, four months later, Mexico joined the Organization for Economic Cooperation and Development (OECD) and acted as a founding member of the World Trade Organization (WTO).

Along with those important achievements, Mexico has also entered into free trade agreements (FTAs) with Bolivia (1995), Costa Rica (1995), Venezuela and Colombia (better known as the "Group of Three" — 1995), the Interim Accord with the European Community (1997), Nicaragua (1998), the Expansion to the Economic Complementation Accord executed with Uruguay (1999), Israel (2000), the European Community and its Member States (2000) and Guatemala, Honduras and El Salvador (better known as the "North Triangle" — 2000). Additionally, Mexico is currently negotiating trade pacts with Singapore, Japan, South Korea and Mercosur (Argentina, Uruguay, Paraguay and Brazil). In early November 2000, Mexico finalized negotiations with the countries comprising the European Free Trade Area (Liechtenstein, Switzerland, Norway and Iceland). Likewise, Mexico is a promoter of the Free Trade Area of the Americas expected to be launched by 2004/2005. Completing these important developments, Mexico has a growing network of bilateral investment treaties (BITs) with several countries, including several European countries.[1]

A recent landmark decision of the Supreme Court of Justice of Mexico (not entirely binding since it is not considered "jurisprudence") held that international treaties have priority over federal laws, and are only subject to the Mexican Constitution. This decision changes a former interpretation that federal laws and international treaties had the same standing. The main reason for this new ruling was essentially that international commitments are assumed by the Mexican State but, at the same time, commit all Mexican authorities before the international community. In other words, Mexico's

1 Mexico has currently executed eighteen bilateral investment treaties, thirteen of them with Member States of the European Community.

President is authorized by Article 133 of the Constitution to sign international treaties, but they must be ratified by the Senate in order to come into effect. Thus, this significant criterion sends a clear message that Mexico is prepared to enforce those commitments entered into with the international community.

Within this context, it is essential to describe what the commercial relationship with the European Community (EC) really is. Mexico has entered a new commercial-political cooperation stage, synchronizing the phenomenon of globalization and retaining the path of a free market economy through regional integration. Mexico and the EC and its Member States are not blind as to the importance of commercial diversification, market presence and market access. The new relationship with Europe is not just another FTA, but rather a new momentum for cooperation in other areas. Commerce with Europe, as perceived by Mexico and the EC, is more than just the exchange of goods and services; rather, it is a stage of cooperation in areas such as politics, human rights, democratic principles, culture and technology.

European Community–Mexico and Member States Treaty

Free Trade Agreement: A Common Misunderstanding

The European Community–Mexico and Member States Treaty on Economic Association, Political Coordination and Cooperation Agreement and its Joint Decisions (the Mexico–EC Agreement) are not only a mere FTA.[2] This Treaty involves several other topics and areas that go beyond commercial matters, such as political cooperation, to name just one example.

It is important to recall that the European Union was created with the Treaty on European Union (TEU) signed in Maastricht on 7 February 1992, although it came into effect on 1 November 1993, and was

2 A Free Trade Area seeks free circulation of merchandise among its partners without common foreign protection. A Customs Union seeks free circulation of merchandise too, but that freedom is protected from foreign markets through a common foreign tariff. Finally, a common market brings these elements together and adds, among other things, common policies in agriculture, transportation and coordination in social and fiscal areas. *See* Araceli Mangas Martín and Diego J. Liñán Nogueras, *Instituciones y Derecho de la Unión Europea* (McGraw Hill, 1996).

subsequently amended by the treaties of Amsterdam (1997) and Nice (2000). The nature of the European Union is subject to some debate because, for some authors, it is only a way of describing a set of supranational and intergovernmental cooperation instruments, while, for others, it is a truly international organization. For some, the TEU is the path to be followed to reach the common objective set forth in the preamble of the European Community Treaty of attaining an "ever closer Europe for the people of Europe" and is a step prior to creating a structure closer to a federal or confederate state. As a matter of fact, by 20 June 2003, in Thessaloniki, Greece, the draft for a "European Constitution" created by the 105 delegates under the supervision of Valerie Giscard D'Estang was to have been disclosed.

The TEU modified the constitutive treaties[3] and provided a new legal structure to the system of treaties creating the full *acquis communaitare*. The European Union is an interaction of supranational and intergovernmental forces, which has been explained as a structure resting on three pillars, like the Greek Parthenon. On the one hand, the European Union rests on the first community pillar, which formerly sustained the Union consisting of the European Coal and Steel Community (ECSC),[4] the European Economic Community (EEC) and the European Atomic Energy Community (EAEC), which reinforce its federal or supranational nature. On the other hand, there are two methods of intergovernmental cooperation reflected in the second and third pillars. The second pillar deals with matters related to common foreign and security policy, while the third pillar currently deals with police and judicial cooperation in criminal matters.[5] These matters are not subject to the federal/supranational nature of

3 "Constitutive treaties" refers to the following instruments and their further amendments: (1) European and Coal and Steel Community, or Treaty of Paris, which was signed in Paris, France on 18 April 1951 and came into effect on 25 July 1952; (2) European Economic Community, or Treaty of Rome, which was executed in Rome on 25 March 1957 and came into effect on 1 January 1958; and (3) European Atomic Energy Community, which was signed in Rome and came into effect on the same day as the Treaty of Rome. It is important to note that, even though the European Economic Community Treaty and the European Atomic Energy Community Treaty were both signed in Rome, only the former is widely known as the "Treaty of Rome".

4 As of 25 July 2003, the fifty-year expiration period of this treaty expired.

5 The Treaty on the European Union was further amended by the Treaty of Amsterdam dated 2 October 1997. The third pillar was renamed and "Cooperation in the Fields of Justice and Home Affairs" became "Provisions on Police and Judicial Cooperation in Criminal Matters". The Treaty was amended again in Nice in 2000.

the Institutions of the EC[6] and, therefore, must be dealt with as a means of intergovernmental cooperation whereby the Member States have not delegated any kind of sovereignty to the Institutions.

An important point to bear in mind is that the European Union did not execute a free trade agreement with Mexico, since the former lacks *locus standi* due to not having legal personality. Thus, the mixed agreement[7] signed with Mexico was executed with the European Community represented by the President of the Council of Ministers and by the highest authority of each of the fifteen Member States of the European Community at that time.

Importance of Executing Treaty with European Community

Economic growth makes Mexico a strategic region for investment and the development of trade relations. With its stabilization and structural and political adjustment policies, Mexico has created the conditions for development and growth. The EC is Mexico's second trading partner after the United States, and Mexico is considered by the EC to be the Community's largest Latin American export market.

Given that both Mexico and the EC are open to trade globalization, both have an interest in strengthening relations and further refining the complementary nature of their economies. Mexico is seeking to diversify its sources of supply, technologies, goods, services and capital. For its part, the EC is trying to consolidate and improve its trading and technological position in Latin America, a region with a strong consumer potential, the presence of which decreased before the execution of NAFTA. Significantly, Mexico's NAFTA membership makes it a natural two-way diving board for the two largest economic zones in the world, an alternative not otherwise available considering the huge stumbling blocks that the United States and Europe face in order to have a direct liberalized trade relationship.

---

6 The European Community Treaty, Article 7 (ex-Article 4) provides that there are only five institutions of the European Community: (1) A European Parliament; (2) A Council; (3) A Commission; (4) A Court of Justice; and (5) A Court of Auditors, assisted by other ancillary organs and bodies which attend to specific areas.

7 This is a mixed agreement since part of the authority to execute the treaty lies with the European Community and part with the Member States in certain specific areas where no sovereign assignment has been granted by the Member States to the European Community: Articles 281 (ex-Article 210), 300 (ex-Article 223) and 310 (ex-Article 239).

The Mexico–EC Agreement has as an underlying objective mutual recognition of the importance of market access. The EC acknowledged the great impact of losing an economic and political presence in Latin America, while Mexico cannot allocate all of its expectations to the North American market. Mexico has acknowledged that a diversified economy enhanced through a network of regional trade agreements will allow it to penetrate other markets under beneficial conditions, and will also make the country an attractive place for foreign direct investment thereby creating badly needed jobs.

As mentioned before, Mexico has gone through a modernization and liberalization process of its economy. Mexico achieved unprecedented progress by reducing its custom duties within the GATT framework. It currently applies average aggregate customs tariffs of 10.6 per cent. As of 2000, the country is the fourteenth largest world economy and the second EC trading partner in Latin America after Brazil. In addition, Mexico alone represents thirty-five per cent of exports from the Latin American region. The EC is Mexico's second trading partner after the United States, the latter making up around seventy-five per cent of Mexico's foreign trade.

One of the main concerns of the EC towards Latin America was that the EC's participation in Mexico's total trade decreased from 11.4 per cent in 1990 to 6.1 per cent in 1996, since NAFTA came into force. In gross numbers, EC exports were reduced by thirty-nine per cent, and it was predicted that such a figure would be further eroded without a commercial treaty with Mexico.

The above data is in sharp contrast to the EC's presence in Mexico through foreign direct investment. As figures show, the EC's direct investment in Mexico has rapidly increased during the last decade. As a result, the EC's share of total direct investment rose from six per cent in 1993 to nineteen per cent in 1996, but remains quite modest compared with the United States' share. Currently, the EC's foreign direct investment represents around twenty-two per cent of Mexico's total foreign direct investment and is Mexico's second most important source of foreign direct investment.

On the other hand, contrary to the situation with MERCOSUR, Mexico complements the agricultural products needed in the European market. Approximately eighty-five per cent of Mexican agricultural products go to the United States, albeit that Mexico, at the same time, is an important importer of agricultural products. Thus, this was seen as a twofold opportunity for Europe: on the one hand, Mexico is a great importer of agricultural products and market access is ensured to the EC but, on the other hand, Mexico complements the agricultural products of the EC (mainly through the export of peas, coffee, beer and natural honey).

History of Mexico–European Community Relationship

The commercial and political relationship between Mexico and the EC is not recent. In the 1960s, Mexico decided to formalize diplomatic relations with the then "European Economic Community" (EEC),[8] and thus established a diplomatic mission in Brussels. Notwithstanding the foregoing, the starting point for the institutional relationship between Mexico and the EEC occurred in 1975 through the Economic and Commercial Cooperation Agreement signed in Luxembourg, which may be considered as a "Second Generation Agreement". Both Mexico and the EEC granted each other most-favored-nation status, and they sought to carry out projects of economic and commercial cooperation. This Agreement was not as successful as expected and achieved limited results, but nevertheless was renewed in 1980. Subsequently, Mexico and the EEC signed, in 1987, an Agreement allowing the exchange of notes related to the commercial exchange of textiles. In 1988, an Accord seeking to establish a Delegation of the European Communities in Mexico was signed, and was inaugurated at the end of 1989.

In Luxembourg in 1991, Mexico and the EEC signed a "Third Generation Agreement" which was named the "Cooperation Scheme Agreement". The main aim of this Agreement was to increase cooperation in the areas of commerce, investment, industry, finance, technology and science, public health, the fight against illegal drugs, tourism, the environment, public administration and culture. This Agreement went further than the 1975 Agreement, focusing on promotion of and entrepreneurial cooperation for the development of small and medium-sized enterprises. One of its main shortcomings was that it did not establish real privileges in commercial and investment matters,[9] and the principal advantages

---

8 The European Economic Community further changed its name after the Maastricht Treaty or Treaty of the European Union, which entered into force in 1993. Since one of the aims of the Union was to foster closer links towards a common market, the "economic" reference disappeared and was changed to "European Community".

9 Report on "Europe in Mexico", *Magazine of the Delegation of the European Commission in Mexico*, Year 1, Number 1, 1999.

consisted of the fostering of entrepreneurial cooperation and the intensification of a political dialogue.

On 2 May 1995, Mexico and the EC signed a Solemn Joint Declaration in Paris whereby the parties agreed to further develop their relationship. The goal was the conclusion of a new economic, political and commercial agreement favoring developments in the exchange of goods, services and investments on the basis of progressive liberalization and reciprocal benefits, consistent with the rules of the World Trade Organization. On 8 December 1997, the full legal regime of relationships between the EC and Mexico evolved positively with the execution of two different legal instruments:

(1) The Economic Association, Political Coordination and Cooperation Agreement executed between the EC and its Member States, on the one hand, and the United Mexican States, on the other (also known as the "Global Agreement"); and
(2) The Interim Agreement related to Commerce and Related Matters executed between the EC, on the one hand, and the United Mexican States, on the other (the "Interim Agreement").[10]

The Global Agreement marks the first time that the EC negotiated an agreement of this kind with a Latin American country. This Agreement needed to be ratified by the Mexican Senate, plus the European Parliament and the fifteen constitutional authorities of the Member States. The Global Agreement is a mixed accord, since part of the Agreement belongs to the absolute competence of the European Community, while other areas remain within the Member States' jurisdiction. This Global Agreement is mainly composed of three chapters:

(1) Political;
(2) Cooperation; and
(3) Commercial matters.[11]

---

10 An excellent work regarding the explanation of the Global and Interim Agreements is found in the paper submitted by Elsa Guadalupe Ortega López called "The Evolution of the EC-Mexico Relation: The New Economic Partnership, Political Coordination and Cooperation Agreement". This paper was submitted by the author as a partial fulfillment of the requirements of the Master's Degree in European Legal Studies, Bruges, May 1998.

11 Report on "Europe in Mexico", *Magazine of the Delegation of the European Commission in Mexico*, Year 1, Number 1, 1999, at pp. 16–19.

The political chapter sought to increase the intensity of the political dialogue and, through contact, the exchange of information and consultation. According to the Global Agreement, this dialogue must be kept at the highest political level of the parties. This chapter also includes the convenience of implementing a political dialogue with the European Parliament. One of the most controversial issues is the inclusion of the "Democratic Clause", which is a proviso of a reciprocal nature commonly included in all agreements executed by the EC. This clause allows the suspension of the Global Agreement for lack of compliance with the democratic principles of human rights.

The chapter dealing with cooperation identifies more than twenty different possibilities for cooperation, and an evolving clause allowing the possibility, through mutual consent, for the parties to develop other sectors not identified in the Global Agreement. Cooperation ranges from industrial and entrepreneurial issues, to combined combat against illegal drugs and money laundering, the environment and the fight against poverty.

Finally, the Global Agreement sets forth norms for the mutual liberalization and preferential commercial treatment. Liberalization includes rules on:

(1) Commercialization of goods (tariff phase-out periods) and services;
(2) Progressive and reciprocal abolition of rules restricting the movement of capital and foreign investment;
(3) Government procurement;
(4) Cooperation and coordination in areas of competition to avoid the distortion of competition affecting commerce between Mexico and the EC;
(5) Adequate protection of intellectual property; and
(6) The adoption of a dispute settlement mechanism compatible with the WTO provisions.

Likewise, the Global Agreement creates an institutional mechanism called the Joint Council, which is entrusted with the decision-making and supervision activities of the Agreement. The Joint Council is composed of representatives from Mexico, the Commission for the European Communities and the Member States. The Joint Council is chaired alternately by Mexico and the EC, as provided for in its Internal Regulations.

The Interim Agreement provided a "fast track" method of commencing negotiations towards trade liberalization without having to wait for ratification of the Global Agreement. Since the Interim Agreement involved commercial areas subject to the exclusive competence of the EC, the ratification process would be reduced only to the European Parliament and the Mexican Senate. The Mexican Senate ratified the Interim Agreement on 23 April 1998, while the European Parliament did so on 13 May 1998. The Interim Agreement entered into force on 1 July 1998. Along with the Interim Agreement, the parties agreed to the terms of a joint declaration related to services, the movement of capital and intellectual property in order to negotiate such items on a parallel basis with the liberalization of trade in goods.

The negotiations held by the EC Member States and Mexico to reach the conclusion of the Global Agreement and certain Decisions issued by the Joint Council commenced on 14 July 1998, when the Joint Council of the Interim Agreement was set up. Subsequently, there was one preparatory meeting held between 30 September and 2 October 1998 to establish the agenda and nine rounds of negotiations that ended on 25 November 1999. This process of negotiation can best be summarized as follows:[12]

	Date and Place of the Round	**Main Content of the Negotiation**
1.	9–13 November 1998 (Mexico).	Proposals on trade in goods, rules of origin, safeguards, technical standards, unfair practices, services, movement of capital and payments, competition, government procurement, intellectual property and dispute settlement.

12 The information herein provided was obtained from the website of the Ministry of Commerce and Industrial Development at http://www.secofi-snci.gob.mx/Negociación/Unión Europea/Avances_neg/avances_neg.htm. During the entire negotiations, the Mexican Government kept a "side room" in order to receive the relevant feedback from the industrial, agricultural or commercial sector involved.

	Date and Place of the Round	Main Content of the Negotiation
2.	18–22 January 1999 (Brussels).	Advance in the drafting of legal texts, especially in matters related to competition, intellectual property, government procurement and standards. Parameters for liberalization were laid down.
3.	8–12 March 1999 (Brussels).	Exchange of lists regarding tariff reduction and specific rules of origin. Important advance in the text of the rules of origin, standards, competition, intellectual property and dispute settlement mechanism. Agreement to cover all sectors in the rendering of services.
4.	12–16 April 1999 (Mexico).	Analysis of drafts on market access, sanitary measures and dispute settlement. The EC expressed to Mexico its desire to review the restrictions upon agricultural products entering the EC.
5.	17–21 May 1999 (Brussels).	Competition and intellectual property groups finalized discussion of technical matters. Regarding agricultural products, the parties exchanged information as to the core products to be covered. Important advances relating to standards, government procurement, services and investment were made in the discussion.

	Date and Place of the Round	Main Content of the Negotiation
6.	16–22 June 1999 (Mexico).	Important subjects were discussed: market access, rules of origin, services and movements of capital. The EC demanded "NAFTA Parity" and reiterated its offer to eliminate eighty-two per cent of the tariffs at the entry into force of the Agreement and the rest by the year 2003. Mexico counter-offered with some gradual liberalization to finalize by the year 2007.
7.	19–23 July 1999 (Brussels).	Safeguards, sanitary and zoosanitary measures, customs cooperation and dispute settlement items were concluded at the technical level. Positions in rules of origin kept narrowing their distance. Government procurement reached an important stage to agree to its final text.
8.	7–15 October 1999 (Mexico).	The safeguard chapter was concluded and important advances in agriculture, fisheries, services, movements of capital and payments were made. The EC submitted important suggestions in rules of origin regarding the automotive sector.
9.	18–25 November 1999 (Brussels).	A final agreement was reached.

Overview of Mexico–European Community Agreement

On 20 March 2000, the Mexican Senate approved three international instruments:

(1) The Mexico–EC and Member States Agreement signed in Brussels on 8 December 1997;

(2) The Decision of the Joint Council regarding the Economic Association, Political Coordination and Cooperation Agreement executed between the United Mexican States and the European Community and the Member States, signed in Brussels on 23 February 2000 (the "Decision on EC-MS Competence"); and

(3) The Joint Decision of the Interim Agreement on Commerce and Commerce Related Matters executed between the United Mexican States and the European Community, signed in Lisbon on 24 February 2000 (the "Decision on EC Competence").

These instruments came into effect on 1 July 2000. Currently, they are in full force, since all formalities have been finally and duly complied with by all signatory parties.

The Decision on EC-MS Competence covers aspects of shared competence. This Decision covers topics related to commerce in services, investment, intellectual property and dispute settlement. On the other hand, The Decision on EC Competence covers areas of specific competence of the European Community where no intervention of the Member States is necessary. This Decision deals with the free circulation of goods, government procurement, competition matters, consultation mechanisms in intellectual property and dispute settlement.

The Mexico–EC Agreement includes eight Titles, which are divided into sixty Articles. Title I deals with the scope of the Agreement and provides a clear commitment to democratic principles and fundamental human rights as set forth in the Universal Declaration of Human Rights. This Agreement aims to strengthen the relationship of the parties on a reciprocal basis and that of common interest. To that end, the Mexico–EC Agreement reinforces commercial and economic relations through commercial liberalization in accordance with the WTO Rules and reinforces and broadens cooperation.

Political dialogue is dealt with in Title II. Thus, the parties agreed to institutionalize a more intense political dialogue based on democratic principles and the respect of human rights, including all bilateral and international common interests within the context of the international organizations that the parties belong to. This dialogue will be carried on in accordance with the "Joint Declaration of Mexico and the European Union on Political Dialogue" contained in the Final Act which is part of this Agreement. The ministerial dialogue in the Joint Declaration will be provided within the Joint Council set forth in its Article 45.

Title III provides for commercial aims. Its main objective is to provide a framework to foster the development of the exchange of goods and services, including a bilateral, preferential, progressive and reciprocal liberalization of goods and services. This liberalization takes into account the sensitivity of specific products and service sectors in accordance with the appropriate WTO Rules.

Regarding trade in goods, the Joint Council will decide the measures and calendar for the bilateral, progressive and reciprocal liberalization of tariff and non-tariff barriers as stated in the WTO and Article XXIV of GATT, taking into account the sensitivity of specific products. Such a decision will take into account, among other things, the following:

(1) Scope and phase-out periods;
(2) Customs fees, any other measures of equivalent effect and quantitative and non-quantitative restrictions over imports and exports;
(3) National treatment and prohibition of tax discrimination;
(4) Antidumping and countervailing duties;
(5) Safeguard and surveillance measures;
(6) Rules of origin and administrative and customs cooperation; and
(7) Technical regulations, sanitary and zoosanitary measures and mutual acknowledgment of labeling and certification.

Exceptions to the freedom of transit of goods will be justified on the bases of, *inter alia*:

(1) Public morality, public policy or security;
(2) Protection of the lives and health of human beings, animals and plants; and
(3) Protection of industrial, intellectual and commercial property.

The Joint Council will decide on the necessary measures for the reciprocal and progressive liberalization of commerce regarding services as stated in the appropriate WTO Rules, especially in Article V of GATT, as adopted by the parties. Those measures will enter into effect as soon as adopted.

Movements of capital and payments are covered in Title IV. This Title aims to set forth a framework for the progressive and reciprocal liberalization of the movements of capital and payments between Mexico and the European Community without prejudice to other applicable provisions of this Agreement and other international agreements. The Joint Council will adopt the corresponding measures in order to reach the objectives above in the form of a Decision. This Decision will include the definition, content, extension and nature of the concepts included in this Title. National treatment principles and the scope and transitory periods of the liberalization are to be perfected. The Decision may include a clause allowing the parties to restrict such freedom for reasons of security and public order, public health and defense or difficulties in exchange or monetary policy.

Title V aims to set forth the objectives in public procurement, competition, intellectual property and other provisions related to commerce. Regarding public procurement, the parties will agree on the gradual and reciprocal liberalization of specific public procurement markets. The Joint Council will decide on an appropriate provisions and deregulation calendar. Such a decision will determine the scope, non-discriminatory access to the agreed markets, value of the thresholds and transparent legal procedures, including clear challenge procedures and use of information technology.

The parties agreed to take appropriate steps to avoid distortions and restrictions of competition that could affect commerce between Mexico and the EC. The Joint Council will provide the cooperation and coordination mechanisms for the competent authorities to apply their competition laws. This cooperation will include reciprocal legal assistance, notification, consultation and exchange of information to ensure transparency in the application of competition policies and laws. The Joint Council will decide on the following issues:

(1) Accords among companies, decisions of associations of enterprises and concerted practices among commercial entities;
(2) Any abuse of a dominant position by one or more economic agents;
(3) Mergers between companies;
(4) State monopolies of a commercial nature; and
(5) Public companies and those which have been granted exclusive or special rights.

The parties reinforced the great importance they place on intellectual property rights, including copyright, software programs, databases and connected rights and rights related to patents, industrial designs and geographical indications.[13] The parties committed themselves to establishing appropriate measures to ensure adequate and effective

13 As defined in the Paris Agreement on Intellectual Property Protection and Confidential Information, Article 10*bis*.

protection in accordance with the strictest international standards, including effective methods of achieving that end. Thus, the Joint Council will decide on a consultation mechanism and the kinds of measures to be adopted in accordance with the relevant multilateral intellectual property conventions.

Title VI expresses the will of the parties on cooperation. This Title states that the Joint Council will establish a periodic dialogue aimed at intensifying cooperation through the exchange of information, periodic revision of the evolution of cooperation and the surveillance of sector agreements established in the Mexico–EC Agreement and the possibility to enter into new agreements.

There are specific aims on industrial cooperation, investment promotion, financial services, small and medium-sized enterprises, technical regulations and conformity evaluation, customs cooperation and information issues. Furthermore, the Agreement sets forth the objective of cooperating in the following sectors: agriculture, mining, energy, transportation, tourism, statistics, public administration, the fight against illegal drugs, money laundering and the control of chemical precursors. There are also rules aimed at cooperation in science and technology, education, culture, the audiovisual sector, information and communications, environmental and natural resources, fisheries, social matters and methods for avoiding and superseding poverty and regional cooperation, as well as statements about cooperation with regard to refugees, human rights and democracy, consumer protection, data protection and health. Of significance is the fact that Article 43 of the Mexico–EC Agreement lays down the "evolution clause", which establishes the possibility that the parties may expand the Title on cooperation through mutual consent. Those resources needed to implement the policy on cooperation will be provided by the parties and, therefore, the parties will endorse the European Investment Bank in order to allow continued support for activities in Mexico.

Title VII provides the institutional framework. The Mexico–EC Agreement provides for the creation of a Joint Council entrusted with the application of this Agreement. The Joint Council will meet at the ministerial level at regular intervals, as well as every time that circumstances so require. It will examine all of the main aspects arising out of the scope of this Agreement and any other bilateral or international matters of mutual interest. The Joint Council will be composed of members of the Government of Mexico and members of the

Council of the European Union and of the European Commission. The members of the Joint Council may send representatives in accordance with the Internal Regulations to be established by the Joint Council.

The Presidency of the Council will be chaired alternately by a Member of the Mexican Government and a Member of the Council of the European Union, in accordance with the provisions of its Internal Regulations. To achieve the objectives of the Mexico–EC Agreement, the Joint Council will be entitled to make decisions in those cases established in the Agreement. The decisions to be adopted will be binding, and the parties will take the necessary measures to adopt them. The Joint Council will also be entitled to make pertinent recommendations. Decisions and recommendations will be adopted with the previous agreement of both parties.

The Joint Council will be assisted in its task by a Joint Committee composed of representatives (high officers) of the Government of Mexico and by members of the Council of the European Union and of the European Commission. The Internal Regulations of the Joint Council will determine the obligations of the Joint Committee. It is expressly provided that the Joint Council may delegate any of its authority to the Joint Committee. The Joint Committee will meet once a year, alternating between Brussels and Mexico City upon a date agreed by the parties. The Presidency of the Joint Committee will be held alternately by a representative of each one of the parties. The Joint Committee may also decide on the creation of any other special committee to help it in the implementation of its duties. The Joint Council will decide on the establishment of a specific procedure compatible with the pertinent WTO provisions in order to resolve commercial disputes.

The parties agreed to secure a high degree of protection regarding personal data and any other form of information. They will also agree on a clause on national security. The parties are, therefore, entitled to take measures required to avoid the disclosure of information contrary to the essential interests of their security and the production and marketing of weapons, as long as they do not alter the conditions of competition in matters not having exclusively military ends. In addition, the parties agreed to take measures considered essential to guarantee their security in cases of severe internal disturbance that could endanger civil peace.

The Final Act contains joint and unilateral declarations made simultaneously with the signing of the Mexico–EC Agreement. Double taxation treaties will still be applicable. This Agreement is applicable in the territory of Mexico and the European Community.[14] If one of the parties breaches its obligations in accordance with the Mexico–EC Agreement, it may adopt the appropriate measures. Except in cases of special urgency (substantial breach), it must provide the Joint Council with all useful information needed to review the situation in order to reach an acceptable solution within thirty days. The parties have committed to choose those measures that least disturb the proper functioning of this Agreement. Those measures will be reported immediately to the Joint Committee and will be subject to consultations within the Joint Council, if the parties so agree.

The Mexico–EC Agreement is drafted in double counterparts in the following languages: Danish, Dutch, English, Finnish, French, German, Greek, Italian, Portuguese, Spanish and Swedish, each one being equally authentic. This Agreement was subject to ratification in accordance with the constitutional procedures of each of the parties. It is currently in full effect.

Conclusion

The Mexico–EC Agreement and its Joint Decisions are an important step towards consolidating an important network of commercial and political agreements started by Mexico at the end of the twentieth century. Mexico cannot only rely on its American network (primarily NAFTA) for economic and trade growth. For Europe, it is a return to the American continent, where it had lost hold. Mexico is changing not only from the commercial point of view, but also from the political one. A new elected democratic President has taken office (1 December 2000), reinforcing Mexico's new direction of a market economy with a human face.

14 Currently, there are twenty-five Member States composing the European Community due to the adhesion of ten additional countries from Eastern Europe. The conditions of accession set out in the Treaty on European Union (1993), as amended by the Treaties of Amsterdam (1997) and Nice (2000), provided that the acceding countries must adopt the *acquis communataire*. Therefore, a likely answer is that an enlargement of the European Community will automatically incorporate those ten new countries of the Community into the benefits and obligations of the EC–Mexico Agreement, at least in those areas of exclusive competence of the European Community.

Human rights and democratic principles will continue to be a paramount objective of Mexico. From its perspective, Mexico signed this Agreement not only for what the EC currently represents, but also for what it will become. Market access is a priority and Mexico and the EC and its Member States are aware of that. It is expected that this Agreement will represent a new stage in Mexico's future that, even though started almost four decades ago, has reached its momentum at the very end of the twentieth century. This is the start of a significant chapter in cross-Atlantic relationships, and specific results must be awaited in the near future for further thought and evaluation.

One may expect, for example, to have a rippling effect and for there to be more of these instruments signed with other nations in the hemisphere. However, as in the case of NAFTA, Mexico has taken the lead, while others will follow soon (or at least they have expressed their will to do so). The diplomatic, political and social impacts in the United States and Europe will play a critical role in the timing for all such new deals to come to fruition.

International Consumer Protection in Bulgaria

Milena Rizova and Peter Boyukliev
Deloitte & Touche
Sofia, Bulgaria

Introduction

The legal concept of consumer protection is a relatively new one for Bulgaria. Before the transition to a market economy, there was legislation in place that imposed requirements on the quality of products marketed in Bulgaria. However, such legislation was primarily aimed at controlling production processes rather than protecting individual consumer rights and interests. In 1999, the Consumer Protection and Trading Practices Act (CPTPA) was enacted. Subsequently, secondary legislation on its implementation was also adopted. At present, Bulgarian product and consumer protection legislation is in a process of rapid change and development related to the approximation of Bulgarian laws with European Union (EU) legislation.[1]

Private Law, Administrative Law and Self-Regulation

Currently, the major part of the consumer protection regulations lie in the domain of public law and, more specifically, in the area of administrative law. The latter puts in place the basic requirements for producers, importers and sellers and vests the corresponding rights in consumers aimed at avoiding risks to their health and protecting their economic interests. Some of the gravest malpractices harming consumers constitute criminal offences under the Bulgarian Penal Code. However, the Code is not well adapted to current economic realities, and some of its norms are practically in desuetude. Bulgarian private law also contains certain consumer protection regulations, which

1 Please note that the legislation referred to in this chapter is as at 15 November 2002.

D.Campbell and S.Woodley (eds.), The Comparative Law Yearbook of International Business 2003, 361-437

mainly derive from the general legal principles of tort liability and must be viewed more from the perspective of an individual consumer.

Self-regulation in consumer protection is still relatively weakly developed in practice, although it is accorded an important role by the CPTPA. According to a report of the European Commission on the progress of Bulgaria in the accession process up to the end of 2000, only six non-government organizations of consumers were registered.

Primary Interest Groups

There are several national consumer associations in Bulgaria which are active in the area of consumer protection. These include, among others, the Federation of Consumers in Bulgaria (established in 1990), the Bulgarian National Consumer Association (established in 2000), the Bulgarian Consumer Academy (established in 2001), the Independent Institute for Consumer Protection (established in 2000), the Independent Union of Consumers in Bulgaria (established in 2000) and the Consumer Center for Information and Research (established in 1998). There are also a couple of consumer associations in specific industries, such as the Association for Consumer Protection in Insurance and Banking Services and the Association of Computer Consumers.

Administrative Bodies and Public Law Structure

Administrative Bodies

In general, the monitoring and controlling functions with respect to the application of consumer protection legislation are shared among a number of administrative authorities discussed below.

Ministry of Economy

The Ministry of Economy is the general administrative body in charge of monitoring and controlling consumer protection. The Ministry controls the domestic market and tourist activities. In its capacity as a general administrative body, the Ministry of Economy performs the above functions through a specialized administrative body with specific tasks, namely, the Commission on Trade and Consumer Protection (CTCP).

Commission on Trade and Consumer Protection

The CTCP is the operative administrative body in charge of implementation of the CPTPA. It is a comparatively new administrative body and was established with the coming into force of the CPTPA. The CTCP is a separate body having the status of a legal entity within the structure of the Ministry of Economy. It is a collective body that consists of three persons: a Chairman and two Deputy-Chairmen. The CTCP is backed and facilitated by expert officers, and its administration is headed by a secretary. The administration of the CTCP is territorially divided into one Central Office and nine regional offices, located in the biggest cities across the country.

The CTCP monitors the application of the CPTPA and the secondary legislation on its application. It is authorized to issue compulsory instructions aimed at eliminating infringements of consumer protection regulations, and makes consultations on proposed draft laws related to consumer protection, cooperates with foreign consumer protection authorities and coordinates the activities of other national authorities involved in consumer protection.

National Council on Consumer Protection

Another administrative authority dealing with consumer protection matters is the National Council on Consumer Protection (NCCP).

The NCCP consists of twelve honorary members, six of which are nominated by the government and the other six appointed by associations of consumers. The Minister for Economy is the Chairman of the NCCP. The NCCP does not have a separate administration, but its work is facilitated by the administration of the Ministry of Economy.

The NCCP is vested primarily with consultative functions. It is competent to draft proposals for amending and/or supplementing the consumer protection legislation through the Minister for Economy. It consults the respective administrative authorities on the proper and effective application of the consumer protection legislation. The NCCP also communicates opinions on proposed drafts of legislative acts.

Municipal Consumer Protection Authorities

The CPTPA provides for the establishment of special consumer protection services with each municipal administration. These services have monitoring functions. They are responsible for consulting consumers on consumer protection matters, communicating to the CTCP any relevant information on goods that are dangerous to consumers' health and integrity and approaching the respective authorities in cases of infringements concerning consumers' rights. The municipal consumer protection services are not, however, competent to directly intervene and impose administrative sanctions on the grounds of infringements committed in relation to the consumer protection regulations.

Public Law Structure for Consumer Protection

Consumer protection regulation lies in a relatively broad area of the public law domain.

Constitution

The legal framework of consumer protection is based on the constitutional provision of Article 19, Paragraph 2 of the Constitution of the Republic of Bulgaria, which provides that the law should guarantee all citizens and legal entities equal legal conditions for economic activities by avoiding monopolistic abuse and unfair competition, and should ensure the protection of consumers.

General Legal Regime

The general regime of consumer protection is established by the CPTPA. It specifies basic consumer rights, regulates labeling requirements and lays down price quotation requirements with respect to marketed goods and products. The CPTPA further regulates the safety requirements which must be adhered to when importing and selling goods and products and prescribes the producer's, importer's or seller's obligations in ensuring the servicing of products and goods and guaranteeing their quality within the guarantee period.

A number of ordinances further develop and specify certain basic principles provided by the CPTPA. The general consumer protection regime is further detailed by secondary legislation, which specifies various aspects of the labeling requirements, the price quotation requirements and the safety requirements, as well as other particulars. The most important secondary legislation is as follows:

(1) Regulation on the labeling of non-food products;
(2) Regulation on the requirements for salt when used for food purposes;
(3) Regulation Number 3 on price quotation;
(4) Regulation Number 5 on the establishment, maintenance and use of a national information center for traders in the Republic of Bulgaria;
(5) Regulation on the labeling and presentation of food;
(6) Regulation on the labeling of products made of crystal glass;
(7) Regulation on products imitating food;
(8) Regulation on the requirements for cosmetic products;
(9) Rules on the activities of the Conciliatory Commissions;
(10) Rules on the structure of the Commission on Trade and Consumer Protection;
(11) Rules on the activities of the National Council on Consumer Protection; and
(12) Decree Number 233 of the Council of Ministers on the import-export regime of the Republic of Bulgaria.

Specific Laws

With respect to certain products and services, there is special legislation which may deviate from the general legal regime. As there are many such special laws and regulations, they are discussed in detail below.

Market Regulatory Systems By virtue of Decree Number 41 of the Council of Ministers of 1993, a Regulation has been adopted on the Monitoring and Control of Products and Services of Particular Importance to the Living Standards of the Population and the National Economy. This Regulation introduced unified fixed prices and maximum allowed prices and mark-ups with respect to certain types of products and services. Deviations by producers, importers and sellers from these mandatory requirements are subject to penalties amounting to double the amount of any income earned as a result of infringements of these requirements.

Apart from and in addition to such expropriations, violators are obliged to compensate any damage suffered by any persons affected by their wrongful acts or omissions. Where the affected persons cannot be established, the said amount is to be paid to the national budget. Generally, these specific price-setting and mark-up requirements apply to the following groups of products and services:

(1) Flour;
(2) Bread;
(3) Various types of meat;
(4) Cheese;
(5) Butter;
(6) Rice;
(7) Beans;
(8) Eggs;
(9) Baby food;
(10) Medications;
(11) Public transport;
(12) Heating;
(13) Coal;
(14) Electrical boilers and lamps; and
(15) Shoes other than luxury and official.

Specific price-setting requirements are detailed by special regulations, which are as follows:

(1) Regulation on the maximum allowed retail prices for medicinal products;
(2) Regulation on the setting and application of prices and tariffs for natural gas;
(3) Regulation on the setting and application of prices and tariffs for heating energy;
(4) Regulation on the setting and application of prices and tariffs for electricity;
(5) Regulation on the terms and conditions for the setting and application of prices for tobacco products; and
(6) Regulation establishing the rules for the setting and application of prices for the universal postal services provided by "Bulgarian Posts" EAD.

The specific price-setting requirements are aimed at securing even supply of even quality to the consumer.

Consumer Products and Services Standards

General Regime

Source of Rule

The general regime regulating the standards for consumer products and services, including safety requirements, packaging, labeling and distribution, is primarily set forth in the CPTPA. Additionally, safety requirements are also contained in the Public Health Act and in the Rules on its implementation.

Scope and Application of Rule

The CPTPA puts in place the general legal principle that producers, importers and distributors involved in the circulation of products must place only safe products on the market. Importers and distributors are banned from marketing products which, on the basis of the information they know or should have known, may be considered dangerous.

Material There are no general statutory rules applicable to the material of products, but there is special legislation on the materials used for specific products, which is discussed below.

Fabrication There are no general statutory rules on the fabrication of products, but there is special legislation on the fabrication of specific products, which is discussed below.

Packaging There is no general regime applicable to the packaging of products. However, there a number of other acts and secondary legislation which introduce specific requirements with respect to the packaging of different types of products. These are discussed in detail below.

Labeling The CPTPA contains general labeling requirements which apply to all products placed on the Bulgarian market. Each product presented to consumers must be accompanied by a label in the Bulgarian language, containing at least the following mandatory information concerning the product:

(1) The manufacturer;
(2) The importer (should the product be imported);
(3) The type of product;
(4) Substantial characteristics and features of the product;
(5) The price; and
(6) Instruction manual, if needed.

The label must be placed either on the product itself or on its individual packaging. All the information contained in the label must be legible, true and accurate. Merchants are prohibited from removing or modifying the labels, other markings and relevant information placed on the product by the manufacturer or the importer. Should the contents of the label not meet those prescribed by law, penalties are imposed by the CTCP.

In cases when the type of product does not allow for a label containing the above-listed information to be attached thereto, the merchant is obliged to provide the same information to consumers using other appropriate means or by presenting documents evidencing the relevant circumstances.

Certain types of products that are subject to specific safety requirements must adhere to specific mandatory marking requirements, that is, they must additionally bear a mark of conformity assessment. The mark for conformity assessment must meet certain legal requirements as to its contents, such as including special marking and indicating the code of the accredited conformity assessment expert.

Specific labeling and other marking requirements apply also with respect to imported goods and products which may be considered to endanger human health. These products are listed in a special regulation: Regulation Number 27 on the import of goods important to human health. Upon the import of such products into Bulgaria, a label must be placed both on the individual packaging and on the transportation packaging of the product. Such goods are subject to sanitary control upon import which, among other things, monitors the contents of the labels. Failure to meet the mandatory labeling requirements as to the contents of the label can result in the import of such goods being blocked.

Price Quotation Requirements The general price quotation requirements are regulated by the CPTPA and are further detailed by Regulation Number 3 on price quotation. The seller shall place in advance, on a visible place nearby the product, the price of the product, which must be legible and easy to see and read. Prices should be quoted for a unit or for a piece of product. Different pricing for the same product is prohibited, unless the sale of any of the following is concerned:

(1) Used products;
(2) Products with an expired term, which cannot endanger consumers' lives or health;
(3) Products the features of which deviate from those initially advertised which cannot endanger consumers' lives or health; or
(4) Products being sold off.

Prices must be quoted in Bulgarian Lev.

Regulation Number 3 on price quotation further specifies the price quotation requirements applicable to service providers, restaurants, fast food sites, accommodation sites, parking places and gas stations.

The CPTPA requires that a reduction in prices shall be accompanied by complete and clear information as to the product or services it applies to and the period within which the reduction shall apply. The old and the reduced price should be quoted together in such case. Announcing a general reduction in prices is prohibited if it does not apply to any and all products and/or services delivered to the respective site.

Distribution The CPTPA establishes certain mandatory rules and minimum standards which must be adhered to by all distributors of products, including safety obligations, information obligations, labeling monitoring, price quotation requirements, sale documentation, guarantee documentation, claims under guarantee, liability for defective products, spare parts, unfair terms and pedlary.

Sellers and importers are equally obliged, together with producers, to market only safe products. Upon the consumer's request, the distributor should demonstrate the way in which the product operates and how it must be properly used. A seller is obliged, along with the producer and the importer, depending on who discovers the fact that a product is not safe, to:

(1) Withdraw any product endangering human life, consumers' health and/or property; and
(2) Immediately inform consumers and the controlling administrative authority of the risks inherent in the use of the product which came to light following putting the product into circulation.

The seller shall provide consumers, prior to purchasing a product, with correct, complete, exhaustive and clear information in the Bulgarian language on:

(1) The characteristics of a product, including its contents, packaging, instructions for use and maintenance;
(2) Price and quantity;
(3) Influence on other goods where they are jointly used;
(4) The risks inherent in its normal use and maintenance;
(5) The terms and conditions of the guarantee; and
(6) Expiry date.

Sellers should specifically inform consumers in advance and in an appropriate way, as well as using special and separate places on the site, when selling:

(1) Used products;
(2) Products with an expired term which cannot endanger consumers' lives or health;
(3) Products, the features of which deviate from those initially advertised, but which cannot endanger consumers' lives or health; or
(4) Products being sold off.

The seller shall place immediately near the entrance of his site information on:

(1) Its business name and management seat;
(2) Working hours of the site;
(3) Name of the person directly responsible for running the site; and
(4) The fact that the site is closed outside working hours.

The seller shall make sure that he presents products with labels in the Bulgarian language, and is not entitled to remove and/or modify the labels placed by producers or importers. The seller shall place in advance in a visible place near the product the price of the product, which must be legible and easy to see and read.

The seller is obliged under the law to issue a document evidencing the sale of a product, which should contain at least the following data:

(1) Date of the sale;
(2) Type of the product; and
(3) Price of the product.

When selling a product, the seller shall issue a guarantee document which he has been provided with by the producer. The seller is also free to provide more beneficial guarantee terms himself, in which case he shall issue a separate guarantee document. The seller shall satisfy any claims made under guarantees, during the working hours of the site, from where the product has been bought or at the management address of the seller, unless the guarantee document specifies a different place for such purpose. The seller should bear the transportation costs when moving large-sized products for guarantee repair to and from the service.

The seller can be held liable by consumers for compensation for material damage caused by defective products even when there is no fault on his part for the defect in the product. Such liability may be engaged in cases when the producer or the importer cannot be discovered.

A seller is obliged to present products only if supplies of spare parts and consumables are insured for a term not shorter than the useful life of the products. The inclusion of unfair terms in consumer contracts is prohibited. The object and effects of unfair terms under Bulgarian law are dealt with in more detail below.

A legal definition of pedlary is provided in the CPTPA, stating that pedlary shall mean retail in public places (such as streets, squares, fairs or marketplaces) determined by the municipal authorities which is conducted by or through:

(1) Transport facilities; or
(2) Stalls, tents and other similar facilities.

Home deliveries of purchased or ordered products and the activities of commercial agents are not treated as pedlary. Pedlary of the following products is prohibited:

(1) Products which, due to the specific means of presentation typical of pedlary, could endanger human health;

(2) Medications;
(3) Petrol products and derivatives; and
(4) Products which are expressly prohibited by law as subject to pedlary.

Generally, the terms and conditions for carrying out pedlary are subject to arrangement by special regulations issued by the relevant municipal authorities.

Standing

The CPTPA regulates the types of, the legal grounds for and the legitimate parties to claims that can be brought by consumers for the protection of their rights and legal interests.

Claims under Guarantee Consumers are entitled to make claims under guarantee in the following circumstances, irrespective of whether the producer has offered a guarantee:
(1) Deficiencies in quantity;
(2) Defects in the product — non-conformity of a product that does not ensure the safety of the product or affects its fitness to serve as per the agreed or its usual purpose;
(3) Non-conformity of the product with its advertised size; and
(4) Non-conformity of the product with its advertised trademark.

Claims under guarantee in cases of point (1) and visible defects should be made up to three working days following the purchase of the product. In cases of defects which become apparent within a certain period, claims under guarantee should be made immediately upon their discovery, but not later than the expiry of any guarantee given by the seller or producer.

Upon making a claim under guarantee, a consumer is entitled to request the following:
(1) Rescission of the contract and restitution of the price paid for the product;
(2) Replacement of the product;
(3) Reduction in the price; or
(4) Repair of the product free of charge.

Sellers shall satisfy claims made under guarantee during the working hours of the site from where the product was bought or, alternatively, at the management address of the seller, unless the guarantee document specifies a different place for such purpose. Sellers should bear the transportation costs when moving large-sized products for guarantee repair to and back from the service. The term of the repair is added to the guarantee period.

Should a seller default under a guarantee or not satisfy the claims under guarantee, a consumer is entitled to approach a consumer association, a state consumer protection authority, a conciliatory commission or go directly to court.

Guarantee Undertakings Producers may, but are not bound under law, to make guarantee statements with respect to products placed on the market. The Council of Ministers, however, is authorized to determine certain products which must always be accompanied by guarantee undertakings.

The guarantee constitutes a statement of the producer that the offered product possesses certain qualities and features which will be preserved within a definite period of time should the product be used according to its normal or prescribed use. It is also an undertaking by the producer to bear the consequences in case of non-conformity of the product with such statement by repairing the defects and any damage caused during the guarantee period.

When giving a guarantee for a product, a producer should expressly indicate in the sale document or in the guarantee documentation the duration, terms and conditions of the guarantee. The guarantee period for food products is the same as their expiry term. In any case, the guarantee period commences upon delivery of the product, unless a later date is provided for in the sale contract or in the guarantee documentation. As stated above, a seller may provide his customers with more beneficial guarantee terms and conditions compared with those provided by the producer, which should be evidenced by a separate guarantee document.

Liability for Damage Caused by Defective Products According to the CPTPA, a producer can be held liable by consumers for compensation for material damage caused by defective products even when there is no fault on his part for the defect in the product. The same liability is borne by importers in the case of import of products and, where that producer or importer cannot be established, such liability without fault can be claimed against the seller. The CPTPA provides that, when a number of persons can be held liable for damage caused by defective products, they should be jointly liable.

Only material damage can be claimed for under the CPTPA, which includes losses incurred and lost profits. Claims for non-material damage can be brought on the grounds of general tort law and are awarded following a separate procedure. The amount of material damage claimed cannot include the value of the defective product itself.

In order for a claim for damages under the CPTPA to succeed before court, the claimant must prove:

(1) That he has suffered damage (material only);
(2) A defect in the product; and
(3) A causal link between the defect and the damage.

A producer can exempt himself from liability if he furnishes proof of the following exonerating circumstances:

(1) He has not placed the product on the market;
(2) The defect which caused the damage did not exist at the time the product was placed on the market, but appeared afterwards;
(3) He did not produce and/or distribute the product with the intention of placing it on the market;
(4) The defect is due to compliance of the product with mandatory regulations issued by the public authorities;
(5) The level of scientific and technological progress at the time the product was put into circulation did not allow the defect to be detected; or
(6) He is a producer of a single component of the product and the defect is due to the development and/or fitting of the product by another producer or is due to instructions given by the latter in relation to transportation, safekeeping or exploitation.

The total amount of compensation due from the producer under the CPTPA for damage caused by the same type of defect in identical products resulting in the death or personal injury of several persons is limited to BGN 1-million (approximately Euro 50-million). Where the total amount of any and all compensation due by a producer exceeds this amount, the compensation to which the affected consumers are entitled should be reduced on a pro rata basis in order to meet the limit. The said limit, however, applies only to material damage claimed under the CPTPA.

To qualify for a claim under the CPTPA, a consumer needs to have suffered damage in the amount of at least two minimum working salaries for the country as at the time the damage occurred. When bringing a claim for damages under the CPTPA, the claimant may, should he so desire, make a public announcement of his claim, at his own expense, so that other consumers or consumer associations may join in the claim. Consumers and consumer associations can do so within one month of notification. Any compensation received by a consumer association can be disbursed only for the purposes of protecting the legal interests of consumers.

Any provision in a sale contract exempting or limiting a producer's liability for damage or waiving a consumer's right to claim for damage caused by defective products under the CPTPA is null and void according to law. A producer's liability under the CPTPA can be disallowed or reduced when the injured person or a person under the latter's control has contributed to the damage. When, however, the damage is caused jointly by the defect in a product and the acts or omissions of third parties, a producer's liability cannot be disallowed or reduced.

Claims for damages under the CPTPA can be brought within a limitation period of five years from the date the plaintiff became aware of the damage, the defect and the identity of the producer or importer, but not later than ten years from the date when the defective product was put into circulation.

General Tort Liability It is important to note that, aside from liability for damage caused by defective products as reviewed above, a general tort liability regime exists under Bulgarian law for claiming for damage caused by objects, including damage caused by defects in products. With respect to non-material damage, it is the only regime applicable and, with respect to material damage, it applies subsidiarily, that is, only insofar as a claim for damages under the CPTPA has been disallowed by the court.

Procedures

The CPTPA establishes procedures aimed at avoiding the placing on the market of defective and dangerous products, which are reviewed below.

Withdrawal of Products If the producer, the importer or the seller of a product becomes aware that the product put into circulation is not safe, they are obliged to:

(1) Withdraw the product endangering consumers' lives, health or property from the market; and

(2) Immediately inform, in an appropriate way, the consumers and the CPTC of any and all risks inherent in the use of the product of which he has become aware after placing the product on the market.

Seizure, Ban and Destruction Where the CPTC or the relevant municipal authorities in charge of consumer protection encounter the placing on the market of a product and reasonable doubts exist as to its safety, the Chairman of the CPTC or the mayor of the municipality shall immediately order the product's temporary seizure from circulation. Along with the issuance of such order, a conformity assessment for the product shall be initiated. The conformity assessment will be carried out at the expense of the seller.

The seized product shall be marked with a special marking approved by the Minister for Trade and Tourism. Within twenty-four hours of obtaining the results of the conformity assessment, the Chairman of the CPTC or the mayor of the municipality shall revise the seizure order and, if the results are negative, the respective authority shall ban the circulation of the product or any shipment thereof. Additionally, the authorities shall, if they consider it appropriate, order the withdrawal and destruction of the product at the expense of the seller. The whole procedure of withdrawal and destruction is regulated by Regulation Number 4 of the Minister for Trade and Tourism.

In the case of positive conformity assessment results, the authorities will revoke the seizure order and release the product for free circulation, distribution and sale. In such a case, the expenses incurred through the procedure are to be borne by the relevant authority. The seizure order, ban order and release order are all subject to both administrative and court appeal, where exhausting the administrative appeal system is not a precondition for a court appeal.

Sanctions

The CPTPA provides administrative sanctions, that is, fines and penalties, for the following administrative infringements:

(1) Infringing the labeling requirements, the information obligations, the price quotation requirements or the safety obligations leads to the imposition of a fine of BGN 500 to BGN 3,000;

(2) Infringing the guarantee obligations, price reduction quotes requirements or the prohibition against misleading or incorrect advertisement leads to the imposition of a fine of BGN 1,000 to BGN 15,000;

(3) Any non-compliance with mandatory prescriptions ruled by officers of the relevant authorities in charge of consumer protection will receive a fine of BGN 100 to BGN 2,000;

(4) The circulation of products contradictory to any seizure and/or ban order will receive a fine of BGN 5,000 to BGN 30,000;

(5) Carrying out trade with products and/or providing services without holding a license or permit when such is required will receive a fine of BGN 2,000 to BGN 20,000; and

(6) Infringements of any other provisions of the CPTPA are subject to a fine of BGN 50 to BGN 500.

Except for the sanctions above, the CPTPA provides that the Chairman of the CPTC is entitled to propose the withdrawal and cancellation of licenses and permits to the relevant issuing authorities.

Additionally, where the controlling authorities establish that income has been earned due to wrongful acts or omissions, contradicting the provisions regulating mandatory price formation requirements, the injured person should be adjudicated the equivalence of such income. Additionally, the party in violation should be penalized with double the amount of such income. All of these sanctions are subject to both administrative and court appeal, where exhausting of the administrative appeal system is not a precondition for a court appeal.

Special Regimes

Food

A specific legal regime exists which regulates certain consumer protection aspects with respect to food and food products.

Source of Rule The consumer protection requirements with respect to food and food products are regulated by the following Acts:

(1) Food Act;[2]
(2) Human Health Act;[3]
(3) Veterinary-Medicinal Act;[4] and
(4) Plant Protection Act.[5]

Each of the above Acts is supported by a wealth of secondary legislation. Some of the most important regulations now in force are:

(1) Regulation Number 7 of 8 April 2002 on the hygiene requirements applicable to enterprises that produce or trade in food and the conditions for the manufacture of and trade in quality and safe food;
(2) Regulation on the requirements for the composition of salt when used for food purposes;
(3) Regulation on the requirements for the composition, characteristics and names of baby food;
(4) Regulation Number 15 of 25 April 2002 on the veterinary-medicinal requirements for poultry and the requirements for the production and placing on the market of poultry;
(5) Regulation Number 11 of 11 July 2002 on the norms for the maximum allowed quantities of mycotoxins in food;
(6) Regulation Number 8 of 16 April 2002 on the requirements for the use of additives in food;
(7) Regulation on the definitions of the types of beverages containing spirit, the rules for their fabrication, permitted additives and the conditions for their use;
(8) Regulation Number 23 of 17 May 2001 on the conditions and requirements for the presenting of nutritional information when labeling food;
(9) Regulation on the requirements for labeling and presenting food;
(10) Regulation Number 31 of 24 July 2002 on the veterinary-sanitary requirements for the production and placing on the market of minced meat;

---

2 Published in the *State Gazette*, Issue 90 of 15 October 1999.

3 Published in the *State Gazette*, Issue 88 of 6 November 1973, enacted as of 1 January 1974 and subsequently amended.

4 Published in the *State Gazette*, Issue 42 of 5 May 1999, enacted as of 6 June 1999.

5 Published in the *State Gazette*, Issue 91 of 10 October 1997 and subsequently amended.

(11) Regulation Number 6 of 28 March 2002 on the types of food allowed to be treated with ion radiation and the conditions for such treatment; and
(12) Regulation Number 21 on the specific criteria and requirements for the purity of food additives.

Additionally, it should be noted that the consumer protection legislation is very dynamic, as various regulations in this area are currently being adopted by Parliament and shall come into force in 2003 and 2004, such as, for example:
(1) Regulation on the requirements for sugar when used for consumption by humans;
(2) Regulation on the requirements for juice drinks;
(3) Regulation on the requirements for honey when used for consumption by humans;
(4) Regulation Number 12 of 21 May 2002 on the norms for the maximum allowed quantities of heavy metals polluting food;
(5) Regulation Number 15 of 28 June 2002 on the requirements for the use of flavorings in food;
(6) Regulation Number 1 of 7 January 2002 on plastic materials and objects intended to come into contact with food;
(7) Regulation Number 24 of 17 May 2001 on the hygiene requirements for non-plastic materials and objects intended to come into contact with food;
(8) Regulation on the requirements for cocoa and chocolate products;
(9) Regulation on the requirements for special-purpose food products;
(10) Regulation on dietetic foods for special medical purposes; and
(11) Regulation on the requirements for low-calorie diets used in weight loss.

Scope and Application of Rule To determine its scope of application, the Food Act (FA) gives a definition of food, which includes every stuff or product used for the purposes of consumption by humans regardless of whether it has been processed, half-processed or not processed. Tobacco, medications, narcotic substances, wine and spirit beverages are expressly excluded from the definition of food. The latter are subject to separate specific legal regulations.

The FA requires that food products presented to consumers meet the nutritional value approved for their contents and the maximum allowed quantities of pollution in food as prescribed by law. The manufacture and sale of food containing pollutants in excess of the maximums allowed is prohibited. The use of additives, flavorings and dissolvers in food is generally restricted and is only allowed if:

(1) A proved need of their use exists for achieving a certain technological effect;
(2) The quantities being used are harmless to human health; and
(3) Their use does not mislead consumers as to the type and quality of the food.

The compliance of the composition of food with the norms prescribed by law is assessed by laboratory analysis carried out by experts of the Ministry of Health Care.

The FA requires that all producers of food be registered with the Ministry of Economy. The manufacture of food or food products without such registration is prohibited. Registration requires a set of documents to be presented by the producer, including a permit for putting the manufacturing site into operation and a resolution on the impact of the site on the environment, if applicable. Registration under the FA is evidenced by a special certificate. A special register of food producers is maintained by the Ministry of Economy.

Registration may be cancelled upon the request of the producer, upon termination of its legal personality and due to the following infringements:

(1) Non-compliance with the hygiene of food and good manufacturing and good hygiene practices, resulting in the endangering of human health; and
(2) Repeated non-compliance with the hygiene of food and good manufacturing and good hygiene practices.

When running their business activities, producers are bound to comply with the hygiene requirements applicable to food, as well as good manufacturing and good hygiene practices.

The production and sale of food is prohibited if it:

(1) Contains stuff which is dangerous for human health and could harm people;
(2) Is not good for consumption due to pollution or expiration;
(3) Does not meet the hygiene requirements applicable to food and is not manufactured in compliance with good manufacturing and good hygiene practices; or
(4) Is misleading for the consumer.

The packaging for food is to be made only from materials and objects which:

(1) Do not pollute the food with substances endangering human health; and
(2) Do not change the appearance, taste, flavor and composition of the food.

The packaging must reliably protect the food from its external surroundings and avoid it coming into contact with substances that are dangerous to human health. The substances that are allowed to be used in the fabrication of food packaging are exhaustively defined by Regulation Number 1 of 7 January 2002 on plastic materials and objects intended to come into contact with food. Another regulation dealing with this is Regulation Number 24 of 17 May 2001 on the hygiene requirements for non-plastic materials and objects intended to come into contact with food, which came into force on 6 February 2003. Both regulations deal with certain technical issues concerning the safety of food packaging.

In addition to the general labeling requirements reviewed above, producers and sellers of food are bound to adhere to specific labeling requirements. Labels for food and food products should not:

(1) Mislead consumers in terms of the characteristics of the food, as defined by its nature, origin, identity, qualities, composition, fitness, manufacturing or processing methods and instructions for use, or in terms of influence and qualities which the food does not have;
(2) Contain indications presenting the food as being somehow connected with the prevention or cure of any disease, unless the food does have such proven features and qualities, which is evidenced by a document issued by the Minister for Health Care; or
(3) Suggest that the food has any special feature if all other similar foods have this feature too.

Labels for food or food products should contain:

(1) The name under which the food is being sold;
(2) The ingredients of the food and their constituents and quantities;
(3) Information on gene-modified ingredients, if any;
(4) Expiry term of the food;
(5) Prescribed conditions for keeping the food;

(6) Net weight or volume;
(7) Name, seat and address of the producer, packager or seller of the food;
(8) Origin marking if the lack of such could mislead consumers;
(9) The country of export or the country of processing should the food be imported or been subject to processing;
(10) Lot marking;
(11) Instructions for use, if needed; and
(12) Information on the price.

All of the above data should be legibly and clearly written, located in an easy-to-see place and not be capable of erasing upon storage, use or other operations with the food. When packed together in transportation packaging or in group packaging, a label should be placed on the transportation or group packaging containing information on:
(1) The name under which the food is being sold;
(2) Expiry term of the food;
(3) Name, seat and address of the producer, packager or seller of the food; and
(4) Lot marking.

Apart from the labeling requirements, which are mandatory, food can also be labeled with nutritional information, which is only voluntary. Such nutritional information includes data on the energy value and the composition of the food and statements on certain special nutritional characteristics of the food. Indications as to the energy value and the composition of the food are, however, mandatory in cases where any statements regarding certain special nutritional characteristics are made with respect to the food.

The nutritional information can be basic (which includes energy value and quantities of protein, carbohydrate and fat) or extensive (which includes energy value and quantities of protein, carbohydrate, fat and enriched fatty acids). In addition to both the basic and extensive nutritional information, an indication on the contents of other substances may be given, which are outlined in an exhaustive list.

The opening of a site for selling food requires the obtaining of a permit for putting the site into operation. The general distribution rules reviewed above apply here as well. Any and all processes, premises and persons involved in or somehow concerned with the manufacturing, distribution, sale, storage and transportation of food and food products are subject to control by various authorities, including but not limited to the Ministry of Health Care and its agencies, the Ministry of Economy and the Ministry of Agriculture.

Sanctions The production and sale of food which contains stuff that is dangerous for human health and could harm people, which is not good for consumption due to pollution or expiration, which does not meet the hygiene requirements applicable to food, is not in compliance with good manufacturing and good hygiene practices or is misleading for consumers is penalized with a fine amounting to BGN 500 to BGN 1,500. If such food is produced or sold by a legal entity or a sole trader, the amount of the fine can be between BGN 1,500 and BGN 3,000. Using additives, flavorings and dissolvers which are prohibited from use in the fabrication of food or using excessive quantities of allowed additives, flavorings and dissolvers is subject to a fine of BGN 250 to BGN 500. If this is done by a legal entity or a sole trader, the amount of the fine can be between BGN 500 and BGN 1,000.

Using materials and objects that come into contact with food despite being prohibited for such purposes, using packaging that leads to changes in the outer appearance of food or its flavor or taste or using packaging which facilitates the pollution of food is subject to a fine of BGN 250 to BGN 500. If this is done by a legal entity or a sole trader, the amount of the fine can be between BGN 500 and BGN 1,000. Infringing the labeling and advertising requirements applicable to food is subject to a fine of BGN 250 to BGN 500. If this is done by a legal entity or a sole trader, the amount of the fine can be between BGN 500 and BGN 1,000.

Producers that manufacture food without being registered with the Ministry of Economy are subject to a fine of BGN 500 to BGN 1,000. If the producer is a legal entity or a sole trader, the amount of the fine can be between BGN 1,000 and BGN 1,500. Failure to comply with good manufacturing and good hygiene practices in relation to food, resulting in the endangering of human health, can lead to a fine of BGN 200 to BGN 1,500. If this is done by a legal entity or a sole trader, the amount of the fine can be between BGN 1,500 and BGN 3,000. The same fines apply for the import of food that deviates from the requirements provided for in the FA and in the secondary legislation on its implementation.

Non-compliance with mandatory prescriptions issued by the respective controlling authorities is subject to a fine of BGN 250 to

BGN 500. If a legal entity or a sole trader is involved, the amount of the fine can be between BGN 500 and BGN 1,500. All of these infringements are penalized with higher fines where they are committed repeatedly, a repeat infringement being one that is committed within one year of the enforcement of the administrative sanction.

Drugs

Source of Rule The manufacture, import, wholesale and retail distribution, use and export of human medicinal products are subject to heavy regulation in Bulgaria, which is in line with Directive 2001/83/EC on the Community Code Relating to Medicinal Products for Human Use.

The main source of rule is the Medicines and Human Pharmacies Act.[6] The application of the Medicines Act is supported by a number of regulations for its implementation, including among others:

(1) Regulation Number 29 of 14 December 2000, issued by the Minister for Health Care, on the Conditions and the Procedure for Granting Permits for the Marketing of Medicinal Products;
(2) Regulation Number 17 of 19 April 2001, issued by the Minister for Health Care, on the Requirements for the Data Contained in the Documentation for Obtaining a Permit for the Use of Medicinal Products;
(3) Regulation Number 7 of 22 June 2000, issued by the Minister for Health Care, on the Mandatory Information Placed on the Packages of and the Leaflets Accompanying Medicinal Products and Instructions for the Use of Medical Tools;
(4) Regulation Number 12 of 14 July 2000, issued by the Minister for Health Care, on the Conditions and Procedure for the Classification of Medicinal Products which are Dispensed with or without Medicinal Prescription;
(5) Regulation Number 13 of 14 July 2000, issued by the Minister for Health Care, on the Conditions and Procedure for the Approving of Advertisements for Medicinal Products;
(6) Regulation Number 16 of 9 June 1995, issued by the Minister for Health Care, on the Procedure for Registering the Prices of Medicinal Products, and Regulation of 13 July 2000, issued by the Council of Ministers, on the Maximum Retail Prices for Medicinal Products Permitted for Use;

6 Published in the *State Gazette*, Issue 36 of 1995, with subsequent amendments.

(7) Regulation Number 5 of 21 June 2000, issued by the Minister for Health Care, on the Conditions and Procedure for Blocking Medicinal Products and Market Withdrawal by Manufacturers, Warehousing for the Wholesale of Medicinal Products, Pharmacies, Drugstores and Medical Institutions; and

(8) Regulation Number 28 of 14 December 2000, issued by the Minister for Health Care, on the Conditions and Procedure for Destroying, Recycling or Use of Drugs for Other Purposes.

Scope and Application of Rule The composition of each medicinal product is approved when the permit for its use is issued. Each manufacturer must ensure that the composition of its manufactured medicinal products conforms to the permit for its use and remains constant with regard to quantity and quality. The manufacture of medicinal products may be carried out by legal entities which have been duly licensed by the Executive Drugs Agency at the Ministry of Health Care. Legal entities may be licensed to manufacture medicinal products which have been duly permitted for use by the Minister for Health Care. The fabrication of medicinal products which have not been permitted for use or the characteristics of which differ from the permit is forbidden.

The fabrication of medicinal products must be carried out in accordance with good manufacturing practices for medicinal products. Good manufacturing practices for medicinal products are a set of rules adopted by the Minister for Health Care which govern all aspects of the manufacturing process for medicinal products, including personnel, premises, equipment, materials, documentation and quality control. The compliance of manufacturers of medicinal products with the good manufacturing practices for medicinal products is supervised and controlled by the Executive Drugs Agency.

The packaging of medicinal products must consist of immediate packaging which is in immediate contact with the product and/or an outer package inside which the immediate packaging is placed. The package must always be accompanied by a package leaflet. The sale of medicinal products without a leaflet is forbidden unless the product is sold with no outer packaging and the information from the leaflet is inscribed on the immediate packaging.

The mandatory data that needs to be inscribed on both the immediate and the outer packaging of medicinal products is set out in Regulation Number 7 on the Mandatory Information Placed on the Packages of and the Leaflets Accompanying Medicinal Products and Instructions for the Use of Medical Tools. The following particulars must appear on the outer packaging of medicinal products or, where there is no outer packaging, on the immediate packaging:

(1) The name of the medicinal product;
(2) The medical substances expressed qualitatively and quantitatively per dosage unit using their common names;
(3) The pharmaceutical form and the quantity in one unit;
(4) A list of the ingredients known to have a recognized action or effect;
(5) The method of use;
(6) A special warning that the medicinal product must be stored out of reach of children;
(7) A special warning, if this is necessary for the medicinal product;
(8) The expiry date expressed as "expiring on: month/year";
(9) Special storage precautions, if any;
(10) Special precautions for the disposal of unused medicinal products or waste materials from medicinal products, if necessary;
(11) The name and address of the holder of the permit for use of the medicinal product;
(12) The number of the permit for use of the medicinal product;
(13) The manufacturer's batch number; and
(14) Method of prescription and, in the case of self-medication, instructions on the use of the medicinal product.

All data on the packaging must be in the Bulgarian language, except for the name of the medicinal product, which must also be inscribed in Latin. All data must be readable and comprehensible. It may not contain misleading names and designations and should not deviate from the data approved when the product was permitted for use.

Regulation Number 7 also determines the mandatory data that must be included in the package leaflet placed in the outer packaging of the product. Specifically, the leaflet must indicate the following:

(1) The name of the medicinal product;
(2) Full qualitative and quantitative composition of the product;
(3) Pharmaceutical form and contents in one unit;
(4) Name and address of the holder of the permit for use of the medicinal product and name and address of the manufacturer, if different;
(5) Pharmaco-therapeutic group or type of activity;

(6) Therapeutic indications;
(7) Information that is necessary before taking the medicinal product, including contra-indications, special precautions for use, forms of interaction with other medicinal products and other forms of interaction, special warnings with respect to the product's use by certain categories of patients, effects on the ability to drive vehicles or to operate machinery and details on the ingredients;
(8) Information on the proper use of the product, including dosage, method and route of administration, frequency of administration, duration of treatment, action to be taken in the case of an overdose, course of action to take when one or more doses have not been taken and an indication, if necessary, of the risk of withdrawal effects;
(9) Description of the undesirable effects which can occur from the normal use of the medicinal product and, if necessary, the action to be taken in such a case;
(10) Reference to the expiry date indicated on the label, with a warning against using the product after that date; and
(11) Date upon which the package leaflet was last revised.

The leaflet must be in the Bulgarian language. It is acceptable that the leaflet be in several languages, provided that one of them is Bulgarian and the information in all versions is the same.

The wholesale distribution of medicinal products is carried out by individuals and legal entities who are duly licensed by the Minister for Health Care. The retail distribution of medicinal products is carried out by pharmacies which are licensed by the Minister for Health Care. Medicinal products, manufactured locally, may be distributed for sale if:

(1) They have been permitted for use;
(2) They are accompanied by a batch quality certificate and permission for sale of each particular batch, both issued by the product's manufacturer; and
(3) Their maximum sales price is registered with the Ministry of Health Care.

The sale of certain locally manufactured medicinal products, however, such as vaccines, toxins and biotechnological products, can be carried out only on the basis of an explicit permit for the sale of the product issued by the Executive Drugs Agency. Imported medicinal products may be distributed for sale if each respective batch of the product is accompanied by:

(1) A quality certificate issued by the manufacturer; and
(2) A permission for sale issued by the Executive Drugs Agency to the product's importer.

An advertisement for medicinal products designated for use by consumers must have prior approval from the Executive Drugs Agency. Once granted, the approval for an advertisement is effective and valid for the term of the product's permit for use. The contents of the advertisement must conform to the brief description of the medicinal product approved at the time of issuing the permit for the product's use and present only the approved characteristics of the product. The distribution of samples of medicinal products to consumers is forbidden, as is the advertisement of medicinal products which contain narcotic substances.

Procedures The procedure for permitting the use of medicinal products is initiated by the product's manufacturer. If the manufacturer is a non-resident entity, the procedure can be started only if the non-resident manufacturer has a permanent duly authorized representative within the territory of Bulgaria.

When applying for a permit, the manufacturer of a proprietary medicinal product is required to submit the product's specifications. These include the administrative, chemical, pharmaceutical, pharmacological, toxicological and clinical data required by Regulation Number 17 of the Minister for Health Care on the Requirements for the Data Contained in the Documentation for Obtaining a Permit for the Use of Medicinal Products. If the applicant seeks to obtain a permit for use of a medicinal product which is equivalent to a product already in use, the applicant must also present evidence of such equivalence.

A permit for the use of a medicinal product is granted following an assessment of the drug's quality, safety and therapeutic effect made on the basis of an examination of the product's specifications. A permit may be denied if, during the process of the drug's examination, it is established that:

(1) The correct use of the product entails a high level of risk to the person's health;

(2) The drug does not have the stated medical effect, or its medical effect does not correspond to the medical effect described in its specifications; or
(3) The product's composition does not conform to the composition stated in the drug's specifications in quantity or quality.

The permit is issued for a period of five years and may be renewed for another five-year term. It becomes effective as from the date of its registration in the registry of permitted medical products maintained by the Executive Drugs Agency. The permit may be terminated before the expiry if its term if a non-resident manufacturer of the product removes its representative office from Bulgaria. It may also be cancelled before the expiry of its term if the medicinal product:
(1) Fails to demonstrate its stated quality;
(2) Does not have the stated medical effect;
(3) Has unacceptable and undesirable side effects; or
(4) Was permitted for use in breach of the applicable law.

A new permit for use is required in case of:
(1) A change in the type or quantity of the medical substances;
(2) A change in the medical form and type of activity; or
(3) The adding of a new therapeutic indication or amending of an existing one.

The permit does not relieve the manufacturer of a medicinal product of its liability for damages in cases where there is a harmful impact upon people's health. Holders of permits for the use of medicinal products are required to notify the Executive Drugs Agency of any serious unexpected adverse effects caused by the product. Such notification must be made to the Agency within fifteen days from receiving the complaint from the user. Permit holders are further required to submit reports to the Executive Drugs Agency on the unexpected adverse effects caused by their products. These reports are submitted on a regular basis as follows:
(1) During the first two years following the date of receiving the permit, every six months;
(2) During the next three years of the validity of the permit, every twelve months; and
(3) Every fifth year from the issuance of the permit, together with the documentation for its renewal.

In addition, it is within the sole discretion of the Executive Drugs Agency to require such information at any time. The Agency is required to organize a system for registration, analysis and summary of unexpected adverse effects and interactions which occur during the course of use of the medicinal products.

Medicinal products may be suspended and withdrawn from the market only if the competent authorities have documentary information on any of the following:

(1) Non-compliance of the product with quality, efficiency and safety requirements;
(2) Non-compliance of the product with the terms and conditions of the permit for its use, including unexpected adverse effects on patients occurring during the course of correct administration of the product;
(3) Manufacture or import of products in breach of the Medicines Act;
(4) Non-compliance of a product's packaging and/or leaflet with the Medicines Act; or
(5) Cancellation of a product's permit for use.

On a national level, the Director of the Executive Drugs Agency is competent to issue rulings for the suspension and withdrawal of medicinal products. On a regional level, this competence falls within the domain of the directors of territorial hygiene agencies. Rulings may also be issued by manufacturers and importers of medicinal products with respect to products which were manufactured or imported by them.

If grounds for suspending a medicinal product exist, a written ruling must be issued to the manufacturer or the importer of the product to suspend its distribution and sale. If the product entails a high level of risk for consumers, the public must be informed through the Bulgarian Information Agency not to use the suspended products. Upon receiving a ruling for the suspension of its product, the manufacturer or the importer is obliged to immediately cease its sales. There is a further obligation, within forty-eight hours from receipt of the ruling, to:

(1) Instruct in writing the persons who were supplied with the product to stop its use and sale; and
(2) Inform the competent authorities of the action undertaken, the persons who were supplied with the product and the number of packages supplied.

In critical situations, the period of forty-eight hours may be reduced to twenty-four.

Based on the examination performed and the testing of the product, the competent authorities must issue a ruling on the suspended product. The ruling may either release the suspended batch of the product or require that the suspended batch be withdrawn from the market. The ruling for release or withdrawal of the suspended batch must be issued within thirty days from the date of the first ruling for suspending the batch of the product. Upon receiving a ruling for withdrawal, the manufacturer or the importer of the batch must arrange for it to be withdrawn within a period of thirty days. If the permit for use of the product has been cancelled, the withdrawal must take place within a period of seven days.

Sanctions The Medicines Act provides for a number of administrative sanctions which may be imposed by the competent authorities in case of violations of the provisions of the law. These sanctions include:

(1) Fines in the range of BGN 300 to BGN 10,000 which are imposed for a variety of violations, such as the manufacture and sale of medicinal products which are not permitted for use, the sale of medicinal products in packages or with leaflets which do not comply with the statutory requirements, the sale of expired medicinal products, the sale of medicinal products at prices which are higher than the maximum prices and the advertisement of medicinal products in breach of the law;
(2) Suspension of the right of medical specialists to practice their profession for a certain period of time which may be imposed on specialists who manufacture or sell medicinal products containing narcotic substances without a permit for use or perform or allow the performance of clinical research in breach of the law;
(3) Closure of premises for the wholesale or retail distribution of medicinal products if the distribution is carried out in breach of the law; and
(4) Confiscation of medicinal products which are manufactured or distributed and sold in breach of the law.

Motor Vehicles

The sale and distribution of automobiles, tractors used in agriculture and forestry and certain spare parts for them are subject to specific consumer protection regulations.

Source of Rule The relevant regulations are contained in the Traffic Act and a number of Regulations issued by the Minister for Transport, the Minister for Agriculture and Forestry and the Minister for Economy. These Regulations specify some requirements with respect to the "type approval" procedures to which motor vehicles are subject.

Scope and Application of Rule The Traffic Act regulates the placing on the market of new:

(1) Motor vehicles, which are defined as vehicles furnished with motors to move them, except railway vehicles;
(2) Automobiles, which are defined as non-railway vehicles used for carrying passengers and freight or for pulling other vehicles;
(3) Trailers, which are defined as vehicles pulled by motor vehicles;
(4) Tractors used in agriculture and forestry, which are defined as motor vehicles for specific activities, such as pulling freight trailers;
(5) Components;
(6) Systems; and
(7) Spare parts.

The composition and fabrication of the above products are subject to the general safety requirements, as well as the regulations under the Traffic Act. The products mentioned can be placed on the market only following a "type approval" examination procedure, which assesses to what extent the respective product meets the technical requirements applicable to it.

Due performance of the consumer protection requirements applicable to motor vehicles and provided in the Traffic Act are subject to control by the Minister for Transport and Communications, the Minister for the Interior, the Minister for Regional Development, the Minister for Healthcare and the Minister for Agriculture and Forestry, who may appoint experts to take charge from within their agencies.

Procedures Except for the general procedures discussed above, the Traffic Act provides that a "type approval" examination procedure be passed prior to placing the products listed above on the market.

Sanctions As the listed products are subject to specific technical requirements assessed by a "type approval" procedure, non-compliance with the applicable consumer protection requirements is penalized using the sanctions envisaged in the Technical Requirements for Products Act. The placing on the market of products that do not meet the safety requirements or that have not passed a conformity assessment examination procedure, as prescribed in the Regulations under the Traffic Act, is subject to a fine of BGN 5,000 to BGN 15,000, unless the Regulations provide for heavier sanctions.

Electrical Appliances

Source of Rule Currently, Bulgaria does not have effective legislation that establishes product and consumer protection rules on electrical appliances. Extensive legislation in this area has already been adopted and promulgated, but not all of it has yet come into force. Such legislation includes:

(1) Products' Technical Requirements Act (PTRA),[7] which came into force on 2 December 2002;

(2) Regulation on the Substantial Requirements and the Assessment of Conformity of Electrical Equipment Designed for Use within Certain Voltage Limits,[8] which came into force on 14 January 2003 and is largely based on Directive 73/23/EEC of 19 February 1973 on the harmonization of the laws of Member States relating to electrical equipment designed for use within certain voltage limits; and

(3) Regulation on the Substantial Requirements and the Assessment of Conformity of Household Electric Refrigerators, Freezers, Appliances for Storage of Frozen Products and Combinations thereof,[9] which will come into force on 4 March 2004 and is largely based on Directive 96/57/EC of 3 September

---

7 Published in the *State Gazette*, Issue 86 of 1 October 1999 and subsequently amended.

8 Adopted by the Council of Ministers and published in the *State Gazette*, Issue 62 of 13 July 2001.

9 Adopted by the Council of Ministers and published in the *State Gazette*, Issue 84 of 3 September 2002.

1996 on Energy Efficiency Requirements for Household Electric Refrigerators, Freezers and Combinations thereof.

Scope and Application of Rule The component parts of electrical appliances should be made in such a way as to ensure that they can be safely and properly assembled and connected. Electrical appliances must be designed and manufactured in such a way as to guarantee protection against certain hazards, subject to their proper use and adequate maintenance. Manufacturers of electrical appliances need to develop and prescribe measures which are aimed at ensuring that:

(1) Individuals and domestic animals are adequately protected against the danger of physical injury or other harm which might be caused by direct or indirect electrical contact;
(2) Temperatures, arcs or radiation which would cause a danger are not produced;
(3) Individuals, domestic animals and property are adequately protected against non-electrical dangers caused by the electrical appliances; and
(4) The products' insulation is suitable for all foreseeable conditions.

Manufacturers of electrical equipment must undertake all necessary measures in the process of manufacture to ensure that the manufactured products conform to their technical specifications and the substantial requirements applicable to such products. The essential characteristics of an electrical appliance, the recognition and observance of which will ensure its safe use, must be marked on the appliance. If such marking cannot be placed on the appliance itself, then the information should be contained in accompanying instructions.

The manufacturer's name or trademark should also be printed clearly on the electrical appliance. If this is not possible, the information should be indicated on the product's packaging. There should also be a mark on the electrical appliance denoting its compliance with the applicable substantial requirements and standards. The mark is in a standard form, and the responsibility for its placing on the products lies with the person who places the electrical appliance on the market.

Electrical appliances must be accompanied by a declaration of conformity issued by the person who is placing the product on the market. The declaration of conformity should be in the Bulgarian language and must include certain data prescribed by the regulations for the implementation of the PTRA.

Procedures The supervision of the conformity of electrical appliances with mandatory requirements and standards is carried out by the State Agency on Metrology and Technical Supervision. If it is established that certain electrical appliances do not comply with the substantial requirements and standards, or if certain appliances are not accompanied by the required documentation for certifying their conformity, the competent authorities may order the withdrawal of the products from the market. If conformity is not achieved, the competent authorities may rule that such products be destroyed.

Sanctions Fines may be imposed on individuals and legal entities who place electrical equipment on the market in breach of statutory requirements.

Tools

Currently, there are no product and consumer protection rules applicable to tools in Bulgaria. Thus, the general consumer protection regime discussed above applies.

Textiles

Source of Rule Currently, special rules on textiles are found in Regulation Number 27 on the Import of Goods of Importance to Human Health.[10] Additionally, there are two more regulations:

(1) Regulation on Labeling and Nomenclature of Textile Products,[11] which came into effect on 1 January 2003; and
(2) Regulation on Dangerous Chemical Substances, Stuffs and Products Subject to Prohibition or Restrictions for Sale or for Use,[12] which came into force on 1 January 2003.

---

10 Published in the *State Gazette*, Issue 75 of 25 August 1995.
11 Published in the *State Gazette*, Issue 2 of 7 January 2002.
12 Published in the *State Gazette*, Issue 69 of 17 July 2002.

Scope and Application of Rule Regulation Number 27 on the Import of Goods of Importance to Human Health deals with the import procedure and the formalities aimed at ensuring the safety of certain imported textile products. The Regulation on Labeling and Nomenclature of Textile Products imposes mandatory requirements with respect to the labeling and names of textile products, while the Regulation on Dangerous Chemical Substances, Stuffs and Products Subject to Prohibition or Restrictions for Sale or for Use expressly prohibits certain chemical substances from being used in the fabrication or composition of textile products.

The composition of textiles must meet definite purity requirements provided in the Regulation on Labeling and Nomenclature of Textile Products. When textile products are fabricated by a craftsman, he must be duly registered in a special Register of Craftsmen. The import of certain textile products into Bulgaria must follow a procedure for obtaining a sanitary permit. The import of some textiles requires that an additional sanitary report be obtained. No specific packaging rules apply to textiles, however.

In addition to the general labeling requirements discussed above, persons placing textiles on the market are bound to follow specific labeling requirements. With respect to these labeling requirements, textile products are divided into three groups:

(1) Textile products subject to the mandatory labeling requirements;
(2) Textile products which are excluded from the mandatory labeling requirements; and
(3) Complex textile products consisting of a number of items of the same composition that can be labeled with a common label.

The first group of textile products must always be accompanied by labels, unless they are not intended to reach end consumers or they are subject to public procurement, in which case the information that must be contained in the label can only be included in the technical documentation of the textile products.

The name indicated on any textile must follow and cannot deviate from the nomenclature list set out by the Regulation on the Labeling and the Nomenclature of Textile Products. The name, description and composition specification of the fabrics must be indicated on the label legibly, in an easy-to-read way and using even text. If any information is given which is additional to the minimum required under the said Regulation, it must be given separately, but is not to be included in the label unless it refers to trademarks or the names of the producers. Including various descriptions and particulars in the label is permissible only as far as they are accepted in usual trade practice.

The second group of textile products, which are listed in a special enclosure to the said Regulation, do not need to be labeled but, irrespective of that, if they are labeled, then they must meet certain requirements. The third group of textile products can be labeled with a common label describing all of the items separately of which the product consists, but this is allowed only insofar as the composition of the separate items is the same.

Generally, no specific rules apply to the distribution of textile products, so the general distribution rules discussed above apply.

Under Bulgarian law, each municipal council is free to regulate the terms and conditions for selling goods from open outlets. Therefore, it is possible that different requirements and restrictions apply to the distribution and sale of some types of textile products in the different municipalities. In the Sofia Municipality, the Regulation on the Terms for Carrying Out Commercial Activities in the Territory of the Sofia Municipality applies, which prohibits the sale of certain types of textile products from open outlets or at open marketplaces, such as knitted fabrics and underwear.

Control over the implementation of the specific requirements as to the names and labeling of textile products is given to the Consumer Protection and Trading Practices Commission, with all its regional offices, and the municipal consumer protection authorities.

Procedures The Regulation on Labeling and Nomenclature of Textile Products regulates various technical examination procedures for the carrying out of laboratory and other analyses of fabrics and textiles. From a legal point of view, however, it is the general legal procedures above which also apply with respect to textile products.

Sanctions No specific sanctions are provided with respect to the manufacture and sale of textile products.

Toys

Source of Rule Specific legal requirements with respect to toys are regulated by the following acts:

(1) Regulation Number 3 on Hygiene Requirements for the Fabrication and Sale of Toys;[13]

(2) Regulation on the Substantial Requirements and Conformity Assessment of Toys,[14] which was enacted on 14 July 2002;

(3) Regulation Number 27 of 17 August 1995 on the Import of Goods of Importance for Human Health;[15]

(4) Regulation on the Labeling and Nomenclature of Textile Products,[16] which came into effect on 1 January 2003; and

(5) Regulation on Dangerous Chemical Substances, Stuffs and Products which are Subject to Prohibitions or Restrictions for Sale or Use,[17] which came into effect on 1 January 2003.

Scope and Application of Rule The Regulation on the Substantial Requirements and Conformity Assessment of Toys (RSRCAT) gives a legal definition of the term "toys" to determine the products subject to specific regulations. Toys are any and all products and/or materials that are evidently intended to be used for playing by children below fourteen years. The said Regulation contains a list of various products which are expressly excluded from the definition of toys. Depending on their nature, qualities and specifications, toys can be classified into different groups, such as functional toys, chemical toys, professional toys or fixed toys. Specific rules apply to these groups, which shall be outlined below.

Both the RSRCAT and Regulation Number 3 on the Hygiene Requirements for the Fabrication and Sale of Toys contain mandatory provisions regulating the composition of toys and the materials to be used in their fabrication. The materials must be entirely safe and harmless. Certain stuffs and materials are expressly prohibited from being used in the fabrication of toys. Recycled materials are also not allowed to be used, and maximum allowed quantities are introduced for certain toxic substances. There are detailed technical

13 Published in the *State Gazette*, Issue 25 of 1 April 1988.

14 Published in the *State Gazette*, Issue 62 of 13 July 2001.

15 Published in the *State Gazette*, Issue 75 of 25 August 1995.

16 Published in the *State Gazette*, Issue 2 of 7 January 2002.

17 Published in the *State Gazette*, Issue 69 of 17 July 2002.

requirements for the composition, form and construction of toys, which are all aimed at ensuring adequate safety for children, depending on their age.

Toys cannot be fabricated at home, unless otherwise expressly allowed and as far as the fabrication is carried out by disabled persons. All persons involved in the fabrication of toys shall pass initial and regular medical examinations and are obliged to wear working clothes. Compliance with the substantial safety requirements applicable to the design and fabrication of toys is attested in different ways, depending on whether the Bulgarian standards, which introduce the harmonized European standards applicable to toys, are followed or not. These different regimes are reviewed below.

The packaging of toys must be carried out on premises that meet necessary sanitary and hygiene requirements. Any toy must be packed in appropriate packaging, which is not allowed to be damaged upon the sale of the toy. The packaging of toys must not expose children to the danger of suffocation.

In addition to the general labeling requirements reviewed above, producers and sellers of toys are bound to follow specific labeling requirements. Labels on toys must contain the name and/or commercial name and/or the trademark of the producer or the importer and its exact address. The labels must also contain conformity marking evidence that the substantial safety requirements have been duly complied with, either by adhering to the Bulgarian standards introducing the harmonized European standards for toys or by satisfying the conformity assessment procedure described below.

Where the size of the toy does not allow the above data to be placed on its packaging or on the toy itself, this data must be indicated in a special leaflet accompanying the toy. The minimum age of the consumer must also be indicated on the toy or on its label or packaging, as well as the necessity, if any, for the toy to be used under the supervision of a parent or responsible adult.

Additionally, labels on toys and/or their packaging or attached instructions for use must contain appropriate and legible texts, warning consumers of the risks related to their use, as well as the measures for their avoidance.

Toys that are intended to be used by children aged over thirty-six months shall contain an express indication of this fact in their labeling. Functional toys (such as those used in the same way and for the same purposes as machines or tools used by adults and often represented as miniature versions of the real thing) must indicate that they are to be used only under the direct supervision of a responsible adult. These toys must be accompanied by operation and safety instructions.

Toys which contain dangerous substances or stuffs, as well as chemical toys (such as chemistry or photography sets) must be accompanied by an indication of their dangerous nature. The operation instructions must, in this case, indicate the appropriate first aid measures in case of emergency and the fact that they must be kept away from children of a lower age than that appropriate for the toy.

Roller skates or skateboards for children must be accompanied by an indication that they must be used with protective equipment. Toys that are to be used in water must be accompanied by an indication that the depth of the water must be below the height of the child and that the supervision of a responsible adult is necessary.

Toys can be placed on the market:

(1) Freely, if their producer has complied with the Bulgarian standards, introducing the harmonized European standards for toys, and has placed a conformity marking on the toy indicating that fact; and
(2) Following a conformity assessment procedure prescribed by the RSRCAT, if the producer has not complied with the Bulgarian standards for toys, together with the placing of a conformity marking on the toys indicating that they are in conformity with a sample which has been subject to a "type approval" examination procedure.

The obligations of a producer who places toys on the market applying option (1) above are limited to keeping a full technical dossier of the respective toy, which must be preserved for a minimum of ten years and presented to the controlling organs when requested. A producer who applies option (2) above must go through a "type approval" examination procedure. This is carried out only by specialized licensed experts. The procedure ends with the issuing of a "type approval" examination certificate or with a refusal to issue such certificate.

In the latter case, the licensed expert is obliged to immediately notify the consumer protection and market monitoring authorities. If such certificate is issued, the toys can be placed on the market after placing on them the appropriate conformity marking indicating that the toys are in conformity with a sample which has been the subject of a "type approval" examination procedure. In this case, the identity code of the licensed expert who has carried out the conformity assessment examination procedure must also be included in the conformity marking.

Compliance with the consumer protection aspects of the production and marketing of toys is subject to control mainly by the State sanitary control authorities, the Consumer Protection and Rules of Trade Act and the State Standardization and Metrology Agency, as well as other relevant authorities.

Procedures Except for the general procedures discussed above, the legislation on consumer protection requirements applicable to toys and, more specifically, the RSRCAT establish a special procedure for the licensing of experts who are authorized to carry out conformity assessments under the "type approval" examination procedure. These experts are licensed by the Minister for Health Care, and their licenses are valid for a period of three years. The activities of the licensed experts are subject to supervision by the Ministry of Health Care.

Sanctions Non-compliance with the hygiene and safety requirements applicable to toys is subject to a fine of BGN 5 to BGN 150 and, in the case of repeated infringement, the amount of the fine is between BGN 140 and BGN 300. The placing on the market of toys that do not meet the safety requirements, or that have not passed a conformity assessment examination procedure when such procedure is necessary, is penalized with a fine of BGN 5,000 to BGN 15,000.

Non-compliance with the mandatory conformity marking requirements is subject to a fine of BGN 300 to BGN 800 for natural persons and BGN 500 to BGN 1,000 for legal entities. Placing toys on the market with a conformity marking, but without them having passed the required conformity assessment examination procedure, is subject to a fine of BGN 3,000 to 8,000 for natural persons and BGN 5,000 to BGN 10,000 for legal entities. Failure to keep a full technical dossier of the respective toy for a minimum of ten years, as prescribed by law, or a refusal to present documents when requested by the controlling authorities is penalized with a fine of BGN 2,000 to BGN 10,000.

Deviating from the mandatory labeling requirements applicable to toys is subject to a fine of BGN 200 to BGN 500 for natural persons and BGN 300 to BGN 1,000 for legal entities. Selling toys without a conformity marking is subject to a fine of BGN 500 for natural persons and BGN 1,000 for legal entities.

Insurance

Source of Rule The rules on consumer protection in the area of insurance are primarily found in the Insurance Act[18] and the Commerce Act.[19] There are also a few other relevant provisions in the regulations for the implementation of the Insurance Act, such as the Regulation on Insurance Brokers and Insurance Agents.[20]

Scope and Application of Rule Bulgarian insurance companies and local branches of foreign insurance companies are required to obtain a license for carrying out insurance activities in Bulgaria. The license is issued by the National Council on Insurance following a recommendation of the Insurance Supervision Agency. The license comprehensively indicates the types of insurance which may be offered by the licensed insurer. Insurers who are involved in life and accident insurance are not allowed to engage in other types of insurance. Insurers who carry out non-life insurance may not offer life insurance.

There are a number of requirements concerning insurers' corporate status and structure which are designed to ensure their financial stability and transparency of ownership. Insurers must be organized in the form of joint stock companies or cooperatives. They must observe the minimum share capital requirements based on the type of insurance or reinsurance activities carried out by each insurer. Insurers are allowed to issue only registered shares, which entitle their owner to one vote in the General Shareholders' Meeting. The acquisition and disposal of certain shareholder stakes in insurance companies must be notified in advance and approved by the Insurance Supervision Agency. All shareholders who own more than one per cent of the insurer's share capital are required to prove the origin of the capital.

All members of insurers' managing bodies and actuaries must meet certain mandatory qualifications and other criteria in order to be appointed to these positions. Compliance with mandatory requirements must be proven before the Insurance Supervision Agency grants its approval for each candidate to be appointed to and registered for the respective position.

---

18 Published in the *State Gazette*, Issue 86 of 11 October 1996.

19 Published in the *State Gazette*, Issue 48 of 18 June 1991.

20 Published in the *State Gazette*, Issue 111 of 21 December 1999.

Insurers have various obligations to provide reports and information to the Insurance Supervision Agency on a regular basis on their insurance activities and financial situation.

The assignment of an insurance contract or portfolio from one insurer to another requires prior approval from the Insurance Supervision Agency. The insured must be duly informed of the assignment and its terms. Within sixty days from receiving the notice of assignment, the insured has the right to terminate the insurance contract. Upon such termination, the insured under a life insurance policy is entitled to receive the premium reserve accumulated as of the date of the termination, while the insured under a property insurance contract is entitled to the part of the insurance premium which corresponds to the remaining term of the contract.

Transformations of insurers involving mergers, acquisitions and divisions are also subject to prior notification and approval by the Insurance Supervision Agency. Those insured with insurers undergoing a process of transformation are entitled to receive information on the transformation and on the terms and conditions of their new insurance contracts.

There are safeguards for the interests of the insured in case of liquidation or insolvency of the insurer. In the case of insolvency or liquidation of an insurer carrying out life insurance, the court may, upon the request of the Insurance Supervision Agency, appoint a second trustee, other than the one appointed to take charge of the insurer's estate and to collect his debts. The main responsibility of the second trustee is to protect the interests of the insured. The claims of the insured are deemed submitted if entered in the books of the insurer, that is, no particular action on the part of the insured is required to submit his claims in the course of bankruptcy or liquidation proceedings. The claims of the insured are privileged over the claims of the insurer's other creditors.

The activities of insurance brokers and agents are monitored and controlled by the Insurance Supervision Agency. Insurance brokers must be licensed by the Insurance Supervision Agency and registered in the register of insurance brokers maintained by the Agency. They are obliged to conclude all their agreements with clients in writing, record such agreements in a special register and provide clients with information on the entries in the register whenever required. Insurance brokers are not allowed to receive insurance compensation on behalf of their clients unless explicitly authorized to do so. Insurance brokers may not assign their obligations under contracts with clients except when the client grants permission for such assignment.

Insurance agents do not need a license, but must be authorized by an insurer to carry out certain insurance-related activities, which are comprehensively listed in their authorization. An agent's authorization to act on behalf of an insurer must always be in writing. Each insurer must maintain a list of its insurance agents, which is submitted to the Insurance Supervision Agency on a monthly basis. Each insurer must supply its insurance agents with signs and documents which legitimize the agent as such in the eyes of the public.

Insurance brokers and agents have the obligation to protect the interests of the insured, provide consumers with relevant information as to the terms of the insurance contract and explain to them the meaning of the insurance terms. If the broker or agent fails to comply with this obligation, the insured may seek compensation for any damage suffered. The Insurance Act requires all insurance brokers and agents to obtain insurance coverage for their professional liability to third parties.

The Insurance Act comprehensively sets out and defines the types of insurance that insurers operating in Bulgaria may offer. The license of each insurer indicates the types of insurance that the respective insurer is authorized to conduct. If an insurer wishes to offer types of insurance which are not included in its license, an additional license from the Insurance Supervision Agency is required.

At the time of licensing the insurers for conducting certain types of insurance, the Insurance Supervision Agency also approves the general terms and conditions that will govern the insurers' contracts with their customers. Insurers are required to strictly apply the approved general terms and conditions of the insurance contracts in their business and are not allowed to alter or modify those general terms and conditions.

Following recent amendments to the Commerce Act,[21] the insurer is obliged to provide all persons who are interested in concluding insurance contracts with information on the relevant insurance. This information must be provided in a suitable written form before concluding the insurance contract. The pre-contractual information due from the insurer must cover the following issues:

(1) Business name of the insurer;

21 Published in the *State Gazette*, Issue 96 of 11 October 2002.

(2) Registered seat and address of the insurer's branch office which will conclude the contract;
(3) Insured risks, exempted risks and opportunities for amending the insurance contract according to the general terms and conditions approved by the Insurance Supervision Agency;
(4) Terms and procedures for terminating the contract;
(5) Terms and procedures for the payment of premiums, the consequences of failure to pay premiums and the terms and conditions for the payment of compensation or the insured sum;
(6) Calculation and distribution of bonuses, if any;
(7) Procedure for the out-of-court settlement of disputes between the parties to the insurance contract if such is available; and
(8) Other terms and conditions which are specific to life or property insurance contracts.

If the insurance contract is concluded by an insurance broker or agent, the obligation to provide pre-contractual obligation lies with them. Insurers, insurance brokers and agents also have the obligation to provide certain information to the insured throughout the term of the insurance contract, such as changes in their business name, registered seat and address or the status of bonuses.

Procedures According to recent amendments to the Insurance Act,[22] a Reconciliation Commission will be established to deal with reports and complaints from customers. Everyone will be entitled to approach the Commission and report violations committed by insurers. The members of the Commission will be responsible for explaining the rights and obligations of the insured and persons who are interested in obtaining insurance, reviewing reports and complaints submitted by customers in connection with violations by insurers and mediating out-of-court settlements for disputes between insurers and their customers. All proceedings before the Commission will be free of charge.

The statements of the Commission on the insured's reports and complaints will not be binding on the parties involved in the procedure before the Commission. After receiving the statement of the Commission, the parties will still be entitled to submit their dispute to court. The insured is entitled to approach the Insurance Supervision

22 Published in the *State Gazette*, Issue 96 of 11 October 2002.

Agency with reports on and complaints of violations committed by insurers if, within a period of three months from the submission of such reports and complaints to the Reconciliation Commission, the latter has not taken appropriate action. Reports and complaints submitted to the Insurance Supervision Agency are reviewed by the Audit and Financial Supervision Department. No anonymous reports and complaints are reviewed. Following the receipt of reports or complaints, the Agency carries out an investigation and, if violations are revealed during the investigation, sanctions are imposed on the insurers and their responsible officers.

If an insurer breaches its contractual obligations under an insurance contract, the insured may also submit a claim to the court.

Sanctions Depending on the violations committed by insurers, the administrative sanctions that may be imposed on them are fines and withdrawal of their insurance license. Fines are charged for violations such as:

(1) Deviation from the general terms and conditions, the tariffs or the reinsurance programs approved by the Insurance Supervision Agency;
(2) Refusal to enter into a mandatory insurance contract after instructions from the competent authorities; and
(3) The conduct of insurance activities in breach of the insurance license.

The insurance license may be withdrawn for a number of reasons, including unlawful refusal of the insurer to pay insurance compensation, failure to respect the voluntary character of insurance and a material breach of the applicable laws.

Travel

Source of Rule The rules on travel packages and consumer protection in connection therewith are contained in the Tourism Act (TA).[23] The TA regulates, among other things, package travel contracts concluded between consumers and organizers and retailers of travel packages. The provisions of the TA on travel packages are based on Directive 90/314/EEC of 13 June 1990 on package travel, package holidays and package tours.

---

23 Published in the *State Gazette*, Issue 56 of 7 June 2002.

Scope and Application of Rule Group and individual travel packages may be organized and offered for sale within the territory of Bulgaria by package organizers and retailers who have obtained a license. The licenses required for package organizers and retailers are issued by the Minister for Economy for an indefinite period of time. All licenses issued to package organizers and retailers are entered into the National Tourist Register maintained at the Ministry of Economy. A part of the information in the Register, including the name of the license holder, its registered address, the scope of its licensed activities and the reference number of its license, is publicly available, and anyone interested is allowed access thereto.

Package organizers and retailers are required to provide consumers with written information which indicates:

(1) The price of the package denominated in local currency and the method of payment;
(2) The means of transportation and category of transport used;
(3) The dates of departure and return;
(4) The place of departure and return and route of travel;
(5) The type of accommodation, its location and category;
(6) The number of nights included in the package;
(7) Whether a minimum number of persons is required for the package to take place and, if so, the deadline for informing the consumer if this number is not achieved; and
(8) General information on passport and visa requirements, as well as any medical and sanitary requirements concerning the travel.

Before concluding a travel package contract, package organizers and retailers are required to supply consumers with:

(1) The terms and conditions of the contract in writing;
(2) Detailed information on passport and visa requirements and the periods for obtaining all required documents; and
(3) Detailed information on health and sanitary formalities required for the journey and the stay.

The above obligation for additional information does not apply in cases of last-minute reservations or organized travel contracts.

Package organizers and retailers are required to present the following information in writing to the consumer after concluding the contract, but at least seven days before the start of the journey:

(1) The name, address and telephone number of the organizer's and/or retailer's representative in the place of destination or, if

there is no such representative, of local agencies in the place of destination which may assist a consumer in difficulty;
(2) The times and places of intermediate stops and transport connections;
(3) The type and category of transportation used and details of the place to be occupied by the traveler in the transportation vehicle;
(4) The insurance policies issued in connection with the performance of the contract; and
(5) Information on the optional conclusion of an insurance policy to cover the cost of cancellation by the consumer or the cost of assistance, including repatriation, in the event of accident or illness.

All information supplied to consumers must be in the Bulgarian language. The information must be comprehensive, accurate, legible and should not contain misleading statements.

Package Travel Contract The package travel contract must be in writing. It needs to include the following elements, which are mandatory if applicable to the package sold:
(1) Date and place of concluding the contract;
(2) Identification data on the organizer or retailer and consumer;
(3) Means, characteristics and categories of transport to be used, the dates, times and points of departure and return, travel destinations, time of arrival and length of stay;
(4) Where the package includes accommodation, its location, type and category, as well as the number of nights;
(5) Type and category of restaurants where meals will be served, as well as number and type of meals included in the package;
(6) Visits, excursions, transfers and other services included in the package's total price;
(7) Special requirements of the consumer which were agreed before the conclusion of the contract;
(8) Price of the package denominated in Bulgarian Lev, other payments not included in the package price and the term and method of payment;
(9) Indication of the possibility of price revisions and the procedure for calculating revisions;

(10) Final deadline for the consumer to withdraw from the contract without penalty or to notify the organizer or retailer of his intention to assign the package to a third party;
(11) Penalty payable by the consumer if the latter withdraws from the contract after the expiry of the agreed period of time;
(12) Minimum number of participants if such is required for the package to take place and, if so, the deadline for informing the consumer if this number is not achieved and that the package may be cancelled;
(13) Obligation of the organizer or retailer to inform the consumer if revision of the contract becomes necessary; and
(14) Requirements with respect to form, procedure and terms for the making of claims by the consumer.

The package prices agreed in the contract may not be subject to change unless the contract expressly provides for the possibility of revision and states how the revised price is to be calculated. In such cases, revisions can be made solely to allow for variations in:
(1) The transportation costs;
(2) The fees chargeable for certain services; or
(3) The exchange rates applied to the particular package.

The agreed price may not be increased during the twenty days immediately preceding the stipulated departure date.

If the organizer significantly alters any of the essential terms of the contract, the organizer or the retailer is obliged to notify the consumer immediately of such change. An increase in the price of the package by more than five per cent is considered a significant alteration of the essential contract terms. Under such circumstances, the consumer is entitled to accept the alteration to the terms of the contract by signing an annex to the contract or to withdraw from the contract without penalty. The consumer must notify his decision to the organizer or retailer within three days from receipt of the notice, but not later than the start of the journey.

If the consumer decides to withdraw from the contract, he is entitled:
(1) To take a substitute package of equivalent or higher quality where the organizer and/or retailer are able to offer him such a substitute;

(2) To take a substitute package of lower quality and to receive from the organizer or retailer a refund of the difference in the price; or
(3) To be refunded the sums paid under the contract within a seven-day period from the date upon which the organizer or retailer received the notice of the consumer's withdrawal.

Irrespective of the option chosen by the consumer, the latter is always entitled to claim compensation from the organizer or retailer for any damage he suffered as a result of the improper performance or non-performance of the contract.

If the organizer cancels the package before the date of departure, the consumer has the same rights as in the case of a significant alteration to the essential contract terms discussed above. However, the consumer will not be entitled to seek damages if the cancellation of the package:
(1) Was made because the number of persons enrolled for the package was less than the minimum number required and the consumer was informed of the cancellation within the period indicated in the contract; or
(2) Was caused by *force majeure*, excluding overbooking.

The consumer may assign his rights and obligations under the travel package contract to a person who satisfies all the conditions applicable to the package. The assignment can be effected if the consumer notifies the organizer or retailer of his intent to assign the contract within the term agreed in the contract. In case of assignment, the assignor and the assignee are jointly and severally liable to the organizer or retailer for the payment of the agreed package price and for any additional costs arising from such assignment.

The consumer must immediately communicate any failure in the performance of the contract which occurred during the journey or the stay to the supplier of the services concerned and to the organizer and/or retailer of the package. The complaint must be in writing or in any other appropriate form. In cases of complaint, the organizer and/or retailer or his local representative, if there is one, must make prompt efforts to find an appropriate solution.

The organizer is liable to the consumer for the proper performance of the obligations arising from the contract, irrespective of whether such obligations are to be performed by that organizer or by its contractors. Such liability may not be excluded by the organizer, and any such waiver of liability made in the contract or otherwise is considered invalid.

The organizer is exempt from liability if the failure to perform or the improper performance of the contract are caused by:

(1) The consumer;
(2) Actions of third parties unconnected with the performance of the contract which were unforeseeable or unavoidable; or
(3) *Force majeure* or an event which the organizer or its contractors, even with all due care, could not have foreseen or forestalled.

In the situations under points (2) and (3) above, the organizer is responsible for providing prompt assistance to a consumer in difficulty.

Bulgarian law states that the maximum amount of compensation for damage which may be payable by the organizer in the case of non-performance or improper performance of the contract is to be agreed in the contract. However, such maximum amount may not exceed three times the price of the package. The limitation of liability clause does not apply to damage resulting in personal injury.

Mandatory Insurance As of 1 January 2003, all package organizers must obtain an insurance policy securing their liability for damage caused by their failure to pay contractors, including by reason of insolvency and bankruptcy. In particular, the insurance policy will have to cover:

(1) The refund of all amounts paid by the consumer under the travel package contract before departure;
(2) The refund of the difference if, during the journey, the consumer was provided with only part of the services agreed upon in the contract; and
(3) Reimbursement of expenses incurred by the consumer in returning to the point of departure.

The failure of a package organizer to obtain the mandatory insurance will represent a legal basis for the withdrawal of its license by the Minister for Economy.

Sanctions The sanctions that may be imposed for breaching the provisions of the TA include fines, temporary closure of tourist outlets and withdrawal of the license of package organizers and retailers. Depending on the violations, fines are in the range of BGN 100 to BGN 30,000. They may be imposed for violations such as acting as a package organizer or retailer without obtaining a license, entering into contractual relations with a package organizer or retailer who does not have a license, the provision of misleading information to consumers and the failure to provide consumers with the terms of the package contract in the Bulgarian language.

Mail Order

Currently, mail order is not subject to detailed consumer protection regulations, but there are still certain rules which are applicable.

Source of Rule Specific legal requirements with respect to mail order are contained in the CPTPA and also in Regulation Number 3 on Price Quotation.

Scope and Application of Rule According to the legal definition, mail order can cover standard letters or advertisements in the press, catalogues, telephone calls, radio, video telephone, electronic messages, fax and television. The CPTPA provides certain mandatory requirements with respect to the contents of offers made by mail order. It also ensures minimum protection standards for consumers approached by mail order companies by giving them statutory rights to reject goods or services accepted by mail order within a prescribed term.

Regulation Number 3 on Price Quotation extends the application of the general price quotation requirements to products sold by way of mail order.

Financial services, vending machine sales, regular deliveries of food products, auctions and contracts for the construction or sale of immovable property or relating to other property rights over immovable property, as well as contracts with telecommunications operators through paid telephone lines, are expressly excluded from specific legal regulation regarding mail order.

As mail order is a specific selling practice, the labeling requirements which would generally apply to the contents of labels are, in this case, applicable to the contents of the offer made by mail order as it is this that gives the necessary information to the consumer. In view of that, and in order to secure the legal rights and interests of consumers approached by mail order, the CPTPA regulates the mandatory requirements that each offer made by mail order must adhere to. Such offer must contain information on:

(1) The trader;
(2) The basic characteristics of the product or service;
(3) The price;
(4) The quantity;
(5) Any expenses and costs that are not included in the price;
(6) The way in which payment should be executed by the consumer;
(7) The performance terms and conditions;
(8) The delivery terms and conditions;
(9) The right of the consumer to reject the goods or services;
(10) The terms and conditions for returning the goods or rejecting the service; and
(11) The term of validity of the offer.

The fact that products are distributed by mail order does not exclude them from legal requirements which may be applicable to them because of their nature. If such specific requirements and/or procedures apply, they must be duly complied with in each specific case prior to beginning distribution of the products by mail order.

In addition, the CPTPA guarantees the statutory right of every consumer approached by mail order to reject the goods or services offered in this way. This right cannot be cancelled or waived. The consumer is entitled to exercise this right within seven days of receiving the goods or the binding offer for services. The said term commences on the day following the receipt of either the goods or the binding offer for services. However, if the consumer is not expressly informed of this right in the mail order itself, the seven-day rejection term shall commence as of the date of his notification of the right. Compliance with mail order rules is subject to control by the Commission on Trade and Consumer Protection.

Procedures Except for the general procedures discussed above, the legislation regulating the consumer protection requirements applicable to toys and, more specifically, the RSRCAT regulate a special procedure under which experts are being licensed and authorized to carry out conformity assessment under the "type approval" examination procedure. Experts are licensed by the Minister for Health Care, and their licenses are valid for a period of three years. Licensed experts are subject to current control on the way they perform their activities. This control is exercised by specialized officers of the Ministry of Health Care.

Sanctions Non-compliance with the above mail order requirements is penalized with the general sanctions provided in the CPTPA.

Testing

Voluntary and Mandatory Testing

Voluntary Testing

All individuals and legal entities may request that certain products, materials and substances be tested. The tests are conducted upon the payment of a fee. Testing of products and materials which affect people's health is performed at the laboratories of the sanitary control authorities. Testing for compliance with technical standards and requirements is conducted by the laboratories of the standardization and metrology authorities. In certain cases, duly licensed private laboratories are also authorized to conduct tests and analyses.

Mandatory Testing

There are certain groups of products which must be formally tested before they are introduced for the first time onto the market. These primarily include medicinal products, cosmetics and household chemicals. There are also other products which do not undergo mandatory tests before being placed on the market, but are subject to ongoing sanitary and/or technical control for compliance with mandatory standards while they are marketed. These primarily include food, electrical appliances and toys.

The manufacturers and importers of products which must comply with certain technical standards and requirements need to ensure the conformity of the products placed on the market with such standards and requirements. For this purpose, they are obliged to establish appropriate procedures for testing and certifying the products' conformity prior to placing the products on the market.

Preliminary Testing Clinical research for medicinal products is governed by the Medicines Act and Regulation Number 14 on the Terms and Procedure for Conducting Clinical Trials of Medicinal Products on Humans, adopted by the Minister for Health Care. At present, all medicinal products which have not been permitted for use within the territory of Bulgaria must be clinically tested. The conduct of clinical trials must have prior approval from the competent medical authorities. Clinical trials are performed under the supervision of qualified doctors in compliance with good clinical practice. The results of the clinical research are submitted to the competent authorities when applying for a permit to use the product in Bulgaria.

The preliminary testing of cosmetics is set out in Regulation Number 34 on the Sanitary Requirements for Cosmetic Products issued by the Minister for Health Care.[24] Under Regulation Number 34, cosmetic products manufactured in Bulgaria and imported from abroad are subject to preliminary tests. The tests are conducted by the competent sanitary authorities and are intended to establish the products' compliance with the mandatory standards. The Regulation, however, does not provide detailed rules and procedures for such preliminary testing.

New legislation in the area of cosmetics has been introduced by Regulation Number 26 on the Requirements for Cosmetic Products issued by the Minister for Health Care,[25] which comes into force on 7 July 2003. Regulation Number 26 establishes more detailed rules concerning the testing and assessment of the safety of cosmetic products. It requires that labels on cosmetic products indicate whether the product has been tested on animals and prohibits the marketing of cosmetic products which were tested on animals after 30 June 2003.

The preliminary testing of household chemicals is governed by Regulation Number 35 of 1 September 1995 on the Sanitary Requirements for Household Chemical Products issued by the Minister for Health Care.[26] Under Regulation Number 35, household chemicals

24 Published in the *State Gazette*, Issue 82 of 13 September 1995.

25 Published in the *State Gazette*, Issue 60 of 6 July 2001.

26 Published in the *State Gazette*, Issue 83 of 15 September 1995.

manufactured in Bulgaria and imported from abroad are subject to preliminary tests. The tests are conducted by the competent sanitary authorities and are intended to establish the products' compliance with the mandatory standards. The Regulation, however, does not provide detailed rules and procedures for such preliminary testing.

Ongoing Testing and Control Ongoing testing and sanitary control over products, substances and materials which may adversely affect people's health are governed by the Health Act[27] and the Rules for its Implementation.[28] Under the Health Act and the Rules for its Implementation, the sanitary authorities are responsible for controlling the conformity of marketed products, substances and materials which may adversely affect people's health with mandatory specifications, requirements and standards.

Sanitary authorities are entitled to take samples of the products subject to control for testing and analysis. The samples must always be taken in the presence of the affected party or its representative. A protocol for taking the samples must be drawn up and signed, and the samples must be packed and stamped in such a way as to ensure their authenticity. The results of the testing are reflected in a report which is served on the affected party. The affected party may either agree with the communicated results of the testing or require a second test. The second test is carried out in the presence of the affected party, and the results thereof are final and binding. On the basis of the test results, the sanitary authorities may undertake various actions, which are discussed below.

There are special rules and procedures with respect to the ongoing testing and sanitary control of medicinal products, cosmetics, household chemicals, toys, food products, fruit and vegetables and food supplements.

Ongoing testing and control over products for compliance with mandatory technical standards and requirements is regulated by the Products' Technical Requirements Act,[29] which came into force on 2 December 2002. Under the Act, the testing of products for technical control purposes is effected by the State Agency for Metrology and Technical Supervision. With respect to construction products, testing

---

27 Published in the *State Gazette*, Issue 88 of 6 November 1973.

28 Published in the *State Gazette*, Issue 31 of 19 April 1974.

29 Published in the *State Gazette*, Issue 86 of 1 October 1999.

for technical control purposes is performed in cooperation with the Minister for Regional Development and Urbanization.

The controlling authorities are authorized to take samples of the products for conducting tests when the declaration of conformity and the technical specifications of the product are not sufficient to establish conformity of the product with the mandatory standards and requirements. If, as a result of the conducted tests, the products are found not to conform with the mandatory standards and requirements, the controlling authorities will undertake the measures discussed below.

Special Regimes Bulgarian law establishes special regimes for ongoing testing and control with respect to certain products, such as medicinal products, plant protection products, construction materials and fruit and vegetables. The testing of medicines which have already been permitted for use in Bulgaria is conducted under Regulation Number 27 of 1 December 2000 on the terms and procedures for taking samples of medicines for laboratory testing, performing the tests and the payment therefor issued by the Minister for Health.[30] Under Regulation Number 27, the testing of medicines which have already been placed on the market is performed jointly by the Executive Agency on Medicines and the sanitary authorities. The testing performed by the competent authorities is aimed at ascertaining the conformity of the tested medicine with the established pharmacopoeia and the specifications approved when the medicine was permitted for use.

The testing of fresh fruit and vegetables for conformity with quality standards is regulated by Regulation Number 9 of 26 March 2002 on the quality requirements and control of conformity of fresh fruit and vegetables, issued by the Minister for Agriculture and Forestry.[31] Under Regulation Number 9, the testing of fresh fruit and vegetables is performed by the Ministry of Agriculture and Forestry. The testing for conformity with quality standards of fresh fruit and vegetables designated for import or export is mandatory.

30 Published in the *State Gazette*, Issue 101 of 12 December 2000.

31 Published in the *State Gazette*, Issue 42 of 24 April 2002.

Distribution and Effect of Test Results

Distribution and Effect of Preliminary Tests

Where products must be tested before they are placed on the market, the test results are submitted to the governmental authorities that are competent to allow the sale and use of the products in Bulgaria. The submission of the results from the mandatory tests, together with evidence that the tests have been conducted by duly authorized organizations in accordance with the required procedures and practices, is a precondition for reviewing an application for a permit for the sale and use of the product in Bulgaria. Based on the submitted test results, the competent authorities assess the efficiency and safety of the product and make a decision on issuing a permit for its sale and use within the territory.

The above procedure has primarily applied to medicines which are introduced for the first time onto the Bulgarian market but, with respect to other products, such as cosmetics and plant protection products, this procedure has become fully applicable following the coming into force of the new legislation concerning these products.

Distribution and Effect of Ongoing Tests

Testing for Sanitary Control Purposes If the sanitary authorities, after conducting tests and analyses of food or other products which may affect people's health, establish that certain products are not suitable for use or consumption, they may ban the use and storage of such products and order their destruction or processing and use for other purposes. The instructions of the authorities are served on the affected party and are carried out in the presence of a sanitary inspector.

Testing for Technical Control Purposes As from 2 December 2002, the authorities on metrology and technical supervision will be authorized to order withdrawal from the market of products which, as a result of the conducted tests and analyses, proved not to comply with the substantial requirements and standards of the law. The authorities will also make available to the public information concerning the non-conformity of certain products with the substantial requirements and standards of the law. In particular, the data that must be provided to the public includes:

(1) Type and quantities of non-compliant product;

(2) Trademark of product;
(3) Hazards and risks associated with the use of the product;
(4) Test results;
(5) Measures undertaken; and
(6) Persons who placed the product on the market.

If, following a product's withdrawal from the market, it is repaired so that it complies with the substantial requirements and standards, the product may be placed back on the market after conducting the appropriate tests for conformity. If the product cannot be repaired to comply with the substantial requirements and standards, the persons who placed it on the market are responsible for destroying them at their own cost and expense under the supervision of the competent authorities.

Advertising Claims

Advertising activities in Bulgaria are subject to various restrictions and regulations. Different aspects of advertising activities are regulated in the following acts:

(1) The CPTPA;
(2) Competition Protection Act;
(3) Radio and Television Act;
(4) The FA;
(5) Gambling Act;
(6) Attorneys Act;
(7) Narcotic Stuffs and Precursors Control Act;
(8) Regulation Number 13 of 14 July 2000 on the Terms and Conditions for Approval of the Advertisement of Medicines;
(9) Regulation Number 13 of 17 April 1998 on the Registration of Veterinary Medicines;
(10) Regulation Number 32 of 29 January 1997 on the Official Archives of Notaries Public and Notary Offices;
(11) Regulation on the Requirements for the Activities of Investment Companies; and
(12) Regulation on the Requirements for the Composition, Features and Names of Baby Food.

Comparisons

Misleading and Unfair Advertising

The general consumer protection regime of advertising is provided in the CPTPA. Generally, the CPTPA prohibits misleading and unfair advertising. Misleading advertising is defined as any advertising which is so made that it misleads, or could mislead, its addressees and which, due to its misleading character, could influence their economic behavior. Unfair advertising is defined as any advertising which:

(1) Contains elements of discrimination based on sex, race, religion, nationality, political beliefs, age or physical or mental abilities, or which impairs human dignity;
(2) Is aimed at causing frustration or fear or which relies upon such feelings or on the lack of experience on the part of consumers;
(3) Inappropriately uses predictions on the future or promises easy profits;
(4) Confuses consumers by presenting products or services in a way similar to that of recognized producers;
(5) Could cause moral or mental disturbance in children; or
(6) Frequently refers to superiority qualities of the product or services which are not substantiated and which cannot be checked.

The advertiser and the advertising agency are always jointly liable to consumers for misleading or unfair advertising. Each consumer is entitled to claim in court for:

(1) The prohibition of misleading or unfair advertising;
(2) Damages suffered as a result of misleading or unfair advertising; and
(3) An announcement in the media, at the cost of the advertiser, of the court decision regarding the misleading or unfair advertising, provided that the latter has come into full force and effect.

Additionally, the Competition Protection Act prohibits, when advertising a product or service, the non-disclosure of its substantial defects or features. The advertising of products or services which are not on the market or are of insufficient quantity is also prohibited, as well as misleading price reduction announcements.

Comparative Advertising

The Competition Protection Act prohibits:

(1) Ascribing, by means of advertising or otherwise, of non-existent features to products or services, comparing them with products or services of competitors;
(2) Ascribing, by means of advertising or otherwise, of non-existent defects to the products or services of competitors; and
(3) Advertising of products or services which look, are packed or are named in such a way that mislead or could mislead consumers with respect to their origin, producer, seller, place and method of fabrication, quantity, quality and other substantial features.

Media Channels

Media channels regulations are contained in the Radio and Television Act. These regulations deal with, *inter alia*, the content of advertisements, the program schedules of the electronic media, the time allowed for advertising during the different hours of the day and the maximum allowed frequency of advertising.

Advertising via electronic media should comply with the fair competition regulations. It cannot be used for encouraging behavior that is harmful to the health or mentality of citizens or to the environment. Advertising containing explicit pornography and advertising provoking violence or public disorder is prohibited, as well as advertising which is based on national, political, ethnic, religious, racial, sexual or other discrimination. Advertising containing subconscious suggestions and hidden advertising is also prohibited. Hidden advertising is defined as such that is made in broadcastings which are not intended for advertising purposes. The state emblem and the national anthem cannot be used in advertising.

Generally, advertising in the electronic media is limited to fifteen per cent of the programming time for each day, but not more than twelve minutes per hour in cases of self-promotion, that is, self-advertising by the respective radio or television station. The total duration of advertising is limited to:

(1) Fifteen minutes in twenty-four hours and four minutes in one hour for Bulgarian National Television — Bulgarian National Television is, however, allowed to use a third of the total advertising entitlement between 7pm and 10pm;

(2) Six minutes in one hour for Bulgarian National Radio;
(3) Six minutes in one hour for other public radio and television operators; and
(4) Fifteen per cent of the programming time for each day and twelve minutes in one hour for commercial operators.

The restrictions under points (1) to (3) above do not apply to advertising included in broadcastings that reflect art, cultural or sporting events of national or international importance. The Radio and Television Act also provides other more specific exceptions.

Target Audiences

Children

The Radio and Television Act differentiates basically two target audiences: children and minors. The Act prescribes that advertising which is targeted at children or in which children participate and which contains anything that could negatively influence their physical, mental or moral development should be avoided. Children's programs cannot be interrupted by advertising.

Minors

Advertising which is targeted at minors or in which minors participate is prohibited from having any erotic content. Advertising targeted at minors must adhere to certain minimum requirements and standards, for example, it should not:

(1) Urge minors to buy products or use services by taking advantage of their inexperience or trustfulness;
(2) Take advantage of the specific trust minors have in parents, teachers and others;
(3) Show minors in dangerous situations; and
(4) Persuade minors, directly or indirectly, to urge their parents to buy the products or services being advertised.

The advertising of alcoholic beverages cannot be targeted at minors and is prohibited from being broadcast during programs for minors. Minors are not allowed to participate in such advertising.

Product-Related Advertising Restrictions

The Radio and Television Act provides a series of restrictions for advertising various products and services. Such restrictions are contained in a number of other acts as well. Express statutory prohibitions are imposed for the advertising of the following products and services:

(1) Narcotic substances and stuffs;
(2) Tobacco and tobacco products;
(3) Substances used in veterinary medicine which are not registered in Bulgaria;
(4) Plant protection substances and products which are not registered in Bulgaria;
(5) Gambling games;
(6) Attorneys and their services;
(7) Notary publics and their services; and
(8) Medication that is subject to strict prescription procedures by doctors.

Specific legal restrictions apply to the advertising of the following products and services:

(1) Plant protection substances and products which are registered in Bulgaria can be advertised only according to the terms of their registration;
(2) Alcoholic beverages can be advertised only provided that the advertising meets certain legal requirements as to its content;
(3) Baby food can be advertised only in scientific and other specialized programs; and
(4) Services provided by investment companies are subject to strict legal requirements.

Standard Terms (Adhesive Contracts)

General

Applicability

Under Bulgarian law, a company can adopt standard terms of business to apply to its contracts with consumers. However, the rule is that such standard terms of business will be binding on consumers only if the latter have explicitly accepted the terms in writing. If the contract requires written form for validity, the standard terms are binding only if a copy of them has been handed to the consumer in advance.

In a limited number of cases, expressly prescribed by law, standard terms of business may govern the relationship with consumers irrespective of whether they were provided to and/or accepted by the consumer. Such is the case with operators of postal services, which are only required to publish their general terms and conditions in one daily newspaper and place copies of such terms and conditions in the premises where the services are rendered.

Unfair Terms

Bulgarian consumer protection legislation declares that unfair terms of contracts between merchants and consumers which are not individually negotiated are null and void. Unfair terms are generally defined as clauses which, contrary to the requirement of good faith, cause significant imbalance of the parties' rights and obligations to the detriment of the consumer. A term is not individually negotiated if it is drafted in advance and the consumer has been unable to influence the substance of the term, particularly in the context of adhesive contracts. All terms representing the standard terms of business of a merchant are regarded as not individually negotiated.

The Bulgarian Consumer Protection Act contains an indicative and non-exhaustive list of the standard terms which may be regarded as unfair. The list is entirely based on the list of terms which may be regarded as unfair attached as an annex to Council Directive 93/13/EEC of 5 April 1993 on unfair terms in consumer contracts.

Bulgarian law does not have special rules applicable to the sale of goods and services to consumers. This is why the following outline of the main aspects of standard terms of business and adhesive contracts will be based on the general rules and principles of Bulgarian civil and commercial law.

Delivery and Payment Terms

Delivery

The seller is obliged to deliver the purchased goods to the buyer in the same condition as they were at the time of the purchase. The purchased goods must be delivered together with all their accessories. Furthermore, the seller must deliver all of the purchased goods together — the buyer is not required to accept partial delivery. If the goods have produced any fruit since the date of the sale, all such fruit must also be handed over to the buyer.

Payment

The buyer has the obligation to pay the purchase price for the purchased goods. Bulgarian law requires that the payment of the purchase price be made together with the delivery of the goods and at the place where the goods are delivered, unless the parties agree otherwise. If the parties agree that the purchase price for the goods will be paid at a later date following the delivery of the goods, the buyer shall be liable to pay interest to the seller accrued on the amount of the purchase price for the goods from the date of their delivery if the goods have produced fruit since that date.

If the buyer fails to pay the purchase price at the time the goods are delivered to him, the seller may cancel the contract of sale, at its discretion, by notifying the buyer within seven days of the cancellation. If the buyer fails to pay the purchase price after the goods have already been delivered to him, the seller is entitled to require the buyer to return the goods within a fifteen-day period provided that the goods are still with the buyer and in the same condition as at the time of their delivery.

Risk

Under Bulgarian law, the risk of loss or damage to the goods passes from the buyer to the seller simultaneously with the transfer of title to the goods, unless the parties have agreed otherwise. When the seller and the buyer have agreed on the sale and purchase of a specific good, the risk of loss or damage to the good passes from the seller to the buyer from the time of conclusion of the contract of sale. If the seller and the buyer have only agreed on the sale and purchase of a certain type of good, the risk of loss and damage passes to the buyer as from the time the parties determine the specific good which will be delivered or at the time of the delivery of the good to the buyer. In cases where the delivery of the good is to be made in a place which is different from the place where the seller is based, the risk passes to the buyer from the moment the good is handed over to the carrier or forwarder, unless otherwise agreed by the parties.

Title

The main obligation of the seller under a contract of sale is to transfer title to the agreed goods free and clear of any rights and security interests in favor of third parties. Title to the goods passes from the seller to the buyer according to the rules for transferring risk of loss or damage to the goods discussed above.

Bulgarian law establishes the principle that title to a good may be transferred only by the owner of the good. Accordingly, if the seller does not have title to the goods that are the subject of the contract of sale, he cannot transfer and the buyer cannot acquire title to the goods. If, as a result of the failure of the seller to transfer title to the goods, the buyer is deprived of the purchased goods, he is entitled to rescind the contract of sale and to receive back from the seller the purchase price for the goods, together with all costs and expenses incurred by the buyer as a result of their purchase, maintenance and improvement and compensation for any damage suffered. The seller is exempt from liability if the buyer was aware of the rights of third parties at the time of purchase.

In order to protect the rights of buyers of movable property, Bulgarian law provides that a buyer who has purchased a movable property item for the payment of a price on a legal basis without knowing that the seller was not the owner of the item will acquire title to the item irrespective of the fact that the seller was unable to transfer such title. This rule does not apply if:

(1) The item has been lost or stolen; or
(2) The contract for sale of the item must be in the form of a notary deed or requires notarization of the parties' signatures.

Conformity

The seller is obliged to deliver goods to the buyer which are in conformity with the contract of sale. The buyer is entitled to receive the contracted goods in the same condition as they were at the time of their purchase. If the buyer and the seller have agreed on the type of goods to be delivered, the seller must deliver goods of the same quality agreed with the buyer. If the seller and the buyer have not agreed on the quality of the goods, the seller is obliged to deliver goods of average quality. If the contract of sale was based on a sample, the seller must deliver goods which have the same qualities as the sample.

However, if the buyer is unable to present the sample, the goods delivered by the seller are presumed to be of the same quality as the sample.

The seller is liable to the buyer if the delivered goods have defects which considerably reduce their value or their fitness for the goods' customary or agreed use. The seller is liable for such defects even if it was not aware of the defects. The seller is exempt from liability if the buyer knew of the defects of the goods at the time of their purchase.

Rejection

The buyer is obliged to examine the goods for defects within a reasonable period of time after their delivery and to notify the seller immediately of any defects found during the examination. With respect to consumers, their claims for shortages and apparent defects in the purchased goods must be submitted to the merchant within three days of the purchase of the goods. If no notification or claim is submitted to the seller, the goods are considered to be accepted by the buyer.

In cases of hidden defects in the goods, the buyer may notify the seller and exercise its rights against him at the time of discovering the hidden defects, but not later than six months following the delivery of the movable property items. With respect to consumers, claims for hidden defects may be submitted at the time of discovering the defects, but before the expiry of the warranty period for the goods.

Replacement

If the goods have been agreed by type, the buyer may require that the seller replace the defective goods with goods which have no defects and conform to the contract of sale. In addition, the buyer may claim compensation for any damage suffered as a result of the delivery of defective goods.

Refund

Alternatively, the buyer may return the defective goods and demand repayment of the purchase price, together with any costs incurred by the buyer as a result of the purchase. The buyer is also entitled to receive compensation from the seller for any damage suffered as a result of the delivery of defective goods.

Warranty

The manufacturers of goods may provide a warranty for the goods which are offered on the market, but they are not obliged to do so. Manufacturers who offer a warranty for their goods are required to indicate the warranty's terms and conditions in the contract of sale or the warranty documentation. Retailers of goods that are warranted by their manufacturer are required to provide the warranty to consumers who purchase the goods. Retailers may provide warranties on more preferential terms and conditions than those given by the manufacturer, but these must be issued in a separate document.

The warranty period starts to elapse from the receipt of the goods, provided that the parties have not agreed otherwise. Irrespective of whether a good is sold with or without a warranty, the consumer is entitled to file a claim with the merchant if the good is defective.

Service

All merchants are required to ensure that there are spare parts and materials for all goods offered by them on the market for the time of their useful life. They may, however, be relieved of this obligation if consumers are expressly warned at the time of sale that there will not be spare parts or materials available for the purchased product during its entire useful life.

Reasonable Pricing

Price Information

The general legal regime on price information and price quotation is established in the CPTPA and Regulation Number 3 on Price Quotation.

General

As already mentioned above, each seller shall place, in advance, in a visible place near the product the price of the product, which must be legible and easy to see and read. Prices should be quoted per unit or per piece of product. Different pricing of the same product is prohibited, unless the following products are concerned:

(1) Used products;

(2) Products with an expired term which cannot endanger consumers' health;
(3) Products the features of which deviate from the ones initially advertised and which cannot endanger consumers' health; and
(4) Products being sold off.

Prices must be quoted in Bulgarian Lev.

Regulation Number 3 on Price Quotation further specifies the price quotation requirements applicable to service providers, restaurants, fast food sites, accommodation sites, parking places and gas stations. Certain other products and services are also subject to specific price quotation requirements, which are reviewed in the respective sections on the special regimes for consumer products and service standards.

Price Reduction Quotes

The CPTPA requires that a reduction in price shall always be accompanied by complete and clear information as to the product or services it applies to and the period within which the reduction applies. The old and the reduced price should be quoted together. Advertising a general reduction in prices is prohibited if it does not apply to any and all products and/or services delivered at the respective site.

Residual Controls over Extortionate Prices

Fixed and Maximum Prices

Generally, any Bulgarian producer or distributor is free to determine the prices of its products or services as it finds appropriate. There are, however, certain products or services which, due to their importance to the welfare of the population, are subject to mandatory price-setting requirements. As mentioned above, the Regulation on the Monitoring and Control of Products and Services of Particular Importance to the Living Standards of the Population and the National Economy introduced unified fixed prices and maximum allowed prices and mark-ups with respect to certain types of products and services.

Deviations from these mandatory requirements are subject to penalties amounting to double the amount of any income earned as a result of infringements of these requirements. Additionally, violators are obliged to compensate for damage suffered by any persons affected by their wrongful acts or omissions. If the affected persons cannot be established, the said amount is to be paid to the national budget. Generally, these specific price-setting and mark-up requirements apply to the following groups of products and services:

(1) Flour;
(2) Bread;
(3) Various types of meat;
(4) Cheese;
(5) Butter;
(6) Rice;
(7) Beans;
(8) Eggs;
(9) Baby food;
(10) Medications;
(11) Public transport;
(12) Heating coal;
(13) Electrical boilers and lamps; and
(14) Shoes, other than luxury or official.

A number of other products and services are also subject to specific price setting requirements, outlined in separate regulations, such as:

(1) Regulation on the maximum allowed retail prices of approved medications;
(2) Regulation on the setting and application of the prices and tariffs for natural gas;
(3) Regulation on the setting and application of the prices and tariffs for heating energy;
(4) Regulation on the setting and application of the prices and tariffs for electricity;
(5) Regulation on the terms and conditions for the setting and application of the prices for tobacco products; and
(6) Regulation establishing the rules for the setting and application of the prices for the universal postal service provided by "Bulgarian Posts" EAD.

The specific price setting requirements are aimed at securing even supply of even quality for the consumer.

Competition Law

Prices are also subject to certain competition protection requirements, which are aimed not only at protecting fair competition between producers and sellers, but also at protecting consumers' rights. Any agreements determining recommended resale prices are prohibited and, if such are concluded in spite of the prohibition, they are deemed null and void.

Enterprises that offer contracts of the same type applying general terms and conditions may agree in advance their terms and conditions, but only provided that the free determination of prices by each of the enterprises is not restricted and, therefore, the legal interests of consumers are not affected.

Sales on the domestic market of considerable quantities of products for a continuous period of time below cost are prohibited.

Installment Payments and Consumer Credit

General

Bulgarian law does not have comprehensive rules to protect the interests of consumers when they purchase goods on credit or use installment payments. There are several relevant provisions on consumer protection in such transactions, but they are not sufficient to create adequate safeguards for consumer interests.

Rates

There are no mandatory rules and regulations on the rates which may be applied in consumer credit transactions. It is within the sole discretion of the parties to agree on the applicable interest rates.

Disclosure

When granting consumer credit, banks are required to provide information on the applicable current interest rate per annum, the principal amount of credit given, the criteria for determining a floating interest rate, if applicable, and any other expenses associated with the obtaining of credit. The information must be provided in writing at the time of concluding the consumer credit agreement.

Cancellation

If goods are sold on credit, the seller may cancel the contract of sale if the buyer fails to pay the installments for the purchase price as agreed. However, the seller is not entitled to cancel the contract of sale if the installments due by the buyer do not exceed one-fifth of the purchase price of the goods. This rule applies irrespective of any agreement of the parties to the contrary.

If the contract of sale is cancelled, the buyer is obliged to return the goods to the seller and the seller is obliged to return the amount paid by the buyer for the goods. Nevertheless, the seller may require the buyer to pay remuneration for the use of the goods, which is in addition to any damage caused by the buyer to the seller as a result of the cancellation of the contract of sale. An agreement between the parties that the installments made by the buyer will be kept by the seller as compensation for the damage resulting from the cancellation of the contract of sale is null and void.

Trade Descriptions and Occupational Licensing

Scope and Application

Under Bulgarian law, certain professional occupations, being regarded of high importance to the health and safety of the population or to the legal interests of Bulgaria's citizens, are subject to special minimum educational standards or to licensing procedures.

Minimum Educational Standards

Minimum educational standards are aimed at ensuring even quality in the performing of certain professional activities, which should best guarantee the interests of consumers. Such minimum requirements are introduced by a number of regulations, which deal with, *inter alia*, the total duration and contents of the learning schedule, the minimum hours of lectures and seminars for each subject included in the schedule and the distribution and sequence of subjects throughout the whole course. These requirements must always be adhered to in order for a university to be able to grant valid and recognized higher education diplomas to ensure that the quality of professionals is guaranteed.

Currently, such minimum requirements are provided for the following professions, which are defined as "regulated professions":

(1) Pharmacists;
(2) Therapists;
(3) Health care experts;
(4) Lawyers;
(5) Public administration experts;
(6) Doctors; and
(7) Dentists.

Occupational Licensing

In addition to the above minimum educational standards, certain professions are subject also to separate licensing procedures. Graduating from higher school does not automatically give the right to practice these professions. The additional licensing procedures are aimed at attesting certain practical skills and abilities of the professionals. Not all professions and occupations which are subject to licensing procedures are subject to minimum educational standards, however.

Currently, specific licensing procedures are applied with respect to the following occupations:

(1) Crane operators;
(2) Plant seed producers;
(3) Operators of stem and boiler machines;
(4) Lawyers;
(5) Elevator mechanics;
(6) Operators of agricultural and forestry machinery;
(7) Construction designers;
(8) Welders;
(9) Drivers;
(10) Professional fishermen;
(11) Teachers;
(12) Securities brokers;
(13) Producers of wine and spirits;
(14) Compact disc manufacturers;
(15) Producers and wholesale distributors of medications;
(16) Persons employed in tourist activities; and
(17) Construction supervisors.

The licensing procedures differ significantly, as each of them is adapted to the specific practical skills, knowledge and approach inherent to the respective profession or occupation.

Sanctions

Non-compliance with the minimum educational standards usually results in the diplomas granted by universities not being recognized as legitimate diplomas and, therefore, graduates holding such diplomas will not be able to practice their respective professions or occupations. In most cases when there is a subsequent occupational licensing procedure, such graduates will not be able to qualify for participation therein.

Non-compliance with the mandatory occupational licensing procedure and the practicing of a profession or occupation without having passed such procedure can lead to heavy sanctions. In most cases, the sanctions will be fines or depriving an individual or legal entity of the right to carry out a given occupation or activities for a specified term. In certain situations of grave violation, however, criminal sanctions can also be imposed. There is a general criminal sanction provided in the Bulgarian Penal Code, which provides that the performing of a profession or occupation without being licensed under the applicable procedure should be penalized with imprisonment of up to one year or, alternatively, with a fine of up to BGN 300.

When the profession or the occupation is related to health care, the sanction is imprisonment of between one and three years and a fine of between BGN 100 and BGN 300. In less dangerous cases of persons performing medical activities without having the required license and when criminal punishment is inappropriate, administrative sanctions can be imposed consisting of a fine of between BGN 50 and BGN 500 and double that amount in case of repeated violations.

The performing of other professions and occupations which are subject to mandatory occupational procedures without passing the latter also leads to sanctions, which are, in most cases, fines of different amounts, depending on the specific profession.

Implementing Consumer Rights

Information

Merchants are obliged to provide consumers, prior to purchase and upon request, with detailed information on the product, including its characteristics (such as ingredients, packaging, instructions for use, spare parts and maintenance), purchase price, quantity, precaution instructions, terms and conditions of warranty, if available, and expiry date. If the information is provided in writing, it must be in the Bulgarian language. Merchants are also required to demonstrate, upon the request of a consumer, how the product operates and its proper use.

Merchants must provide preliminary information on and designate special areas for the display of products on sale, second-hand products and products the date upon which has expired or which deviate from their specifications, both of which do not endanger the lives or health of consumers.

Merchants must place, close to the entrance of their retail outlets, signs which indicate the name and business seat of the merchant, the working times of the retail outlet and the name of the person responsible for the outlet. If the outlet is closed, this should be indicated on the outlet's entrance. The information provided by merchants must be correct, complete, exhaustive and clear to understand. Merchants are not relieved of their obligation to provide information to consumers if they have not received the necessary information from the products' manufacturers or importers.

Material Incentives

Product liability under Bulgarian law covers only actual material damage, including lost profits, caused to the consumer by a defect in the product. A consumer who suffers damage from a defective product must successfully prove the existence of the defect, the damage suffered and the causal connection between the defect and the damage.

Bulgarian law does not allow for the awarding of punitive damages.

Moral damage suffered by consumers as a result of defects in products is not covered by product liability either. Such damage may be claimed for by consumers under the general civil law procedure. The compensation awarded by Bulgarian courts for moral damage is comparatively small.

Class Actions

A claim for protecting collective consumer rights and interests may be filed by an individual consumer, a group of consumers, an association of consumers or the Commission on Trade and Consumer Protection. By filing the claim, the claimant may demand that the court adjudicate the violation of the CPTPA or other legislation protecting the rights of consumers and/or rule on the suspension of such violation. The claimant has the right to publicize the filing of the claim following the instructions given by the court. Within a one-month period from publicizing the claim, each consumer who is affected by the alleged violation of the consumer laws may state before the court that he wishes to join the collective claim against the violation or to proceed with his claim independently in separate legal proceedings under the general rules. The ruling of the court on such collective claims is effective and binding on the claimant, the person who violated the law and the consumers who were affected by the violation and did not express their desire to protect their interests independently in separate legal proceedings.

Associations of consumers are entitled to file a claim for damage caused to consumers as a result of breaching the applicable consumer laws and regulations. The association initiating the claim has the right to notify the other consumer associations of the claim in the manner prescribed by the court. Each consumer association is entitled to join the claim within a one-month period from the notification of the claim. If the claim was joined by several consumer associations, the compensation for damage is awarded to all of them jointly and must be used solely for protecting the rights of consumers. At present, there is a very limited number of court precedents, if any, on collective claims for protecting consumers' rights and interests.

Streamlined Procedures

The CPTPA states that certain disputes between merchants and consumers are to be resolved by reconciliation commissions which are established by the Minister for Economy. The reconciliation commissions consist of three members, including one representative of the regional body of the Commission on Trade and Consumer Protection, one representative of the association of traders and one representative of the consumer association. The Minister for Economy determines the seat and the territorial jurisdiction of reconciliation commissions, as well as the list of individuals who may be appointed as members of such commissions.

The role of reconciliation commissions is to assist traders and consumers to resolve certain disputes. Under Bulgarian law, reconciliation commissions are not competent to resolve disputes by rendering decisions which are binding on the parties.

Reconciliation commissions may assist consumers in settling disputes on warranties, consumers' rights to claim in connection with goods and services and unfair contractual terms. Reconciliation commissions have territorial jurisdiction which is determined by the Minister for Economy. The procedure before the commission is initiated by a consumer living within the territorial jurisdiction of the commission and is free of charge. Should the procedure have a successful outcome, the parties to the dispute sign a settlement agreement. If the settlement agreement is breached by either party, the other party may submit the dispute to the competent court.

Technical and Material Support Groups

Consumers have the right to establish consumer associations to support and protect their consumer rights and interests. Consumer associations are established in the form of non-profit organizations. If they have more than 300 members, governmental and municipal authorities are obliged to assist them in their activities. Consumer associations are entitled to:

(1) Be informed of draft legislation which will affect consumer rights and interests;
(2) Inform the competent authorities of infringements of consumer rights; and
(3) Approach the court in cases of infringement of consumer rights and interests.

INDEX

A

B

C

D

E

F

G

H

I

J

L

M

N

O

P

S

T